CW00729683

ABOUT THE AUTHOR

Bob Wurth is the author of five books on the Asia-Pacific region. They include *Justice in the Philippines* (ABC Books, 1985), *Saving Australia* (Lothian, 2006), *1942: Australia's greatest peril* (Pan Macmillan, 2008) and *Capturing Asia* (ABC Books, 2010). A former ABC foreign correspondent and manager for Asia, and later ABC manager for Queensland, he was the 2009 visiting scholar to the John Curtin Prime Ministerial Library at Curtin University, Perth, and a fellow of the Australian Prime Ministers Centre, Museum of Australian Democracy, Canberra, in 2008–2009 and again in 2010–11, for research for this book in Canberra, Singapore, Tokyo, London and Cambridge.

For more detail of his books and to contact the author, see www.bobwurth.com

Also by Bob Wurth

1942

BOB WURTH

The
BATTLE
for
AUSTRALIA

A nation and its leader under siege

MACMILLAN
Pan Macmillan Australia

First published 2013 in Macmillan by Pan Macmillan Australia Pty Limited
1 Market Street, Sydney

Copyright © Bob Wurth 2013
The moral right of the author has been asserted

All rights reserved. No part of this book may be reproduced or transmitted by any person or entity (including Google, Amazon or similar organisations), in any form or by any means, electronic or mechanical, including photocopying, recording, scanning or by any information storage and retrieval system, without prior permission in writing from the publisher.

National Library of Australia
Cataloguing-in-Publication data:
Wurth, Bob, 1947–

Battle for Australia: A nation and its leader under siege /author, Bob Wurth.

ISBN: 978 1 74261 205 8 (pbk)

Curtin, John, 1885–1945.
World War, 1939–1945 – Australia.
World War, 1939–1945 – Campaigns – Pacific Area.
Australia – Politics and government – 1939–1945.

940.5426

Every endeavour has been made to contact copyright holders to obtain the necessary permission for use of copyright material in this book. Any person who may have been inadvertently overlooked should contact the publisher.

Typeset in 13/15 pt Granjon by Post Pre-press Group
Printed in Australia by McPherson's Printing Group

Cartographic art by Laurie Whiddon

Papers used by Pan Macmillan Australia Pty Ltd are natural, recyclable products made from wood grown in sustainable forests. The manufacturing processes conform to the environmental regulations of the country of origin.

This book is dedicated to:

Ethel Jeanie Campbell, nee Ritchie: sister of likely lads soldier Henry Ritchie and his brother, seaman David Ritchie, of Gordon in Sydney, both Australians killed at war

and

Toshiro Takeuchi of Manazuru, Japan: a peaceful young Japanese army conscript sent to Manchuria in 1945, fortunate in never being required to fire a shot in anger, who later became world president of the YMCA and, much later, my wise friend.

CONTENTS

FOREWORD

In his fifth book, Bob Wurth has turned his attention to the history of Australia and its political leadership in the dark days of World War Two.

Here we find the compelling story of a leader fraught with anxiety, and a nation in peril. John Curtin is depicted with all his human frailties – a man weighed down by physical and emotional illness, while being only too aware of the immensity of the military threat faced by Australia in 1942.

Few men would have been so tested as Curtin was during that time. Yet for all the heartache he endured, what shone through were his courage and vision. His foresight in appreciating that we could no longer depend on the United Kingdom for our national security led to his announcement of 'an outstanding departure from Australia's international relations that would ring through future decades' – the alliance with the United States of America that remains the cornerstone of Australia's strategic and defence policy settings to this day.

The carefully researched content of this book fills an important gap in our knowledge of this critical period of Australian history. For, seventy years after the bombing of Darwin and the invasion of New Guinea, we are still learning about what happened and just how beleaguered we were.

The Battle for Australia is also an outstanding political biography. The portrait of Curtin is evoked with drama and sympathy, and there is a fascinating counterpoint with Churchill that gives us new perspectives on the leadership of the time.

This is a significant addition to the annals of Australian history. I congratulate Bob Wurth on a scholarly but eminently readable book.

Her Excellency the Honourable Quentin Bryce, AC CVO
Governor-General of the Commonwealth of Australia

PREFACE

Images of a leader

The imagery of Prime Minister John Curtin as the resolute Australian war leader thundering in demand of a greater war effort and guiding the nation towards victory over Japan is imperfect. Curtin did successfully rally Australians. But the imagery is flawed and so too was the leader. There are other images of Curtin: visions of the prime minister wrapped in a rug, nerves on edge, energy sapped, deeply brooding in the dark of his temperance hotel room. Or of the national leader in January 1942, fleeing from the centre of the nation's defence operations in Melbourne at one of the most critical times of his prime ministership to take a slow train to Western Australia to rest in what one wartime army officer called 'sheer desertion'. And the spectre of the nation's war leader on his way home, stranded by floodwaters in the barren wilderness of the Nullarbor, connected to the world only by the dots and dashes of Morse code, while the Australian territory of Rabaul in New Guinea fell to a massive Japanese invasion and the defence of Malaya crumbled.

Or Curtin, in February 1942, two days after the fall of Singapore, addressing a huge rally in Sydney's Martin Place, thumb in vest pocket, virtually shouting at the throng, warning: 'our fighting forces stand between us and the invasion of our country'. The masked truth is that the prime minister was in acute pain, close to collapse and within the hour would be admitted to St Vincent's Hospital with nervous strain, a Perth newspaper reporting Curtin 'overcome temporarily by the weight of war responsibility'.

How accurate that headline turned out to be. Behind the façade of the war leader is the black dog of depression, afflicting Curtin since his younger years as a campaigner against military conscription. Before Curtin came to power in October 1941, his conservative predecessors had sent the cream of Australia's armed forces overseas in the service of Great Britain and they exercised little control over how and, often, where the Australian forces were used. With the entry of Japan into the war, the difficult yet essential task of reasserting Australia's need to defend Australia, a concept that seems unquestionably obvious today, fell to Curtin. With it came his great clashes with Prime Minister Winston Churchill. The British prime minister distorted the truth in his efforts to keep the primary focus on Nazi Germany and Italy. Here now is the popular image of a clash of wills between two Allied leaders, but what was not appreciated at the time is that both men were blighted by the same black dog.

Churchill kept from Curtin, for more than five months, the fact that the entry of Japan into the war in December 1942 had not altered Churchill's 'Beat Hitler First' doctrine. Churchill told an open session of the House of Commons in January 1942: ' . . . there is no question of regarding the war in the Pacific as a secondary operation'. Yet in a secret session of Parliament three months later he said: ' . . . I now leave the lesser war – for such I must regard this fearful struggle against the Japanese – and come to the major war against Germany and Italy'.

As Japan quickly occupied a vast arc of territory generally northwards of Australia, Curtin's fear of an invasion of Australia became a very real image in his mind and a recurring nightmare. Because he had followed Japan's brutal subjugation of the Chinese people, and then the Indo-Chinese, he knew it was likely that Australia would be next. Senior American officers in Australia and some in Washington, and Curtin's defence chiefs, agreed. But Churchill was determined to keep the focus on Germany. 'Do you think you are in immediate danger of invasion in force?' he asked Curtin, commenting condescendingly, 'It is quite true that you may have air attacks but we have had a good dose already in England without mortally harmful results'. He later said: 'We do not see here that the Japanese would get great advantages by invading Australia in force'.

Yet privately Churchill told King George VI at Windsor Castle, 'Burma, Ceylon, Calcutta and Madras in India, and part of Australia, may fall in to enemy hands'. Meanwhile Australia's governor-general Lord Gowrie revealed to the king: ' . . . people are realising at last that attack, or invasion of Australia, is a possibility that may occur in the near future'. In fact Churchill agreed that Japan would try to establish bases in northern Australia, as he told the secret session of parliament, but not Curtin: 'No doubt the Japanese will do their utmost to threaten and alarm Australia and to establish lodgements and bases on the northern part of Australia in order to procure the greatest locking up of Allied forces in that continent'.

Moreover, Churchill, at least initially until reason and logic prevailed, convinced President Roosevelt that the Far East and the southern Pacific were indeed secondary theatres of the World War and for crucial months John Curtin, at his most vulnerable, felt terribly alone. A haggard and gaunt prime minister walked the corridors of Parliament House, stricken by worry about whether to defy Churchill and bring the troops home from the Middle East. Curtin desperately wandered the grounds of the Lodge, haunted by the thought of troopships being torpedoed on their way home. The imagery of Curtin rarely changes: the man tensely monitoring the great battles to keep Japan from Australia's door. Even when the tide turned, and his party won re-election in 1943, his anxiety was unrelieved. He was burdened by a difficult Cabinet team with only a few good men around him who he could count on. He had a few ministers who were zealots and who tried to undermine him when he was down. He was also hampered by a minority of trade unionists, especially some wharfies and miners, who failed to grasp the reality of a nation at war. The leader's stress mounted and the illnesses increased, eventually consuming him.

And the final image: Curtin was released from hospital in 1945 after recovering from a heart attack and returned to the Lodge into the waiting arms of his loving wife, the unassuming Elsie, who preferred their little bungalow in Cottesloe to the Lodge. Curtin looked around at the lovely garden, as though it would be his last glance at the roses. It was. He was carried upstairs to his bedroom on a stretcher by ambulance officers, never to come down again alive. Finally, some considerable time later, he told Elsie: 'I'm ready now' and died that night. Japan still had not surrendered.

There was an image of sadness about John Curtin. Far from the perfect leader, he nevertheless successfully did the job that Australia needed. He was 'for Australia' when it mattered and when some other Australians, influenced by thoughts of Empire or of self-indulgence, frankly weren't.

Bob Wurth

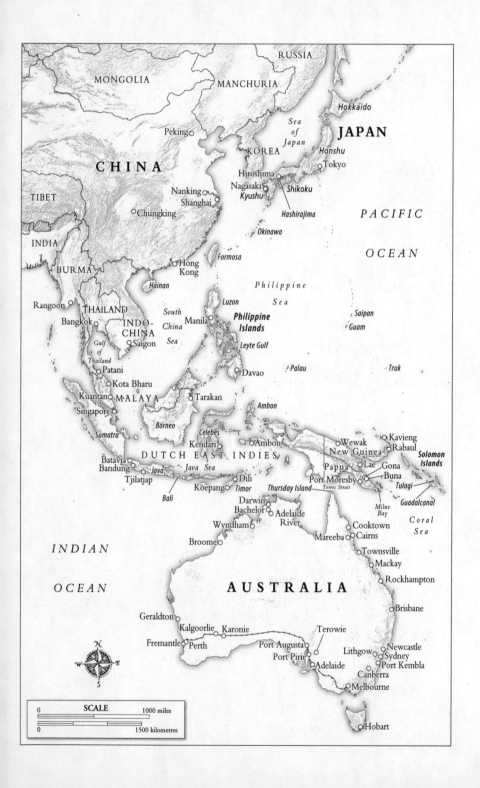

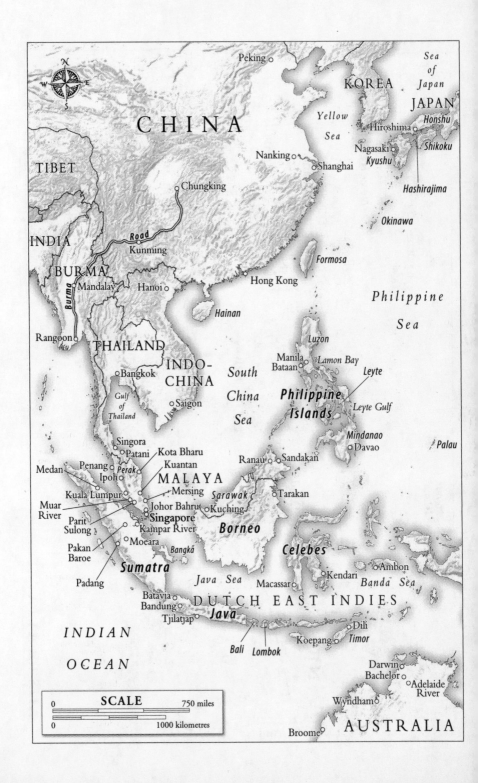

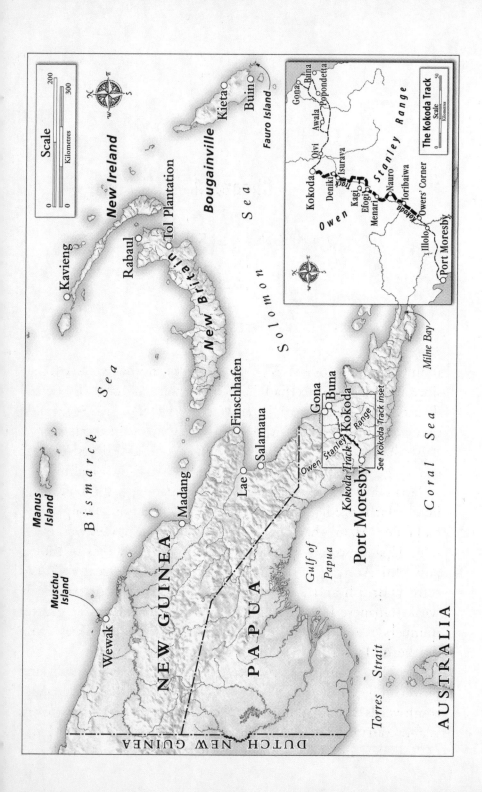

Chapter 1

MAN ON THE BRINK

John Curtin felt unable to go on. It had been just over six weeks since Japanese forces had launched their colossal downward thrusts through East Asia and across the Pacific. Seemingly they were unstoppable. Aged fifty-seven and prime minister of Australia for the last 107 days, Curtin was under great stress and teetering on the brink. The last six weeks had been appalling.

Japan had sent great American battleships to the bottom in Pearl Harbor. Thailand had accepted occupation. Hong Kong had fallen. Manila had been taken and the Philippines was under siege. Japanese troops were overwhelming British forces, including powerful Australian contingents, in Malaya. Retreat followed retreat. British and Australian air defences were comparatively weak. Japanese pilots flying superior aircraft and in far greater numbers were quickly gaining supremacy in the skies from northern Malaya south to the British base of Singapore.

On the ground, despite bitter fighting, well-trained and powerful Japanese forces were successfully pushing their way southwards through jungle and plantations towards the Singapore island. Burma had been invaded. The Dutch-governed islands of Sumatra and Java were immediately threatened. And now

1

Rabaul, on the big New Guinea island of New Britain, was about to be overwhelmed. That immediate looming scenario sent shivers down the spines of those in Australia who knew the truth: that the beautiful tropical town of Rabaul, with its big, deep harbour, would become a Japanese stepping stone towards the ill-defended Australian base of Port Moresby, sitting on the coast of Papua just to the north-east of Australia's Cape York Peninsula.

Australia at home was militarily terribly weak. The continent with its small population was significantly exposed, its best troops fighting with Britain in the Middle East and North Africa or in the air over Europe and its small navy widely scattered around the globe. Australia lacked all the most modern armaments. It had no aircraft that truthfully could be called fighters. It had no tanks. It had few powerful ships in Australian waters. There was even a significant shortage in Australia of basic rifles for the army.

Japanese carrier-borne aircraft had just made a devastating raid on Rabaul and invasion was expected there at any minute. Following the advice of his defence chiefs, Curtin had endorsed the abandonment of some 1400 relatively inexperienced Australian airmen and soldiers, as well as nurses who chose to stay, in Rabaul. There had been ample time to evacuate the Australians to safety but now they would have to face a powerful and cruel Japanese invasion force alone. Curtin from his youth had fought with all his energy against war. Now, as Australia's war leader, the Rabaul decision tore at the very fibre of his lifetime beliefs and brought him great personal agony and tension. It was a decision that would come to plague him. Curtin's colleagues had seen the symptoms before and were alarmed. A doctor in Melbourne had advised Curtin to rest. The prime minister's first reaction was that this was utterly impossible. Everything was about to reach a terrible climax close to home in Australia's mandated territory in the New Guinea islands.

On Wednesday 21 January 1942, Curtin's war cabinet was meeting in the bluestone Victoria Barracks building in South Melbourne, which housed the nation's Defence Headquarters, to deal with an endless stream of urgent and often alarming reports on Japanese victories and the threat to Australia's north. Curtin had missed the previous day's war cabinet meeting, which discussed, among other things, the evacuation of 'surplus and non-essential' civilians from coastal areas of Australia. At this time Britain's prime minister Winston Churchill in London was being difficult when it came to Britain supplying desperately needed reinforcements for the Far East (South-East Asia).

In recent weeks clashes via cable with Prime Minister Churchill had become ever more pronounced and acerbic. Curtin no longer couched his messages in diplomatic niceties because he rightly believed that stopping Japan was far from foremost in Churchill's mind. Curtin engaged in a poisonous exchange of urgent and secret cables with Churchill, in an attempt to secure Britain's promised reinforcement of the Far East, especially for the so-called fortress of Singapore, and to ensure that Australia had a say in the wider direction of war. Churchill and his ministers and defence chiefs were treating Curtin and his ministers as mere colonials whom they expected to heed British advice and direction, no matter how cavalier some of Churchill's military adventures were, nor how flawed and dangerous to Australia's national interest.

The war cabinet meeting agreed to tell Churchill that his plan for the coordination of the war against Japan was hopeless as far as Australia was concerned.

In the sound-proofed war cabinet room Curtin reluctantly gave in to medical advice and the urging of his close ministers and agreed to go home to the suburb of Cottesloe, north of Fremantle, Perth. Curtin long held a fear of flying and opted to take a slow train across the vastness of the Australian continent, taking all the precautions he could to remain in touch. The ministers promised to keep Curtin in constant communication, which in reality was barely possible across vast and empty stretches of the continent.

Curtin flatly refused to surrender the reins by appointing an acting prime minister. His deputy was the army minister Frank Forde, a loyal yet somewhat uninspiring colleague who was never a serious contender for the leadership. While Curtin was away, Forde would chair the war cabinet and the Advisory War Council, which included opposition members, and would remain in Melbourne with the defence chiefs at Victoria Barracks. The prime minister's trip to Perth would be sold to the public as necessary for important defence consultations in Western Australia. Curtin would, in fact, have limited discussions with the army commander in Perth, but he could have done so by telephone from Canberra or Melbourne.

Curtin's flight occurred at the most inopportune time imaginable for a war leader to abandon the helm of government. It underscored the state of Curtin's mind and health, and how close Australia had come to losing a prime minister at the crucial hour. Every day an army officer in the top-secret war cabinet room would pull down a roller map to plot the latest Japanese advance. The map provided disturbing evidence of the threat facing Australia.

Just over a month earlier Curtin himself had warned all Australians to be perpetually prepared:

On guard against the possibility, at any hour without warning, of air raid or invasion . . .

*

John Curtin had a remarkable journey to become the nation's war leader in 1941 during the Second World War. He had grown up in Victoria in poverty through the depression of the 1890s, when the poorest faced actual starvation in the slum suburbs of Melbourne. Those fortunate enough to have jobs often suffered appalling working conditions. Young Jack Curtin, as he was known for many years, attended one school after another in Victoria as his father, a former policeman, managed or worked in various country and city hotels. The family was in Melbourne when Jack turned fourteen in 1899 and began looking for work. For the next five years Curtin was unable to find permanent employment. He lived off part-time jobs and most of any pay he received went to his struggling Irish-born parents.

As a youth, Curtin became passionate about the plight of the poor and the unemployed. It was an era in which workers could be sacked for wanting to join a union or for asking for a wage rise. There was no payment for time off due to sickness, no or few annual holidays, and no compensation for accidents.

Around the turn of the century when Jack Curtin was fifteen, he was worldlier than many a Melbourne man. In his free time his retreat was the Melbourne Public Library, where he discovered the world of ideas, politics, history and the power of words. As a teenager Curtin began fulminating at the Yarra bank speakers' forum about the poverty and injustice he had witnessed and the warmongering he had read about. In 1901 he joined the Political Labor Council, the forerunner of the Labor Party in Victoria, even before he had reached voting age.

Curtin eventually secured employment as a clerk with the Titan Manufacturing Company in South Melbourne in 1903, working the usual six long days each week. Life was difficult but he found time for enjoyment with the Victorian Socialists' Party, then in the halcyon days of revolutionary socialism. Curtin loved the dances, picnics, rowing on the river, and silly games with the girls of the socialist movement. He played for the Brunswick Football Club and also the local cricket club. He began to attend socialist committee meetings, writing commentaries and giving Sunday night lectures.

In 1911 Curtin's advocacy took a new direction He became secretary of the Timber Workers' Union of Victoria, a role into which he threw himself, with frequent travel to remote timber camps and sawmills. He quickly made a name for himself as an innovative young unionist.

*

The man who would become John Curtin's ally yet antagonist in the early years of the Second World War had an utterly different upbringing. Arriving at Blenheim Palace is a breathtaking experience. The birthplace of Winston Spencer Churchill in the Oxfordshire countryside is a majestic mansion and a beautiful estate crafted into the finest English country park. Blenheim Palace is the seat of the dukes of Marlborough, and Winston Churchill's father was the second son of John, the 7th Duke of Marlborough. Churchill frequently stayed at Blenheim, especially as a boy, but it was never his permanent home.

Churchill's relationship with his mother and father was loving, yet somewhat ambiguous:

> My mother always seemed to me a fairy princess; a radiant being possessed of limitless riches and power. She shone for me like the Evening Star. I loved her dearly – but at a distance.

His father once accused Churchill, who was doing badly at school, of being a 'social wastrel'. Churchill hated the harsh regime of school and performed poorly. He entered Harrow School, Middlesex, at twelve and spent four and a half years there, three in an army class, after which he gained entry to the Royal Military Academy at Sandhurst. He went to India with a cavalry commission in 1895 and won early fame, both as a soldier and a war correspondent. He covered the Cuban revolt against Spain in 1895 and then the British campaigns in India and the Sudan, and in South Africa during the Boer War, where he was a newspaper correspondent with an officer's commission.

In 1901 Churchill became a Conservative member of the House of Commons, but he proved something of a radical among the Tories. In 1904, at the age of thirty, Churchill dramatically crossed the floor of parliament to sit as a member of the Liberal Party. The Liberals were elected to office the following year and Churchill was appointed under-secretary of state for the colonies and later became a member of the cabinet. In the summer of 1909 the German Kaiser asked Churchill to visit him for the second time to witness German manoeuvres. The Kaiser, wrote Churchill to his wife Clementine, was very friendly. More than anything Churchill was overwhelmed by the might of the German military:

Much as war attracts me and fascinates my mind with its tremendous situations – I feel more deeply every year – what vile and wicked folly and barbarism it all is.

*

In Melbourne, the horror of a coming war was a frequent topic of Jack Curtin's speeches and writings in the Socialist Party. He spoke often of 'the international war policy played by the international gang of capitalists'. When the First World War arrived on 28 July 1914, accompanied by pro-British flag-waving and patriotic parades in Australia, Curtin became one of Australia's leading campaigners against military conscription of young men. At first there were plenty of Australian volunteers for the war. In 1914 the male population of Australia was less than three million, yet almost 400,000 Australian men volunteered to fight. At the time the Defence Act would not permit compulsory service beyond the shores of Australia, but a threat to the 'Mother Country' was considered a threat to Australia. At the outset the recruiting stations were besieged. Only the fittest were accepted and many a despondent would-be soldier was turned away. Young men, especially boys from the bush with good riding skills who had never been far from home, joined city boys decked out in their uniforms for the coming grand adventure. Australian war historian Ernest Scott wrote that 'enthusiasm is at boiling point'.

Curtin was confidently running for election as the Labor Party candidate for the federal Melbourne seat of Balaclava in the Australian parliament in September 1914, but the war with Germany, he thought, had changed everything: 'Until the war tore like hell through Europe, we were making it [Balaclava] the most vital campaign in Australia – we had a continent wondering.' In fact Curtin never stood a chance in the conservative seat, standing against the premier of Victoria, William Watt, who won easily. Curtin's excessive drinking contributed to his defeat and his subsequent melancholy state. Curtin had gone missing one night before his major policy speech at the St Kilda Town Hall and had to be pulled together by friends before launching his campaign, in what was described as an alcoholic daze. His heavy drinking probably started when he became secretary of the Timber Workers' Union, where union business was often discussed in a pub. Losing the election was a deep disappointment and Curtin's drunkenness and stress increased. There was so much he had wanted to do and say as a member of the Australian parliament, and now his plans were dashed, partly by his own hand.

Curtin turned his attention towards the war with Germany and military conscription in Australia. He began sounding like a pacifist, although he said he was not. Indeed, he described pacifism as 'inherently fallacious' because force had and would continue to 'rule the world'. Curtin would never call for an end to Australians wishing to take up arms voluntarily, as he believed heartily in the defence of Australia. Nevertheless, he regarded war as a hateful and avoidable barbarism.

Australia's share in the coming sacrifice would emerge as significantly disproportionate for a remote country with such a small population. An Australian Imperial Force (AIF) was assembled for overseas duty. One of Australia's first moves was to send the Royal Australian Navy (RAN) to seize German wireless stations in the south-west Pacific. Armed parties captured the German administrative centre of Rabaul, an action that cost the lives of six Australians. Within a few weeks most of German New Guinea, Bougainville and the Admiralty Islands had been occupied by Australia.

At the outbreak of the First World War the men recruited into the AIF were sent to Egypt to meet the threat the Ottoman Empire (modern-day Turkey) posed to British interests in the Middle East and to the Suez Canal. In London, Winston Churchill, then first lord of the Admiralty, came out in favour of an unlikely strategy to force a passage through the Dardanelles Strait, the narrow waterway in north-west Turkey connecting the Aegean Sea to the Sea of Marmara, separating Europe at the Gallipoli peninsula from the mainland of Asia. Turkey had closed the strait to shipping. Once Turkish forts on the peninsula were captured, the plan was for the Royal Navy to sail north, link up with a Russian force in the

Black Sea, and capture the Turkish capital of Constantinople (now Istanbul). The Balkans would then join the British and French, open a new front and complete the encirclement of Germany.

Winston Churchill's adventurous proposal in the Dardanelles would become an unmitigated disaster. At dawn on 25 April 1915, more than 16,000 Australians and New Zealanders landed on the peninsula from large rowboats and other small craft. They soon found themselves at a small bay to the south of the planned landing zone of Ari Burnu, now known as Anzac Cove, and under deadly fire from the high slopes above. The catastrophe began to unfold at 4.30 am.

In the months that followed the intended invasion became a series of brave yet futile attacks, bringing constant death and injury all around through bullet and shell, and, with poor food and putrefying corpses, widespread sickness. The Anzacs mostly clung to the rocky coastal hills and cliffs. It did not take long for Australia's disaster to unfold publicly. In a letter made public, Australian correspondent Keith Murdoch (father of newspaper magnate Rupert Murdoch) alerted the Australian prime minister, Andrew Fisher, to the growing calamity at Gallipoli:

> It is undoubtedly one of the most terrible chapters in our history. Your fears have been justified.

*

At thirty Jack Curtin was a man driven by the appalling state of the world. Increasingly he saw the war as a capitalist plot fostered by arms manufacturers. In 1915, as the war escalated with killing on an unimaginable scale, he was serving his fifth year as secretary of the Amalgamated Timber Workers' Union of Victoria. Curtin had thrown everything into his union role and had achieved much for the timber workers. But the union work and his electioneering had taken a toll, as did his heavy drinking. He wrote darkly in the winter of 1915 to friends about war and his own distress. He was at home at Brunswick in Melbourne. It was night, the fire had gone out and he sat alone writing under the light of a candle:

So I am cold and disturbed and planning the way seems more difficult than it used to be. I have looked at the clock and it ticked me no comfort and I have turned over one or two books in a sort of help me spirit and it is no good. Life at this point is dangerous.

Curtin wrote a confused letter on 6 July 1915, addressed simply to 'Dear Friends', lashing out at the world's injustice and madness:

Ah! Yes! Capitalism is having its most splendid frolic and to the great carnival we are all welcomed and they who stay away are quietly brought along. Here instead of bats and marbles and dolls and swings for blue-eyed smiling gold-locks there is shriek of shrapnel and scream of pain, and their [sic] is the swish of bullets and the thud of falling corpses. Instead of happy days and songs reaching to the sky there is [sic] twenty million men locked in drunken blood-clasp at each other's throat . . .

His bitterness was enhanced by the fact that he saw most Labor supporters accept the war as inevitable and necessary. Curtin's friends knew he was headed for a mental and perhaps physical breakdown.

In October 1915, the diminutive and outspoken William Morris Hughes, known as Billy, took over as the Australian Labor Party prime minister from Andrew Fisher. Hughes was in favour of conscription to feed the insatiable British war machine and Curtin began organising rallies and making rousing speeches against conscription. In 1916 he was charged at Brunswick Court with having failed to enrol for basic military training at his local drill hall and sentenced to three months' imprisonment. Under pressure, the government ordered that Curtin be released after only three days. He would soon write to his then girlfriend, Elsie Needham:

I am glad to have gone in. It nerves our hearts and steels us to the great cause.

But the hint of cowardice directed at those who didn't enlist would have lodged in Curtin's mind and agitated him.

*

With Churchill's Gallipoli campaign turning into a disaster, mounting concerns surfaced in October 1915 during a meeting of the British Government's Dardanelles Committee, chaired by Prime Minister Herbert Asquith. Churchill himself broached the inevitable subject, as the minutes read:

> . . . if it proved that we could not hold Gallipoli we must go, but he would be no party to our going unless it was proved that there was no other course.

Asquith seized the moment and commented that 'details of evacuation should be thought out' and evacuation from the Dardanelles was approved by the British Government the same month. Nothing whatsoever had been gained at Gallipoli but a lasting admiration for the combatants. In November 1915 Churchill was excluded from the Dardanelles Committee. Churchill tendered his resignation from the Asquith Government. He took the prime minister's daughter and Churhill's friend, Violet Bonham Carter, into his room, as she later related:

> He . . . sat down on a chair – silent, despairing – as I have never seen him. He seemed to have no rebellion or even anger left. He . . . simply said, 'I'm finished.'

Australia's official war historian, Charles Bean, later wrote a biting commentary:

> So, through Churchill's excess of imagination, a layman's ignorance of artillery, and the fatal power of a young enthusiasm to convince older and more cautious brains, the tragedy of Gallipoli was born.

Clementine would later record her husband's anguish:

The Dardanelles haunted him for the rest of his life. He always believed in it. When he left the Admiralty, he thought he was finished . . . I thought he would never get over the Dardanelles; I thought he would die of grief.

Yet Churchill never publicly admitted guilt. The failed Dardanelles campaign cost 28,150 Australian casualties, including 8709 deaths. New Zealand lost 2721 killed and 4752 wounded. France lost an estimated 10,000, India 1358 and Newfoundland 49. British troops suffered enormously, with 21,255 killed and 52,230 wounded. Turkey's casualties were 86,692 killed and 164,617 wounded.

On 7 May 1916 Churchill re-entered the House of Commons. In March 1917 the British Government's Dardanelles Commission inquiring into the military defeat released a report to parliament, but it was not published in full until after the war. The inquiry's conclusion was that the difficulties of the Dardanelles operation had been much underestimated from the start. Winston Churchill, as first lord of the Admiralty, had been a key proponent of the operation, but he escaped the censure of the parliamentarians on the commission, some of whom were his friends. The report was an immediate stimulus to his political career. In July 1917, Churchill, then an ordinary member, was unexpectedly elevated by Prime Minister David Lloyd George to the position of minister for munitions. He was back in business as a war planner, although on a much tighter leash.

. *

Public meetings in Australia for and against conscription were becoming rowdy and violent. Accusations of cowardice and treason flew against anyone opposing the war. John Curtin became the recipient of much public abuse, sometimes from returned soldiers attending his public meetings. But the grog and depression had him in a grip. He was admitted to a convalescent hospital at Lara near Geelong. Curtin's old political mentor, federal parliamentarian

Frank Anstey, on 2 July 1916, hoped Curtin would 'stick it to the limit':

> Don't hurry. Never mind what the others say. There are a few among the toilers of this State who would grieve to see you go down at the Pit and delighted to see you climb out reborn. And John, one last word; don't hate yourself, despise yourself or be ashamed of yourself or ashamed to face others. There is no redemption that way. John drunk was a damned nuisance, but he was even a better man than thousands sober, and John sober is the Nestor [mythical Greek warrior] of them all.

As the carnage in Europe continued and Australia suffered heavily in battles like Pozières, Prime Minister Billy Hughes spoke of the war with Germany as a direct threat to Australia; giving support to 'our boys' became the national catch-cry. Hughes enthusiastically promised Britain ever greater numbers of Australian troops for the war machine. Australia, he declared, 'could not leave her men at the front without trained reinforcements'. Hughes called a national referendum to introduce compulsory military conscription, but Curtin and his supporters won the referendum. Hughes then tried to introduce conscription regardless. The left wing of the Australian Labor Party strongly opposed conscription and Hughes's relentless advocacy in favour of it would split the Labor Party. Hughes was expelled from the party and established the short-lived National Labor Party, which became known as the Nationalist Party.

*

Overseas the fighting went on, often in appalling weather and despite staggering losses, until November 1917. Finally, with the armies stuck in muddy fields churned up by the artillery fire, the bloody offensive came to a ragged close. The offensive was named after the village that had become the last objective – Passchendaele. Total casualties at Passchendaele were atrocious: about 275,000 British and Commonwealth and about 200,000 German.

The Commonwealth casualties included some 38,000 Australians and 5300 New Zealanders who were either killed, wounded or reported missing.

*

Curtin moved in and out of a haze of grog, conflict, stressful work and his usual anxiety. He desperately wanted a clean break from Melbourne. He left Port Phillip in February 1917 having secured the position of editor of a union-owned newspaper, the *Westralian Worker*, in Perth. He promised one of his benefactors, Labor parliamentarian Hugh Mahon, that he would 'strive to justify that respect which has to do with my personal conduct'. The newspaper blossomed under Curtin's editorship, which allowed him free range for his often strident and outspoken political views. He was a prolific columnist and his long essays attracted a strong readership.

On 21 April 1917, Curtin married Elsie Needham in the district registrar's office in Leederville, Perth. They set up home at Cottesloe, near Fremantle. The two had met in Hobart in 1912. Elsie was the daughter of a socialist agitator and former Methodist pastor, Abraham Needham, who had taken a liking to the younger Curtin. Elsie had a strong interest in politics through her father and was considered to be a decent, intelligent woman, attending political meetings but having no serious political ambitions of her own. She was often referred to as 'homely' and was a strong, steadying influence on the firebrand activist. There was never a pretentious bone in her body.

*

The war slowly ground to an end with the capitulation of Germany. From a population of just 4.8 million almost 332,000 Australians had served overseas in the war. Of these 61,520 who served in Australian units were killed. Another 156,000 were wounded, gassed or taken prisoner. There was no record of the number of Australian men whose lives were irretrievably wrecked, while physically they appeared normal. At war's end John Curtin, like so many others, had difficulty comprehending a calamity of such appalling magnitude:

History has no parallel to the destruction that has been occasioned. The toll demanded of life and limb; the price paid in anguish of spirit and bafflement of high hopes; the suffering; the terrific mortality of the actual combatants; the actual and potential devitalising of civilisation itself, is too vast a computation for living men to make.

Curtin's depression was never far from the surface. In 1919 he stood for federal election for the Labor Party in the conservative seat of Perth. He received a good deal of abuse from those objecting to his anti-conscription advocacy during the war. The election campaign was a disaster and he was soundly beaten, while the National Labor Party government of Prime Minister Hughes was triumphant.

At the time Curtin was also coping with the death of his father and the loss of his close friend, railways unionist Frank Hyett. Curtin suffered a nervous breakdown and he did not recover quickly. He took two weeks' rest in the country town of Narrogin, south-east of Perth, but once home he still required several months' more rest before resuming his busy schedule as editor of the *Westralian Worker*.

Elsie Curtin witnessed her husband's decline:

> I hoped that if he could turn all his energies into one channel it would be better for him. How right I was proved after the election campaign. The strain of electioneering while he still carried on his Worker [newspaper] job was too much. 'Dad' lost the election and his health. He developed neurasthenia and had to take six months' complete rest.

Neurasthenia is an obsolete medical term used to describe a vague disorder marked by chronic and abnormal fatigue and moderate depression. Curtin veered between moods of high optimism and deep melancholy, according to wife Elsie:

> He would wake up in the morning at peace with the world and I'd start my household chores with a light heart. By lunchtime

I would be treating him with the blend of sympathy and 'Come now, things aren't as black as that', which I learnt through the long months was the best mixture. He'd seem to improve for a while and I'd think he was really better. Then he'd slip back into despondency again.

Curtin made several attempts to take the train east, but on one occasion in 1920 he had to turn back after seeking medical advice at Kalgoorlie. The following year he pulled out of a union conference in Brisbane. The *Bulletin* magazine reported that on doctor's orders, Curtin had 'eschewed politics for the present' and reduced his literary output from twenty columns a week to fifteen. In 1922 Curtin was ill yet again. Prolonged public speaking and constant heavy smoking apparently affected his throat, and his doctor forbade him from addressing public meetings for a month.

Despite the restrictions on his life, and after his failure in 1925, Curtin was eventually elected to the House of Representatives on 17 November 1928, when he won the seat of Fremantle as an opposition Labor Party member during the period of the government of Prime Minister Stanley Bruce. Curtin had developed some respect for the workings of the League of Nations in solving international problems. He began to moderate some of his more radical political views. He believed in consultation and thought constant industrial action was of dubious advantage.

In 1929 Curtin failed in his bid to be elected to the cabinet of James Scullin. His history of drinking binges counted against him. He lost his seat of Fremantle in 1931 but regained it in 1934. When Scullin resigned as leader of the Labor Party the following year, Curtin was elected leader over the favourite, Frank Forde, by one vote.

*

The horror of a new world war became more likely when two important events occurred on 17 October 1934 – one in London and the other in Berlin. Both highlighted the deteriorating international situation for democracies. In Berlin, German cabinet ministers took an oath that Herr Adolf Hitler was to be the absolute ruler of Germany for life. In London for 'naval conversations', the commander of Japan's 1st Air Fleet, Rear Admiral Isoroku Yamamoto, announced that Japan had a 'cut-and-dried plan' to replace the 1922 Washington Naval Treaty system sponsored by the League of Nations that had restricted Japan to a quota of only three new capital warships to every five built each for Britain and the United States. Japanese militarists had big things in mind, not least a massive and modern expansion of the Japanese fleet, as Yamamoto wrote to a naval friend:

I sense the day might not be so distant when we shall have Britain and the United States kowtowing to us.

John Curtin, one of his party's best orators and clear thinkers, had become an effective party leader in the House of Representatives. He was soon beset with challenges at home and abroad.

By 1937 Japan was on a campaign of military aggression in China, determined to expand her colonial empire just as the West had done. But on 5 October 1937, President Franklin D. Roosevelt, looking to Japan, finally took a stand against what he termed 'the present reign of terror and international lawlessness':

Without declaration of war and without warning or justification of any kind, civilians, including women and children, are being ruthlessly murdered with bombs from the air ... Nations are forming and taking sides in civil warfare in nations that have never done them any harm.

Japanese troops pursued the Chinese towards the capital city of Nanking, burning villages and towns on the way. By late November the Japanese were attacking Nanking, a city of half a million people, via three routes, murdering and raping as they went. American newsman Edgar Snow witnessed the fall of Nanking as Chinese attempted to escape through a narrow gate:

Scenes of utmost confusion ensued. Hundreds of people were machine-gunned by Japanese planes or drowned while trying to cross the river, hundreds more were caught in the bottleneck which developed at Hsiakuan gate, where bodies piled up four feet high . . .

Japanese officers allowed their men to slaughter civilians unchecked for six long weeks, as Snow reported:

Anything female between the ages of ten and seventy was raped. Discards were often bayoneted by drunken soldiers. Frequently mothers had to watch their babies beheaded, and then submit to raping . . .

In his mind's eye John Curtin had visions of another terrible world war. In 1937, while sitting on the beach at Cottesloe, he told his daughter Elsie he had stopped wondering if Japan would ever invade Australia: 'The only question to be answered now is *when*.'

*

On 3 September 1939, Prime Minister Robert Menzies sat before a microphone and spoke words that filled many Australians listening on the wireless with dread. Germany had invaded Poland. Menzies said it was his 'melancholy duty' to inform listeners that Great Britain had declared war upon Germany 'and that, as a result, Australia is also at war'. To Menzies, Great Britain going to war had triggered an automatic response from Australia, even though he had visited Nazi Germany in 1935, commenting:

The best guarantee of peace in Europe would be the concessions of some power and self-respect to Germany and the best guarantee in the Far East a friendly alliance with Japan.

Menzies in 1938 had misjudged Hitler, believing, like many, that appeasement could provide a permanent solution to the crisis:

If we could persuade Germany that we were prepared to give her justice, we might drive out the evil spirit of suspicion and hatred.

Curtin had also dabbled in appeasement and had been most cautious about offending Germany and Japan. In 1935 he had made an isolationist speech, warning that it was sheer folly for Australia to become involved in European disputes: 'Our business is to keep Australia aloof from the wars of the world.'

*

In the inter-war years Winston Churchill never wavered in sounding the alarm about the threatening military build-up and the aspirations of Nazi Germany. He correctly foreshadowed the increasing power and ruthlessness of Chancellor Adolf Hitler. On the other hand, by early May 1940, British prime minister Neville Chamberlain had lost considerable support from his own party for his mishandling of the European crisis, his continual appeasement of Hitler and the country's lack of preparedness for war. It became all too much. Chamberlain called for Churchill on 10 May and intimated that Churchill should be prime minister as Chamberlain had lost the confidence of the House of Commons. Churchill was summoned before King George at Buckingham Palace and took over the leadership of Great Britain at its gravest hour. In his war histories, Churchill wrote that he went to bed at 3 am as the new prime minister conscious of a profound sense of relief:

> At last I had the authority to give directions over the whole scene. I felt as if I was walking with destiny, and that all my past life had been but a preparation for this hour and for this trial. Eleven years in the political wilderness had freed me from my ordinary party antagonisms. My warnings over the last six years had been so numerous, so detailed, and were now so terribly vindicated . . .

On 16 July 1940 Hitler issued a directive for Operation Sealion, the invasion of Britain. But first the Royal Air Force (RAF) had to be eliminated. Hitler ordered the German air force, the *Luftwaffe*, to 'overpower the English Air Force' by 15 September. The intention was to cut Britain's coastal supply lines and draw the RAF's fighters into battle over the Channel where they could be destroyed. Attacks on shipping were followed by raids on British radar installations and on RAF airfields in southern England.

Air Chief Marshal Sir Hugh Dowding had been able to make preparations. Churchill would later say that Dowding's Fighter Command deserved the highest praise: 'the generalship have shown an example of genius in the art of war'. Nevertheless, Dowding said events had startled the RAF:

> The German arrival on the Channel surprised us. The enemy was only twenty miles away and we had to fight from airfields organised when the Rhine was the frontier.

Nearly 3000 RAF personnel would serve with British Fighter Command in the course of the Battle of Britain, of whom nearly 600 were from the British Dominions and from occupied European countries. Thirty-five Australians fighter pilots flew combat operations during the Battle of Britain, of whom ten were killed in action. Flight Lieutenant Paterson Hughes from Cooma, New South Wales, shot down fifteen German aircraft and shared the destruction of three others. Hughes died when shooting down his fifteenth victim. Hughes was twenty-two when he died. Churchill famously said of the protectors of Britain, 'Never in the field of human conflict was so much owed to so few.'

*

Britain was now fighting a war on many fronts, with the defeat of Hitler uppermost in Prime Minister Churchill's mind. His disastrous Greek campaign resulted from Britain's guarantee to support Greece if attacked by the Germans. But the Allied forces were vastly outnumbered. Australia and New Zealand, which provided most of the troops, were not involved in the planning of this campaign.

When German forces invaded Greece in April 1941 they faced Australian, Greek, British and New Zealand troops as part of a Churchill defence plan. Without adequate equipment or proper air cover the Allies were overwhelmed and forced to make a fighting withdrawal. Many were evacuated to Crete, where they faced a German airborne invasion. More than 600 Australians lost their lives in the Battle for Greece and Crete while some 5000 became prisoners of war.

After Greece and Crete, Churchill planned what he called 'the Syrian adventure'. When the commander of the British forces, General Archibald Wavell, protested at such an ill-considered invasion, Churchill said Britain must not shrink from running 'small scale military risks'. Churchill told parliament on 7 May that as painful as the Allied losses in Greece were, the Empire forces had much to be proud of and he would do the same thing again if necessary.

With a sheltered deep-water harbour, Tobruk on the eastern Mediterranean coast of Libya was long a well-fortified key Italian naval outpost. The Italian defence perimeter was attacked by the 6th Australian Division on the morning of 22 January 1941 and the town fell the next morning, resulting in 27,000 Italian prisoners and the capture of over 200 artillery pieces. Forty-nine Australians were killed. The 6th Division pressed on beyond Tobruk and the 9th Australian Division was moved into Libya in February to garrison territory captured by the 6th. But the Germans launched a major offensive and an Allied retreat towards Egypt commenced. The 9th Division fell back on Tobruk and was subsequently encircled. This began what became known as 'the siege of Tobruk', which lasted from April to December 1941 and ended only when the Germans called it off and withdrew. The following year, after all Australians had left, the Germans attacked Tobruk again in force and captured the stronghold from the British.

*

War with Japan was becoming ever more likely in the Australian spring of 1941. But Australia's home defence was increasingly being compromised by the significant demands from Britain for Australian soldiers, sailors and airmen to fight in Europe, the Middle East, the Mediterranean and North Africa.

Japan's forces had been trained and tested in the country's attacks on China from the mid-thirties onwards. Japan more recently had occupied the Vichy French colonies of northern Indo-China, and then southern Indo-China, in what now includes Vietnam. The Japanese also asserted their authority over the former French colonies of Cambodia and Laos. In 1941 the way was being paved for the occupation of Siam (now Thailand) and British Burma. But these were not the main prizes. Malaya (now part of the broader Malaysia) had huge supplies of rubber and tin. There was also plentiful oil on British Borneo. A southward thrust in Malaya through the rubber plantations and jungle could present Japan with the great prize of the British trading island of Singapore, long considered a fortress securing the seaways of South-East Asia. Occupation of Singapore would almost certainly lead to the capture of the oil-rich Dutch East Indies (now Indonesia) and a vast stretch of scattered but strategically important islands of New Guinea and others to the south nearer to Australia, which was unprepared, underarmed and undermanned.

For decades Australia's defence strategy had relied on the security of British interests in Asia, principally the big naval base at Singapore, which was long viewed as a sufficient deterrent against any potential enemy in the East. As the threat from Japan grew, Australia's 2/20th Infantry Battalion had embarked for Singapore in February 1941. On arriving in Singapore they moved into south-west Malaya (now part of Malaysia). At the end of August the battalion redeployed to the port of Mersing on the east coast. Mersing was seen as a potential Japanese landing point. Additionally, battalions of the 27th Brigade had sailed to Singapore at the end of July 1941 and also had moved into Malaya to prepare for a possible Japanese attack.

*

Due to the difficulties in getting home to Western Australia from Canberra, Curtin often remained in the national capital between sitting sessions of parliament. In Canberra Elsie Curtin had few close friends and her husband was perpetually busy. Leaving her friends in Western Australia was 'one of the most painful wrenches experienced in her life'. As time went on, and as Curtin's political star rose, Elsie's visits to join her husband in Canberra became less frequent.

Curtin greatly missed his wife and family living on the other side of the continent. When he did return home he took the train because of his fear of flying. A slow and tiring train journey of four days or more would often mean that when he got home, his stay would be brief before he made the long return journey, changing to as many as five or six trains because of the different rail gauges before reaching Canberra.

As opposition leader in 1941 John Curtin was under pressure from members of his own party to topple the government of Robert Menzies, given that the balance of power in the House of Representatives was held by two independents. Labor frontbencher Herbert 'Doc' Evatt, who had come to parliament from the High Court bench, was especially keen on Curtin making a move and was in negotiation with the independents – and at one stage even Menzies himself – trying to arrange a national government that might include Labor. But Curtin wanted no joint national government like Britain's and was in no hurry to try to form government. He was still trying to mend major splits within the Labor Party.

War news around the globe seemed to deteriorate by the day. Australians were away fighting in the air over Europe, in the Middle East, the Mediterranean and North Africa. As Japan aligned herself to the Axis powers, small Australian forces, mostly inadequately armed and supported, had been despatched to islands close to northern Australia. Militarily, it was a death sentence for many who would face far greater enemy numbers. The outlook was bleak and worrying by the end of September 1941. Curtin privately conceded his woes in a letter to his wife at this time.

He longed for his family, home life and a degree of normality, which – like so many Australians going to war – would become a thing of the past:

My Dearest,

Saturday is your birthday and here at Canberra I am not able to arrange anything. But I wish with all my heart I was at home to share the day with you. May it be a happy day and may it have very many happy repetitions. Of course it is a timetable and records what we do not like to feel. I find I am growing old, as the song says. We cannot avoid what life brings. To me the finest occurrences have been you and the two children. I dreamed about [son] Jack last night. I'm afraid my nerves need a rest. And here crisis follows crisis and there is no spell at all. More than ever before my nature is crying out for a holiday from strife. What with Royal Commissions, debates in the House, the conflict and conferences in the caucus, and the too-neglected work of the War Council I find myself dragged into the commonplace and not able to attend to what would be worth doing.

But enough of complaint. Let me look at the credit side. And you alone have supplied that. I have had a kindly life. You have given me a deep well of content and met the urges of my nature completely. I have had supreme happiness in your love and love-liness. And no man has ever had more than that.

I cannot do more now as the Executive is waiting. We have the budget to consider and I am sick of millions for that and for this and everybody assuming no one should pay and that the thin air gives money and not oxygen. All my love and all my heart and all my gratitude for all you have been and are, the wife – the stout-hearted, sweet natured wife – of my manhood and the beloved of my soul.

Your loving husband, John xxxxxxxxxxxx

Chapter 2

JAPAN STRIKES

On 29 August 1941 Arthur Fadden, an earthy and affable Queenslander who got on well with Curtin, despite them being political opposites, became prime minister. Menzies had desperately wanted to return to Britain to help direct the war effort from London. There is evidence that Menzies had designs on a primary role in British politics. Menzies' United Australia Party supported his bid to travel again to London, although the leader was unpopular with many parliamentary members. The Labor Party, however, refused to endorse the visit. Under increasing pressure Menzies had resigned and Fadden, from the conservative Country Party, assumed the leadership of Australia.

A new political crisis was building in Canberra as Prime Minister Fadden prepared to present his first budget while doubting if he had the numbers to get it through parliament. It is telling that Curtin felt so low on this day, for he knew that the time had come for the Australian Labor Party to make its bid to form government. Harold Cox, political reporter in Canberra for the Melbourne *Sun*, had spent many long nights in Curtin's office where Curtin, stressed out, would lie on a couch for long periods on end, chain-smoking and complaining about his headaches and neuralgia. Curtin had been in no hurry to challenge for the leadership of the nation. He knew that even if he became prime minister, he would need to rely on independents to hold power at a time when Germany and Italy were expanding their conquests and Japan was clearly preparing for war.

In the early hours of 2 October 1941, the morning before the crucial vote in the House of Representatives, Cox walked down the almost deserted Labor corridors. It was after midnight when he was confronted by Curtin with the sort of information any political reporter would kill for, as Cox explained:

> Curtin, whom I knew very well, stopped me and said 'Harold, I wouldn't have thought this possible, but from something I've heard in the last hour, I think I'm going to be prime minister by this time tomorrow'.

Arthur Fadden described his own meeting with Curtin:

> On the day the vote was to be taken Curtin called on me on his way to lunch. 'Well boy,' he said, 'have you got the numbers, I hope you have but I don't think you have.' I replied, 'No John, I haven't got them. I have heard that Wilson spent the weekend at Evatt's home, and I can't rely on Coles.' Curtin said 'Well, there it is. Politics is a funny game.' Wryly I replied, 'Yes, but there's no need for them to make it any funnier.'

Curtin wasn't being polite when he hoped that his opponent had the numbers. He had been under constant pressure from some of his senior colleagues, especially the ambitious Doc Evatt, to challenge the government on the floor of parliament, but was strangely reluctant to do so.

Soon a telegram boy parked his pushbike against the white picket fence of a modest cottage in Jarrad Street, Cottesloe, and knocked on the front door, handing Elsie Curtin a telegram from Canberra:

THIS IS YOUR BIRTHDAY GIFT COLES AND WILSON ARE PROVIDING
IT THEY HAVE ANNOUNCED THEIR INTENTION OF VOTING FOR OUR
AMENDMENT AND THE GOVERNMENT WILL BE DEFEATED LOVE JOHN

Arthur Fadden later complained that Robert Menzies, still leader of the United Australia Party and a senior member of the government, had sat in the House of Representatives in silence, allowing the tide to swirl against the new Fadden Government:

> When the [budget amendment] vote was called the two Independents, [Arthur] Coles and [Alexander] Wilson, crossed the floor to join the Opposition and the Government was defeated. I returned my commission to [Governor-General] Lord Gowrie and advised him to send for Curtin.

Fadden's government was defeated on 3 October in a censure motion moved by Curtin. Fadden's reign lasted 'forty days and forty nights', as he later put it.

There were many who doubted Curtin's ability to govern. Don Whitington, the senior political reporter in Canberra with Sydney's *Daily Telegraph*, later wrote that Curtin did not want office and had been prepared to remain in opposition until the next election:

> Curtin's health was expected to prove unequal to his new responsibilities. The Labor Party was not expected to hold together.

*

At home on Saturday 4 October Elsie Curtin, celebrating her fifty-first birthday, spent most of the time on the telephone taking congratulatory messages and speaking with the press. She said her husband had called from Canberra to tell her there would be no election, which pleased her, mindful of the stress electioneering caused him. The Curtins' daughter Elsie, aged twenty-three, shared the calls and the care of Mrs Curtin's 83-year-old mother, who lived with them. A Melbourne *Herald* reporter appeared surprised to see Curtin's wife doing domestic chores: 'Mrs Curtin has solved the Australian domestic service problem – she does the work herself!'

Curtin took the portfolios of prime minister and defence coordination. Frank Forde was elected as Curtin's deputy and minister for the army. Among other appointments, Ben Chifley, a good friend, became treasurer. Doc Evatt, a High Court judge for almost ten years, became attorney-general and minister for external affairs handling foreign issues. Among the portfolios directly concerned with the war, the navy and also munitions portfolios went to Norman Makin; air and civil aviation to Arthur Drakeford; aircraft production to Senator Donald Cameron; supply and development to Jack Beasley; war organisation of industry to John Dedman; and labour and national service to the militant rabblerouser, Eddie Ward, who would plague Curtin for much of his prime ministership. While Curtin allocated portfolios he was not able to appoint his cabinet members, who were selected by the parliamentary ALP caucus. This procedure would not be changed for decades.

Curtin had been handed a poisoned chalice. He suddenly realised that Australia was hopelessly underarmed, desperately short of warplanes, warships and army equipment. Britain made promises to help equip Australia and to reinforce Singapore and Malaya, but little of substance happened. While the growing threat of war from Japan hung over the new government, Australian casualties in the war with Germany and Italy were mounting rapidly. While Australia had not undergone the savage, indiscriminate bombing suffered by England, the country had suffered significantly. Since the outbreak of war in 1939, 2113 Australians had been killed, 5043 wounded and thousands taken prisoner.

Curtin's stresses were often a concern for the governor-general, Lord Gowrie (Sir Alexander Gore Arkwright Hore-Ruthven, 1st Earl of Gowrie), who had known Curtin personally from the time he became leader of a fractious and disorganised opposition in 1935. Curtin would often go to Government House and spend quiet afternoons and evenings with the Gowries. The governor-general told King George VI in a letter soon after he swore in Curtin as prime minister:

> I know Mr Curtin well and I have every confidence in his integrity – his judgment and his anxiety to do only what is best for Australia and for the successful prosecution of the war. But his health is not good. He has a difficult team and there are ambitious men in his Party anxious for the prime ministership, so his path will not be easy.

Curtin cabled Churchill soon after his swearing in to assure him of his full cooperation with the British Government and those of the other dominions:

> In particular we will devote our energies to the effective organisation of all our resources so that we may play our part in bringing victory to the Empire and our allies.

Churchill responded, 'You may be sure that we shall work with you on a basis of most intimate confidence and comradeship.' Any comradeship would rapidly decline. The British leader was already miffed at Australian attempts to help direct British Empire war policy. Churchill had a friend in Lieutenant General Sir Henry Pownall, whom he called 'a first rate man'. Pownall was vice chief of the Imperial General Staff in the War Office and kept a rather forthright and revealing personal diary that appears dismissive of Australian concerns, a trait that became standard fare in Whitehall. Six days after Curtin was sworn in as prime minister of Australia, Pownall's diary entry of 13 October had this to say:

> The new Government is Labour, some of whom have distinct tendencies towards isolationism, so we may have trouble. Indeed we had the same with the previous Government where first Menzies, and then for a short time Fadden, insisted that the

Australian division in Tobruk should be relieved. Winston was very angry with them but he couldn't shake them.

The Curtin Government vigorously took up a case for withdrawing the last weary members of the 9th Division AIF from Tobruk. The 9th Division, with British artillerymen, had held Tobruk under months of heavy German assaults during 1941. The first portion of the 14,000 AIF force was relieved in August with the second relieved in September and October.

General Pownall wrote caustically that the Australian commander in the Middle East, General Thomas Blamey, 'seems to have played a fairly low game in giving military advice to his Government' without telling British commanders in the Middle East:

> The Dominions are quite ready to take more than their share of the glory and advertisement, but if they think they are approaching equal shares with us in tasks and casualties there is the devil of a fuss.

Britain's Far East commander-in-chief, Air Chief Marshal Sir Robert Brooke-Popham, arrived in Melbourne from Singapore to address the Advisory War Council on 16 October. He had been commander-in-chief in charge of land and air forces since November 1940. It was a strange meeting. Brooke-Popham initially spoke optimistically about Malaya 'growing from strength to strength, as was Burma and Hong Kong'. He boasted that British air forces could handle any Japanese aircraft. Japan had superiority in aircraft numbers, but not in quality, he believed. The American-designed Brewster Buffalo fighters in the RAF in Malaya were 'superior to the Japanese'. Admittedly there was a shortage of long-range bombers, but more were promised for 1942, he assured Curtin.

Curtin immediately was highly sceptical. He had already received expert advice to the contrary. In reality, pilots discovered that the Buffalo was no match for the Japanese aircraft. Curtin quietly demanded to know what had happened to a proposed expansion program of 336 aircraft for Burma, Malaya and Borneo that had been adopted by British chiefs of staff in April. Brooke-Popham replied that there were about 180 aircraft now in hand. He did not add that most were obsolete and their crews had received little training. Curtin kept seeking answers. After some debate Brooke-Popham opened up, suddenly and surprisingly admitting that he had made 'all representations short of resigning' in his efforts to secure additional air power for the defence of Malaya and Singapore. He felt that the British chiefs were not neglecting the Far East 'and probably they made a fair allocation from the resources available'. His true thoughts were expressed much later:

> It is a long way from Whitehall to Singapore and so there was a natural feeling of isolation and we were apt to feel neglected . . . the Far East was regarded as a place to which tired officers could be sent. Although we were ready to welcome war-weary pilots for the sake of their experience, Malaya is not a place in which officers who are physically and mentally exhausted can recuperate, nor could we afford to carry passengers.

Before going to war, Japan had accused Australia of 'encirclement of Japan' by sending troops to Malaya in 1941. Curtin now went public in a press statement with his mounting concerns about the British defence of the Far East. He spoke of 'ominous portents' on the Pacific horizon, which threatened to bring the conflict to the very doors of Australia:

> Australia wants peace in the Pacific. She is not a party to any policy of encirclement and never has been nor will she be guilty of any act of aggression . . . Nevertheless, if need be she is fully resolved to defend herself to the utmost of her capacity.

Lieutenant General Sir Iven Mackay, recalled from Palestine, was appointed commander-in-chief, Australian Home Forces.

The more he examined the Japanese threat and the home defence situation, the more concerned he became. In late October 1941 he found Australia:

> virtually naked, militarily . . . because all I can see is more than 12,000 miles [19,000 kilometres] of Australian coastline, and so little wherewithal for defending the points that really matter.

*

Labor's euphoria at taking power, together with a good deal of public support for Curtin in the community, was undermined by militant unionists who demonstrated little concern for the fact that Australia was at war. Even as Curtin was being sworn in as prime minister in October, storemen, wharf labourers and railwaymen in Darwin were striking against the army handling its own waterfront cargo. As a result, they decided not to handle cargo associated with the Australian army, which included building material urgently needed for the construction of quarters for troops arriving to defend Darwin. In Melbourne a strike over wages was threatened at the Commonwealth Aircraft Corporation; while at Lithgow, inland from Sydney, 4500 workers at the Commonwealth Small Arms Factory went on strike because four men had continued working during a previous stopwork meeting. At South Maitland, coalminers went on strike, but stayed in the pit, claiming insufficient payment. In Brisbane, strikers at the Ipswich railway workshop were ordered back to work by the Industrial Court in a dispute over rates of pay for fifth-year apprentices. All of these disputes occurred within two days of Curtin's appointment as prime minister.

The former militant unionist and now minister for labour, John 'Eddie' Ward, blamed the Darwin dispute on the army. Ward saw that orders were given to the army to discontinue using troops to unload cargo at Darwin. Ward generally took the workers' side, regardless of the merits of any dispute. He had been minister for only two weeks during the plethora of strikes when he told a public meeting:

I have no fault to find with the workers. I have discovered a great deal of the delays and irritation existing in many workshops has not been due to lack of drive by the workers to give the maximum effort, but to irritation tactics by employers who are overbearing to the workers.

Army Headquarters in Melbourne, which censored the letters written by servicemen, received stark accounts of how the enlisted men felt about the strikers during November 1941, including a letter penned by an unidentified member of the Royal Australian Artillery in Rabaul:

It hits us mighty hard when we read papers from down South and see that thousands are striking for more pay etc., shorter hours, more privileges and so on. I've heard some of the boys say they would like to go back and shoot the strikers. They are nothing but traitors or saboteurs against the war effort . . . Dirty rats.

A similar response was read in a letter from a member of the Army Postal Unit in Darwin:

The wharfies go on strike every other week and now this . . . they tell the Brig[adier] just what he has to do. The military must not unload a thing. Not a gun down to a nail. The rotten . . . should be machine gunned – that's what I think anyhow.

*

When Curtin became prime minister, he had initially received encouraging news from special envoy to Britain Sir Earle Page, who was in Singapore. Page was a conservative politician and former prime minister, appointed special envoy by the previous government. While inspecting naval installations and coastal defences, Page was appalled to find that little had been done by October 1941 to strengthen naval and air force defences:

I was so concerned at the obvious deficiencies revealed that I made the strongest possible representations to the conference [of defence chiefs] for substantial naval and air reinforcements without delay.

The defence chiefs in Singapore authorised a cable to London stressing that the only real deterrent to further Japanese aggression would be a British fleet based at Singapore. Page travelled to London and met Prime Minister Winston Churchill on 5 November, stating bluntly:

We in Australia think the sands of the Japanese crisis may run out in days . . . Could not that [military] aid be sent forward immediately to prevent disaster?

Page had already discovered that the protection of England from German bombing and invasion had absolute priority, while the Middle East was considered next in importance. Singapore was important as a 'main fleet base', he was told. But there was no eastern fleet and few effective aircraft. It quickly became clear to Page that the British defence chiefs gave Singapore and Malaya low priority. Indeed, the Churchill Government, in June 1940, had signalled that if Japan altered the 'status quo', the Royal Navy would have insufficient resources to fight the Japanese in the Pacific:

it is most improbable that we could send adequate reinforcements to the Far East, we should have to rely on the United States of America to safeguard our interests there.

But Page soon breathed a sigh of relief when Prime Minister Churchill revealed that the modern battleship the *Prince of Wales* and the battle cruiser the *Repulse* were being sent to Singapore. Churchill also promised 'all necessary aid to ensure the safety of Australia and New Zealand'. Page didn't know that the great warships would have no air cover and that Britain would contribute little to the threat against the Antipodes.

*

On 5 November 1941 Japan took a fateful step. In Tokyo Emperor Hirohito entered an imperial conference at his palace. Japan's political and military leaders jumped to attention and bowed deeply. Hirohito would remain silent during the entire conference. The new prime minister, General Hideki Tojo, was an aggressive, hard-line militant who was called, within the Imperial Army, 'The Razor'. Between 1935 and 1937 Tojo had been head of the fascist gendarmerie, the dreaded and ruthless Kempeitai, a secretive army force that arrested civilians without warrant and often tortured and killed them on any suspicion. Tojo's next posting was chief of staff of the Kwantung army which was still involved in a brutal war against the Chinese and was continuing to occupy more Chinese territory. His appointment was the first time a general on active service had become prime minister of Japan.

Tojo had met with the Emperor before the conference to report that the government and the armed forces had decided to begin preparations for war. Hirohito had agreed to the preparation for war, but asked that every effort be made to negotiate with the United States over sanctions against Japan. When the conference in the Imperial Palace opened, Tojo took charge. He said that since the last imperial conference when it had been decided 'not to avoid war' with the United States, a special effort had been made to achieve success in diplomatic negotiations. But no agreement had been reached. Now, during discussions that lasted nearly four hours, the emperor's representative, Yoshimichi Hara, president of the privy council, asked for precise details of what a southern operation would entail if negotiations in Washington broke down. The army's chief of staff, General Hajime Sugiyama, responded:

> Targets of this operation are military and air bases in Guam, Hong Kong, British Malaya, Burma, British Borneo, Dutch Borneo, Sumatra, Celebes, the Bismarck Island, and small islands southwest of the Bismarck Islands.

This included Australia's mandated territory of New Guinea. The Australian territory also included the large island of New

Ireland opposite New Britain. General Sugiyama thought Japanese forces would make short work of their opponents:

> There are other forces in India, Australia and New Zealand, which I assume would participate sooner or later. The Army will carry out operations under these conditions in cooperation with the Navy, and its major efforts will be made in the Philippines and Malaya. The operation is planned to start in Malaya and the Philippines simultaneously and then to move towards the Netherlands East Indies . . . the entire operation will be completed within five months after the opening of the war.

Negotiations with the United States would continue, but the imperial conference on 5 November made the decision that 'the time for resorting to force' would be set for the beginning of December 1941. A Japanese Combined Fleet top-secret order on the same day listed 'areas expected to be occupied or destroyed' as eastern New Guinea, New Britain, the Fiji islands, Samoa, the Aleutians, Midway and 'strategic points in the Australia area'. Admiral Yamamoto said these were 'areas expected to be occupied or destroyed as quickly as operational conditions permit'.

General Tojo, in summing up, feared that Japan would become 'a third-class nation after two or three years if we just sat tight' and did not go to war. A further imperial conference of 12 November 1941 agreed that:

> Our Empire, in order to resolve the present critical situation, assure its self-preservation and self-defence, and establish a New Order in Greater East Asia, decides on this occasion to go to war against the United States and Britain . . .

*

Sir Earle Page in London in late 1941, continued to press for reinforcements for Singapore. War cabinet meetings revealed to Page the startling and ongoing British inattention to the Far East. Reviewing deficiencies in air strength in Malaya, the Joint

Planning Committee was far from helpful, firstly stating that 'adequate forces' had to be kept in England for protection against bombing and invasion, even though the Battle of Britain had ended over a year earlier. If air strength were augmented in Malaya, it could only be done at the expense of the Middle East and 'this could not be contemplated unless it became absolutely necessary'. Page accompanied Churchill on a three-day tour of devastated areas of England, where Churchill proved influential because on 10 November Page sent a personal cable to Curtin in Canberra:

> You will be pleased to learn that Churchill today at Lord Mayor's Banquet made public the despatch of the heavy British fleet to protect British interests in the Pacific and Indian Oceans and has also promised all necessary aid to ensure the safety of Australia and New Zealand.

Page had argued that the air strength at Singapore ought to be augmented, 'even at the expense of other theatres.' But Churchill said the transfer to the Far East of forces currently engaged against Germany and Italy would be a grave strategic error as they might remain inactive for a year:

> The correct strategy was to move forces from theatre to theatre as the situation changed. Our forces could be most useful employed in the Middle East and a victory [there] would have a big effect in keeping Japan back . . .

Yet too many unanswered questions hung over British and American responses as to how they would react if Japan entered the war. Dissatisfied, Page made his way to the Air Ministry for what would become a deeply worrying private meeting with the chief of the air staff, Air Chief Marshal Sir Charles Portal:

> My talk with Sir Charles Portal produced some astonishing opinions. He admitted that Singapore was inadequately defended, but regarded this as a political rather than a military question. If it

became necessary, or if the appropriate measures were applied, he could, he said, release six Blenheim squadrons from the Middle East without unduly affecting operations in that theatre.

It was only then that Portal let slip to Page the British defence thinking that was at the heart of Churchill's Far East policy:

My diary account of our interview records that Portal expressed the incredible view that, if Singapore were lost, *it could be picked up again later*. Moreover, he thought it possible that Britain would not fight if Japan invaded the Netherlands East Indies, a course which would bring Japanese troops within 400 miles [644 kilometres] of Darwin.

Page was aghast at the thought of Singapore being allowed to go under only to be recaptured at some later date. Yet this ruthless approach towards the Far East and the region all the way down to Australia and New Zealand was precisely the concept that war planners in London and Washington were beginning to embrace. Page said he 'warmly retorted' to the British air chief that Britain would show herself quite unconscious of the nature of opinion in Australia and New Zealand if she adopted this attitude:

By refraining from action in the Indies, she could, at a critical stage, split the Empire asunder.

One of Britain's prominent official war historians, Major General Stanley Woodburn Kirby, said that as long as the Churchill Government gave priority to the Middle East and to aid for Soviet Russia before security for the Far East, the Air Ministry could not find additional aircraft for Malaya. The result, he thought, was that the prime minister and the chiefs of staff 'may well be considered guilty of unjustified complacency'.

As war with Japan loomed, Winston Churchill misled Prime Minister Curtin and the Australian Government about the true state of British priorities in the Far East. Churchill's absolute priority concerned operations against Germany. The fact that operations such as those in the Middle East included a high percentage of Australian servicemen did not give the Australian Government a modicum of extra consideration, nor a meaningful say in the allocation of resources in the higher direction of the war.

Churchill knew the extent of the threat to Singapore. While the Middle East fighting continued, he had advice from a trusted general that Japan was likely to make an effort to capture Singapore in the near future. Churchill's close assistant, General Sir Henry Pownall, made an important prediction in his diary on 15 November 1941. He believed that Japan would go to war soon and that Singapore would be an early target. Yet Churchill had told Sir Earle Page only three days earlier that if Britain moved forces to the Far East they might 'remain inactive for a year'.

Two days later Churchill appointed Pownall as the new commander-in-chief Far East, replacing Air Chief Marshal Brooke-Popham, who had fallen from favour with his many requests for assistance. But because of the crisis, Brooke-Popham would continue in his role into 1942. Pownall must have known that Churchill was, at best, misguided about the Far East, or in fact was wilfully deceiving the new Australian Government.

According to General Pownall, the British Government was relieved to leave the management of negotiations with Japan to the United States. Pownall indicated that Britain wasn't 'too worked up' about Japan in the Far East, although in his diary on 20 December 1941 he wrote that 'we've under-estimated the Jap . . . he is a far better fighter than we ever thought'.

*

In Japan, Foreign Minister Shigenori Togo said the time for negotiations with the United States was drawing to a close. Western sanctions against the Japanese economy were now beginning to hurt and projections on the future use of natural resources such as oil and on production pointed to Japan gradually being crippled. Prime Minister Hideki Tojo gave the broadest hint imaginable of Japan preparing for imminent war when he addressed the national diet in Tokyo on 17 November. Japan now faced a situation where she must decide her course 'for generations to come' as 'a grave and pregnant situation' menaced Japan in the South Pacific:

> One hardly needs to explain that an economic blockade, as between non-belligerents, constitutes a measure little less hostile in character than armed warfare.

*

The war with Germany came closer to Australia when a great naval tragedy occurred off the coast of Western Australia. Rory Burnett was a twelve-year-old schoolboy when he farewelled his father, Captain Joseph Burnett, the commander of the light cruiser HMAS *Sydney*. Burnett was to re-join his ship in Fremantle in 1941. Rory Burnett, who later became a commodore, never forgot his father's farewell:

> I remember my father's parting words at the tram stop in St Kilda Road as he was seeing me off to school: 'Remember to be a leader and not a follower and always use your initiative.'

Curtin had been prime minister for less than seven weeks when he received news that HMAS *Sydney* and her 645 men were overdue. On 24 November Curtin was told that the navy had been calling the cruiser continuously by wireless transmission without response. Curtin was informed that a British tanker had picked up twenty-five German seamen on a raft 115 nautical miles (212 kilometres) north-west of Carnarvon, Western Australia. He was told a search by aircraft over the Indian Ocean had failed to locate the *Sydney*. The German seamen were from the raider the *Kormoran*. The rescued survivors said their ship had been sunk in an action with the *Sydney*. Of the 399 men on the *Kormoran*, 318 had survived. On 25 November Curtin took senior political reporters into his confidence, as recorded by the Melbourne *Herald*'s Joe Alexander in his diary that night:

> Curtin gave us certain bad war news affecting ourselves today. We were forbidden to discuss the matter with anyone excepting our editors. It will become a great sensation when it becomes known.

On 28 November Alexander wrote again in his diary:

> The captain of the Hun raider [Theodor Detmers of the *Kormoran*] has been taken and he says the *Sydney* fired two torpedoes but missed. The raider fired three, one of which hit the *Sydney*. The raider's crew left before the raider blew up and the *Sydney* was last seen steaming over the horizon ablaze.

Both vessels were destroyed in the firefight. Curtin put a blanket ban on the release of any information about the *Sydney* in the hope that survivors might be found:

> I couldn't bring myself to make the announcement. I couldn't bear to think of the shock the news would mean to relatives and friends of the crew. So I went to Government House and talked to the Governor-General. He comforted me . . .

By late November Curtin couldn't withhold the information any longer and issued a statement saying the cruiser had been in action with a heavily armed enemy merchant raider, which she sank by gunfire, according to survivors from the enemy vessel:

> No subsequent communication has been received from HMAS *Sydney* and the Government regrets to say that it must be presumed that she has been lost. Extensive search by air and surface units to locate survivors continues.

Soon, speaking in strict confidence, Curtin told political reporters of his fears, as Joe Alexander recorded in his diary:

Curtin's story still left a great element of mystery but he is convinced that through carelessness or a conviction of invincibility, the *Sydney* took risks.

*

Around this time Curtin received a terse complaint from Churchill saying that External Affairs Minister Evatt had been critical of his government in public for not declaring war on Finland, Hungary and Romania. Churchill insisted that 'inevitable divergences' between the two countries be kept secret. It was a strange time for the British prime minister to be carping about Evatt's wording when so much more was at stake in the Far East. Curtin had no intention of being lectured by Churchill and quickly responded:

> We assume that your Government welcomes our independence of thought and advice rather than that we should wait on you for guidance and support. The latter would be most unhelpful to you and would be equally unhealthy from an Australian national viewpoint.

Curtin had more urgent issues on his mind. He feared that Japan was intent on war, as Joe Alexander noted in his diary on 30 November:

> There is extreme pessimism about the prospects in the Pacific. Japan is ready for action apparently.

*

Japanese leaders solemnly entered the East Room of the Imperial Palace in Tokyo on Monday 1 December 1941. It was a formal high chamber, its walls covered with silk embossed with the imperial chrysanthemum emblem. Emperor Hirohito was seated at a slightly raised dais before a silk screen. Officers in their dress uniforms and white gloves sat on one side of long tables, stiffly facing each other, not the Emperor. Prime Minister Tojo outlined the events that had led to this imperial conference. He said the 25 November deadline for an agreement with the United States had passed; America's consistent policy had been to thwart the establishment of a new order in East Asia. Others made statements in support of war. Tojo concluded that the Japanese Empire 'now stood at the threshold of glory or oblivion':

> Once His Majesty reaches a decision to commence hostilities, we will all strive to meet our obligations to him, bring the government and the military ever closer together, resolve that the nation will go on to victory, make an all-out effort to achieve our war aims, and set His Majesty's mind at ease.

Hirohito nodded in agreement. Army Chief of Staff General Hajime Sugiyama noted that the Emperor displayed not the slightest anxiety: 'He seemed to be in a good mood. We were filled with awe.'

The Foreign Office in Tokyo that day sent a coded cable of advice to its embassy in Washington:

> to prevent the United States from becoming unduly suspicious we have been advising the press and others that though there are some wide differences between Japan and the United States, the negotiations are continuing.

Soon Japanese embassies around the world, including Australia, were instructed to abandon the use of code machines and dispose of them along with top-secret cables and files.

Urgent communications were now taking place between Whitehall, Singapore, Washington and Canberra as to whether action to protect the Kra Isthmus, linking the Malay Peninsula to the Asian mainland, should be taken immediately. Churchill, in his memoirs, made it clear that the Far East was of lesser importance than British interests:

It was rightly decided, both on military and political grounds, that we should not complicate the course of events by striking first in a secondary theatre. On December 6 it was well known both in London and Washington that a Japanese fleet of about twenty-five transports, eight cruisers and twenty destroyers were moving from Indo-China across the Gulf of Siam [Thailand]. Other Japanese fleets were also at sea on other tasks.

*

Australian military intelligence informed Prime Minister Curtin that they had received reports of the Japanese burning papers at the consul-general's residence at Point Piper in Sydney, the commercial secretary's residence in Canberra and the Japanese minister's residence at Auburn in Melbourne. After dinner on Friday 5 December Curtin met senior political reporters at the Victoria Palace Hotel in Little Collins Street, Melbourne. Curtin stayed there because in those days it didn't serve alcohol. In a small smoke-filled sitting room in the hotel, Curtin revealed his deep concern to the journalists over reports that a Japanese expeditionary force was sailing from Indo-China south-west into the Gulf of Siam. He said he would remain in Melbourne over the weekend to monitor developments. War cabinet and defence chiefs had already been meeting in an urgent session at Victoria Barracks. Newspapers the following day, Saturday 6 December, headlining 'grave developments' in the Far East, reported the continuing steady southward movement of the Japanese expedition. Japan would not explain the destination of the ships. Newspapers also reported the almost certain breakdown of the lengthy negotiations that had been going on in Washington to prevent war between Japan and the United States.

During the day a distracted Curtin visited old friends in East Melbourne. They thought he was restless and terribly disturbed. Curtin startled them by saying, 'I've got to go back. Big things are happening.' A message from Singapore via London had read:

Two escorted Japanese convoys sighted. First convoy twenty-five merchant ships escorted by six cruisers and ten destroyers . . . Second convoy ten merchant ships with escort of two cruisers and ten destroyers . . .

Two Royal Australian Air Force (RAAF) Hudson bombers made the initial sightings of the Japanese invasion force. The first Hudson crew thought the Japanese ships were heading for the east coast of northern Malaya as they were 265 nautical miles (490 kilometres) from Kota Bharu, steering due west. Flight Lieutenant John Ramshaw of Melbourne and his observer, Flying Officer Don Dowie, with two gunners circled the ships from a considerable height for many hours, as Dowie later noted:

Using broken cloud cover we shadowed them as they moved north. Suddenly they altered course and headed back south. The squadron kept an eye on it and throughout that day and the following day – 7 December – as it steamed closer to Khota Bharu.

The commander of the Malaya operation, General Tomoyuki Yamashita, was aboard the *Shinshu Maru* – for intelligence purposes also known as the *Ryujo Maru* – a heavily armoured, specially built ship carrying landing barges that would be launched from gates at the stern and from the sides. Yamashita immediately sent a message to Japanese headquarters at Saigon (Ho Chi Minh City):

Enemy planes shadowing our ships. They seem to have come from Borneo.

Soon after Yamashita sent another signal to Saigon:

British planes shadowing us still. Cannot know if they have sent radio signal to Singapore. If so, British will be expecting us and preparing defence line. Plan will proceed as ordered.

Following a prepared plan, the invasion convoy turned into the Gulf of Thailand to make the British think Malaya was not the target. Shortly after, the RAAF aircraft turned away. As they disappeared over the horizon the convoy turned back on its original course. The correction put the Japanese back on track to hit the east coast of southern Thailand or northern Malaya. Another Hudson, piloted by Flight Lieutenant James Emerton of Melbourne, also spotted Japanese ships in the same area heading in the direction of Kota Bharu, although the two Hudsons never saw or made contact with each other. Emerton's Hudson quickly flew into the clouds and headed for his base at Kota Bharu as an armed float plane took off from one of the warships.

On Saturday afternoon, 6 December notices flashed on cinema screens in Singapore recalling all naval men to their ships. The big show was on at last and men seemed keen for action. Soon shore patrols rounded up all servicemen in uniform telling them to report for duty. Australian war correspondent Ian Fitchett said Australia's AIF troops up-country in Malaya were toiling on defence works in rain and steamy heat. Many miles of coastline and vital points inland had been wired and mined, he said. Roads, bridges and strongholds had been constructed by the AIF soldiers who were in an excited state:

> The Diggers' slouch hats have long since become a sodden mass of felt, almost shapeless in the rain, but they are still worn with a distinctive air ... The men are in high spirits. Their watchword: 'here is where we may have to fight; get ready!'

That Saturday night Joe Alexander of the Melbourne *Herald* took Curtin's press secretary Don Rodgers to dinner at the Australia Hotel in Collins Street. Alexander was experiencing the thrill and dread of being a journalist at the heart of critical but menacing developments. Over dinner Rodgers gave Alexander the latest information, which the reporter recorded in his diary:

We are on the brink of war with Japan. These are exciting and tragic but wonderful days in Melbourne. There is a stimulus in being in touch in this way. The Ministers are all very anxious but not fearful. There is an atmosphere of great strain and of sleepless nights but all are thankful while awaiting the deadline. If Japan takes the plunge it means fearful perils for Australia.

The tension mounted over the weekend. Radio broadcasts and Sunday newspapers told of the Japanese armada's advance in the Gulf of Thailand. More defence cables with information on sightings of the convoys came in to Army Headquarters at Victoria Barracks. The number of merchant troopships in the convoys was revised upwards to forty-three. But conditions for reconnaissance deteriorated; Brooke-Popham, awaiting reinforcements in Singapore, commented, rather alarmingly, to his chiefs in London:

Conditions for reconnaissance were very bad and there can be no real certainty that ships seen were an expedition.

Brooke-Popham had made an unforgivable miscalculation. Japan's incredible assault across Asia and the Pacific was underway and he had been forewarned of what was approaching. The RAAF crews off the Malay Peninsula knew precisely what they had seen and reported. After the crew of the first RAAF Hudson to spot the Japanese ships landed at the Kota Bharu airstrip, their commanding officer told them to get a good night's sleep because they were going to be busy very soon. Flying Officer Don Dowie said they took off at one o'clock the next morning, Sunday 7 December. The Japanese ships were now immediately off the Malaya coast and the Australians began to bomb them:

We bombed up the aircraft again and our crew led the second attack. We picked what appeared to be a cruiser and released our bombs at mast head height. That's all I remember. I woke up in the sea supported by my Mae West life jacket. A16–94 [the RAAF Hudson] was lost without trace of the crew. By an amazing stroke of good fortune an empty native *prau* floated towards me in the strong current. I managed to grab it and climbed aboard.

Dowie was captured by the Japanese and finished up on the dreaded Burma railway. The captain of the Hudson, Flying Officer John Ramshaw, was among those killed. The captain of the second Hudson that found the convoy, Flight Lieutenant (later Wing Commander) James Emerton, would be killed fighting the Japanese over New Britain in 1944.

The defenders of Malaya had only 158 aircraft on 7 December, many of them woefully outdated. The RAAF Hudson bombers were relatively new and effective but others were not, like the RAF's twenty-four obsolete Vickers Vildebeest biplane bombers first built in 1928. As General Sir Henry Pownall would later state, the Vildebeests were 'really quite useless'. At least five Vildebeests were shot down over the next few days.

In Singapore the staff of the Combined Operations Room badly confused the intentions of the convoy off the Malay Peninsula. The sighting by Emerton in the second Hudson was taken to have been of two cruisers, ten destroyers and twenty-five transports. Since it seemed that the first force, reported by Ramshaw, had rounded Cape Cambodia and was heading north-westerly into the Gulf of Thailand and not towards Malaya, it was presumed the other forces should be following it.

*

Australia was now on full alert but, in many ways, the country was still living a dream. Sydney's *Sunday Telegraph* boasted in an editorial that Australia, with the Americans, Britons, Chinese and Dutch, had less reason to fear the future than the Japanese themselves: 'Inch by inch Japan was edging along a branch that could be cut.' An adjoining feature headlined 'Japan's air force isn't first class' pointed out that the nearest Japanese air base was 2650 miles (4265 kilometres) from Sydney and well out of bomber range. Besides, Japanese aircraft 'did not stand up well to hard use in active service' and independent experts were 'not impressed by the

quality of Japanese airmen'. It was mostly regrettable myth, reinforcing the notion that the 'little yellow men', as Australians often
called the Japanese, were no real threat despite their recent years of
brutal wartime experience in China and their massive armaments.

The British in Singapore continued to misinterpret Japanese
intentions towards Malaya. Dominions Secretary Lord Cranborne
(Robert Gascoyne-Cecil) cabled Curtin:

> information received is not yet sufficient to establish whether
> Japanese are making for (1) Kra Isthmus (Thai-Malaya border
> region), (2) Bangkok, (3) Anchorage in Indo-China between
> Cambodia Point and Thailand border. Admiralty advice last
> mentioned possibility can by no means be excluded.

*

While world attention was riveted on the Japanese warships and
troopship armadas in the Gulf of Thailand, secretly, highly skilled
and war-tested Japanese naval airmen were in high spirits aboard
six Japanese first-line carriers – the *Akagi*, the *Kaga*, the *Soryu*, the
Hiryu, the *Shokaku* and the *Zuikaku* – about 600 nautical miles
(1110 kilometres) north-west of the Hawaiian island of Oahu.
With over 420 aircraft, the carriers, support ships and men constituted by far the most powerful carrier strike force ever assembled
for war. This fearsome armada was rapidly steaming to within
striking distance of the US base at Pearl Harbor. The airmen had
been awoken with a radio message from the commander-in-chief
of the Combined Fleet, Admiral Yamamoto, who had visited the
Emperor, and had been told:

> The task facing the Combined Fleet is of the utmost importance
> and the whole fate of our nation will depend on the outcome . . .

Yamamoto, about to leave the Inland Sea aboard the battleship
the *Nagato*, his flagship, had the Emperor's message relayed to the
carrier strike force as it neared its attack location north of Hawaii.
Yamamoto included his own exhortation:

I have reverently accepted the Imperial command and assured His Majesty that all the officers and men of the Combined Fleet would devote themselves unsparingly to the achievement of the mission, to satisfy His Imperial Majesty's wishes.

Talks between the Japanese and US governments had been getting nowhere. There was one final meeting scheduled at Japan's request between Japanese special envoy Saburo Kurusu and Ambassador Kichisaburo Nomura in Washington with Secretary of State Cordell Hull. Mamoru Shigemitsu, who would become Japan's foreign minister in the last two years of the war, summarised the situation succinctly in his memoirs:

As for the negotiations, there were limits to the concessions that Japan could make. So long as the Army and Navy were confident of the issue, they could see no reason to compromise at the expense of their self-respect.

An American-educated Japanese diplomat of the time, Toshikazu Kase, who was pro-Western in his outlook, especially after a four-year posting to London, later wrote that he tried to arouse the active interest of the British Government in the negotiations 'which, after all, materially affected the British Empire'. He said the British ambassador in Tokyo, Sir Robert Craigie, readily agreed that he should pass his requests to Whitehall, but Craigie was 'rather bluntly told to keep silence', since the United States knew what was best:

This was most unfortunate. If the British Government had played a more active role in the negotiations, the outcome might have been quite different.

In London the chief of the air staff, Air Chief Marshall Sir Charles Portal, composed a reassuring cable to Brooke-Popham in Singapore intended to inspire:

You know the limits in numbers and in equipment which necessity has set to your resources but we are confident nevertheless that your squadrons by their skill, gallantry and determination will overcome all handicaps and win enduring fame for themselves and their service.

It was Sunday evening in Australia and pre-dawn in Hawaii; the Japanese strike force with its six carriers neared its attack position 316 miles (508 kilometres) north of Oahu. An extraordinary distance away – some 6700 miles (10,700 kilometres) – commanders of the Japanese expeditionary force in the Gulf of Thailand were nearing the great Malay Peninsula and were relieved to discover lights burning along the Thai and Malay coastline as though they were not expected. The first landings were in rough seas at Kota Bharu, at 1.45 am on 8 December 1941, forty minutes earlier than the raids on Pearl Harbor. Soon after the Kota Bharu landings, Japanese troops also landed at Patani and Singora on the south-eastern coast of Thailand.

*

John Curtin went to sleep in his room at the Victoria Palace Hotel on Sunday night, 7 December, expecting to soon hear of a Japanese attack on Thailand. He had recommended that British forces, including Australian troops in Malaya, should 'go in first' but he would come to believe that Churchill had prevaricated, having divided his war cabinet on the issue. Curtin had given senior political reporters a top-secret briefing. Joe Alexander quoted Curtin on Churchill's attitude:

It amounted to this – 'Unless America collaborated, Britain should let Thailand rip'. This is disturbing and forecasts another terrific condonation by the Allies of Japanese aggression.

Japanese carriers north-west of Hawaii swung into the wind in the pre-dawn darkness and swarms of aircraft began taking off. Captain Mitsuo Fuchida of the Imperial Japanese Navy

Air Service led the first wave of attack aircraft to reach Pearl Harbor:

> I peered intently through my binoculars at the ships riding peacefully at anchor. One by one I counted them. Yes, the battleships were there all right, eight of them! But our last lingering hope of finding any carriers present was now gone. Not one was seen. It was 0749 when I ordered my radioman to send the command, 'Attack!' He immediately began tapping out the pre-arranged code signal: TO, TO, TO . . .

Japanese aircrews achieved complete surprise when they hit American warships, airfields and installations on Oahu shortly before 0800 local time. The navy air bases at Ford Island and Kaneohe Bay, the marines airfield at Ewa and the Army Air Corps fields of Bellows, Wheeler and Hickam were all bombed and strafed. Of the more than ninety ships at anchor in Pearl Harbor, the primary targets were the eight battleships: the *Arizona*, the *California*, the *Maryland*, the *Nevada*, the *Oklahoma*, the *Pennsylvania*, the *Tennessee* and the *West Virginia*. Twenty-one ships of the US Pacific Fleet were sunk or damaged. American aircraft losses were 188 destroyed and 159 damaged. Most were hit before they could take off. American dead numbered 2403, including 68 civilians. There were 1178 military and civilian wounded. Japanese losses were not considered heavy. Twenty-nine planes, less than 10 per cent of the attacking force, failed to return to their carriers. The only good fortune for the Americans was that the three aircraft carriers of the Pacific Fleet, the *Lexington*, the *Enterprise* and the *Saratoga*, were safely at sea during the Japanese raids.

After the Pearl Harbor news, General Douglas MacArthur's commander of the US Far East Air Force in the Philippines, Major General Lewis H. Brereton, had been desperate to have his planes bomb the Japanese base on Formosa, but several times was prevented by MacArthur from doing so. When Brereton finally got permission to attack, a fiasco ensued. His fighter planes, already aloft and circling for some time, needed to land to refuel. With the fighters being refuelled and the bombers lined up in neat rows at Clark Field, the Japanese made their devastating attack, catching the US air fleet on the ground some nine hours after the Pearl Harbor attack. The attack destroyed 142 aircraft, or about one-third of the US fighter strength and over one-half of the US bomber strength in the Philippines. The surviving bombers were flown to Australia. The surprise at Manila was completely incomprehensible, wrote the US naval historian Samuel E. Morison.

In Washington US Secretary of State Cordell Hull received a telephone call from special envoy Saburo Kurusu, who sought an urgent appointment for himself and Ambassador Kichisaburo Nomura with Hull at one o'clock. Nomura and Kurusu arrived over an hour late. Just before they arrived President Roosevelt telephoned Hull to say that the Japanese had attacked Pearl Harbor. Hull called the Japanese ambassadors into his room. They were not invited to sit. They apologised for the delay and handed Hull a long fourteen-part document. Hull already knew the gist of the document's contents from secret intercepts of Japanese cables but made a pretence of looking at it. The rambling message did not declare war but informed Hull that negotiations had closed. It said Japan's hope of preserving peace in the Pacific had been lost and in view of the US Government's attitude it was 'impossible to reach an agreement through further negotiations'. Hull put the document down and spoke very deliberately:

In all my fifty years of public service I have never seen a document that was more crowded with infamous falsehoods and distortions – infamous falsehoods and distortions on a scale so huge that I never imagined until today that any Government on this planet was capable of uttering them.

Nomura was about to speak. Hull put up his hand and nodded to the door and the Japanese diplomats trailed out.

In Melbourne the Australian Information Department's listening post, which had been set up to monitor the world via short-wave receivers at Mont Park near Melbourne, relayed flashes from world broadcasting networks to Curtin's Victoria Palace Hotel throughout the night. Curtin was asleep at 5.30 am when a monitor picked up the faint words 'and have now attacked Pearl Harbor in addition to the bombing of Manila reported a few minutes ago'. Further war reports began flooding in. At 7.40 am a report was received from Malaya saying that the Japanese were attempting to land from five ships off Kota Bharu on the east coast of Malaya near the Malaya-Thai border. Another message was picked up saying Singapore was being bombed. The BBC soon had news from Hawaii, saying that 150 planes had taken part in the raid on Pearl Harbor and that a naval engagement was in progress. The engagement was a search for submarines.

During this frantic period of grave early morning reports into Victoria Barracks came a curt and unequivocal cable from the Admiralty in London:

COMMENCE HOSTILITIES AGAINST JAPAN REPEAT JAPAN AT ONCE.

Before light Curtin's press secretary Don Rodgers knocked on the door to Curtin's hotel room and read the prime minister a brief report. Curtin looked at Rodgers through tired eyes and said simply, 'Well, it has come. Call war cabinet for 11 o'clock.'

A kind of calmness had overcome John Curtin. Ross Gollan, respected political reporter for the *Sydney Morning Herald*, wrote about it for the Monday 8 December edition. Gollan said there once was a theory that Curtin would not be able to stand up to the strain of prime ministership for more than a couple of months. He said minor illnesses of a nervous origin had attacked Curtin whenever heavy political weather had arrived. But now, according to Gollan, all Curtin's closest observers briefly saw a changed man:

The plain fact about Mr Curtin since he took the prime ministership is that the bigger the matter that has come to him, the more

decisive has been his handling of it – the more the load of work and worry upon him, the better his apparent physical trim.

From the general observations of his secretary, Fred McLaughlin, Curtin probably was calm:

It seems that his fullest strength flows out when there is the most imperative need for it, both in the struggles of Parliamentary affairs and under the more severe strain of vital decisions on which immense consequences may depend.

As the pressure increased, the image of the robust war leader was as illusory as it was transitory.

Chapter 3

OUR DARKEST HOUR

Bewilderment, anger and slowly mounting fear were the initial reactions among Australians to Japan's audacious attacks across East Asia and the Pacific. There were many who thought the Japanese, long considered inferior in almost everything, could readily be pushed back. 'The Japs must want to commit suicide!' was a common, uninformed comment heard on street corners where people gathered in groups. Flashes and disjointed snippets of overseas news broadcasts were being picked up and repeated. A broadcast from New York said Japan was in a state of war with the United States and Britain. A report from Boston said there had been a heavy loss of life and much damage in Hawaii. In Melbourne a cyclist with a ladder on his shoulder peddled past a crowd yelling: 'The Japs are at us!' The hubs of towns and cities around Australia were soon crowded with the curious and anxious. People gathered around newspaper sellers on street corners seeking the latest special editions. Radios in shops and homes were much in demand. 'Now we're in the thick of it' seemed to be a growing consensus. 'It will clear the air anyhow,' someone volunteered. Another said, 'The boys in Malaya won't be idle any longer.' The thousands of Australian troops in Malaya were, in fact, preparing for the fight of their lives.

Crowds gathered early at Melbourne Town Hall where a public meeting had been called to raise funds to replace the cruiser HMAS *Sydney*. When a radio blared the popular tune with the words 'The Yanks are Coming', the crowd clapped enthusiastically to the music, glad that America was in on the new Pacific war. Men rushed to enlist in the AIF at the army's recruitment offices in the town hall. The national anthem was sung in the streets with fervour by hundreds as the willing new recruits pushed forward. Bank clerks, council workers, shop assistants and many others were among the long queues of young men formed at the temporary recruitment centre in Martin Place in Sydney and at many other centres around Australia.

Australia had been at war with Germany and Italy since 1939. But now a new enemy had moved in force much closer to home. For almost another year a major part of the AIF would continue to fight in the Middle East and Australian airmen would fight in the skies over Europe until the end of the war, but Japan suddenly was the enemy that really mattered most.

*

Bombs began falling on strategic defence locations and densely populated areas of Singapore as seventeen Japanese bombers droned over the island in the pre-dawn darkness at about 4 am on 8 December. The city was not prepared. Sirens wailed but streetlights remained on. The Japanese bombers from Saigon mostly struck British air and naval facilities, but bombs also hit the financial centre Raffles Place, killing sixty-one people and injuring more than 700. Many of the casualties were British Gurkhas assembled there. Catherine Butcher, the daughter of a soldier serving in Malaya, was living in Singapore's Tanglin Barracks when she heard the first bombs drop:

> From then onwards there was panic with everyone trying to leave the Island. My friends were all evacuated. The bombing continued both day and night. We had to stay under the billiard table because there was nowhere else to go. Then there was this

tremendous explosion. The building seemed to shake and Amah got a mattress, put it on top of me and she then lay on top of that to protect me with her body and I shouted out 'Goodbye Mummy; I'll see you in heaven'. But luckily it must have been a very near miss.

Othman Wok was a schoolboy in Singapore:

I saw people dying on the road, people injured and buildings on fire and tumbling.

*

In the House of Commons, Churchill told a hastily assembled parliament that the Japanese had attempted a landing on the coast of Malaya without warning and had bombed Singapore and Hong Kong. In view of these 'wanton acts of unprovoked aggression, committed in flagrant violation of international law' Britain had declared war on Japan. Churchill said the Japanese in northern Malaya had been immediately engaged by British forces:

When we think of the insane ambition and insatiable appetite which have caused this vast and melancholy extension of the war, we can only feel that Hitler's madness has infected the Japanese mind, and that the root of the evil and its branch must be extirpated together.

*

The Australian war cabinet met on a floor above the nation's Defence Headquarters at Victoria Barracks. Defence chiefs gave brief reports, most of which were deeply unsettling for Curtin and his ministers. All Australian shipping to the north was falling back on Rabaul and Port Moresby. The troopship SS *Katoomba* was at sea carrying troops towards Rabaul but their numbers would be hopelessly inadequate to defend the strategic town and harbour. Australia's special team of coastwatchers in the islands, who worked for the Intelligence Division of the RAN, based in

Melbourne, had been warned to exercise special vigilance. Cable traffic between Australia and Singapore had been cut, presumably by bombing, and wireless transmitters were carrying the additional traffic.

In the midst of this shock and surprise, Labor ministers were now confronted by angry defence chiefs with serious complaints about the industrial situation on the Darwin waterfront. Vice Admiral Sir Guy Royle demanded urgent action to alleviate the waterfront delays which were 'seriously prejudicing defence measures at Darwin'. The war cabinet agreed to despatch the minister for labour, Eddie Ward, and a conciliation commissioner to Darwin to 'take all necessary steps to ensure the speedy handling of material required for defence purposes'. Ward and the commissioner hurried north, but the industrial problems remained.

Prime Minister Curtin agreed to an army recommendation that AIF troops be despatched to Koepang (Kupang) on Timor island, north-west of Darwin across the Timor Sea. The 2/40th Battalion departed Darwin by ship two days later, but no air cover could be provided for most of the journey. The army's chief of general staff, Lieutenant General Vernon Sturdee, said the army was considering sending two battalions of reinforcements, possibly each up to 1500 men, to Rabaul and Port Moresby.

Then came the hammer blows for Curtin. Significant new military shortages were revealed to the war cabinet. These included serious deficiencies in artillery, anti-tank guns, light machine guns, Bren guns, transport vehicles and rifles. General Sturdee disclosed that some troops in 'rearward areas' would receive rifles on a 'reduced scale', which was a calming way of saying that many infantry recruits at barracks across Australia were training without a rifle. An RAAF report said there was a shortage of 250-pound (113-kilogram) bombs, not to mention the shortage of reliable aircraft, which had been well documented. Curtin and the war cabinet ministers reacted with alarm. They asked the defence chiefs to quickly draft a report on Australia and adjacent areas, estimating possible forms of attack, scale of defences needed and current strengths and preparedness. The acting chief of the Naval Staff, Commodore John Durnford, assured the war cabinet that an air attack on Australia from Japanese aircraft carriers was not likely. Although Australia was short of escort ships, there were sufficient warships to deal with armed merchant or limited cruiser attacks, he said. Durnford warned that an attack on Rabaul was possible.

There was a sudden shock realisation of Australia's vulnerability. The nation's propensity to send much of its defence capability to Britain, the Middle East and the Mediterranean was coming home to haunt defence planners and the government. Ministers belatedly began to question why Australia had so much of its defence resources overseas when Japan was such a threat. The question of the return of a Sunderland flying boat squadron from Britain and a fighter squadron from the Middle East was debated, as the minutes recorded:

> Reference was made to the paucity of our own air resources and the value of these squadrons here and in the Far East.

The RAAF at this time stated that it had only 177 first-line aircraft in Australia, Durnford said. The figure was quite misleading. After initial clashes it would be discovered that none of the aircraft in Australia could be relied on to match the Japanese. Most of the aircraft were Hudson bombers, which performed good service in coastal reconnaissance and light bombing raids. There were slow Brewster Buffalo fighters, Catalina flying boats used mostly for reconnaissance, and the obsolete Wirraway being produced in growing numbers. Beaufort bombers were only trickling off production lines in Australia. Curtin was not the only minister reeling from the reality of the situation.

*

In Tokyo the Imperial Navy announced that Japanese naval planes had bombed air and military bases in Hawaii, Singapore, Davao in the Philippines and on America's Guam and Wake islands. Japan's Domei news agency reported that Japanese forces had started attacks on British forces in Thailand and were driving them across the border into Malaya. Another Domei report said a surprise dawn landing had occurred on the Malay Peninsula at Kota Bharu on the north-western coast. In a broadcast from Tokyo, Prime Minister Tojo said that 'brave military and naval forces were defying death' in the field of battle. He said that should Japan have submitted to American demands, the prestige of the Japanese Empire would have been compromised.

*

Prime Minister Curtin in Melbourne broadcast that Australia was at war with Japan. The formal declaration would be signed the next day. Australia's vital interests were imperilled and the rights of free people had been assailed, he said. The Pacific Ocean had been 'reddened with the blood of Japanese victims'. He predicted that these wanton killings would be followed by attacks on the Dutch East Indies and on Australia and New Zealand, 'if Japan can get its brutal way':

> The thread of peace has snapped – only the valour of our fighting forces, backed by the very uttermost of which we are capable in factory and workshop can knit that thread again into security.

Australia would be held as a citadel for the British-speaking 'race' and as a place where 'civilisation' would persist. With building emotion, Curtin's renowned oratory came to the fore with a stark warning:

> Each must take his or her place in the service of the nation for the nation is in peril. This is our darkest hour. Let that be fully realised.

One of the worrying issues now was to ensure adequate representation of Australia's point of view on matters of high policy. In London, Australia's special representative Sir Earle Page proposed that he should have open access to all discussions, secret plans, war cabinet meetings, defence committee meetings and to Prime Minister Churchill himself. Churchill would agree to something much less, but initially was irritated by Australia's demands for direct representation in the higher decisions of war.

Churchill was not prepared to divert much-needed modern aircraft and reinforcements to the Far East in significant quantities. Instead, he had put his faith in a great battleship and a battle cruiser:

> We had lost the command of every ocean except the Atlantic. Australia and New Zealand and all the vital islands in their sphere were open to attack. We had only one key weapon in our hands. The *Prince of Wales* and the *Repulse* had arrived at Singapore.

The ships had arrived six days earlier with Singapore under daily attack. Later Churchill was propped up in bed going through his red boxes of state papers when the telephone rang at his bedside. It was the first sea lord, Admiral Sir Dudley Pound, and Churchill thought his voice sounded odd:

> He gave a sort of cough and gulp, and at first I could not hear quite clearly. 'Prime Minister, I have to report to you that the *Prince of Wales* and the *Repulse* have both been sunk by the Japanese – we think by aircraft. Tom Phillips [Vice Admiral] is drowned.' 'Are you sure it's true?' 'There is no doubt at all.' So I put the telephone down. I was thankful to be alone. In all the war I never received a more direct shock . . . As I turned over and twisted in bed the full horror of the news sank in upon me. There were no British or American capital ships in the Indian Ocean or the Pacific except the American survivors of Pearl Harbour, who were hastening back to California. Over all this vast expanse of waters Japan was supreme, and we everywhere were weak and naked.

Before sailing north from Singapore Admiral Phillips had asked for fighter cover but was told there was none to be had. On the early evening of 9 December, despite poor weather, Japanese reconnaissance planes found his ships, forcing Phillips to change course back to Singapore. But he then changed course again to the north when he heard of the Japanese landings. Japanese aircraft first sank the *Repulse* with torpedoes and then turned on the *Prince of Wales* with torpedoes while other aircraft dropped bombs. Both ships went down with huge loss of life. Lieutenant Albert Jacobs escaped the *Repulse*:

> I was trying to swim in a heavy type of overall suit, buckskin shoes, and a service-type respirator complete with a jar of anti-gas ointment, eye-shades, etc . . . I heard a loud cheer go up from the men swimming around me. They were looking back, and on looking round I saw *Repulse* with her bows vertical, gently sliding below the surface stern first.

Curtin's secretary, Fred McLaughlin, recalled Curtin's rather stoic reaction the next morning:

> Following so quickly on what was then the great – seeming the perhaps irreparable – disaster at Pearl Harbor, his night had been one of great anxiety and care. But his step was firm as he set off for his office; and in reply to a tentative suggestion of concern . . . Mr Curtin replied: 'Nobody squeals about being a few goals down at half time.'

Curtin cabled the Churchill Government for an urgent appreciation of the Far Eastern situation from British chiefs of staff. Given Australia's commitment to Malaya, a somewhat impertinent reply soon came from the secretary for dominion affairs, Lord Cranborne, saying his government understood Curtin's wish, but 'things are moving so fast' that a telegram draft in the morning was often out of date by the evening. He added 'we are hard at work examining the situation'. Cranborne was dismissive of Curtin's concern and urgency, saying Australia's special envoy Sir Earle Page would 'no doubt tell you how we view the general situation confronting us'. Cranborne then had the audacity to point out that Japan was not the principal enemy:

> We must not forget that Germany, who is still the main enemy, is in serious and increasing difficulties both in Russia and Libya.

Besides, Cranborne said, there was no immediate large-scale threat to Australian territory, and much less to New Zealand. Curtin was outraged. He didn't regard the Far East as a subordinate theatre of war and was determined not to accept such arrogant offhandedness. Churchill at this time was getting ready to sail to the United States to meet with President Roosevelt. Despite the loss of the great ships off Malaya, Churchill's mood was now rather buoyant. After months of attempting to get America involved in the war, the Pearl Harbor attack had remedied that problem. On 12 December Churchill cabled Roosevelt with the observation: 'I am enormously relieved at turn world events have taken.'

Japanese forces quickly overcame British and Indian defenders on the north-eastern Malaya border with Thailand. The Allies were forced to withdraw to positions south of the important airstrip and base at Kota Bharu, from where the Australians had operated, but the base was soon abandoned. The Melbourne *Herald*'s Joe Alexander, wrote anxiously in his diary on 10 December:

> Our chances of survival are slender now ... God help us and above all God Bless Britain. Went to sleep with a heavy heart tonight mindful of all my sins and oppressed by a sense of disaster. These are terrible times but we must face them. In a flash Sydney has become as vulnerable [as] London – or Coventry. It is unbelievable. All Britain's refusals to face the consequences of Japanese aggression since 1931 have come to this lamentable pass.

A grim situation faced Australia's home defence. Australia had a four-division expeditionary force – the second Australian Imperial Force (AIF). Three divisions, the 6th, 7th and 9th, were serving in the Middle East or North Africa. Australia was barely equipped to defend itself. However, it did have several militia divisions, which would soon be pressed into action. In Australia the militiamen were disparagingly called 'The Chockos' or the 'Chocolate Soldiers' by the AIF. The Chockos had been called up for service and had not volunteered like those in the AIF. Initially, the militia, also known as the Citizen's Military Forces (CMF), was restricted by the Defence Act to service in Australia, which the government interpreted as also meaning Australian territories.

Private Norm Scowen of the 55/53rd Battalion recalled that the only difference with the AIF was that they wore shoulder patches with the word 'Australia':

> You'd be on the train and it would be half full of AIF and half full of Chocos, see there wouldn't be any brawls or anything. They might have a sling at each other . . .

There were 1563 CMF soldiers manning fixed defences on Thursday Island, and at Townsville and Brisbane, which meant Queensland's north was particularly vulnerable. Thursday Island and surrounding islets, only 164 nautical miles (304 kilometres) across a string of islands from south-western Papua and New Guinea, were especially open to occupation. Queensland's massive coastline of 8293 miles (13,346 kilometres), was defended by just 16,400 CMF soldiers. The Northern Territory had a total strength of only 6670 troops, with two militia battalions and an AIF independent company moving north from South Australia. Darwin was within easy range of Timor in the Timor Sea and many islands to the east in the Arafura Sea. Western Australia likewise was despairingly exposed, especially along its vast coastline and the almost empty north. There were 1900 men in coastal forts with a total of 8180 scattered troops defending a coastline of 12,968 miles (20,870 kilometres).

The vast lands and islands of Papua and New Guinea were also poorly defended. In the whole of the territory of New Guinea (excluding Papua) plus the Solomon Islands and the New Hebrides, there were but 2158 Australian troops, both CMF and AIF. The majority were based at Rabaul on New Britain. At Port Moresby, in the territory of Papua, there were 1088 men. Australia was wide open to powerful forces now pressing southwards. The war cabinet approved proposals to bolster the Australian army, which then had 132,000 full-time men. The new target was an extra 114,000 men plus an additional 5000 for the Volunteer Defence Corps for full-time duty on coastwatching and aerodrome defence. Around this time a group of senior officers who had recently given distinguished service in the Middle East were recalled to lead militia formations or fill staff positions. They included Lieutenant General Iven Mackay, who became general officer commanding Home Forces, and Brigadier Sydney Rowell, appointed to the General Staff with the rank of major general.

Curtin was desperate to instil into the minds of Australians the imminent danger from the Japanese. He sounded the alarm on 11 December at a lunch in Melbourne to promote war savings bonds:

Today the war rages in Australian waters; the enemy is seeking the earliest possible hour in which he can set foot on our soil.

A toughened Curtin said the government would make the decisions, and there must be no argument about them:

No man should drive a car for the purpose of pleasure. Not one gallon of petrol must be wasted, or one ton of coal misused. If to-night, or to-morrow night, I see a repetition of what I saw last night a vast glow in the sky of this capital – or if I hear of it in other capital cities – it will stop thereafter as a result of decisions the Government will make.

In London, the vice chief of Naval Staff, Vice Admiral Sir Henry Moore, beavered away on his papers in the underground communications centre, which was a concrete maze containing offices, plotting rooms and the Cabinet War Room off Horse Guard Parade alongside St James's Park. In front of him was a card, placed there on the orders of Churchill with a message attributed to Queen Victoria during the Boer War:

> Please understand there is no depression in this house and we are not interested in the possibilities of defeat. They do not exist.

Deep in the reinforced bunker Admiral Moore worked quietly on a document headed 'Future British Naval Strategy'. Moore's assessments of 14 December 1941 give insight into the magnitude of the opposition Curtin was about to face in his urgent efforts to reinforce the Far East and Australia. The British naval strategy's first consideration was on the Atlantic and keeping open British sea communications. After the Atlantic, next in importance was the Indian Ocean, because, as Admiral Moore saw it, on this rested the ability to supply armies in North Africa, the Middle East and Russia. Further down the list of naval priorities came the Far East and the Pacific. Britain would play a part in the Far East – Australia's near north – but with important terms and qualifications:

> to reinforce Singapore if the local situation permits and to proceed to the assistance of Australia and New Zealand.

Moore acknowledged that Britain's vital interests included the security from seaborne attack of Australia and New Zealand. But it was an afterthought in the scale of things. Moore deduced that a Japanese attack on Australia and New Zealand was unlikely 'unless the Japanese make Singapore untenable for our fleet'. There was only a reluctant token acknowledgement of numerous past promises:

> but if a real threat to Australia or New Zealand arises we must implement our pledges and proceed with the fleet to their aid.

Admiral Moore, however, heavily qualified what constituted a 'real threat' of invasion:

> There may be pressure by Australia, possibly as a result of raids by the enemy into Australian waters, to make us change our object before a real threat of a large scale attack arises. This must be resisted.

The hope of the new British naval strategy was that the Pacific should be left to the Americans, although for the moment there was not much chance for 'forward action' by the US navy, still reeling from its losses at Pearl Harbor. With no available resources in Australia, Curtin tried to get help for Rabaul. In mid-December he made a plea to President Roosevelt to come to Australia's aid in the Pacific Islands, including Rabaul, without success. Admiral Moore, in a revealing last paragraph, appears to have had an awful after-thought: what indeed might happen if Australia was abandoned:

> Moreover the consequences to Imperial unity of a Japanese attack on Australia and New Zealand unopposed by a strong British fleet are incalculable.

Six days after receiving Admiral Moore's recommendations, with Churchill in Washington, the chief of the general staff, Sir Alan Brooke, chaired the war cabinet's Chiefs of Staff Committee. The committee acknowledged that the position in Malaya was 'very serious' and that the Japanese advance towards Singapore must be disputed 'inch by inch':

> But should we, in spite of all our efforts, be forced out of Malaya, we must make every effort to hold the other essential points in the East Indies [Indonesia], retention of which provides a barrier to the Indian Ocean and Australia.

The committee generally agreed with Admiral Moore's naval strategies. It proposed the rushing of army reinforcements to Malaya and Burma as soon as possible. The committee also agreed that the Australian Government should be approached to despatch one Australian division from Palestine to Malaya. The committee also wanted to maintain the strong flow of air force pilot and maintenance trainees from Australia and New Zealand to Europe. From the outset Australia had agreed to provide an incredible 28,000 RAAF personnel to Britain under the Empire Air Training Scheme.

Meanwhile, Curtin's war cabinet struggled with competing priorities and limited trained manpower. On 15 December the war cabinet recommended that Australia's key priority be the defence of the big industrial centres of Newcastle, Sydney, Port Kembla and the giant munitions plant inland at Lithgow, all vital to war production. This region had nearly 4000 troops on fortress duty and the whole state of New South Wales had 43,807 men in the army. Darwin was listed as the next in defence importance, followed by the islands to the north-east of Australia. Rabaul, with its big harbour at a strategic point on New Britain, was another important consideration.

The speed and array of Japanese landings around the South Seas, as they called the massive region, were bewildering. The Japanese quickly captured the mainland off the British island of Hong Kong and by 13 December all British troops had retreated to Hong Kong island. Five days later Japanese troops crossed the harbour and landed on a wide front on the island. Surrender would be only a matter of time. The Japanese were keen to capture the oilfields in British Sarawak on the island of Borneo, east of Singapore. They landed in the south of Borneo on 15 December with another landing near Kuching nine days later. In the Philippines Japanese troops landed in the north on Luzon Island on 10 December with further landings at Legaspi much further south. They were met by American and Filipino forces under the command of the US's General Douglas MacArthur. On 20 December another Japanese force landed at Davao, even further south on the island of Mindanao.

Britain's new Far East commander-in-chief, General Sir Henry Pownall, had arrived in Cairo travelling somewhat slowly en route to Singapore. Reading cables, Pownall was 'not convinced' that the battle was going well in Malaya. The Japanese had landed in Thailand and Malaya and had moved southwards. 'They need pushing in to the sea,' he wrote in his diary, 'and the longer they stay ashore the harder it is going to be to do it.' He privately blamed Churchill for the loss of the *Prince of Wales* and the *Repulse,* sent against the invaders without air protection:

> But Winston *would* do it. He said to me that he'd had to over-come a lot of Admiralty resistance before he could get it done. Now we've lost two of them.

Japan's thrust into Malaya was succeeding on three main fronts with the defending troops constantly being outflanked and with-drawing. There was concern that British forces might be cut off in the north. Churchill sent a message to his military assistant General Hastings Ismay demanding that the security of the naval base at Singapore have absolute priority over holding mainland Malaya:

> Beware lest troops required for ultimate defence Singapore Island and fortress are not used up or cut off in Malay Peninsula. Nothing compares in importance with the fortress.

British and Indian forces in Malaya's north soon became committed to a continuous process of southward retreat, accom-panied by delaying actions in the hope that reinforcements might arrive. The Australian commander in Malaya, General Gordon Bennett, who had been with the first landing at Gallipoli in 1915, sent a message about the British command to Army Headquarters in Melbourne:

> I have seen a total absence of the offensive spirit, which after all is the one great remedy for the methods adopted by the Japanese . . . The position has arrived where something must be done – urgently.

Bennett feared that Malaya was becoming 'another Crete'. He strongly urged that at least one AIF division be transferred from the Middle East to Malaya. Australia's chief of the Naval Staff, Vice Admiral Sir Guy Royle, on secondment from the Royal Navy, had just returned to Melbourne from Singapore and gave first-hand reports of British air defence and land defences in Malaya that had 'completely failed'. Without aircraft carriers the position in the Far East was precarious. There were twenty-nine British torpedo bombers in Malaya, Royle said, which could have done great damage to the Japanese warships and troopships during the landings on 8 December, but none of the torpedo planes had attacked and he didn't know why. Members of the Advisory War Council chaired by Curtin were appalled, pointing out how often the Australian Government had stressed the need for Britain to strengthen air defences in Malaya.

An irate Curtin left the 16 December meeting and dictated a blunt cable to Churchill saying Royle's report 'fills us with great concern'. Convoys of troopships off Malaya should have been easy prey, he said, but there appeared to be no concentration of striking forces to deal with them:

> It is desired to point out that we have done all we can in making available three squadrons towards the air defence of Malaya and two for the Netherlands East Indies.

Churchill responded dismissively without directly addressing the situation in Malaya, saying Sir Earle Page in London would have 'the fullest opportunity for knowing all essential facts and putting forward suggestions'. He said a force of four aircraft carriers with cruisers was being organised for action in the Indian Ocean, but there was no reference to naval or air reinforcements for the Far East. Churchill said Burma had been placed under General Archibald Wavell, who had served in the Middle East, and General Sir Henry Pownall was relieving Air Chief Marshal Sir Robert Brooke-Popham, 'who is not up to job at Singapore'.

In fact General Pownall felt the same anger and frustration as Curtin about the lack of air power in Malaya. Pownall, in Calcutta

(Kolkata) en route to Singapore, wrote bitterly in his diary of Churchill's dominant sway over British decision-making:

> He didn't believe that the Japs would come into the war – not yet at any rate. For once his long range vision was at fault, and badly. As a rule his 'hunches' (as distinct from his day to day strategy) are pretty good. Not this time. I only hope we shall not pay dearly for the mistake. Singapore has got to be held, for to lose it may mean losing Australia, if not New Zealand. I don't mean losing them to the Japanese, but to the Empire, for they will think themselves let down by HMG [His Majesty's Government] at home. That would lead to quite unpredictable results.

Around this time General Bennett wrote a personal letter to the minister for the army, Frank Forde. He was disturbed that a British division had withdrawn from its position in the Malay state of Kedah, bordering Thailand:

> This withdrawal is the more perturbing because it has been brought about by the attack of one division of Japanese only. It seems to me that on the slightest provocation, withdrawals are ordered, not so much by the junior commanders as by the Higher Command itself.

Bennett said senior British officers in Malaya were not fit for the job. He believed the situation in the north was overstated by the British:

> I have found the [British] higher command so panicky that they are discussing a withdrawal to Johore [adjoining Singapore island] itself. In fact I am led to believe that it has gone beyond the discussing stage and has already been decided.

Bennett said the Japanese had control of the air. He claimed that the AIF, which was based in Johore state, 'will stand firm and will not retreat one yard, no matter what the opposition'.

The Royal Navy had now largely abandoned the Far East. Churchill was pressing the Americans to assume responsibility for communications to the east, 'right up to the Australian or New Zealand coast'.

The US army was moving ahead with plans to deliver limited aircraft and other weapons to Australia. They were not, however, intended for the protection of Australia but for the relief of the Philippines, where General MacArthur's forces, having evacuated Manila, were retreating to the Bataan Peninsula near the northern entrance to Manila Bay. Brigadier General Dwight D. Eisenhower (later the US president) of the War Plans Division on the General Staff wrote to US army chief General George C. Marshall that Australia should be only a transit point:

> Build up in Australia a base of operations from which crucial supplies [planes and ammunition] and personnel can be moved into the Philippines – probably entirely by air. Speed is essential . . . Move carrier with Army pursuit planes, pilots, ammunition and bombs from San Diego to Brisbane, Australia.

But the Japanese were rapidly seizing control of land and air in the Philippines. The situation in Malaya was deteriorating markedly. Bennett cabled General Vernon Sturdee in Melbourne to report a British retreat in the north from Kedah south into Perak and again called for an Australian division from the Middle East to save the situation. Prime Minister Curtin was informed, and on 20 December he cabled London with a message for Churchill in Washington. He said it was paramount that he know precisely what resources would be committed to stop the Japanese:

> Now that the actual threat has come and the enemy is making substantial progress on several fronts, we must press for it to be boldly met and hope it will not be attempted by dispositions of a 'penny packet' nature.

By 20 December 1941 the British had all but written off Malaya and Singapore. A memorandum was drawn up on that day by Field Marshal Sir Alan Brooke who said Britain couldn't send a fleet with fighter support to Singapore, even though he admitted that the position in Malaya was 'very serious'. He acknowledged that British air forces in Malaya were meagre and that land forces were heavily outnumbered. Although it was of the 'greatest importance to hold Singapore', to Brooke the outlook seemed inevitable:

> should we, in spite of all our efforts, be forced out of Malaya, we must make every effort to hold the other essential points in the East Indies, retention of which provides a barrier to the Indian Ocean and Australia.

The unlikely British plan now was to base a fleet in the Indian Ocean, which 'may well have to relieve Singapore or repel a threat to Australasia'. Brooke must have known that these suggestions were pipedreams. British attention was already moving away from Singapore and reports were sought on how Sumatra and Java in the Dutch East Indies could be reinforced.

Curtin and his ministers faced the reality of Singapore, the Dutch East Indies and all the territories and islands to the south potentially being lost to the Japanese juggernaut, with Australia itself being raided and bombed at the very least. Australia's official representative in Singapore, Vivian Bowden, scorned by high British officials because of his lowly diplomatic rank (he was previously a government trade representative on the island), cabled Canberra saying the air forces in Singapore were not capable of mounting successful attacks. Bowden said the best fighter available for the defence of Malaya was the Buffalo, but it had a low ceiling and couldn't even reach Japanese fighters. He said Penang on the west coast of Malaya was 'already virtually abandoned'. Bowden recommended seeking assurances from the British Government that Malaya would 'not continue to be regarded as a secondary theatre of war' and that reinforcements and supplies of modern arms and equipment would be rushed to Singapore:

Am convinced that unless reinforcements of modern aircraft and operationally trained personnel are sent immediately Singapore will before long be in gravest danger.

The Australian war cabinet began ramping up Australia's home defences, approving half a million pounds for air raid precautionary measures in government factories. Elements of the Australian press were now able to bypass rules forbidding criticism of the war effort and attacked British authorities for their conduct of the war. *The Argus* in Melbourne took the lead:

the man in the street is at last beginning to realise that he has been let down by men who have committed the same mistake that Britain has committed so many times in this war ... Critics of British conduct of the war were not welcome in Malaya a while ago, but critics are now plentiful among the British themselves.

The British high commissioner in Canberra, Sir Ronald Cross, saw anti-British views in Australia as 'infuriating and deplorable' and inspired by ministers of the Curtin Government. With a background in Toryism, Cross was firmly opposed to Curtin's politics. He was disgusted at senior Australian politicians holding Australia blameless for the war situation while believing that reverses in Malaya were 'simply the consequences of British stupidity and incompetence':

A stranger might suppose, moreover, that for the first time Australia was asserting her independent viewpoint, driven to so doing because [it had been] badly let down by dunderhead British generals.

Cross informed the dominions secretary Lord Cranborne in London that the time had come to 'fight for British prestige in Australia'. Cranborne was unimpressed with Cross, at one stage saying that his high commissioner had 'taken to lecturing Australian ministers as if they were small and rather dirty boys'.

At this time the British press also questioned British decision-making. Critics included the *Daily Express* in London:

> Beyond doubt, Australia and New Zealand view the Japanese threat in a graver light than Britain, which is natural because, while Dominion troops are overseas, the people of the Dominions face a danger of a Japanese invasion of their homes.

The Times of London joined the British press chorus:

> Allies in the Pacific are paying dearly for miscalculations and unpreparedness. They cannot afford to allow Japanese encroachments to stretch so far that a recovery of lost positions will be long and strenuous.

But on his delayed arrival in Singapore, the new British Far East commander-in-chief, General Pownall, was appalled by the situation in the air:

> I think the Air Ministry have distinctly neglected this part of the world. At the beginning of the operation there were here less than 200 of the 330 odd [aircraft] which constitutes the authorised scale. Some half of the 200 are now out of action and we are very thin . . . we can carry out only a light scale of bombing and that only at night.

Churchill had churned out strategic position papers at sea while en route to the United States. One nominated 1943 as the year when Britain and America would send expeditions to recover 'places lost to the Japanese', because it would be at a time when Britain was 'intact and more strongly prepared against invasion than ever before'. In fact Britain had been well able to meet German attacks on British soil by the end of 1941. The serious threat of an invasion had long passed.

Churchill's position papers were very much aimed at engendering US support for the main thrust against his predominant enemy, Hitler. On arrival the British prime minister moved into the White House in Washington and quickly established a friendly and easy working relationship with the president and his senior advisers. Churchill's physician, Dr Charles Wilson (later Lord Moran), who had travelled with Churchill to Washington on the *Prince of Wales*, recorded in his diary that Churchill in the United States seemed like a younger man. The prime minister, he mused, must have known that if America stayed out of the war, there could only be one ending. But now, suddenly, the war was as good as won and to be prime minister of England in a great war at this time, recorded Wilson, was beyond even Churchill's dreams. 'He loved every minute of it.' But Wilson indicated that Churchill had one great fear – that Japan, rather than Germany, might become the primary focus of attention of the US forces. Wilson had been present for dinner at Chequers when Churchill heard news on the radio that Japan had attacked the American fleet at Pearl Harbor:

Since that moment it has never been out of his mind that America's entry into the war might mean a change in her strategy: [Quoting Churchill] 'They may concentrate upon Japan and leave us to deal with Germany. They have already stopped the stream of supplies that we were getting.'

He completed a paper on the Pacific front at the White House and gave it to Roosevelt before Christmas. The highly secretive paper would contain no immediate hope for Curtin in Australia, or for those commanders fighting in the Far East. Churchill said the Allies would not have the power to fight general fleet engagements. His plans sounded distinctly defeatist but in reality had more to do with Britain's home defence priorities:

We must expect therefore to be deprived one by one of our possessions and strong-points in the Pacific and that the enemy will establish himself fairly easily in one after the other, mopping up the local garrisons.

Yet in this interim period, as Churchill termed it to Roosevelt, there must be 'stubborn resistance at each point attacked and efforts should be made to slip supplies and reinforcements through as opportunities offered.' The aim was to force the enemy to make ever larger overseas commitments far from home, extending them, straining shipping resources and providing vulnerable targets, especially to Allied submarines. Churchill said he did not wish to discourage the United States from regaining its naval power in the Pacific, nor discourage it from 'the precise secondary overseas operations', possibly meaning the Philippines, so long as the 'absolute first priority' was in Europe.

At this crucial time Australia's Sir Earle Page in London might have had an opportunity, and certainly it was his duty, to sway British policy away from directing its efforts so fundamentally towards the defeat of Germany. Yet Page, increasingly under Churchill's influence, left London for almost a week from 22 December 1941 to spend Christmas with relatives in Belfast.

The US movement of weapons to Australia began, but General Eisenhower's initial enthusiasm had waned and it was a trickle in comparison to the amount needed. Four ships with some 4000 American troops aboard landed at Brisbane on 22 December. Some US merchant ships began to arrive in Australia carrying aircraft in crates, but they had to be assembled, as available skilled staff permitted, and the establishment of production processes took time. One division of US troops that arrived in Australia was quickly despatched by General George Brett for the defence of New Caledonia. The speed of the Japanese advance in the Philippines, together with Japan's rapidly growing dominance of the air over the Philippines, meant that the intended supply operation to these islands was delayed, and then became impossible. There would be very gradual but significant benefits for Australia in the US failure to rearm its embattled forces in the Philippines. But time was slipping away.

*

The Malayan campaign was already looking like a rout for the British, Australian and Indian defenders. On 22 December British troops were withdrawing over the Perak River near Ipoh. They destroyed road and railway bridges north of Kuala Kangsar and a pontoon bridge near Ipoh as they retreated. On the same day General Pownall relieved Sir Robert Brooke-Popham as commander-in-chief Far East, although the change would come too late to have a major impact.

Further south, troops of the 2/20th Battalion, part of the 8th Division AIF, at Mersing on Malaya's east coast in northern Johore state, were anxious to come to grips with the enemy. The battalion had been at Mersing since August, having left Sydney in early February 1941. Mersing was an attractive tropical town surrounded by plantations and villages nestled under coconut palms. The beaches along the river mouth made an excellent landing zone. The troops had spent most of their time at Mersing preparing defences for an expected landing by the Japanese.

Private Henry Ritchie, twenty-six, of Sydney, a member of A Company of the 2/20th Battalion, wrote to his sister Ethel in Sydney on 22 December from what he described as 'the front line' on the coast, where the company was camping in weapons pits. Ritchie wrote that a Japanese convoy spotted coming down the Malay coast had been turned back:

> But believe me they'd have got a hot reception as we are fairly well equipped and felt confident of ourselves. We are a likely crowd, even though I say it myself, although I suppose there'd have been a few dirty pants afterwards. But I expect we will cop something sooner or later and then here's hoping for all the luck in the world.

Luck would be in short supply. A Company's Lieutenant Frank Gaven didn't share Private Ritchie's confidence. He is recorded by his battalion association as saying that A Company had 'insufficient weapons, insufficient ammunition, insufficient written instructions and insufficient time to train a sufficient number of personnel'. It would be almost a month before the Japanese infantry would arrive at Mersing and Private Ritchie would get his long-awaited crack at the enemy when it came in overwhelming numbers. Initially the 2/20th Battalion suffered from heavy aerial bombing and machine-gun attacks. They tried firing back at aircraft with their .303 rifles until ordered to stop wasting ammunition. Private Ritchie was soon in the thick of things.

A Company carried out a highly successful and audacious ambush of the advancing Japanese troops and inflicted many casualties before pulling back. The retreating Australians destroyed the large concrete bridge over the Mersing River, but the Japanese quickly rebuilt it and continued southwards. South of Mersing Australian artillerymen urgently radioed for air support and requested a drop of small arms and drugs for the wounded. A slow old RAF Vickers Vilderbeest biplane eventually flew over and dropped the small arms and drugs among the Japanese. According to Gunner Russell Braddon, the aircraft then dropped a large bomb in the middle of the Australian perimeter in a rubber plantation and killed a group of Diggers. After heavy fighting, in which the Australian artillery killed large numbers of Japanese, the 2/20th were ordered to retreat.

*

The top-level talks in faraway Washington would now make no difference to Japan's ability to advance at a cracking pace. As Australia's minister in the United States, Richard Casey, reported, Churchill was discussing military, air, naval and supply matters in all theatres of the war with Roosevelt at all hours. Churchill clearly misrepresented the true situation in Malaya, speaking confidently of Singapore's ability to hold out for another six months and of efforts to strengthen Burma. The British were pleasantly surprised. Despite Pearl Harbor, the Americans agreed substantially to maintain the 'Beat Hitler First' doctrine, as Churchill's chief military assistant General Ismay noted:

We had not expected our American friends to see eye to eye with us on this question without considerable argument . . .

While President Roosevelt would accept this policy, gradually some important voices in Washington, and in time General Douglas MacArthur, would begin to criticise the US interpretation of the strategy. General Joseph Stilwell, known for his derisive and outspoken personality, was the senior tactical commander in California at the time of Pearl Harbor. In his diary in December he described Roosevelt as a 'rank amateur in all military matters' who had been 'completely hypnotized by the British'. Stilwell was scornful of the United States taking the offensive in the Atlantic rather than the Pacific:

and what will the USA think of a government that abandons the Philippine Islands and the Netherlands East Indies to their fate? The British and the Russians argue that Germany is the real menace, and that once we pull her down, everything else is simple. But meanwhile Japan makes it most difficult to visualise how we are going to knock her out unless we keep her out of the East Indies.

But the general thrust of the policy would hold for several years. In the interim, there would be terrible and ongoing Allied tragedies all over the Asia-Pacific region.

*

In Canberra, Prime Minister Curtin received a copy of another alarming message from Australian commander General Bennett in Malaya to his chiefs in Melbourne. Bennett said British troops were tired and depleted and had no reserves to meet further Japanese attacks. Fresh retreats seemed certain, even involving British troops at Kuantan, about halfway down the east coast to Singapore. Bennett noted that the lost ground must be regained when the advance was checked:

This will require at least three divisions in my opinion. Again strongly urge that at least one of our divisions from Middle East be sent here as early as possible.

In the Philippines a big invasion force including eighty-five transport ships was landing at the southern end of Lingayen Gulf north of Manila in another Japanese spearhead. They were attacked by just four Fortress bombers that had flown from Brisbane. The huge Japanese thrust quickly pressed on southwards towards Manila to be joined by another Japanese force that had landed at Lamon Bay, on the east coast of Luzon Island, catching many of the Americans in a giant pincer movement. Already that Christmas Eve the roads to Bataan Peninsula around the northern waterfront of Manila Bay were choked with retreating soldiers and civilians.

*

Canberra was hot and smoky with summer bushfires burning on the hills around the capital. Mindful of his son's training in the RAAF at remote Geraldton in Western Australia, Curtin decided to entertain six RAAF airmen from Western Australia who were stationed at the air base in Canberra at the Lodge on Christmas Day. He called the local RAAF base but the telephonist didn't believe it was the prime minister on the line. So Curtin left his number for them to call back. The airmen were most grateful for the lunch, one of them writing to Curtin:

As obscure members of His Majesty's Air Force we realise that of all the Powers, only in Australia could such an event happen as you prepared for us. We feel that your gesture was truly consonant with the freedom of thought and action of this great country.

At Cottesloe, Elsie Curtin and her mother and daughter had Christmas lunch alone. On the mantelpiece was a telegram sent from Canberra two days earlier:

MY DEAREST THIS IS THE FIRST CHRISTMAS WE HAVE NOT BEEN
TOGETHER IT TEARS MY HEART YET OUR TASKS MAKE US OBEDIENT
TO THEIR HIGH DEMANDS AND WE DO THEM WITH ALL OUR MIGHT
STOP I PRAY YOU A GOOD CHRISTMAS HEAVEN GUARDING YOU ALWAYS
YOUR LOVING HUSBAND JOHN

At the White House on Christmas Day Churchill responded bitterly to Curtin's 'penny packet' jibe about Far East defences, saying he did not share Curtin's view that there was 'danger of an early reduction of the Singapore fortress', which he said 'we are determined to defend with the utmost tenacity'. Churchill concluded grandly and mischievously:

You may count on my doing everything possible to strengthen the whole front from Rangoon to Port Darwin. I am finding co-operation from our American allies. I shall wire more definitely in a day or two.

Every allowance had to be made for the state of mind into which the Australian Government was thrown by the hideous efficiency of the Japanese war machine, Churchill condescendingly later wrote of this time in his memoirs:

The command of the Pacific was lost; their three best divisions were in Egypt and a fourth at Singapore. They realised that Singapore was in deadly peril, and they feared an actual invasion of Australia itself . . . A mass exodus into the interior and the organising of a guerrilla without arsenals or supplies stared them in the face. Help from the Mother Country was far away, and the power of the United States could only slowly be established in Australasian waters.

Churchill didn't believe the Japanese would invade Australia across 3000 miles (4828 kilometres) of ocean. Yet the speed of the Japanese advance meant that the enemy would be in Timor 447 miles (719 kilometres) from Darwin in less than two months.

That Christmas Day the British and Canadian defenders of Hong Kong island had been forced back to the end of the Stanley Peninsula. They were out of mortar bombs and machine-gun ammunition, and food and water was in short supply. A large number of wounded had been taken to St Stephen's College at Stanley. Canadian padre Captain J. Barnett was walking through broken glass and whizzing bullets into the main ward of the makeshift hospital when the Japanese burst into the building. 'As they came in I saw them bayonet wounded soldiers in bed,' he recalled. In outrages that would be repeated elsewhere, the Japanese drove their bayonets repeatedly into the defenceless, sick or wounded patients. Two European doctors rushed forward to stop them. Both were immediately shot and bayoneted dozens of times. Japanese soldiers then went through the hospital ward in a frenzy, killing more than fifty wounded in their beds. Four Chinese and three British nurses were dragged outside, raped and then murdered. The atrocities in Hong Kong would continue under Japanese occupation.

As the joint military conference got underway in Washington the US chief of the army air forces, Lieutenant General Henry 'Hap' Arnold, told British chiefs he couldn't let the Philippines fall:

> I stated that we must build up our air strength in the Philippines, Australia and the Dutch East Indies as rapidly as possible . . . and that we would cram into Australia such airplanes, combat crews and other air force personnel as is possible to get there by air, by boat or any other way until we had built up for General MacArthur a total of eighty heavy bombers and about 160 to 200 operating pursuit craft.

The initial plan was to help General Douglas MacArthur beat off the Japanese invasion of Manila, but the Japanese were rapidly advancing from different directions. MacArthur was forced to evacuate the capital and move his headquarters to the island of Corregidor at the entrance to Manila Bay. The rocky island fortress, with its big guns, was being constantly bombed and strafed. MacArthur had been promised by radio that every effort was being made to send him reinforcements:

> But during the year-end conference in Washington, which again reaffirmed the Allied 'Hitler first' strategy, I received this message: 'It now appears that the plans for reaching you quickly with pursuit plane support are jeopardised.'

Publicly, Curtin put a positive spin on the Washington talks. Perhaps his briefings from the Australian envoy in Washington, Richard Casey, who would soon be working for Churchill, were deficient. Curtin said in a national broadcast on 26 December that he was 'greatly encouraged by the growing reinforcements that will be ranged on our side'. But the Australian Government, he said, had never been satisfied with the air position in the Pacific:

> The meeting at Washington shows that the democracies are fully alive to the need for cohesive action in directing the Pacific operations.

In reality they were not, but demands flooded in from Washington for details reports, facts and figures. Curtin wrote to his wife Elsie in Perth that his Christmas week had been heavy going. Inward and outward cables putting the Australian view on each and every item under discussion in Washington had been 'staggering'.

President Roosevelt gave some encouragement that his country would come to the aid of the Pacific when he opened a new Beam direct radio-telegraph link between the United States and Australia on 26 December 1941 with this message to Australians:

> We give you our assurance that we consider the safety of your great Commonwealth as a definite essential in every plan of defence and every plan of offensive action against our common foes.

At best, Roosevelt was looking ahead in years. Churchill, responding to an earlier cable from the Australian prime minister, told Curtin that he had diverted the 18th British Division to Singapore, and it was rounding the Cape of Good Hope in American transports, along with Indian reinforcements.

Churchill would not share Curtin's view that there was any danger to the so-called Singapore fortress. He repeated to Curtin that air support was already on the way. He said Roosevelt and the defence chiefs of Britain and the United States were impressed with the importance of maintaining Singapore and were anxious to move a continuous flow of troops and aircraft through Australia for the relief of the Philippines. But should the Philippines fall, said Churchill, President Roosevelt was agreeable to 'troops and aircraft being diverted to Singapore'. Fine words, but largely it wouldn't happen.

At this time there were no plans for American offensive actions in the south-west Pacific. Well before Roosevelt's words were spoken, *The Herald* in Melbourne had asked Prime Minister Curtin to pen an article looking ahead to 1942. The task actually fell to Curtin's press secretary, Don Rodgers, who knew Curtin's thinking better than anyone. Curtin clearly agreed with Rodgers's words for the draft article, published on 27 December, headed 'The Task Ahead'. For a nation of only seven million, Curtin's New Year message was a bold outburst at Allied planning that declined to consider Japan as a primary enemy:

> we refuse to accept the dictum that the Pacific struggle must be treated as a subordinate segment of the general conflict.

Curtin then went on to announce an astounding departure from Australia's international relations that would ring through future decades:

> Without any inhibitions of any kind, I make it quite clear that Australia looks to America, free of any pangs as to our traditional links or kinship with the United Kingdom. We know the problems

that the United Kingdom faces. We know the constant threat of invasion. We know the dangers of dispersal of strength, but we know too, that Australia can go and Britain can still hold on.

We are, therefore, determined that Australia shall not go, and we shall exert all our energies towards shaping a plan, with the United States as its keystone, which will give our country some confidence of being able to hold out until the tide of battle swings against the enemy.

According to Don Rodgers in a later explanation, Curtin's message was framed at a time when the British Government thought that if Australia was lost, the nation could be recovered later, along with Britain's other 'possessions' in the Pacific. Churchill seethed when he read Curtin's New Year's newspaper message looking to America 'free from any pangs'. He told Curtin that he had been 'greatly pained in all my labours by the harsh tone' that characterised Curtin's various messages:

I hope you will not mind my saying that you have really not begun to feel the weight of this war or even begun to experience the danger and suffering under which the people of Great Britain have long been proud to live . . . I do not understand the reason for this mood of panic which I am sure is not shared by the people of Australia.

If hostile speeches continue to be delivered by members of your Government against the mother country and the present war direction I should be quite ready to address a broadcast to the Australian people. I feel confident of their generosity and enduring goodwill.

Churchill restrained himself from implementing such a divisive threat. He wrote in his memoirs:

It was my duty to make the fullest allowance for the alarm which racked the Commonwealth Government and the dangers which beset them.

On 19 January 1942 Churchill cabled Curtin again saying he bore no responsibility for the 'neglect of our defences' and the policy of appeasement that preceded the outbreak of war while he was out of office. He said the Japanese had gained the temporary command of Pacific waters and no doubt there would be 'further grievous punishment to face in the Far East'.

None of this helped Curtin or Australia. Curtin wanted guarantees in return for Australia's considerable contribution to the war effort to date overseas, not mere hopes for the future.

Chapter 4

ABANDONING AUSTRALIA

The Japanese fleet soon ranged almost unhindered across a vastness of the Pacific. The landing parties in the Philippines at Lamon Bay and Lingayen were now halfway to their objectives, including the capital Manila. On New Year's Eve General Tomoyuki Yamashita's 25th Army forces were continuing to smash their way southwards down the Malay Peninsula towards Singapore. They were a fearsome, well-trained enemy that had overcome road barriers, ruined bridges and ambushes and had continually encircled the British, Australian and Indian troops in bitter clashes. Japanese aircraft were dominating the air over Malaya. Now Yamashita put 1500 men of the 5th Division in barges to land behind the Allied forces. The Japanese landed well to the north, yet British commanders saw the landing as a frightening development and ordered further evacuations to the south. On New Year's Eve Yamashita was pleased to be breathing the warmer air of southern Malaya. He wrote in his diary of his brimming confidence:

My duty is half done, although success is still a problem. The future of my country is now as safe as if we were based on a great mountain. However, I would like to achieve my plan without killing too many of the enemy.

The chief of staff of the Combined Fleet, Admiral Matome Ugaki, on the battleship the *Nagato*, similarly quietly celebrated the New Year, reflecting on how smoothly operations were progressing. Ugaki wondered whether the United States and Britain would recover their strength sufficiently to fight 'a great decisive naval battle', which is what the Imperial Navy wanted:

Anyway, the future is filled with brightness. The course of events during the year will determine the fate of the war, so we must work hard, exerting every effort. The main thing is to win, and we surely will win.

In Washington on 31 December, the chiefs of staff of Britain and the United States formulated a groundbreaking agreement, which would have significant repercussions for Allies in the Asia-Pacific region. The 'cardinal principle' of British–American strategy, established in conference at Washington, would be that only the 'minimum of force necessary for the safeguarding of vital interests in other theatres' should be diverted from operations against Germany. They agreed to 'defensively hold' Hawaii, Alaska, Singapore, the Malaya Barrier, the Philippines, Rangoon and the Burma Road, and they thought it 'necessary to maintain the security' of Australia, New Zealand and India, and to support China. All of these were listed as 'long range' defensive objectives but in reality many points in the Far East were already in the process of being overwhelmed.

The Washington talks also agreed to exclude Australia and its territories from the newly created joint South West Pacific region for which the US fleet at Honolulu, or what remained of it, was responsible. Churchill had sent details of the unified command to Curtin, saying the arrangements were 'designed to safeguard Australia's interests and safety'. Curtin and the Australian defence chiefs bridled at the proposal, saying in a snippy cable that the attitude of the US and British planners was 'quite out of harmony' with Churchill's assurances on Australia's safety:

> Our view of these proposals is that their adoption would result in Australia and New Zealand being isolated and left to defend the Australia area without allied assistance and with entirely inadequate naval, military and air resources thereby endangering the line of sea and air communications between the United States and Australia.

A testy Churchill a few days later complained to Curtin about constant Australian requests for assistance in the Far East, telling Curtin that it was only a little while ago that the Australian leader was 'most strongly urging the highest state of equipment' for the Australian army in the Middle East. Churchill deeply resented the Australian interference in the important Washington discussions, saying:

> Night and day I am labouring here to make the best arrangements possible in your interests and for your safety, having regard to other theatres and other dangers which have to be met from our limited resources.

It was the equivalent of saying 'just trust me'. Curtin had complained that the new command structure to meet the Japanese set up by General Archibald Wavell, known as ABDA (American, British, Dutch and Australian forces), only reached the coast of northern Australia, excluding the rest of the country. Churchill responded that Wavell's ABDA Command was limited to the fighting zone where active operations currently were proceeding. This did not mean that vital regions would be left without protection. ABDA covered an impossibly vast area from Burma and Thailand to Malaya and the Philippines down to the tip of northern Australia. It was a command intended to take control of the so-called 'Malaya Barrier' but in reality the 'barrier' was disintegrating.

Churchill said he was pressing for the American navy to assume responsibility for the islands right up to the Australian and New Zealand coasts, but warned:

Obviously if we cannot persuade the Americans to take over, we shall have to fill the gap as best we can but I still hope that our view will be accepted.

Assuming responsibility in a 'holding operation' and pouring in vital war resources were two entirely different matters. Churchill had discouraged America from investing significant capability in the South West Pacific at the expense of Europe. Their 'Beat Hitler First' policy strictly limited any offensives and even support for countries in the path of the Japanese rampage. At best it allowed for some US raids and operations by submarines if 'favourable opportunities arose', but only limited offensives. Fortunately there was one influential senior American officer who was keen to grab those 'favourable opportunities' and turn them into significant offensives. The commander-in-chief of the US fleet and chief of naval operations, Admiral Ernest J. King, realised that the Pacific had a much greater potential as a naval theatre for successful operations than Europe, and began to justify additional forces for the Pacific on the grounds that they were required to safeguard vital interests.

In his extensive history of US naval operations, Samuel Eliot Morison, a friend of President Roosevelt who was made a rear admiral, wrote of the immediate plight Australia and New Zealand faced:

Nobody seemed able to stop the Japanese and in Washington there was even serious talk of abandoning Australia and New Zealand to the enemy. But, as King told the president, 'We cannot in honour let Australia and New Zealand down. They are our brothers, and we must not allow them to be overrun by Japan'. And the president agreed.

Australia and New Zealand can be thankful to Admiral King. When the leadership and defence hierarchy of Britain and the United States was all but deserting Australia and New Zealand, King began influencing a reluctant Roosevelt and secretary of the navy, Frank Knox, to bring about some meaningful offensive actions in the Pacific, which would begin during 1942. In the interim, one of King's first moves was to establish advanced bases to keep open the lines of communication between the United States and Australia. These included new island bases strung across the Pacific at places like Efate, Espiritu Santo, Fiji and New Caledonia. King would later write:

> The establishment of those bases, which have been in constant use as fuel and troop staging stations, and as distribution points for material and supplies, was in large measure responsible for our ability to stand off the Japanese in their advance towards Australia and New Zealand. Without them we should have been at such disadvantage that it is doubtful if the enemy could have been checked.

There was concern that, if not pressed by the United States, Japan's next move might be to drive through Burma into India and link up with the advancing Germans, possibly invade Siberia or even invade Australia and New Zealand, according to Morison. Faced by this dilemma, by March 1942 the US joint chiefs would at last recommended a limited deployment of American forces in the South West Pacific with the object of securing the Antipodes.

*

In Singapore, the newly appointed British commander-in-chief, General Sir Henry Pownall, now fully realised the strength of the enemy and how the Japanese as fighters had been badly underestimated:

> Our policy was to avoid a war with Japan as long as we could (*or to make America cause it*, if it was to happen) and we calculated

on that policy succeeding (or if it didn't succeed on America bearing the brunt). With all our other commitments I don't believe that however highly we had rated the Japs as fighters we would have been caused terribly to improve the condition of our Services in the Far East. We just hoped it wouldn't happen. And it did.

In Malaya, the Japanese were making intensive air attacks as they thrust down the western part of the Malay Peninsula. The Allied forces were constantly falling back to make another stand, this time south of Ipoh. On Christmas Eve, Curtin and Evatt were rocked by an assessment of the situation from Australia's representative in Singapore, Vivian Bowden, who cabled that the deterioration of the air position in the Malayan defence was 'assuming landslide proportions' and was likely to cause a collapse of the whole defence system. He said modern British fighters were expected to arrive on the island, but they would not save the situation because they were in crates and would take weeks to assemble under danger of bombing. British policy had now dictated that fighter and anti-aircraft defence be limited to Singapore island, which deprived forward troops in Malaya, including the AIF, of protection against Japanese aircraft. Bowden said the only thing that might save Singapore was the immediate despatch of large numbers of troop reinforcements by air plus the latest powerful aircraft flown in from the Middle East:

Anything that is not powerful, modern and immediate is futile. As things stands at present fall of Singapore is to my mind only a matter of weeks.

Bowden's desperate requests would never be met. The Australian commander, General Bennett, also pressed headquarters in Melbourne for the urgent transfer of an infantry division from the Middle East. He was promised something less – a machine-gun battalion and 1800 reinforcements. Inspecting his troops near the front, he found officers serving Christmas lunch to the men at tables, with the men light-heartedly calling the officers 'boy'. Bennett wondered 'if they realised that would soon be fighting for dear life'.

*

War production was slowing in Australia as a result of industrial strikes by essential workers. This included 100 employees of the Commonwealth Aircraft Corporation and workers at the Lithgow Small Arms Factory. On Saturday 27 December Curtin had called together in Canberra a conference to establish an Australian Industrial Relations Council. Curtin made an impassioned address saying that peacetime industrial processes must be overtaken by wartime practises. He frankly admitted that Australia's fighting forces lacked equipment that would give them parity with the enemy:

> Our men have been fighting a somewhat unequal struggle. It is most certainly a handicapped struggle from the standpoint of preparation. We have to overtake this gap. We have to produce feverishly and with all our might . . .

*

These were anxious days for Australia. The Japanese were successfully storming southwards while also pushing through Burma at a time when Australian forces were scattered across the globe. The Australian 8th Division was fighting hard and falling back in Malaya.

Churchill would much later attempt in his memoirs to explain why Australians were so anxious about Japan:

> They saw themselves exposed to the possibility of direct invasion . . . The new foe could strike straight at Australian homes. The enormous coastline of their continent could never be defended. All their great cities were on the seaboard. Their only four well-trained divisions of volunteers . . . and all their best officers were far away across the oceans . . . Can we wonder that

deep alarm swept Australia or that the thoughts of their Cabinet were centred upon their own affairs?

In reality Australia was doing more to provide for Britain's security than the reverse. In early 1942 Churchill, taking a lofty view, was frustrated with Australia's lack of a 'true sense of proportion' in world strategy. But Curtin had put Australia, under direct threat, first. The prime minister and the leader of the opposition, Arthur Fadden, were working closely together on national defence. They had a deep respect for each other and the opposition was well represented on the Advisory War Council, which had real power.

The governor-general, Lord Gowrie, in a broadcast on New Year's Day, foreshadowed that 1942 would be the most critical year in Australia's history:

> It is this Homeland, this free and honoured soil, which is now in danger of invasion by a savage and ruthless foe. This must not – this shall not – happen . . . It is the time for calmness and courage, for willing courage and intense and organised effort.

The Japanese were seemingly unstoppable. In Malaya they had now thrust further south along the important railway link towards Kuala Lumpur, the centre of government. British troops had withdrawn from their positions south of Ipoh and were preparing new positions further south. Japanese aircraft were dropping crude leaflets on Australian troops attacking the British and calling on Australians to surrender. Singapore was under dire threat and was being bombed constantly. The Philippines' capital Manila had been occupied. General MacArthur and his American and Filipino troops fought on in Bataan and Corregidor but the outlook was bleak. In Batavia, the Dutch administration warned the population to prepare for an invasion of the East Indies.

In Australia, civilian volunteers were out everywhere in coastal cities and towns filling sandbags and digging trenches. In Sydney, the volunteers were working alongside local council workers and home troops. Municipal councils and other civil authorities were lending men, plant and materials to speed urgent work. Money was being allocated for more air raid shelters in city and suburban areas. They were being opened in basements, subways, reinforced buildings and on vacant lots and parkland. In cities like Sydney and Melbourne, staff gave up their weekends to work on the sandbagging of city buildings. The façades of some city office buildings were being protected with reinforced brick walls. The tall sandstone clock tower on the General Post Office in Sydney's Martin Place, seen as a landmark for enemy pilots, was taken down in case it was hit by a Japanese bomb, which would wreck Australia's biggest communications centre below.

Having committed to 'Europe first', Churchill and Roosevelt with their defence chiefs had to decide what was worth saving. In Washington, Churchill's doctor, Sir Charles Wilson, wrote in his diary that he sometimes wondered if the prime minister felt the full weight of the decisions he had to make:

> It is as if Winston has a family of twelve children and there is not enough food for all of them – some of them must starve to death. He has to decide which.

*

Australians got a shock on Sunday 4 January 1942 when Japanese Mitsubishi bombers of the Imperial Navy's 24th Air Flotilla began bombing Rabaul, the beautiful Australian-administered town on the island of New Britain. Japanese planners had long decided Rabaul, with its large, deep harbour, would make an excellent major air and sea base for its strategic location.

On 4 January there were two bombing raids on Rabaul intended to damage or destroy airfields and aircraft. Rabaul was poorly protected by the small Lark Force, the 2/22nd Battalion that had arrived in April 1941. It had combined with the local unit of the New Guinea Volunteer Rifles, and a coastal defence battery, an anti-aircraft battery and a field ambulance contingent.

A key role of Lark Force was to protect the airfields at Lakunai and Vunakanau, and the seaplane base at Rabaul. But Lark Force was poorly equipped and hopelessly undermanned. As the first bombers flew over, youthful troopers fired two anti-aircraft guns, one with a damaged barrel. None of their shots neared the enemy aircraft. Among the bombs dropped were anti-personnel 'daisy cutters', seventeen of which landed around the Rapindik Native Hospital, killing fifteen Tolais and causing horrific injuries to another fifteen. In all thirty New Guineans were killed in the raid that day. There were no casualties among the Australians. At dusk four-engined Kawanishi flying boats dropped more bombs, all of which missed their targets in the fading light. The Japanese air raids on Rabaul continued every two days, making it clear that the operations were leading to an invasion.

*

On Monday 5 January a weary and depressed Prime Minister Curtin wrote to his wife Elsie a melancholy saga of his battles with Churchill and of his stress:

> The war goes very badly and I have a cable fight with Churchill almost daily. He had been in Africa and India and they count before Australia and New Zealand. The truth is that Britain never thought Japan would fight and made no preparations to meet that eventuality. In addition they never believed air power could outfight sea power and there is no early possibility of air support. In Australia we have to produce our own aircraft. Notwithstanding two years of Menzies we have to really start production. But enough, I love you, and that is all there is to say.

Curtin's concerns wore him down mentally and physically. His initial calmness and steadiness in taking government had deteriorated. There is strong evidence to suggest that in early 1942 he folded, for at least some weeks, under distress at the possibility of a Japanese invasion and his inability to do enough about it. Some of Curtin's close associates began wondering if his nerves would hold. It was now obvious to his colleagues that his stress levels were rising markedly. The *Sydney Morning Herald*'s political correspondent, Ross Gollan, noted that a minority of ministers in the Curtin Government were 'overworking themselves in order to carry the whole Ministry', while others were demonstrating signs of 'not only persistent inefficiency but also of developing obstructionism'. Curtin was, in fact, under enormous pressure.

The day after writing of his woes to Elsie, Curtin composed another blistering and insistent cable to Churchill. He was upset that Churchill had not responded to Australia's request for a seat on any appropriate joint body considering higher Allied war strategy and direction. Australia would be a base in the South West Pacific theatre, he emphasised, and an Australian voice should be heard in councils of Pacific strategy:

> Australia is involved in a vital struggle for the security of our homeland and all that we have built up in this part of the world.

On 8 January Churchill sympathised with Curtin's feelings, but he explained that the United States entering the war against Japan 'most favourably' affected the issue 'in the final struggle'. Almost as an aside, he said he thought the United States 'would be quite willing' to reinforce Australia's home defence troops with 40,000 or 50,000 Americans, providing the shipping could be provided. He concluded with a barbed remark questioning Curtin's deep anxiety and perhaps his fortitude:

> Do you think you are in immediate danger of invasion in force? It is quite true that you may have air attacks but we have had a good dose already in England without mortally harmful results.

The following day Churchill and his personal staff arrived in Florida for a rest. Sir Charles Wilson described Churchill wallowing in the warm blue ocean of Florida and basking 'like a half-submerged hippopotamus in a swamp'. Inevitably, Churchill's black dog of depression surfaced, as Wilson noted in his diary:

> The P.M. was on his best behaviour in Washington. Now he is suffering from a sharp reaction. He does not like making important decisions, especially when he finds himself lined up with the Americans against his own Chiefs of Staff, and the strain mounts . . . at any rate he has had plenty of time here to work off steam.

Churchill told his staff and Dr Wilson that he had sent a stiff telegram to Curtin:

> The situation in Malaya was making Australia jumpy about invasion. Curtin was not satisfied with the air position. He had renewed his representations to London in blunt terms. The P.M. fulminated in his reply. London had not made a fuss when it was bombed. Why should Australia? At one moment he took the line that Curtin and his Government did not represent the people. At another that Australians came from bad stock. He was impatient with people who had nothing better to do than criticise him.

Wilson said the significance of Churchill's outburst was not lost on him and for that reason he didn't worry about the Australians:

> I knew that he had been persuaded to tone down the cable before it was sent . . . this particular patient needed rest. He was just hitting out blindly, like a child in a temper.

*

In the Imperial Japanese Navy there was uncertainty, but not anxiety, about where to strike next, and Australia was one of the invasion targets being considered. It had seen nothing but victory since Pearl Harbor and victory bred contempt for enemies temporarily on their knees. Combined Fleet chief of staff, Vice Admiral Ugaki reflected on the discussion aboard Admiral Yamamoto's flagship about where to strike next:

> We shall be able to finish first stage operations by the middle of March, as far as the invasion operation is concerned. What are we going to do after that? Advance to Australia, to India, attack Hawaii, or destroy the Soviet Union at an opportune moment according to their actions? I have decided to have staff officers study it.

Ugaki wasn't alone in looking towards Australia in the next stage of the Japanese operations. Rear Admiral Shigeru Fukudome, chief of the 1st Division (Operations) of the Navy General Staff, thought it was vital to adopt 'aggressive operational leadership', forcing the enemy to take the defensive:

> Underlying this basic policy was support for the invasion of Australia, the main area from which the United States would launch counter-offensives against the Japanese. This was leadership of stage two operations through offensive strategies in the Pacific Ocean area, strategies that it was hoped would hasten the end of the war through naval surface battles in the region.

Another admiral would soon come forward with a prepared blueprint for invading Australia. He was Rear Admiral Tamon Yamaguchi, commander of the 2nd Carrier Division, a close friend of Admiral Ugaki. Yamaguchi believed the American Pacific fleet must be challenged at the earliest opportunity in a decisive battle. His blueprint included plans for a lightning naval and air construction program to allow Japan to participate in widespread invasions across the Indian and Pacific oceans starting from May 1942. Yamaguchi proposed that during June and July, landings be made on Fiji, Samoa, New Caledonia,

New Zealand and northern Australia. Midway, Johnston and Palmyra islands would be occupied in November and December while Hawaii would be invaded and occupied from December 1942 or January 1943. He proposed using three task forces comprising fourteen carriers.

The issue of what to do about Australia produced the first major internal clash of philosophies within the Imperial General Headquarters in Tokyo. This was the name for the combined command facility for Army and Navy General Staff in Tokyo, but in fact there was no single combined facility, indicative of the level of ongoing antagonism between the army and navy.

On Saturday 10 January, Australia and New Zealand were discussed at a liaison conference between senior ministers and armed forces representatives in Japan. Noting the anxieties and fears of the people of Australia and India following Japan's military successes, the meeting decided to bring greater pressure to bear on Australia and New Zealand. This invovled the disruption of communications, including air and sea lanes, between Britain and the United States to 'break Australia's tie' with both countries. The conference had decided to brew anti-war sentiment among Australians by intensifying propaganda activities together with military operations.

At the outbreak of the war Japan did not contemplate invading Australia and India but was content to sever their links with Britain and America. But, as Colonel Takushiro Hattori, head of the operations section of the Army Department, later recalled as the southern invasion operations progressed and future conquests were studied, the Imperial Navy began seeing advantages in invading Australia, which raised 'major problems' for the army. The trend would be towards further strategic offensives, promoted mainly by the Imperial Navy. The navy's attitude towards Australia hardened significantly, according to Hattori:

the Navy, including the Navy General Staff and the Navy Ministry, strongly favoured adopting a positive policy and insisted on the invasion of Australia. Briefly, the Navy's contention was that in the prosecution of a protracted war, being on the defensive was disadvantageous, and that it was highly desirable to keep the enemy on the defensive.

The Japanese navy believed Australia was the most vital base the Americans could use for a counteroffensive against Japan. But the army was deeply wary, according to Colonel Hattori:

Contrary to the Navy's stand, the Army's main interest was in establishing a durable and effective national structure for the prosecution of a protracted war, by remaining on the strategic offensive as originally planned.

As the army saw it, Australia covered an area about twice the size of China and had a population of about seven million. Roads and other communications were by no means well developed. The Japanese army was also wary of the fighting spirit of the Australians, as Hattori said:

If the invasion is attempted, the Australians, in view of their national character, would bitterly resist the Japanese to the end. Also, because of geographic conditions of Australia present numerous difficulties, in a military sense, it is apparent that a military venture in that country would be a difficult one.

The Imperial Navy in time reluctantly agreed with the army on these objectives, but during the next critical months the navy clung to the idea of an occupation of the great southern land and planned to raise it again when the timing was right.

Prime Minister General Hideki Tojo, facing prosecution for war crimes in Tokyo after the war, was widely quoted as saying there were never any plans to invade Australia. A member of the imperial family, Prince Naruhiko Higashikuni, had sat on conferences of the military councillors in the presence of the Emperor just before the war, asking probing questions as to how Japan could sustain a war against Britain and the United States. Higashikuni, an army general who had served in China and who would briefly lead Japan as prime minister in the last days before the end of the war, records in his diary, as the Japanese were quickly pushing down in Malaya in early 1942, that he advised Prime Minister Tojo:

> I think Singapore will fall soon . . . Japan should advance nego-
> tiations with Chiang Kai-shek's government and start peace
> overtures with Britain and the United States. We must end this
> war without further delay.

Higashikuni records that Tojo was defiant:

> I think we will have few problems occupying not only Java but
> Sumatra and also Australia if things go on like this. We shouldn't
> think about peace at this time.

*

Holding the Australian administrative centre of Papua, Port Moresby, from the Japanese was crucial. The town, with its good harbour, is situated on the southern coastline of the Gulf of Papua facing Australia to the south. Moresby lies only 348 miles (560 kilometres) from Thursday Island at the northern tip of Australia's Cape York Peninsula. What was particularly worrying about a Japanese occupation of Port Moresby was the fact that the twin-engined Mitsubishi bombers could easily hit towns and cities all the way down the central Queensland coast. Thus Cooktown, Cairns, Townsville, Mackay, Rockhampton and other centres would have been vulnerable.

Initially Australia reinforced Port Moresby in a shoddy fashion. The 49th Infantry Battalion had arrived in the first week of December 1941. From the start of January 1942 the 39th militiamen and the 53rd Infantry Battalion joined the 49th. The soldiers were young and inexperienced, and their training meagre. Their troopships had been incompetently loaded. Tents, cooking gear and mosquito nets were at the bottom of holds. Peter Ryan had enlisted in the army in 1941 at the age of eighteen. He wrote that there was little in the way of a tactical plan for the defence of Port Moresby and that at first troops were employed more as labourers than as soldiers. After the first air raids in early 1942, discipline deteriorated and soldiers looted civilian property. The RAAF in Moresby in January could muster only six Hudsons, two Catalinas and two Wirraways.

*

US navy historian Morison had already been surprised at the talk in Washington about abandoning Australia and New Zealand. Less than two weeks into 1942, Curtin and his ministers, the press and a great many Australians were deeply alarmed when the two politicians managing the naval affairs of their respective nations in Britain and the United States both made almost simultaneous public speeches that played down the war with Japan as a secondary consideration for the Allies. Their alarming statements clearly were a result of the 'Beat Hitler First' policy and had the appearance of being loosely coordinated. The insensitive and undiplomatic remarks stunned many, not least in Australia and New Zealand. The comments began with a speech on 10 January by Churchill's first lord of the Admiralty, Albert Alexander, a Labour MP in the national coalition government. Alexander clearly emphasised the Allied war priority as Germany, despite recent Japanese victories. He said Britain should never take her eyes off the Axis Powers in Europe:

> If we knock them (the Germans) out we can do what we like with Japan afterwards. In the meantime we must hold on to the Far East. We have a duty towards out kith and kin in the Commonwealth.

Alexander said the combined strength of the British and American fleets in the long run would 'see us through, but it will take a little time'. Two days later the US secretary for the navy, Frank Knox, known for his bluntness, addressed a conference of mayors in Washington:

> We know who our greatest enemy is. It is Hitler and Hitler's Nazis; Hitler's Germany. It is Hitler we must destroy. That done, the whole Axis fabric will collapse. Finishing off Hitler's satellites will be easy by contrast.

Knox told the mayors not to expect 'favourable dramatic developments of triumphant American full-scale naval engagements in the Pacific' in the near future because of the wide distribution of US naval forces. The suggestion that countries defeated by Japan might be recovered later – originally raised by Churchill in one of his memorandums to his chiefs on 18 December 1941 – caused widespread anger in the Antipodes. Editorial writers on Australian newspapers were indignant with both men for relegating the Far East and the Pacific to the status of minor theatres of war. *The Argus* said the remarks now made it apparent that 'impregnable' Singapore was gravely endangered. *The Age* said British authorities apparently believed Singapore to be of secondary importance. The truth was out.

'What's all the hullabaloo about?' Knox asked Australia's minister to Washington, Richard Casey. Casey said he believed there was concern and resentment in Australia that the war against Japan was seen as a sideshow. Knox asked Casey to reassure Australia that there would be no slackening of American effort in the war against Japan, when in fact the effort, apart from the fighting near Manila, had barely begun. Knox soon would say that he had been misunderstood:

> We dare not turn our backs on either front . . . [but] We must not confuse history with strategy. The main enemy historically may not be the first enemy strategically . . .

Time magazine called the Knox statement 'stupid' and 'the last straw'. The issue would continue to simmer in Australia.

*

Brigadier General Eisenhower had been grappling with war planning and wrote in his diary that it was hard to get anything done for Australia:

Dive bombers arrived minus essential parts; base facilities are meagre; other expeditions, directed by politicians, interfere, notably [two of Churchill's war plans] Magnet and Gymnast. But we're getting some things on the road to Australia.

Eisenhower said limited pursuit and bomber aircraft had arrived in Australia. By 12 January he was able to say that 21,000 Americans would be despatched for Australia in nine days' time, but he didn't know if he could get all their equipment and supplies to them. He saw the Far Eastern situation as critical and thought proposed offensives in Europe should be dropped and Britain forced to retire from Libya:

Then scrape up everything everywhere and get it into NEI [Netherlands East Indies] and Burma. We mustn't lose NEI, Singapore, Burma line; so we ought to go full out saving them.

The advance guard of the Americans arriving in Darwin found the labour situation on the Darwin docks appalling. One of the senior US officers, Brigadier General Julian F. Barnes, was invited to address the War Council in Melbourne on 12 January. He complained that Darwin was now a fortress area and liable to be attacked at any time. A freighter, the SS *Holbrook*, carrying American artillery equipment, had waited for three weeks to be unloaded at the Darwin dock because 'civilian labor was not employed to the fullest advantage'. Barnes had wanted to use US troops to do the unloading but a Commonwealth Government regulation hampered this. Barnes said delays at Darwin had stranded two other ships destined for Darwin at Townsville. Curtin promised to sort out the problem. What no one knew on that day was that Japanese submarine *I-121* was sowing mines off Darwin that would sink US ships. Another sub, the *I-123* would do the same two weeks later. Both subs also had a mission to begin severing Australia's trade routes wherever possible.

Random industrial stoppages affecting essential war industries were increasingly becoming a blight on Australia at war. Striking workers, especially watersiders, were often acting against the directives of their own union executives. In a national broadcast the president of the South Australian Labor Council, Ken Bardolph, appealed to workers in war industries to exert their last ounce of energy for 'the battle of production'. The Curtin Government's inability to control militant workers left it looking weak. Following a continuing wave of strikes in the coal industry, stronger National Security Coal Regulations were introduced on 12 January. Curtin warned that the government would ban stoppages and impose penalties equally on workers and employers who caused strikes over frivolous matters. New emergency conditions were tough not only against striking miners, but also on mine owners and managers. Yet mines remained idle in New South Wales, an overseas ship was held up in Sydney Harbour with waterside workers refusing to unload it, and engineers at a small arms factory were on strike. The *Barrier Miner* at Broken Hill editorialised, 'Perhaps when the bombs begin to fall industrial peace will be achieved.'

Curtin held off using his tough new industrial powers. He and his ministers, including the minister for labour, Eddie Ward, were negotiating urgently with all sides of the mining industry. On 15 January the government received word that a stoppage was planned for the following week that would hold up for a day all road transport in the Melbourne metropolitan area. Curtin worked the phones behind the scenes. The outrage grew. *The Courier-Mail* came out with an editorial – 'Australia Has its Traitors' – describing strikers as 'miserable scabs on their fighting comrades' holding back supplies vitally needed on the Pacific front.

On Saturday 17 January Curtin acted. He directed the chief of the Naval Staff, Admiral Sir Guy Royle, to requisition an Allied ship carrying soda ash that had been delayed for some days in Sydney and to use naval personnel to unload it immediately. Curtin angrily attacked men who would not work:

> The men who are not in the fighting forces and who at the same time will not work are as much the enemies of this country as the directly enlisted legions of the enemy.

Within a few hours on that Saturday, Curtin received word that men would be available to unload the disputed ship on Monday morning, which they did. Curtin told the navy to withhold strike-breaking action.

Curtin's showdown was welcomed by the press but it did not stop further strikes, despite the government's powerful new regulations. Striking coalminers at the Old Bulli Colliery on the New South Wales south coast returned to work on the Monday morning but 1500 miners employed in Maitland, Cessnock and one another mine on the south coast went out on strike.

*

Singapore was under constant aerial attack with bombs dropping all over harbour, airfield and city areas. Allied aircraft, mostly inferior to the Japanese planes, had suffered enormous losses on the ground and in the air, but the commander-in-chief of the Far East in the ABDA Command, General Sir Henry Pownall, was pinning his hopes on the arrival of new Hurricane fighters. Soon many of the Hurricanes would be destroyed with the surviving fighters being flown out to defend the East Indies. General Pownall on 19 January shifted his headquarters from the Dutch capital of Batavia (now Jakarta) to the hill town of Lembang near Bandung, where the climate was cooler and there were better working conditions. The first Japanese bombing of Batavia occurred a fortnight later. In Lembang General Pownall, like Curtin, harboured private doubts about the ability to hold Singapore, writing in his diary on 19 January:

As a result of Wavell's last visit there, we withdrew to the northern border of Johore [state], but they've pushed us back from that now ... I'm quite sure that with good and well trained troops we could take tea with these Japs, which makes the whole thing infuriating. Apart from the Australians we have practically none left now in Malaya.

It was planned that two Australian divisions of the AIF were coming from the Middle East to Malaya as reinforcements, but as Pownall noted in his diary, they would not start to leave until the beginning of the next month:

It's going to be a very tough fight and we haven't much ground behind us now – only 60 miles [96 kilometres] or so. Whereas three weeks ago we had more than 200 [322 kilometres].

The Far East commander-in-chief now worried about keeping the vitally important sea and air communications open from Darwin to Java. He noted the extensive Japanese victories east of Singapore, including Mindanao Island in the southern Philippines, Tarakan Island near the north-east tip of Borneo and even further south, the Japanese occupation of the Celebes (Sulawesi):

From these places they doubtless intend to push further south, Ambon probably being their next objective.

Ambon, in the Molucca Islands west of the New Guinea mainland, certainly was in the immediate firing line.

*

The Japanese were still regularly bombing Rabaul. Their fleet from Truk Island to the north was coming south and their reconnaissance aircraft were everywhere in the islands. Those remaining in Rabaul knew what was coming.

Curtin was so incapacitated by stress and anxiety that at this critical time he could not even attend the war cabinet meeting on Tuesday 20 January. His deputy, Frank Forde, chaired the meeting in his place as Curtin saw a doctor and rested. As the day went on the news from Rabaul would have contributed to Curtin's malaise. Australia's Lark Force of some 1400 men, the 'hostages to fortune', plus a smaller New Guinea volunteer force, knew invasion was imminent.

Just after noon on the same day a planter and coastwatcher, Cornelius Page, on Tabar island north of Rabaul reported twenty Japanese Zeros flying over his plantation towards Rabaul. An hour or so later a naval rating at Victoria Barracks ripped off a message from a teleprinter and took it to his superiors. It was a cryptic message from Rabaul, via Port Moresby, sent by the fiery wing commander of RAAF 24 Squadron, John Lerew, and would soon reach the prime minister:

> Waves of enemy fighters shot down Wirraways. Waves of bombers attacking aerodromes. Over one hundred aircraft seen so far. Front seat gunnery on Praed Point.

There were 109 Japanese aircraft in the major attack. Praed Point was the location of the small Australian battery of six-inch (15-centimetre) guns at the northern entrance to Blanche Bay, a deep harbour surrounded by active volcanoes. Top-secret reports pouring into the Combined Operational Intelligence Centre in Melbourne that day and night, copied to Australia's defence chiefs and passed on as summaries to the government, revealed the deteriorating situation.

Japanese planning was continuing at a furious pace to turn sleepy Rabaul into one of Japan's greatest air and sea bases in the South Seas, with plans for the construction of many new airstrips, supply dumps and a vast network of underground tunnels and bunkers to protect the Japanese and their stores from the inevitable Allied bombing raids.

The abandonment of Rabaul by Curtin and his defence chiefs was a clear sign of Australia's significant military weakness. The chiefs – the Chief of the Air Staff Burnett, the Chief of the

General Staff Sturdee, and the acting chief of the Naval Staff Durnford – had recorded that they did not consider reinforcement of Rabaul possible 'in view of the very great hazard and difficulties' in transporting troops from the mainland despite urgent, almost pleading messages from Australian officials in the town. One administration official, Harold Page, had pleaded earlier with Canberra to evacuate the last civilians from Rabaul aboard a Norwegian freighter, the *Herstein*, which had been ordered to take on a load of copra. Page unaccountably was told, 'no one is to take the place of copra on the *Herstein*'. The ship had ample time to escape and to save the lives of many Australians before the arrival of the Japanese. The defence chiefs commented, 'With our limited resources we are bound to concentrate on tasks of a higher priority.' The chiefs knew full well what the likely outcome would be:

> In making this recommendation we desire to emphasise the fact that the scale of attack which can be brought against Rabaul from bases in the Japanese mandated islands is beyond the capacity of the small garrison to meet successfully. Notwithstanding this, we consider it essential to maintain a forward air observation line as long as possible and to make the enemy fight for this line rather than abandon it at the first threat.

Curtin and his cabinet could have overruled the military chiefs to prevent unnecessary slaughter, but felt obliged to go along with the recommendation.

The defenders of Rabaul hadn't seen Zero fighters before. They were stunned by their speed, climbing rate and the prowess of the well-trained pilots. The Japanese Zeros were in every way better than Australia's so-called 'first-line fighter', the newly built but already outdated Wirraway.

As the Japanese descended, pilots in two RAAF Wirraways were already in the air and another three proceeded to take off. Only two made it. After a quick burst of fire from a Zero, the first Wirraway went screaming towards the water belching flame and black smoke. Flying Officer John Lowe and his observer, Sergeant Albert Ashford, both aged 26, were the first pilots to die. Zeros soon pounced on another lumbering Wirraway. Pilot Officer Albert Claire and Sergeant George Herring, who was flying the plane, were both hit in the legs. The Wirraway, with a damaged tail, spiralled out of control but Herring managed to belly flop down at the Lakunai strip. Both were pulled out before Zeros poured more fire into the aircraft. Sergeant Charles Bromley and his observer Sergeant Richard Walsh had just taken off from nearby Vunakanau when six Zeros attacked their Wirraway. Bromley, nineteen, was killed instantly. Walsh tried to jump before the aircraft hit the water but his parachute failed to open and he was killed. The pilot of another Wirraway that had just taken off, Sergeant William Hewitt was hit in the knee by a bullet. His observer, Flying Officer Jack Tyrell, bailed out and landed in a tree. Hewitt managed to land the damaged aircraft. Another Wirraway landed after hiding in cloud. Yet another, manned by pilot Robert Blackman, twenty, and his gunner, Sergeant Stanley Woodcroft, was last seen in combat with several Zeros and was missing. Eight Wirraways had been destroyed. An Australian flying boat was also shot down. One Japanese bomber was shot down by anti-aircraft fire. Wing Commander Lerew in Rabaul sent a brief message about the grim situation and asked: 'Will you now please send some fighters?'

An RAAF officer replied: 'Regret inability to supply fighters. If we had them you would get them.'

Lerew signalled back:

Wirraways and Hudsons cannot be operated in this area without great loss and sacrifice of skilled personnel and aircraft . . . As fighters cannot be obtained only one course if services of trained personnel valued. Only three undamaged aircraft remained – two Wirraways and one Hudson.

The Hudson, loaded with wounded, and the two Wirraways were flown to Port Moresby.

John Curtin took the news hard. He keenly felt any decision where Australian servicemen and women were placed at high risk. Abandonment of Rabaul was worse – almost crippling – for him because the Australians in effect were told to stay, 'make the enemy fight', report on what was happening and either be captured or killed. Observation reports could have been supplied from a safe distance by trained Australian coastwatchers in New Britain and New Ireland.

*

One man observing Curtin in Melbourne around this time was Geoffrey Sawyer (later a lawyer, academic and historian) who was head of the overseas broadcast service, Radio Australia, with its headquarters in Melbourne:

> Curtin struck me at that time as being a very frozen sort of person. Terribly overwhelmed by the problems that were on his shoulders and so afraid of giving himself in any way to anybody around . . . he then had relatively recently given away grog. He was still I would say in late 1941 and early 1942 a reformed drunkard. I understand that later on he threw that off and that that no longer was a bother, but it certainly was then.

Curtin's press secretary, Don Rodgers, recalled that Curtin's problems with alcohol occurred much earlier, while his boss was in opposition:

> My conclusion is that he was never a drunkard as such, or even an alcoholic. I think he was what's called a cheap drunk and because of the political turmoil of the time and the fact that his Party was headed for certain defeat, he was probably what might also be called a crying drunk.

Rodgers, who knew Curtin more intimately than Sawyer, saw his boss as an emotional man:

He had unfortunately a streak of Irish forebears in him of what a doctor later told me was black melancholia and he'd go right into the depths ... when this melancholia descended on him he would go for long walks, quite often unaccompanied but sometimes he'd take myself or the secretary with him. He had had the ability to rise very quickly and he did rise to great heights.

Curtin's colleagues in Melbourne had urged him to take immediate leave. There is no record of their discussion, apart from a fleeting newspaper reference to the prime minister being 'unwell' and the concern of his colleagues. But clearly his closest ministers were worried that he might break down and be unable to continue.

In smouldering Rabaul, Wing Commander John Lerew received a signal that emanated from Victoria Barracks, ordering 'all available aircraft' to attack the approaching enemy fleet. What a joke! The small air base was a shambles from the recent raids. Lerew, exasperated, now had one Hudson bomber and, with some fast work, possibly one damaged Wirraway at his disposal to meet the onslaught. After a curt exchange of signals Lerew sent his final message. When it reached Victoria Barracks the cipher staff puzzled over the meaning because it was in Latin: 'Nos morituri te salutamus.' It was a Roman gladiators' salutation, 'We who are about to die, salute you.'

Squadron intelligence officer, Flight Officer Geoffrey Lempriere, helped bury the dead in Rabaul from the previous raid and returned to Lerew's office:

Not only did we grieve for the loss of the men who had been killed, we were saddened and frustrated by the failure of the Australian authorities to understand what was happening in Rabaul.

They did understand but now they could do little.

Australian coastwatchers were now reporting that four enemy warships and 'other vessels' had been sighted south-west of Kavieng, on the northern tip of New Ireland, steaming on a course for Rabaul. Senior officers at Victoria Barracks were in urgent consultation with the war cabinet without the prime minister present. Curtin thought the loss of Rabaul would threaten Port Moresby, numerous islands and even the east coast of Australia. His every inclination was to become deeply involved in handling the emerging catastrophe, but he knew mentally and physically he couldn't go on without rest. Curtin's doctor had told him he must take a break. His close colleagues had seen the effects on their leader and insisted that Curtin go home to Western Australia for short break. He had very reluctantly agreed, but stubbornly refused to briefly surrender the prime ministership to his deputy. It was agreed that Curtin should go home to Cottesloe and that Don Rodgers would put out a short press statement saying the prime minister hadn't seen his son John and daughter Elsie since the previous August, which was true. Now his flight from stress and anxiety was planned, his transport organised, his family informed, his ministers and doctor insistent, yet his doubts remained ever present and nagging while Australian territory was about to be taken by a massive enemy force.

Chapter 5

FLIGHT OF A PRIME MINISTER

The monumental tragedy unfolding was a nightmare for John Curtin. From his first-floor office window in the old bluestone Victoria Barracks Defence Headquarters, he gazed out over St Kilda Road into the parkland and gardens opposite. Workmen were digging zigzag trenches through the lawn in case of Japanese air raids. Just to the right he could see the great Shrine of Remembrance, evocative of a classic Greek structure with its massive Doric columns, built to commemorate the 19,000 men from Victoria alone slaughtered in what was now called the Great War. The Stone of Remembrance, set like a gravestone, bore the simple words: 'Greater love hath no man'. How ironic that Curtin, the war hater, had now assigned young men to their assured death.

A plethora of appalling news continued to clatter over the Victoria Barracks teleprinters in code. It was Wednesday 21 January 1942. From Malaya it was reported that a high degree of cooperation was occurring between Japanese ground forces and aircraft, which dominated the skies. Another message ominously reported that Japanese battleships were joining aircraft carriers at Truk Lagoon, north of New Britain. Combined fleets including many transports were now concentrating, and intelligence experts believed that a major invasion in the near future was probable. Four Japanese cruisers were spotted in the Bismarck Sea. Intelligence suggested they must be escorting so far unseen aircraft carriers, all heading for Rabaul.

Prime Minister Curtin and his ministers had become visibly shaken by the situation Australia was in. Jack Commins from Sydney, who was sent to Canberra in January 1942 as an ABC federal parliamentary reporter, found an atmosphere of fear:

> The only way I can describe the atmosphere when I arrived in Canberra is tangible. You could feel the tensions in speech with Ministers; you could almost touch their deep concern with the threat and fear of invasion . . . People were fleeing to the mountains, notably refugees who had come out here in 1939; there was a real atmosphere of, if not panic, very much near to it.
>
> We'd sent our best troops overseas, we'd stripped the country of equipment to send with them, yet the Japanese came into the war three months after Curtin had come to power and he was faced with a war on his very doorstep.

The dread only worsened when Curtin's war cabinet ministers were working at Defence Headquarters in Melbourne.

From his office Curtin could see Government House and its tower amid the trees where he would privately meet the governor-general, who was now on his way down from Canberra. The prime minister looked forward to unburdening himself as he had done before. Lord Gowrie was a man's man: sympathetic, engaging, a good listener with no-nonsense advice. Gowrie's fears about an invasion of Australia were precisely the same as Curtin's. For Curtin, it seemed that everything was rushing to a climax. Where it would end for himself, he dared not speculate.

Curtin resumed working on his papers while, just down the corridor, the war cabinet was meeting in a sealed room guarded by two armed soldiers. Curtin's deputy, Frank Forde, also minister for the army, was inside, chairing the meeting and discussing a range of topics, including how and when 'non-essential' civilians might be evacuated from coastal areas of Australia in the face of potential Japanese attacks.

*

Rabaul was now burning. Captain Mitsuo Fuchida, who had led the aerial attack on Pearl Harbor, recalled the ease of the operation on Rabaul:

> Leading a powerful force of ninety bombers and fighters in the Rabaul attack, I saw just two enemy planes. They were attempting to take off from one of the two airfields and were promptly disposed of by our fighters. The second airfield was empty.

Further strikes were carried out against Rabaul's township. Fuchida thought it was all rather ridiculous:

> All in all, the employment of the Nagumo Force in this operation struck me as wasteful and extravagant. If ever a sledge hammer had been used to crack an egg, this was the time.

There were a number of good reasons for capturing Rabaul, as the planning staff officer and baron who later would be the naval commander at Rabaul, Captain Sadatoshi Tomioka, later vice admiral, knew:

> it was an important Australian military base on the north-eastern tip of New Britain, with a good natural harbor and even an air base. The Japanese occupation of Rabaul would afford us an excellent air base for scouting and patrolling the areas to the northeast of Australia, anticipated to be the zone of operations of the enemy fleets.

Tomioka's head in the planning bureau, Vice Admiral Shigeru Fukudome, would later say that all kinds of proposals were being put forward in the navy. Taking Rabaul was part of a navy plan, he said, but some favoured taking territory only as far as Shortland

Island off Bougainville. Later this idea was extended over the entire Solomon Islands group and later even further south-east:

Yes, the idea was considered of taking New Hebrides and even of proceeding to Australia, but those plans were never attempted or incorporated into an order ... [but] after Rabaul was taken and subsequent operations were extended it became more and more clear that a broad area would have to be occupied in order to secure Rabaul.

*

Concluding his talks in Washington, Prime Minister Winston Churchill cabled the ABDA commander-in-chief, General Wavell:

I want to make it absolutely clear that I expect every inch of ground to be defended, every scrap of material or defences to be blown to pieces to prevent capture by the enemy, and no question of surrender to be entertained until after protracted fighting among the ruins of Singapore City.

Wavell responded, 'I doubt whether island can be held for long once Johore is lost.' Almost immediately Churchill turned his thoughts to the holding of Burma and to the reinforcements then on the way to Singapore, especially the Australians, who might best be diverted to Rangoon (now Yangon). On the day Japan was attacking Rabaul with a massive fleet, Churchill asked his chiefs of staff:

What is the value of Singapore above the many harbours in the south-west Pacific if all naval and military demolitions are thoroughly carried out? On the other hand, the loss of Burma would be very grievous ... We may, by muddling things and hesitating to take an ugly decision, lose both Singapore and the Burma Road.

The defence chiefs could see Churchill's point. They would divert reinforcements to Burma if they had the chance. Churchill's musings about leaving Singapore to its fate soon were reported to an alarmed Curtin.

In Melbourne a whiff of imminent disaster hung in the air. Singapore on 21 January was being plastered by Japanese bombs. Gas mains, electrical cables, cold storage plants and communications were put out of action with reports of sixty-four killed and 154 wounded that day. New intelligence cables to Melbourne revealed that a fresh invasion force appeared to be heading from Truk to the Dutch East Indies, just as Curtin had feared.

At 9 am on 21 January a brief report was received in Sydney from Rabaul Radio stating a large number of enemy aircraft were over Rabaul. Kavieng on New Ireland was being attacked from the air, as was Salamaua near Lae and nearby Bulolo on the New Guinea mainland. The radio link between Rabaul and Port Moresby was soon cut. The best the defence chiefs could expect was short reports from the men of the Coastwatch service, often planters and government officers away from Rabaul in the Bismarck Archipelago on plantations or at small government outposts and on islands, sending reports by teleradio of sightings of enemy aircraft and warships. Closer to home, intelligence reports suggested that three of four Japanese submarines had been destroyed in the Darwin area, two by the corvette HMAS *Deloraine* and one each by the corvette HMAS *Katoomba* and the destroyer USS *Alden*. It was thought that up to six Japanese submarines had been operating in the area.

Before leaving Melbourne Curtin had urgent work to complete and a last meeting with his war cabinet. He wrote three separate cables to Churchill in London. Following Curtin's strident complaints about the ABDA area and its failure to cater for Australia's security, the British and US governments had come up with the idea of a new ANZAC area. A major and timely concern for Curtin was the weakness of forces being allocated to the protection of Australia, which he didn't realise at the time was a result of the 'Beat Hitler First' policy. The Australian Government had assumed that with the entry of Japan into the war, previously set priorities against Germany would have been revised to take into account the new threat in the Pacific. Curtin soon received word of a massive raid on Rabaul. His anxiety is obvious in the graphic tone of one cable to Churchill on this torrid day:

> The situation developing at Rabaul at the present moment, where an attack of one hundred aircraft from carriers has just taken place and a possible landing by heavy ships may be pending, point to much stronger forces being required in the ANZAC area than those allocated. The continuance of this southern advance will produce a threat on the flanks of both the line of communications across the Pacific and the land and air route to Darwin from the east coast of Australia.

Mindful of the inability of the Allies to intervene successfully in new Japanese invasions, a frustrated Curtin reminded Churchill that he and Roosevelt had indicated the importance of Australia as a base for American operations. He also pointed to the lack of warships in the Australian region to launch counteroffensives. Curtin then answered an earlier cable from Churchill that had asked the Australian leader, 'Do you think you are in immediate danger of invasion in force?' Curtin replied that it was now a race against time in Malaya. Should Singapore be lost, he said, the prospects of retaining Sumatra would be poor. Control of the Pacific could be won or lost in one fleet action. It would be folly for Australia to suggest that these factors would turn in Australia's favour. Curtin's desperation was now starting to show. As Malaya crumbled, he passed on to Churchill an assessment from Australia's chiefs of staff of the danger of invasion to Australia:

> the direct move towards Australia from bases in the mandated islands grows more probable. This is also likely to take the form of a progressive southward move securing New Guinea, New Hebrides [Vanuatu] and New Caledonia as advanced bases from which to sever our sea communications and from which a major attack could be launched on Australia if and when the strategic

situation in the area of Malaya and the Netherlands East Indies is judged to be suitable.

Curtin starkly warned Churchill:

It is clearly beyond our capacity to meet an attack of the weight that the Japanese could launch.

Latest reports from Malaya said the Allies were losing their foothold to a skilful and well-trained enemy. The Japanese at this time were only 70 miles (112 kilometres) from Johore Bahru, the town facing Singapore island across the narrow straits. At this time the Australian commander in Malaya, General Gordon Bennett, noted that enemy air activity seemed to be growing stronger. Japanese planes had been mercilessly bombing men of the 2/19th Battalion around the Parit Sulong bridge south-east of Muar. In two days' time, with ammunition exhausted, casualties mounting and no chance of relief, a combined Australian–Indian force would strike out east through the jungle for Yong Peng. The 2/19th would be forced to leave its wounded behind.

Curtin took up his pen again to respond to an irritated message from Churchill of a few days earlier. The British prime minister had deemed the Middle East 'a more urgent theatre' than the Far East and the South West Pacific generally. Churchill said he was sending two and possibly three of the Royal Navy's four modern aircraft carriers to the Indian Ocean, commenting hopefully, 'thus the balance of seapower in the Indian and Pacific oceans, in the absence of further misfortunes, will turn in the Allies favour'. Churchill then rather condescendingly lectured Curtin:

We must not be dismayed or get into recrimination but remain united in true comradeship. Do not doubt my loyalty to Australia and New Zealand. I cannot offer any guarantees for the future and I am sure that great ordeals lie before us, but I feel hopeful as never before that we shall emerge safely and also gloriously from this dark valley.

Curtin now took the opportunity to have another swipe at Churchill, who had announced the establishment of a Far Eastern Council in London, over which he would preside. Curtin wrote that all political parties in Australia opposed Churchill's plan, which was 'purely advisory and quite out of keeping with our vital and primary interest in the Pacific sphere'. Curtin said Australia wanted a Pacific War Council established in Washington and again demanded a real say in the higher direction of the war.

*

As Curtin privately pondered his agreement abandoning the Diggers at Rabaul, he was told that a Japanese landing force would invade there at any moment.

Thanks to the dangerous work of the coastwatchers, defence headquarters knew that strong forces of Japanese aircraft were being sighted at a number of points across the Bismarck Archipelago. Japanese landings at Kavieng, Salamaua and Lae would occur in the near future. Much further north on the New Guinea mainland's north coast, Lieutenant Bob Emery, an Australian planter from Lae and a member of the Australian New Guinea Administrative Unit (ANGAU), was guarding Madang's airstrip with a Lewis light automatic machine gun, accompanied by several New Guinean volunteers. Emery spotted planes circling high above and before he knew it the first bomb lobbed right alongside their position:

The gun pit shook, and great clods fell down and bits of rock and lumps of trees flew through the air.

The volunteers scrambled to safety as more bombs fell:

I could look across towards the Madang township itself and there's great clouds of black smoke going up there. I knew that there was a brand new big cargo shed on the wharf at Madang.

A huge supply of copra awaiting shipment was burning. Bob Emery said he grabbed his Lewis gun, which he hadn't fired, and 'went bush'.

*

That day on 21 January Curtin chaired his last war cabinet meeting for some time. In a busy agenda, ministers agreed to the urgent purchase of a multitude of new war equipment, including training aircraft, marine engines, torpedoes and machine guns. He emerged from the meeting to send Churchill yet another cable saying that his war cabinet and defence chiefs now believed it was 'a race against time' to prevent the Japanese from over-running Malaya, where thousands of Australian troops were in the front line. He pessimistically faced the daunting prospect of Singapore and the islands of Sumatra and Java falling to the Japanese, leaving the way to Darwin open.

Curtin had awoken at the Victoria Palace Hotel in Melbourne earlier that morning. In the newspapers he read his disloyal minister for labour, Eddie Ward, grossly misinterpreting the previous day's war cabinet discussion on the fundamental changes to wartime manpower legislation: 'The only way this can be achieved is by complete nationalisation'. The business world was naturally agog and outraged.

Under the manpower legislation the Commonwealth had proposed to keep records on every male eligible to work and to have the power to transfer men from non-essential work, or no work, into war production industries. Ward saw an opening in this change to industrial law to implement drastic industrial policies favoured by those on the far left. Ward's fanciful interpretation of events now was that the government had taken steps to organise labour in Australia and must go the whole hog, with complete nationalisation of industry, which was never the government's intention.

Curtin and Ward sat behind a closed door in the prime minister's office for what was described as 'a long meeting'. Curtin, although furious, made no public comment on Ward's recklessness, but press secretary Don Rodgers later, in calm understatement, told reporters that the talk was 'satisfactory to Mr Curtin, who regards it as the duty of individual ministers to observe and implement in full the will of the Government as a whole'.

*

In the Japanese diet in Tokyo that evening Prime Minister Tojo outlined Japan's war aims, including securing strategic bases in Greater East Asia, thus bringing regions with important resources under Japan's control:

> As regards the Netherlands East Indies and Australia, if they continue their attitude of resisting Japan, we will show no mercy in crushing them. But if their peoples come to understand Japan's real intentions and express willingness to co-operate with us, we will not hesitate to extend them our help, with full understanding for their work and progress.

*

It was time to go home. Curtin and several of his staff rattled down in the old lift to the ground floor of A Block New Wing. They stepped into the courtyard where Curtin's driver waited in the dark in a black Buick. It is not difficult to imagine the turmoil in Curtin's mind. Suddenly he was abandoning the centre of Australia's war effort at the gravest period, heading home on a series of slow trains to the other side of the continent. His loyal and hardworking deputy, Frank Forde, the army minister who inspected troops sporting a pith helmet, assumed Curtin's chair for twelve of the nation's most crucial wartime decision-making war cabinet and Advisory War Council conferences during January and February 1942. Yet despite fleeing the wartime centre of activity and planning for his health's sake, Curtin would get little rest.

It was now clear that Churchill and some of his ministers believed that if British interests in the Empire overseas were lost to Japan, they could be recovered later. Some of President Roosevelt's senior policymakers and service chiefs had precisely the same view about countries overrun by the Japanese. But Curtin believed that while Australia might be recovered after invasion and capture, in the interim the country could be ravaged and Australians decimated. In the promises of Britain coming to Australia's aid, Curtin was being deceived and he now knew it.

The RAAF that evening distributed a statement on the Japanese raids on Rabaul, which included a brief quote from the prime minister, reflecting his frustrations and his state of mind:

> Anybody in Australia who fails to perceive the immediate menace to Australia which this attack constitutes must be lost to all reality. The peril is nearer, clearer, deadlier than before.

Curtin was thinking the darkest thoughts, cogitating morosely on morbid possibilities that soon found expression in what he saw as the need to deny Australia to the enemy with a dreadful apocalyptic scorched-earth policy in which the great progress that Australia had made would, when the time came, be purposely destroyed by Australian hands. Factories, great industrial plants, oil refineries, power and gas plants, all forms of communication and transport, bridges, major roads, dry docks, mines, food supplies, all wilfully blown up, set alight or bull-dozed into rubble. Ships sunk and harbours blocked, aircraft smashed, weapons burnt, sheep and cattle shot and airfields dug up. As Curtin walked out of Victoria Barracks, plans were already being drawn up. The issue was on the agenda for the war cabinet in Melbourne on a preliminary basis the very next day. Only the intervention of General Douglas MacArthur later in March would turn the prime minister away from his dark contemplation of such horrendous and drastic plans. The American would see the scorched-earth policy as part of Australia's mood of 'dangerous defeatism'.

*

Before he left Melbourne, Curtin stopped at Government House to meet with the governor-general, Lord Gowrie. Curtin's wife

Elsie would later write that Lord Gowrie and her husband had 'formed a very real, lasting friendship'. They settled in comfortable chairs before an unlit fireplace in the large, open room. Detail of their private talk was never released, but it is clear that Rabaul and Malaya would have been high on the agenda. Curtin would have been anxious to explain his coming flight to Perth, the views of his doctor and concerned colleagues, and how his trusted senior ministers had insisted he return home to rest. Curtin was suffering from his old and rather vague disorder neurasthenia, marked by chronic fatigue and depression. Had he stayed, exchanging bitter cables with Churchill under the pressure of the Japanese onslaught and the fall of Rabaul, he might well have broken down. His known illnesses, after becoming prime minister, would include psoriasis, pneumonia, gastritis, high blood pressure and neuritis. As one illness cleared up another would afflict him. Historian Michael McKernan makes the point that all were either caused by, or heightened by, stress and worry. Psoriasis, for example, could be an awful and painful skin complaint, leading in its worst forms to arthritis. Indeed it could be fatal. It could have several causes, but a worried, anxious person might be more susceptible.

Curtin would have unburdened himself about the rapidly emerging disasters, especially at Rabaul. Gowrie's reports to King George VI would speak favourably of Curtin's leadership. But Gowrie's letters also recognised that Curtin was on a knife edge.

Bustling Spencer Street station exuded a cacophony of sound and activity on the summer evening of 21 January. Curtin and his staff, including his secretary, Fred McLaughlin, alighted from Commonwealth cars and walked to their train. They were followed by cluster of political correspondents from some of the major Australian newspapers under the watchful eye of Don Rodgers. With the war at such a critical stage and a possible split in Curtin's ministry being tipped by some of the reporters after Ward's antics, they had insisted on travelling with the prime minister. Two great puffing steam locomotives stood on number one platform ready to haul the Overland to

South Australia. Soldiers heading to Western Australia on the same train crowded the platform with their kit bags. Many had been training in Victoria. Securing travel on heavily used major passenger trains was difficult for many civilian travellers, unless on war business, because of troop and supply movements. With a risk of Japanese submarines in the waters around Australia, the Trans-Australian Railway was now a vital and safe transport link between east and west.

Although he had made the trip many times, this was Curtin's first journey across the Nullarbor as prime minister and his first trip home for some five months. The remoteness of the route can be gauged by the fact that an 'all-weather' road had only just opened across the continent. The train journey would be comfortable for Curtin and staff as the Victorian Government had courteously put its special State Car No. 4, built in 1912, at the prime minister's disposal. Curtin entered the carriage via steps in the centre of a covered observation platform at rear of the train. The carriage had been used by the Duke and Duchess of York, now King George VI and Queen Elizabeth, during their trip to Australia in 1927. The Labor prime minister might have felt a little guilty at such indulgence if he hadn't been feeling so poorly. It was all so different from his travel on overnight trains as a young union leader, sleeping on hard wooden benches. Curtin and his staff entered the elegant state car with its dark timber panelling and high pressed-iron ceilings. It had especially wide windows and ornate fittings. There were two big bedrooms with beds that folded into plush leather seating during the day, a dining room, which would also serve as his office, and separate ladies' and gentlemen's bathrooms, each with a bath, shower and toilet. Small sleeping berths were provided for staff.

A whistle shrilled at exactly seven in the evening and the Overland pulled out of Spencer Street station. It would be a journey to remember.

Curtin would often say his train trips over the Nullarbor were the only time he could get away from the telephone. According to his private secretary, Gladys Joyce:

All the way across in the train at every station you'd get cables
and then I'd have to sit up in the bed and decode them.

Normally travelling home by train was 'a little peaceful
trip' but the train that left Melbourne on 21 January offered
anything but. The Overland travelled through the night towards
Adelaide. Curtin settled into a comfortable lounge with his
papers. He had been told that it had not been technically possible
to fit his carriage with a wireless set, so he was content to feel the
sway of the carriage and brush up on correspondence. Curtin
was forced to rely on his deputy Forde to send brief telegrams
on the war, where communications along the track permitted.
Telephone calls were possible, but only to major railway stations.
Sometimes the information was received many hours and even a
day or two after the event. But that day his mind was elsewhere,
the men in Malaya being forced to withdraw towards Singapore
under withering Japanese attacks on the ground and from the
air. In particular he was often reminded of the 1400 'hostages
to fortune' in Lark Force at Rabaul. Late that night Victoria
Barracks had received a message from Rabaul stating that naval
codes had been destroyed and no further intelligence was being
sent. Civilians had moved inland. Dive-bombers had attacked
two airfields. Radio communication with Rabaul stopped early
the next morning. All of this in code would be passed on to
stations along Curtin's route.

That morning, Thursday 22 January, when the Overland
was heading to Adelaide, the commanding officer of Japan's
R Invasion Force, Rear Admiral Kiyohide Shima, could just
glimpse the islands of New Britain and New Ireland through
sudden showers and dense cloud:

As we gradually drew closer to the coastline, we were very much
worried about being taken unawares by the enemy. Indeed, it
was truly by the aid of the gods that we were not troubled by
them.

Assistance from the gods was not required. The Japanese thought the Australians had ten large guns at Praed Point protecting Rabaul. In fact they had two and had little means of stopping a big invasion force. That night the order came to all the Japanese ships to 'make preparations for landing'. Two big flares erupted over Rabaul and Simpson Harbour, lighting up the moonless night. Before midnight on 21 January, landing craft had pulled away from the troopships. Light now came from the volcano Tavurvur, on the edge of the bay near Rabaul's aerodrome, as it belched ash and smoke in one of its regular small eruptions. The streetlights of Rabaul, which the Australians had failed to extinguish, reflected a 'weird beauty into the night sky', according to the Japanese, 'making finding the way relatively easy'.

*

Australian newspapers that Thursday 22 January hit the streets with fearful news of the important battle in the Muar River region in western Johore state in Malaya. Australian correspondents correctly speculated that the Japanese were concentrating for a critical battle for Johore, close to Singapore. The Japanese had been infiltrating Allied lines and evading frontal clashes. The Australians had borne the brunt of the various Japanese attacks when they went to the aid of an Indian Brigade that had been pushed back from Muar River. Elite Japanese Imperial Guards, whose size and stamina surprised the Australians, used encircling movements and regularly came up at the rear of the defenders. They had the advantage of heavy air bombardments and strafing attacks at a time when the Allies had little left in the air. After the Muar River had been crossed, the battle went badly for the retreating Australians, despite a series of brave stands. When a spirited assault was requested to give them space and time to recover, Captain Frank Beverley led his men forward. The words 'Once a jolly swagman . . .' rang out through the jungle as the Australians attacked the enemy and delayed their progress. Lieutenant Colonel Charles Anderson of the 2/19th Battalion had been ordered to destroy his equipment and, with his force, make his way back as best he could around the enemy positions. They discovered that their only avenue of withdrawal was over a bridge near the village of Parit Sulong, which was in Japanese hands.

Colonel Anderson, fearing annihilation, ordered his men to break through the jungle to escape. They left about 150 wounded Australian and Indian troops in the charge of a captain to surrender at Parit Sulong village. What followed was appalling. The Japanese arrived and herded the injured and dazed soldiers together with kicks, usually aimed at their wounds, blows from rifle butts and jabs into the flesh from bayonets. There were about 110 Australians and forty Indians, described by a witness as maimed and bloodstained. Late on the afternoon of 22 January the wounded Australian and Indian prisoners were forced outside, sprayed with machine-gun fire, doused with petrol and set alight. Many were still alive after the shooting. Lieutenant Ben Hackney, of the 2/29th Infantry Battalion AIF, feigned death then crawled to a native hut where he became a horrified witness:

> Rifles and machine guns belched forth a storm of death, a few fell, a group fell . . . The prisoners were then set alight and amid screams and yells of pain, fright, nervousness and delirium, burnt . . .

Three soldiers survived the atrocity. The villagers of Parit Sulong also suffered. Many, suspected of assisting Australian soldiers, were executed or severely mistreated. After the war, the evidence of Ben Hackney was instrumental in bringing Lieutenant General Takumo Nishimura, commander of the Imperial Guards Division, to justice. The general would be hanged for war crimes in 1951.

Two hundred and seventy-one men from the 2/19th would reach the British lines at Yong Peng, but only 130 of their Australian comrades from the 2/29th would make it after ten days of cease-less fighting. The Malaya commander, General Arthur Percival, would write that the Battle for Muar was one of the epics of the Malayan campaign:

Our little force by dogged resistance had held up a division of Japanese Imperial Guards attacking with all the advantages of air and tank support for nearly a week, and in doing so had saved Segamat force from encirclement and probable annihilation. The award of the Victoria Cross to Lieutenant Colonel Anderson of the AIF was a fitting tribute both to his own prowess and to the valour of his men.

Gunner Russell Braddon was twenty when he enlisted in Sydney. After the Muar battle he could not talk of heroics:

According to the war histories – even the Japanese war histories – our little battle, which started on a river bank at Muar and ended in a rubber plantation at Parit Sulong, was a gutsy and splendid one; but to those of us who fought it, our side of it was a shambles. Constantly deprived of the initiative and devoid of tactics, we fought more like rats than heroes.

The Imperial Guards, he wrote, never ceased to bewilder the Australians with their swiftness and daring and never failed to cut the Diggers off from resupply and reinforcements. Like so many Allied soldiers, Braddon would spend most of the war in captivity.

Just before 8 am on 22 January a further massive attack on Rabaul was launched by forty-five fighters and dive-bombers from the carrier invasion fleet. The dive-bombers attacked the Praed Point battery's two guns with bombs and intense machine-gunning. The bombs blasted the battery so heavily that the upper gun collapsed onto the gun emplacement below. Eleven Australians were killed. Troops sheltering below in a dugout were buried alive.

Colonel John Scanlan, commander of Lark Force, ordered his men to fight to the last. But as the town was bombed and the enemy convoy approached, he instructed that demolitions be carried out and the town evacuated. The bulk of Lark Force was sent to the western shore of the harbour where retreat from Rabaul might not be cut off. But little plan had been made for falling back.

*

The Overland stood in the sunshine at Adelaide station for only forty minutes. No coded telegram came through from Rabaul via Melbourne. The premier of South Australia, Thomas Playford, was waiting on the platform to greet Curtin. They talked briefly about manpower problems and how they affected business. *The Advertiser* in Adelaide that morning editorialised on how tardy the people of Adelaide were in complying with blackout directives. Adelaide had been a blaze of lights at night. Reporters gathered around Curtin on the platform and he said he agreed with the newspaper criticism of Adelaide's lethargy, saying all cities in Australia must be blacked out at night.

A few hours after leaving Adelaide, the train came to the end of its journey at Port Pirie. Here everyone transferred to a new train for the journey on the broader gauge of the Commonwealth Railways to Kalgoorlie in Western Australia. The prime minister and his staff transferred to an even more luxurious private car. The Prince of Wales carriage was built for Prince Edward, later Edward VIII, who made the journey in 1920. Curtin used the fine timber-panelled saloon both for dining and meetings. The carriage had a well-equipped kitchen, a bathroom complete with a full-length bath, and four two-berth and two elaborate single-berth sleeping compartments. The saloon opened onto an observation platform. As the train headed north towards Port Augusta, Curtin relaxed a little, reading.

Corporal Sydney Gray, aged twenty-three, of the 2/10th Armoured Regiment, was travelling with other troops in far less comfort. Gray, who would later serve overseas, was among his mates in crude cattle trucks that still reeked of their previous passengers. The conversion consisted of not much more than the installation of hard benches for troops in each van. The servicemen slept rough on the floor on hessian paillasses filled with straw. There were no windows and it was hot, so the men left the wide sliding doors open and often sat dangling their feet from the doorway. The ride was rough owing to the tight springs used to bear the weight of cattle. One van was converted into a kitchen and another had storage for the men's kit bags. Corporal

Gray had been at the Puckapunyal army camp in Victoria and had been granted special home leave to be married to his fiancée, Roma Milbourne of Fremantle. Word came through that flooding much further ahead had cut the railway line, so the troops had ample time to stretch their legs at the next stop, as Gray recalled:

> I walked down to the end of the train and found a very nice 'special' coach attached. As I walked down to have a look, a group of very well dressed civilians came towards me and a voice from the group said, 'Young Syd Gray, I thought you were up north somewhere!' I was staggered. It was John Curtin, prime minister of Australia, who was an old friend and Labor colleague of my father for many years. He came over, shook my hand ... I said, 'I'm going home on special leave to get married on Saturday ... God willing'.

Gray worried that the flooding on the Nullarbor Plain might cause him to miss his own wedding scheduled for the day the train was due to arrive in Perth:

> John said, 'Syd, you know the floods have taken out some of the rails between here and Kalgoorlie and this train might not get through to Kalgoorlie.' I hadn't realised that things were that bad, so I was pretty concerned at that stage. He said, 'Don't start worrying yet, I have to be in Perth by Saturday morning and I will be getting a plane for myself, my friends and staff, and you can be included.' He said, 'I've also rung Elsie, and we're coming to your wedding on Saturday afternoon'.

Curtin invited the young corporal into his special carriage at Port Augusta. The white-jacketed steward rustled up a small meal for Curtin's guest. A table in the saloon was set with a white linen tablecloth, crystal glassware, silver cutlery and a large vase of flowers. A fan mounted high on the wall stirred the hot summer air.

Corporal Gray was suitably impressed. 'We had a long talk, some nice sandwiches and a beer.' When they stepped out onto the platform, other Diggers crowded around the two cheering. Curtin turned to the young soldier: 'You know, Syd, would anyone ever believe that they dumped me last time?' referring to his electoral loss in Fremantle in 1931. Curtin told amused pressmen looking on, 'He's invited me to his wedding in Perth on Saturday and I'll be honoured to be present.' Syd Gray had worked on the *Westralian Worker* newspaper in Perth as an apprentice compositor when Curtin was editor.

Curtin took a few minutes to chat with the political reporters. The talk had to be brief because the reporters needed to lodge their news telegrams at Port Augusta station before the train pulled out. Curtin was sensitive about being away from Melbourne and Canberra at such a critical time. 'I'm prepared to return to Canberra immediately in the event of a national emergency,' he assured them.

The next stretch, comprising the longest segment of straight railway track in the world, would take the passengers across South Australia into Western Australia through the Nullarbor Plain, initially into the great, sandy and often flat and treeless desert region north of the Great Australian Bight. There were twenty-four stops, including watering points for the locomotives, between Port Augusta and Kalgoorlie, a distance of 1051 miles (1691 kilometres). Along the way there were tiny settlements of railway workers and scattered Aboriginal camps. Many of the stops employed just one railwayman, a sort of multiskilled station master with no staff. Over the railway's entire length between Port Augusta and Kalgoorlie the line did not cross one permanent stream, although in the downpours nature temporarily created her own watercourses through dry gullies. The rain had been unusually heavy in recent days.

*

Australia waited anxiously for the expected news of an invasion of Rabaul. Relatives of the 1400 soldiers from Australia were

listening to every wireless broadcast, but there was no news about
the fate of Lark Force. News did come through that Lorengau
on Manus Island had been bombed. Malaya was top of the news.
Malay Chinese and the remainder of the European population
were now fleeing southwards to Singapore, causing enormous
difficulties for a city under withering aerial bombardment. On
22 January some 100 Japanese aircraft bombed and strafed
Singapore, mostly in residential areas. That day and night the
Japanese killed 304 people and wounded another 725, mostly
civilians. Few war planes were left in Singapore to rise against the
invaders. Hospitals were not coping. Services were beginning to
break down. Yet for the British still in Singapore – many of them
civil servants – life went on, with difficulty, almost as normal.
Civilians at night joined officers at the Raffles Hotel on the waterfront. Foxtrots and old patriotic tunes nightly between eight and
midnight were not silenced by the sirens.

*

Mid-afternoon on Thursday 22 January, Victoria Barracks
received a radio message that nine ships were approaching
Rabaul's Simpson Harbour. A later report said the number was
eleven. Then reports came through of another large air raid on
Rabaul involving up to forty-five Japanese aircraft. Damage in
Rabaul appeared to be extensive. Japanese reconnaissance aircraft
were reported over many centres across Papua, New Guinea and
the nearby islands. Fighting of 'a savage nature' was reported in
the Philippines.

On a hot summer's morning on Friday 23 January, the prime
minister's train had crossed over into South Australia and was
racing on the dead-straight track through the sandy limestone
desert of the Nullarbor. There was still no meaningful news
on the fate of Rabaul. It was known that the Japanese were
continuing to press south through Malaya towards the Singapore
island. In the Yong Peng area south of the Muar River the enemy
was advancing quickly on bicycles, on foot and in tanks. Men of
the 2/29th Battalion had been fighting continuously for ten days,

constantly attacked by Japanese dive-bombers. Their commander, General Bennett, in his diary that day, complained that most of the new Australian reinforcements, disgracefully, had received practically no training, such was Australia's military weakness and confusion:

> Some, in fact, have never fired a rifle. The majority had been in camp only a few weeks before embarking for Malaya. The two battalions, who have performed so magnificently, cannot possibly reach the standard of the old units for some months. Unfortunately, my trained reinforcements in Australia were sent to the already crowded reinforcement depots in the Middle East where they were not urgently needed.

Around this time, Lieutenant Arthur Tranter of the 2/29th Infantry Battalion and his men were surrounded in the dark by the Japanese even before any firing could commence. But once it did, the Australians were shooting at gun flashes and shot more of their own men than the Japanese. They then formed a circle and began firing only outwards from it so they couldn't shoot each other. Gunner Russell Braddon noted that when dawn came, it was found that friend had bayoneted friend and .303 bullets had poured so furiously outwards to the other side of the perimeter that they had settled in many Australian limbs. From that night onwards the order was given that the Japanese were to be engaged at night only with bayonets. Some of the Diggers called the inexperienced and often untrained Indian troops the Galloping Gwahlis, according to Braddon, because they had abandoned their trucks, blocking Allied convoys, and run backwards and forwards in absolute panic. There was good reason. Some had never been taught how to fire a rifle and were given quick instruction by the Australians. But even some of the Australians, as young as eighteen, weren't much better off. Lieutenant Tranter would recall that there were Australian soldiers in Malaya who were captured by the Japanese only three months after enlisting in the army. Bitterly, he believed that these young Australian recruits were used as pawns and that their efforts were just a waste of life.

*

After a long, hot haul over the Nullarbor the Trans passed the lonely little outpost at Zanthus and pulled into a stop at Karonie, 69 miles (111 kilometres) short of the big gold mining town of Kalgoorlie, where they were meant to change trains. But Curtin was informed that the train could go no further. As the Trans ground to a halt at Karonie, the resident railwayman reported to the driver, and the word came back down to the prime minister, that men were working on the washaway of the track up ahead. It wasn't known when it would be restored, maybe later in the day. In the meantime, Curtin would sit in frustrating luxury in this hot, barren emptiness with his growing anxieties, fears and loneliness, stranded on the Nullarbor between his war cabinet and Defence Headquarters on the east coast and his welcoming family and friends on the west.

Chapter 6

DESPAIR ON THE NULLARBOR

Karonie is a place few Australians have heard of. Not much has changed since 23 January 1942, when this far-flung speck of a watering stop became symbolic of John Curtin reaching his personal nadir in the emerging drama. The Trans had left the sandy desert country behind and stopped in a patch of poor, partly timbered country, its unwelcoming irregular ridges broken by outcrops of granite that formed low, rounded hills.

John Curtin sat miserably in splendour, under the whirring fans stirring the hot air, holding genuine fears of the enemy at any moment surging down through Australia from the north. Terrible battles would ensue. Everything Australians had built up would be destroyed either by their own hands or the Japanese, and remnants would retreat to the centre; here, where there was nothing to sustain life but water, and even that soon would disappear. Here was the leader of a nation, wallowing in his own misery aboard the elegant false comfort of this pretentious carriage on a train, with Australian Diggers travelling up front in stinking cattle vans; the one time left-wing activist who made indignant speeches over inequality and the slaughter of the First World War; the man who briefly went to jail for refusing to report for military training. Now, when forced to rise to the defence of Australia, he was impotent.

By his own hand, Curtin had temporarily removed himself from control of a nation in peril. The *Sydney Morning Herald*'s Ross Gollan wrote only a few days later that Curtin's extraordinary absence took place in the 'most critical juncture of [Australia's] history':

> It was unfortunate for Australia that the week's most serious developments in the Pacific occurred after Mr Curtin had physically committed himself to his Western Australian tour. He was on his way across the Plain when the mass attacks that began on Rabaul on Tuesday revealed themselves as a prelude to an invasion of the islands . . . a War Cabinet from which Mr. Curtin is absent is not as effective an instrument of Australian national policy as one at which Mr Curtin is present.

Now his only link to his military chiefs, his key ministers and indeed the world was a telegraph pole with a single strand of wire that ran to a little timber waiting shed and office. Inside was a Morse code key connected to the Commonwealth Railways' telegraph network. It was normally used to monitor train movements and pass railway messages. Today it was the sum total of Curtin's lifeline.

As time trickled by and the delay at Karonie became further prolonged, Curtin's frustration knew few bounds. He was restricted and constrained while the prime minister of Great Britain, irresponsibly in Curtin's eyes, both endangered and ignored Australia, her government and her loyal men fighting for 'King and country' as they had duly sworn at the time of enlistment.

Curtin's last report from Rabaul was that communications had been cut with the Japanese about to land. He knew that the force of 1400 had no chance and had almost certainly been overwhelmed if not wiped out.

He was ill and depressed; if ever the black dog came sniffing, it was now. Curtin sat on the train alongside his secretary, Frederick

McLaughlin, a man devoted to Curtin. McLaughlin and the prime minister were working through a sheath of unanswered correspondence when McLaughlin quietly placed a small silver cigarette box on the table, knowing it would please his boss:

'What's this, Fred?'

'It's from Mr David Crone, sir, of Goldsbrough Mort and Company in Melbourne. Mr Crone says and I quote, 'Congratulations from the old football world! What a great job you are doing from the Full-Back Line to the Forward Line! It's all in – and we bet we will kick some goals!'

Curtin's face momentarily lit up. Dave Crone had played a few games for Fitzroy before joining the Blues. He was Carlton's president for years before the war. McLaughlin knew that the prime minister hadn't kicked too many goals himself recently and would be cheered a little. Curtin, who had played as a junior for Brunswick and later had followed Fitzroy, dictated a heartfelt reply greatly appreciating the gift from the 'old football world':

Evidence such as you have given me of support in the difficult tasks which confront me and my colleagues is very gratifying to the Government. I can only assure you that we will continue to do our utmost towards ensuring that the Commonwealth makes the maximum contribution in the struggle in which we are engaged . . .

On the east coast, Curtin's ministers were beginning to demonstrate agitation and their own despair. Deputy Prime Minister Frank Forde, who was chairing war cabinet sessions in Melbourne, was sending ever more urgent missives to Prime Minister Churchill. Overseas communications were mostly sent in Curtin's name. Yet Curtin wasn't writing these important messages, which in essence represented Australia desperately calling for help. For a few vital days the ministers were getting the gist of Curtin's thinking from hurried, scratchy telephone calls or a line or two from coded telegrams. As Forde explained:

Mr Curtin has been advised of the nature of the communications which have been despatched overseas and is fully cognisant of everything that has been done.

One of the messages Curtin received was that unions with members in munitions production, in the face of the war emergency, were planning to take holidays, including the Australia Day public holiday on the coming Monday. Curtin wondered if they were lost to reality. He sent a telegram to the Metal Trades Union Group in Sydney reminding the unionists that the enemy was 'at Australia's doors'.

With Curtin absent, his external affairs minister, Doc Evatt, took a vicious swipe in public at the first lord of the Admiralty, A.V. Alexander, a key proponent of neglecting the war in the Far East:

It now seems clear that the First Lord of the Admiralty, Mr. Alexander, and the few other public men in Britain who gave utterance to contrary sentiments will, at long last, learn the lesson that the defence of Malaya and the Netherlands East Indies is in truth the defence of Britain as well as the defence of Australia . . .

Evatt issued a statement saying Australians refused to believe that the people of Britain were blind to the immediate peril in the Pacific to their own and to the Allied cause:

It is a pity that so much will have to be suffered by gallant soldiers and innocent people to prove that Malaya is not a sideshow but a primary and vital struggle between the Democracies and the Axis Powers.

It is doubtful that Evatt would have tried to consult Curtin before his public criticism of the British Government.

While they continued to wait on the track, Don Rodgers told Curtin that the political reporters aboard wanted to have a chat so they could file stories immediately on arrival at Kalgoorlie. The journalists were invited into the Prince of Wales carriage at dusk. A steward took orders for drinks. It was hot and sticky. The ceiling fans worked overtime. The men sat smoking in comfortable armchairs, taking notes around the mahogany table in the saloon. Curtin had a relationship with these senior political reporters that possibly no other Australian prime minister had before, nor would have after. He would tell them the most 'hair-raising secrets' of the war, as they would describe them. His trust in these men rarely failed. The newsmen referred Curtin to the Japanese prime minister's threat to crush Australia and the East Indies unless they cooperated. Curtin emotionally replied that Australia would consider 'every village a strongpoint, every town a fortress and every man, woman and child a soldier' should Japanese aggression come to the Commonwealth:

> The only Australians who would co-operate with the Japanese would be dead Australians.

Curtin's blood pressure no doubt rose when he was informed that the New South Wales Trades and Labour Council had come out in strong support of minister Ward's proposed nationalisation of Australian industry. In the meantime, serious industrial stoppages continued unabated. While Curtin sat in the Nullarbor, five coalmines in the Hunter region of New South Wales were on strike. Arthur Fadden's opposition spoke of 'the shocking spectacle of idleness on the coalfields while Australia's sons were fighting overseas'.

*

The timing of the prime minister's absence had begun to lead to discontent. Curtin was openly criticised by *The Courier-Mail* in Brisbane as he sat immobilised:

> the Federal Parliament, which has not met for more than a month, is still scattered all over the country, and the prime minister, though he has promised to give consideration to its early reassembly, is on his way to his electorate in Perth.

People were pressing for information on many vital issues and demanding explanations of government policy, the newspaper insisted. But newspapers were simultaneously turning their editorial guns on Prime Minister Winston Churchill and his cabinet for neglecting the Far East. The salvos had the hallmarks of a coordinated press strategy hatched during the earlier part of the rail journey and involving Curtin's wily press secretary Don Rodgers and his close relationship with senior political reporters. He and Curtin had briefed the reporters on Australia's bid for a say in the higher direction of the war in both London and Washington. The newspaper editorials spoke of Australian anger over the relegation of the Far East and the Pacific regions as secondary theatres of war. The *Canberra Times* said the British Government was in grave error if it thought the region was subordinate:

> The idea that Japan can be allowed to move onward from point to point until one day the British Government decides that the time has come to drive them out would constitute an Empire wrecking mistake if it were to abide for another moment in the thoughts of leaders and advisers on the other side of the world.

Curtin's government now had greater justification for recalling Australian troops from the Middle East rather than the Churchill Government 'hoarding men, planes and materials in Britain', the newspaper said. The *Sydney Morning Herald* found it lamentable that Russia and the Middle East had a precedent in receiving war aid. The newspaper spoke of a new threat to Australia 'of unprecedented gravity':

> For every Australian the prospect that the towns and countryside he knows may be visited with the suffering and devastation of armed conflict is one that may well fill him with dismay.

The Argus in Melbourne came out with a scathing editorial 'This must not happen here.' Australia's voice must be heard after previous British military debacles in Greece and Crete, the newspaper said. The policy of sending reinforcements 'too little, too late', it argued, ran a grave danger of being repeated in the South West Pacific. Ships, planes and men should be sent in their thousands. *The Argus* alarmingly foreshadowing potential disaster in the Pacific:

> ... Britain has adopted in Asiatic waters a policy of hesitation and inadequacy which has proved disastrous in other theatres of war. It is likely to be disastrous on this occasion also, and not only to Australia and her fellow Dominion in the Pacific, but to the whole British Empire and to the whole Allied cause.

*

The war cabinet in Melbourne was in emergency session on Friday 23 January. Australian newspapers, as Curtin would have been informed, were dominated by catastrophic news: *The Courier-Mail* headlined with 'Rabaul Believed Taken By Enemy', with sub-headlines, '100 Planes Raid Singapore', 'Invader 100 Miles from Rangoon' and 'Japanese Success in Celebes'. Ministers were skittish, deeply concerned about Japan's seemingly unstoppable advances. Reports coming into Victoria Barracks contained nothing but dire news. Ministers were also furious with Churchill. Frank Forde said he had received a cable from the Australian commander, General Bennett, warning of a 'serious deterioration' of the position in Malaya. The defence chiefs of staff predicted that Japan, after taking Rabaul, would probably begin operations against New Guinea designed to take control of the Torres Strait. This they said would 'seriously affect the flow of supplies to Darwin and the Netherlands East Indies'. The chief of the Naval Staff, Admiral Sir Guy Royle, said it had to be realised that 'we are in danger of invasion as our naval forces are not sufficient to offer effective resistance'. He did not think a public statement now was a good idea, however:

> In the event of invasion people should be told to remain in their homes and allow the military authorities to have control and keep the roads clear.

Royle could only hope that because Japan had so much else on her hands, Australia might not offer an attractive target.

Forde took a break from the meeting to send an urgent demand to Churchill to rush additional supplies of equipment, especially aircraft, to the south-west Pacific. Forde told the waiting press that he would have a long conversation by telephone with Curtin in Perth next day. He said Australia was facing a more serious threat of invasion than ever before, but there must be 'no form of panic or defeatism', only firm determination to throw the enemy back:

> Australians must face up to the cold hard fact that the enemy is now hammering at our gates endeavouring to gain a foothold with the avowed intention of invading our land.

An indication of the alarm in Melbourne was that newspapers said some ministers considered there was an urgent need for 'immediate mobilisation of the whole population in resistance to any Japanese forces' that might try to occupy any part of Australia. Newspapers predicted that a scorched-earth policy on the Australian mainland was likely to be sought within the war cabinet.

Inside the war cabinet meeting the deputy chief of the Air Staff, Air Vice Marshall Bill Bostock, reported that after the loss of eight Wirraways at Rabaul, orders had been issued that the aircraft be no longer used as fighters, although they could be used as dive-bombers. At last there was official admission that the lumbering Wirraway trainers were no match for Zeros and indeed were not fighters. During war cabinet discussions on the need for complete coastal blackouts, Bostock admitted the 'inability of the RAAF to undertake complete reconnaissance to seaward', a rather stunning admission to the assembled ministers.

The anxiety and anger of Curtin's ministers in Melbourne was profound. External Affairs Minister Doc Evatt could see disaster encroaching on many fronts. He said it was a pity that so much would have to be suffered by gallant soldiers and innocent people to prove that Malaya was not a sideshow:

We in Australia have been asked to accept in complete faith the doctrine that in the final hours of crisis the steel walls of the British navy would stand between us and danger. The danger is here . . .

The minister for supply, Jack Beasley, said long-range plans now were 'the height of stupidity' unless the British wanted another Dunkirk, Greece or Crete:

The Japanese are in New Guinea. In New Guinea they are on the threshold of Australia . . . Therefore the fight for Malaya is vital; it anticipates, perhaps averts the last great battle before Australia.

In this highly charged atmosphere in Melbourne, Doc Evatt began preparing a memorable draft cable to Churchill, which would be approved by Deputy Prime Minister Forde, who would sign the draft as 'Acting Prime Minister', which he wasn't. The cable would be sent in the name of John Curtin, who presumably, at some stage during that day, had received the gist of the extraordinary message, although this is not confirmed. The caustic cable was largely Evatt's doing. He made drafts, which Forde at least sighted. Evatt and the government had learned through Australia's special envoy in London, Sir Earle Page, that Churchill was considering evacuating Singapore to the Japanese and as far as possible using the available troops to reinforce Burma. Evatt's cable sent in Curtin's name was unequivocal:

After all the assurances we have been given, the evacuation of Singapore would be regarded here and elsewhere as an inexcusable betrayal. Singapore is a central fortress in the system of Empire and local defence. As stated . . . we understood it was to be made impregnable and in any event it was to be capable of holding out for a prolonged period until the arrival of the main fleet.

Even in an emergency diversion of reinforcements should be to the Netherlands East Indies and not Burma. Anything else would be deeply resented and might force the Netherlands East Indies to make a separate peace.

The cable said the trend in Malaya and the attack on Rabaul were 'giving rise to a public feeling of grave uneasiness at Allied impotence to do anything to stem the Japanese advance.' Churchill would later claim that the 'severe reproach was not in accordance with the truth or military facts.' He was deeply offended by the words 'inexcusable betrayal' penned in Evatt's handwriting, as were the British Government and even Roosevelt. There was no betrayal, Churchill later wrote. But he withdrew his proposal to evacuate Singapore and reconsidered the issue of reinforcements, deciding instead to and sent the largely untrained and very inexperienced British 18th Division to Singapore. Later he would blame the Australian Government in part for the consequences.

*

As Curtin sweated it out in his carriage, his attention often focused on the Australians at Rabaul, about whom he had heard so little. During the tropical night of 23 January in Rabaul, Australian troops waiting beside Vulcan volcano on Simpson Harbour heard the Japanese laughing, talking and even striking matches. As an unnamed Australian defender told a war historian:

> We could see dimly the shapes of boats, and men getting out . . . We allowed most of them to get out of the boats and then fired everything we had.

The Japanese made two attempts to rush the barbed-wire defences in this area but were prevented by the Australian fire. The Japanese then shifted away from the entanglements. Sheer weight of numbers prevented a prolonged Australian defence. The Japanese began infiltrating the shoreline at a number of points. In some places there was no opposition. In a short time the Australians were being overwhelmed and survivors began withdrawing. By 4 am the Japanese were establishing themselves in the once beautiful Rabaul town, adorned with mango trees and frangipanis. Rabaul was a burning mess. Transport ships could be seen discharging more troops. Japanese were landing at numerous places between Rabaul town and the small town of Kokopo, on the bay just to the south-east. Fighting was continuing in many places along the shore but the Japanese were coming through in thousands. Enemy aircraft, flying low, were machine-gunning and bombing retreating Australian troops, and roads, airfields, buildings and the Australian battalion headquarters. Lark Force commander, Colonel John Scanlan, unwisely declared that it was now 'every man for himself'. Officers told men they could either surrender or 'go bush'. With only cursory and incomplete evacuation plans, chaos ensued. Despite conspicuous Australian bravery and stubborn fighting in some quarters, the defence became a tragic and unseemly rout as shocked men, with little preparation, either fled Rabaul or simply surrendered.

By the afternoon organised resistance to the Japanese around Rabaul ended. Scanlan's force split up into small parties. Many withdrew south-west to the island's north coast or south-east down the coast. Lieutenant Malcolm Mackenzie, a navy intelligence officer, reported that occasional food dumps, which recently had been left by the Australians at villages, had been looted. Numerous cars and trucks, some filled with supplies, were abandoned. The Japanese dropped pamphlets, dated 23 January, addressed to the 'Officers and Soldiers of this island':

SURRENDER AT ONCE! And we will guarantee your life. Treating you as war prisoners. Those who RESIST US WILL BE KILLED ONE AND ALL. Consider seriously, you can find neither food nor way of escape in this island and you will only die of hunger unless you surrender.

*

Singapore too was now in a terrible state. Over 100 Japanese aircraft were bombing Singapore each day. A war correspondent for *The Argus*, Rohan Rivett, saw the disaster unfolding:

Bombs, bombs everywhere, bombs whistling down diagonally with an unmistakable scream, bombs bursting on streets, on shops, on houses, on military targets – eighty major raids in twenty-four days in this fair town. A silent city glimmering in the gorgeous full moonlight waiting for the inevitable drone of bombers . . .

The British were living in hope that Singapore could be saved. The commander-in-chief Far East in the ABDA area, General Pownall, based in Lembang, near Bandung, West Java, recorded in his diary that with luck the Japanese might be held off, provided they didn't get into the town of Johore Bahru, just over the water from Singapore island. Pownall rather strangely in his diary at this time launched into bitter condemnation of the Australians:

The Australians, as was inevitable, have now started to 'register', saying they are not adequately represented on the staff here . . . [General] Wavell [ABDA supreme commander] said when he was first appointed that the Australians would be the most difficult of our Allies. Very likely, indeed the telegram from Canberra was distinctly rude.

*

As dark gathered at Karonie, news arrived that the washaway had been repaired. To the relief of everyone, the Trans began to roll westward again towards the big mining town of Kalgoorlie, less than an hour and a half away.

When the Trans pulled into the big railway junction at Kalgoorlie, it was more than four hours late so Curtin was surprised to see hundreds of people lining the platform. They pressed towards the Prince of Wales carriage at the rear. When Curtin appeared on the observation platform, he received an unexpected tonic: a big roar went up from an appreciative crowd. His tiredness from the trauma of the day in the Nullarbor fell away and an invigorated prime minister robustly addressed the throng: 'It is very pleasant to receive a real Western Australian welcome.' The crowd cheered again. Curtin knew they wanted to hear about the war. In what reporters called 'a challenging speech', Curtin in a loud, indignant voice said the Japanese were questioning the right of Australians to occupy their own country:

In the last one hundred years of our occupancy of Australia there has never been a time when the challenge to our occupancy was direct and so menacing. The men and women who pioneered this country endured hardships and privation in the belief that they were building the foundations for a great civilisation. Their spirit has come down to us as an imperishable heritage . . .

The crowd, including many tough local miners, cheered some more when Curtin insisted that Australians would not flinch, no matter how far the Japanese came:

We will have scars of battle and we will suffer casualties, but that grim prospect will no more intimidate us than our ancestors.

There was a place for 'every able-bodied man and woman in Australia', he shouted. Those who could not fight could work 'and there is no excuse for them not working!' One of the pressmen asked whether any Australian city or town would be surrendered to save buildings or to avert bloodshed. Curtin bellowed with an emphatic 'No!' to the delight of the assembly. Australians would not surrender any town or soil to any invader, he thundered, but would 'fight until they die'. Curtin was fortified and defiant. This was not a time for introspection. He relished the chance to shake off anxieties. Civic leaders and union leaders, many of whom he knew, crowded forward to shake his hand. Kalgoorlie miners wanted their grievances to be heard. They feared race riots on the gold fields, saying aliens had most of the well-paid jobs with the younger Australian-born men enlisting for war service. Curtin replied that aliens would be subjected to the call-up for service in pioneering labouring battalions, which cheered the miners. He and his party then made their way to the waiting Westland express. Labor premier of Western Australia, John Willcock, had supplied Curtin with his own special carriage, not as elegant as the Prince of Wales carriage, but roomy and very comfortable. On this last leg and for the first time since leaving Melbourne, the prime minister slept with a belief that Australia was doing everything in its power.

On the morning of Saturday 24 January Victoria Barracks continued to receive dire intelligence reports on the Japanese in Malaya. Reports spoke of extensive Allied aircraft and personnel losses over enemy front lines owing to the Japanese fighter cover and 'lack of sufficient Allied fighter escort'. A report from Kuala Lumpur said a massive 204 enemy planes had been seen over Malaya on one recent day. In southern Burma at Mergui, 600 British army and RAF men with 170 civilians were being evacuated by ship as the Japanese approached. In the East Indies, intelligence predicted Japanese infiltration into Sumatra.

On the other side of the country, everyone wanted a glimpse of the first prime minister from Western Australia. Crowds gathered along the way merely to wave at the train as it passed. At some railway stops people gathered expectantly, hoping to welcome the prime minister home personally and perhaps press his ear with a few quick words. Curtin obliged wherever he could while making brief but rousing impromptu speeches, just as he always answered every letter to his office.

Press secretary Don Rodgers received word at one of the stops that the BBC had broadcast a news item saying the Australian prime minister was returning to Perth on a holiday. Curtin was particularly annoyed, having urged Australians to work through their holidays for the war effort. Rodgers released a press statement for his boss saying, 'It is an absolute lie that I am holidaying.' The truth, however, slipped through Curtin's minder in several publications, including the *West Australian*:

> As the main object of his visit is to afford him a respite from office, the programme arranged for him has been restricted . . .

*

Invasion jitters continued in Melbourne. The war cabinet chaired by Frank Forde had been sitting almost continuously each day. On Saturday morning, 24 January, External Affairs Minister Evatt anxiously asked if the government should begin the preparation of the scorched-earth policy, to be implemented if Japan invaded. War cabinet members wanted a defence report on the subject. Only five months earlier, Evatt had told parliament the Japanese threat had been much exaggerated.

War posters with Curtin's approval began appearing around Australia. 'The Enemy Thunders at Our Gates' said one such poster, using a quote from the prime minister. It featured a diagram of enemy aircraft heading down the east coast of Australia from the New Guinea islands. A message from Curtin urged Australians to stop industrial lockouts and strikes, prevent waste and 'keep a clear head and a quiet tongue'. Another more graphic propaganda poster showed an armed Japanese soldier about to step on to mainland Australia with the warning, 'He's coming south. It's fight, work or perish.'

*

On early Saturday afternoon, the Westland pulled into Perth railway station, a grand two-storey red brick building with cream stucco. It was packed with hundreds of well-wishers, including John Willcock and Curtin's wife and daughter. The crowd surged forward to the special carriage when the train came to a stop. Curtin alighted from the other end and quietly strolled through the crowd from the opposite direction. A few minutes elapsed before Curtin was noticed, a face in the crowd. The crowd suddenly let out three roaring cheers, followed by another for Curtin's wife Elsie. Photographers swarmed to snap Curtin with his family. It seemed that everyone wanted to greet the prime minister personally. With more cheering and hand-shaking, Curtin and party pressed through the throng to the station exit. Local reporters said it was one of the most affec-tionate and stirring welcomes ever given to a public man in Western Australia.

Curtin desperately wanted to go home to his cottage at Cottesloe near the sea, to embrace his family and pat his loyal dog Nip (strangely also his pet name for his wife) and slump into his comfortable yet kitschy lounge chair with ashtray stand at the ready in his book-lined front room. But all that was put on hold. Soon after arriving in Perth Curtin and Elsie, in the same floral frock she wore to the station, walked into the Wesley Church at Fremantle to see Corporal Syd Gray marry Roma Milbourne and leave the church through a guard of honour of Gray's mates from Fremantle's Arthur Head battery. The Curtins went on to the reception, where the prime minister proposed the toast, in his case with something soft, to the newly married couple. The Curtins didn't have time to buy a present, so they gave a cheque for ten pounds.

Home life at 24 Jarrad Street for Curtin would be distracted and fleeting. Staff and reporters hung about the cottage, filling the house and front lawn. Numerous civic, union and political groups clamoured to greet the prime minister. Some arrived unannounced. There were so many invitations his staff amalgamated some proposed functions and made apologies for many others. But despite his illness, Curtin knew his war duty required him to make rousing speeches to inspire his fellow Australians. His war work at home and at his office in town was filled with meetings, telephone calls and cables to and from Melbourne. The distractions shrank his time at home in Cottesloe. He was especially thrilled to see his son John, who had briefly come south from RAAF duty at Geraldton.

*

At the time Curtin was settling in to spend his first relaxing night at home with his family, Imperial General Headquarters in Tokyo announced that enemy resistance in Rabaul and Kavieng in the New Guinea islands had ceased:

The capture of this important position, from where it will be possible to spread our influence to the Australian mainland, is extremely significant in terms of our ability to attack and menace Australia.

Japan's official war history, *Senshi sosho*, records accurately that the capture of Rabaul was a textbook operation of cooperation between the Japanese army and navy. It says the loss of Rabaul and the advance through Malaya had begun to 'impact greatly on the citizens of Australia' with the country's four divisions and best officers serving overseas:

> In fact, the general mood in Australia at that time was one of extreme alarm . . . Defence of the huge expanse of the Australian coastline was absolutely impossible by either sea or sky.

Australia's defence chiefs expected the danger of invasion to remain until the whole of the so-called Malay Barrier, from Singapore to the tip of Cape York Peninsula, was stabilised, or until the Allies had gained supremacy over the Japanese fleet. Neither of those scenarios appeared likely in the foreseeable future. Despite Churchill's cynicism, British intelligence chiefs meeting on 25 January 1942 thought that a major operation by Japan to capture the Australian continent was feasible, although unlikely. But raids by cruisers and armed merchant cruisers were possible at any time 'against one or more of the principal ports on the coast of Australia and New Zealand'. The British Intelligence experts said the Japanese might hesitate before attempting the occupation of a continent such as Australia, although Darwin was seen as a marked target for occupation:

> It seems likely that Japan will, at this stage, be content with endeavouring to isolate Australia and New Zealand without embarking on a major operation to the southward except for the capture of Port Darwin. An attack on Port Darwin is likely in any event.

*

Dread and alarm, if not panic, was now affecting some of Curtin's senior ministers, who feared a direct attack somewhere on the northern Australian coast. They knew that if the worst happened there would be no escape for seven million Australians. Ross Gollan, of the *Sydney Morning Herald*, detected the mood of the ministers in Curtin's absence:

> The war cabinet, it is thought, fully recognises that if Japan did manage to get full control of Australia, she could be ousted only after a period in which things would inevitably occur that would end the chances of the victorious Allies restoring the Australia which we know.

Curtin's ministers, Gollan wrote, were vividly picturing Australians desperately fighting across the countryside:

> They will be white peoples under Japanese attack, having as their only choice either the desperate holding of some parts of their soil, or national annihilation.

There were those who believed that John Curtin and his ministers in those torrid early months of 1942 lacked courage and moral strength in adversity, and even demonstrated cowardice. Journalist Paul Hasluck, who had known Curtin in Fremantle, later became governor-general of Australia. He was a junior official in the Department of External Affairs in Canberra in 1942. He wrote about the fear generated in Canberra about a potential Japanese invasion:

> I now record that my personal observation of the Australian ministers, including the prime minister, at the time of crisis in early 1942, was that they were lacking in fortitude. They were in a state of jitters when bad news came.

Hasluck wrote later in reminiscences that in the first half of 1942 the fear of invasion, and the belief that even Canberra itself was a war target, were very real and he said that this fear spread among the general populace:

My sober summing up in the war history was that the Curtin Government 'consistently acted as though it expected Australians to be scared'. My evidence as a witness drawing on my own observations is that the Government was itself scared.

Another official war historian Charles Bean wrote, in a newspaper in 1949, that the Curtin Government made no attempt to hide its belief that the morale of Australians during the crisis was questionable:

My own impression during the time was that it was shakiest at the top; that some, though by no means all, ministers and officials thousands of miles from the spot . . . failed in their trust of the people.

Bean said Canberra might have been 'in a state of the jitters' but if the Japanese had landed in the north, the world would have seen a guerrilla resistance that would have illuminated Australia's name, 'even if the struggle had finished us off':

Let me hasten to add that I don't specially blame the folk in Canberra. The situation was entirely new to them . . .

James Plimsoll, a public servant who joined Army Intelligence in early 1942 and later became governor of Tasmania, didn't agree that Curtin was scared:

I think perhaps the Government was a bit nervous and uncertain. But that was because, not only of the danger, but because it was a new government . . . I think there might have been not so much panic but uncertainty as to what a government should be doing.

Plimsoll said Curtin worried about the loss of Australian troops at sea without convoy escorts, but added, 'Of course, it's no cowardice on Curtin's part; it was sheer worry about loss of Australian lives and the consequences.'

Japanese thinking in early 1942 in fact was divided on what to do about Australia when so much territory had been gained in victorious battles in such a short time. Supply lines were stretched further than contemplated, shipping vessels were in short supply and there were more immediate priorities than Australia. Japan had some short-term goals but no long-term structured plans as to how far it could expand without leaving itself vulnerable. But with each stunning military success, the war planners, especially and including senior officers of the Imperial Navy, would become bolder and more aggressive and grandiose in their considerations of future operations.

Baron Captain Sadatoshi Tomioka, later Vice Admiral, was chief of the Operations Section of the Navy General Staff and wielded considerable power and influence. He wrote of the Imperial Navy's 'Australia Strategy' in a history after the war. After the initial Japanese victories, Tomioka was particularly worried about Australia becoming a base from which the United States could launch air attacks northwards against Japan. He believed that if the enemy was not yet prepared in 1942 'then we can take Australia':

When they [the United States] looked for the best area to advance from in this war, Australia was the only option in the Pacific . . . If this huge military force set itself up in the vast expanse of Australia and then surged northwards, they would be unstoppable. Hence we needed to either force Australia out of the war or isolate them from America.

Speaking with the army I was told it was not possible to occupy Australia. The army was set up in the north and could not spare another five or six divisions. Given Japan's military strength, such a strategy would be foolhardy. I see, I thought. There is logic in that. It would be foolhardy. But the war has started. We must destroy the enemy. We must win. To win whatever happens we can't permit the enemy to use Australia.

The plans fostered by Tomioka had the support of Vice Admiral Shigeyoshi Inoue, commander of the 4th Fleet, and of his chief of staff, Rear Admiral Shikazo Yano. Inoue's duty was to protect the south-west Pacific from enemy incursions. His area of interest extended to the shores of Australia. Several months of titanic struggle began between the planners and chiefs of the Imperial Navy and those of the Imperial Army. The navy came up with proposals to invade and occupy Australia, and although it had the support of some more cavalier military hotheads, the Imperial Army repeatedly blocked the Australia proposals.

Historian Hiromi Tanaka, who became Japan's foremost expert on the fighting in New Guinea, believes the Imperial Navy behaved quite irrationally:

> You know, some Japanese navy officers thought that letting the Emperor live and survive is the most important thing that needs to be done. They saw their mission as to die beautifully in the battlefield for the empire. Sometimes I wonder if these Japanese were really determined to win the war or not . . . I wonder if they really wanted to win the war.

Japanese propagandists continued to relish the apparent public division between Australia and Britain, gloating over Australian recriminations in the face of the Japanese onslaught:

> with Singapore practically lost, the strategic strongholds of the enemy for the defence of Australia and the Netherlands East Indies has now come to the verge of collapse, for no effective aid can safely reach them in the face of Japanese military, naval and air superiority in the south west Pacific. It is now clear that Great Britain is in no position to aid any country . . .

The official spokesman for Japan's Board of Information, Tomokazu Hori, did his best to widen the gulf between Australia and Britain. He said the 'frantic appeal' of the Australian war cabinet to Prime Minister Churchill and President Roosevelt for planes and ships would go unanswered:

The characteristic blunder of the British Cabinet has proved too much for the people of Australia to bear with ... We must be ready to see a complete collapse of not only Australia and other British possessions but the entire British Empire and the Allied countries.

Curtin in Perth now made a conscious decision to tell the Australian people in the clearest terms how determined he was to ensure that Australia would participate in key Allied decisions affecting Australia:

We make it plain that we claim representation on an Imperial war cabinet so that Australia's voice and counsel might be heard directly in respect to the conduct of the war in total.

Chapter 7

THUNDERING AT THE GATES

John Curtin was now desperate. Australia had not one aircraft that could take on a Japanese Zero. Added to this, the vast bulk of the experienced fighting infantrymen were overseas and many training at home didn't even have rifles. The navy had few major fighting ships in Australian waters. In fact, Australia's home defences were so inadequate the Japanese could have landed successfully just about anywhere on the Australian coast and become entrenched. There was increased concern and a renewed sense of patriotism, but many Australians carried on as usual, spending money on leisure, attending race meetings and taking long holidays at the beach while complaining about increasing government austerity measures. On Monday 26 January, the day after his arrival in Perth, Curtin made a national Australia Day radio broadcast. The gravity of the address shocked Australians, as he intended:

Today, we Australians are faced with a war for survival. The enemy thunders at our very gates. We are now inside the fighting lines. The war has come to Australia. It is the enemy that has done this. Powerful, ruthless, well-prepared as the result of years of planning, he now sends his legions to our doorstep. We, who consistently sprang to assist others in resisting wanton aggression, are now called upon to resist it ourselves.

This gauntlet we accept. All we have, all that we are, all we ever hope to be, is being mobilised in total organisation to meet war with war, and, by our strength and quality in war, ensure the integrity of our country and the survival of Australian authority in Australia for Australians. That means that all of us are now inhabitants of a war station. The old ways of peace are gone.

Curtin might have sounded confident yet was anything but. He would tell President Roosevelt in a cable that same day that Australia simply did not have the means to defend itself. The choice was to make some sacrifice for Australia or Australia would become a complete sacrifice to the enemy. He reiterated his demand for a greater Australian say in the running of the war, demanding 'consultation as equals'. Without naming the obvious target of his toughest barb, Curtin went to the gist of his concerns about Australia's treatment by 'the Motherland':

No single nation can afford to risk its future on the infallibility of one man, and no nation can afford to submerge its right of speaking for itself because of the assumed omniscience of another.

Curtin's worry and stress at the looming threat to the Australian mainland grew by the day. Curtin also sent Roosevelt a copy of a cable he had sent to Prime Minister Churchill requesting that two Australian divisions be returned home from the Middle East. Attached to the cable was a rather desperately worded note personally to the president about the state Australia found itself in:

We are now, with a small population in the only white man's territory south of the equator, beset grievously. Because we have added to our contribution in manpower so much of our resources and materials we now lack adequacy for forces of our homeland on our own soil.

Roosevelt referred Curtin's note to Brigadier General Dwight D. Eisenhower of the War Plans Division. Eisenhower had received a similar message from the then US commander in Australia, Major General Lewis H. Brereton, who said there was 'no, repeat no, adequate defence available' in Australia. According to Brereton the situation was so bad that he thought the United States should impose 'a strong centralised control of internal Australian politics under American influence', an extraordinary proposition but one that would occur, at least partially, through American influences in Australia. Brereton emphasised the 'strong probability' that the American air and sea lanes to Australia would be broken and forecast that the country faced invasion. Eisenhower was taken aback. He noted that the cables from Prime Minister Curtin and General Brereton demonstrated an 'extraordinary uneasiness of mind' on the part of both men. He drafted a message to the Australian Government saying that the War Department was 'acutely aware of the seriousness of the situation' and was sending to Australia 'every fighter airplane for which shipping space is presently available'. But in fact the flow of aircraft to Australia that could be put into the air quickly, and for which shipping and pilots were available, would remain painfully slow. Eisenhower was torn between his strong advocacy of the 'Beat Hitler First' policy and the need to recognise his colleagues' pleas in Australia and elsewhere to take the war to the Japanese.

The gravity of Australia's paltry air defences in late January 1942 can be gauged by the fact that it had not one single operational fighter aircraft that could provide for the defence of Australia, New Guinea or Papua. Australia's eighty Wirraways had been sidelined; used mostly for training purposes. Apart from some ancient machines including biplanes, Australia had only twenty-nine Hudson bombers and fourteen Catalina flying boats, which were no match for their superior Japanese equivalents. Further, a large part of the force was located in the New Guinea area, where losses were now being sustained daily. Kittyhawk fighters, piloted by inexperienced Americans, used Darwin as a staging post for flights to the Dutch East Indies. Curtin in Perth gave these aircraft figures to Churchill in a cable of 27 January, saying he could not emphasise too strongly the urgency of Australia's aircraft needs, adding a line that he could never admit to the Australian people: 'In the air, we are left almost defenceless against our enemies.'

Curtin emphasised Australia's massive contribution to Britain's defence, pointing out that since the inception of Australia's Empire Air Training Scheme at the outset of the war, 6500 aircrew and 2300 ground staff had left Australia for the RAF. In addition, six squadrons of the RAAF were operating overseas. Clearly the Menzies, Fadden and Curtin governments had all sent too much of Australia's meagre defence resources overseas.

*

Annoying yet accurate references to Curtin's illness and stress continued to surface in small paragraphs in newspapers around the country. The *Sun Pictorial* in Melbourne said it had been surprised to hear that Curtin was in Western Australia 'to deal with urgent defence matters':

> We were given to understand that he had gone there for a badly-needed rest, which none would begrudge him, though it might be wished that he had chosen to recuperate in some place less distant from the nation's nerve centres.

The newspaper rightly said it was difficult to imagine any defence matters that would justify the prime minister remaining in Perth 'when the Government may at any moment have to take decisions of far-reaching importance' in consultation with the defence chiefs in Melbourne.

In his anxiety, John Curtin received welcomed stimulus from the people of Perth. On Tuesday 27 January he entered the Capitol Theatre in Perth for a civic reception. As he walked down the aisle the crowd of some 2500 people rose as one and clapped and cheered him all the way to the stage. The extraordinary display continued for several minutes. He stood smiling occasionally, but mostly his expression was serious, which was significant to those who knew him, for he had little joy to impart. The thrust of his thundering speech was that there was no easy way out. It was 'Work or fight!' He said Australians shouldn't be 'snakey' about new wartime regulations, but must rise to the fact that they were facing invasion:

> This Commonwealth, which has never known the heel of an invader, is face to face with the imminent prospect of raids on our coastline and attempts to land enemy forces . . . I should humbug you if I were to deny that the British race was caught napping. It was. I might fool you, but not the enemy, if I were to say that we were prepared for all eventualities.

Curtin's long, thundering exhortation to join the war effort ended with sustained applause and wild cheering before the crowd burst into a chorus of 'For he's a jolly good fellow'. Curtin gave every appearance of being the tough war leader. If only they knew.

*

On the same day as Curtin's rousing speech in Perth, Churchill in London was dealing with renewed depression. With Singapore and the Dutch East Indies gravely threatened, British newspaper editorials were joining the clamour of their Australian counterparts with rising condemnation of the direction of the war in the Far East. There was considerable criticism of Churchill as leader. Some British newspapers called for a reshuffle of the British cabinet. After his talks with Roosevelt and his chiefs in Washington, Churchill believed the 'Grand Alliance' between Britain and the United States was bound to win the war in the long run. But now he also felt that 'a measureless array of disasters', as he termed it, approached with Japanese victories.

Churchill's answer was to go before the House of Commons to deliver a strong speech on his recent work in the United States before seeking a parliamentary vote of confidence in his government. He felt confident of the outcome of the vote and was not prepared to concede the slightest curtailment in his considerable personal authority. He acknowledged the deteriorating situation in the Far East and other bad news, and said there would be many tales of blunders and shortcomings. He emphasised how unlikely it had appeared that Japan would consider going to war with Britain and the United States:

> It seemed very unlikely that Japan would attempt the distant invasion of the Malay Peninsula, the assault upon Singapore, and the attack upon the Dutch East Indies, while leaving behind them in their rear this great American Fleet.

But the record shows differently. Churchill himself on many occasions assessed that Japan might well launch a major war, long before Japan made her mass attacks across the Pacific and the Far East. Churchill said parliament now must decide whether his government was right in accepting, for the time being, a far lower standard of forces and equipment for the Far East while his priorities were Russia and Libya:

> The first obvious fact is that the Far Eastern theatre was at peace and that the other theatres were in violent or imminent war. It would evidently have been a very improvident use of our limited resources – as I pointed out earlier – if we had kept large masses of troops and equipment spread about the immense areas of the Pacific or in India, Burma and the Malay Peninsula, standing idle, month by month and perhaps year by year, without any war occurring . . .

There had never been any suggestion that Britain should have kept 'large masses of troops and equipment' spread about large areas of Asia and the Pacific. The exact reverse applied. The RAF in Malaya had been starved far below its agreed minimum requirements of men and aircraft, especially modern aircraft. The former commander-in-chief Far East, Air Chief Marshall Brooke-Popham, would soon say that there was a feeling of isolation and neglect in Singapore as the Japanese approached. Asia had also been anything but a peaceful backwater. Japan's war in China had raged on since at least 1937 and Japan had occupied northern Indo-China in late 1940. British intelligence chiefs in London in late 1941 had given Churchill detailed assessments of how Japan was likely to thrust southwards with a possible attempt to seize and hold Java and Sumatra southward to Timor.

In the House of Commons on 27 January Churchill addressed Australia's protests about representation at the highest levels of decision-making and the lack of British reinforcements in the Far East and the Pacific. Britain, he said, would not raise any obstacle to the return of the 'splendid Australian troops who volunteered for Imperial service' to defend their own homeland. Churchill added, 'or whatever part of the Pacific theatre may be thought most expedient', a term that might have foreshadowed that Churchill had other plans for the Australian forces in the Middle East. Churchill said Britain had been urging the United States to aid Australia:

I am sure we all sympathise with our kith and kin in Australia now that the shield of British and American sea power has, for the time being, been withdrawn from them so unexpectedly and so tragically and now that hostile bombers may soon be within range of Australian shores.

Churchill's sympathy had a hollow ring. He publicly down-played and disparaged the Curtin Government's concerns about the chances of an invasion of Australia. Japan, he said, was more likely to take the rich prizes of the whole Malay Archipelago, the Philippines and the Dutch East Indies, and seize island bases:

I think they are much more likely to be arranging themselves in those districts which they have taken or are likely to take than to undertake a serious mass invasion of Australia. That would seem to be a very ambitious overseas operation for Japan to under-take in the precarious and limited interval before the British and American navies regain . . . the unquestionable command of the Pacific Ocean.

Churchill said he had made no secret of expected 'severe ill-usage at the hands of the Japanese in 1942'. But when Allied forces regained the naval command of the Pacific and establish effective air superiority 'we shall be able to set about our task in good style in 1943' in Australasia, India and in the Dutch East Indies. Churchill during 1942 repeatedly qualified what he meant by 'coming to Australia's aid' in the event of a Japanese invasion. It became clear that Australia would need a 'serious mass invasion' rather than random Japanese landings before Britain might deploy her forces to Australia, if she had any available. Mere attempts to take Darwin, for instance, probably would not qualify for British support. Despite all this, Britain would do 'everything in human power' to either help Australia, or persuade America to, should Australia face a mass invasion:

> *But there is no question of regarding the war in the Pacific as a secondary operation.* The only limitation applied to its vigorous prosecution will be the shipping available at any given time. [author's italics]

For the Curtin Government, this sounded very much like a gamble with Australia's fate.

*

The day after John Curtin's Australia Day broadcast from Perth, the Australian Government, through Frank Forde in Melbourne, agreed to the creation of an American proposal, the ANZAC Command, after the disintegration, as the Japanese advanced on the East Indies, of the ABDA Command. The ANZAC area took in the whole of the east coast of Australia, Tasmania and New Zealand, the east of the New Guinea mainland island and numerous islands including the Solomons and Fiji. But the naval units available for the new command were exceptionally meagre in comparison to the available Japanese fleet. When the Allied fleet was formed at Suva in the Fiji islands during February, it would consist only of the heavy cruisers HMAS *Australia* and USS *Chicago*, the mostly old light cruisers HMNZS *Achilles* and *Leander* and the destroyers USS *Perkins* and *Lamson*.

*

Many Australian troops as well as remaining government officers and planters at Rabaul who had not been captured on New Britain were now desperately fleeing for their lives from the Japanese on New Britain. Lance Bombardier Jack Holmfield, a member of the 2/22nd Battalion, had counted twenty-two ships coming into Rabaul's Simpson Harbour. After the initial overwhelming landings he was on a machine-gun carrier and had been ordered to go down to the beach and rescue Australian infantrymen. The carrier made two trips down the mountainous roads to the beach. Holmfield said he and his crew didn't fire a shot. They were quickly forced back:

> we were on and off the truck, with the machine-gunning – that was the most frightening part. You were lying down in a little bit of a gutter on the side of the road and a bloody bullet would hit one of those rocks and brrrrring! We were sent there with the impression, or the idea, that we were going to stop the Japs. Well, it was an impossible situation.

Holmfield and his group escaped up the Kokopo Road and then went into the bush and survived on their wits. In an extraordinary epic, he and some of his compatriots walked down the north coast of New Britain. They then sailed to the New Guinea mainland via the Trobriand Islands to the south and finally made their way back to Port Moresby. Many years after his escape from Rabaul, Holmfield still had no time for the man he sarcastically labelled 'the greatest prime minister we've ever had':

> I believe that John Curtin was a real bastard. His was the order to say that we stop there.

Japanese forces were soon engaged in repairing Rabaul's two aerodromes and 'mopping up' the fleeing Australians on New Britain, which they did on foot, by boat and by air. They received intelligence of a large group of Australian troops in the Wide Bay area near Rabaul. The unprepared Australians soon found the escape a living hell. One group of about 160 men had little food and began suffering from malaria, dysentery and tropical ulcers.

Kenneth Ryall was a plantation manager at Kokopo who would spend eleven weeks on New Britain after the Japanese invasion. He survived by living on taro, sweet potatoes and fish, but believed the Diggers didn't stand a chance because they were not accustomed to native food. He saw in every second or third Tolai village all the way along to the south two or three Australian soldiers dying:

> At the food dump at Malalonga, the soldiers had bayoneted all the tinned food with a view to preventing the Japanese from using them. This meant, of course, when the other Australian soldiers came along the food was poisoned. There was no organisation on the part of the civil population or by the military leaders either.

Ten days after the Japanese invasion of Rabaul one exhausted and hungry group reached Tol and Waitavalo coconut plantations in Wide Bay, where they promptly surrendered to the Japanese who had landed by barge to cut off absconders. The prisoners had their hands tied behind their backs and were taken into the jungle. They were systematically shot or bayoneted in the presence or hearing of those who awaited their turn. The waiting victims either saw the actual killings or heard the screams of their mates as the bayonets were being driven home. At one stage after one Digger's screams were heard, a Japanese soldier emerged from the jungle wiping blood from his bayonet with a cloth. The spectacle was so frightful, one of the Diggers next in line broke loose and tried to escape but was cut down by a Japanese officer with a sword. Two Australians, badly bayoneted in the stomach, managed to crawl to a hut, but the Japanese set fire to it and burnt them alive.

A small number of wounded victims, feigning death, managed to escape to later give evidence. Among them was Private Bill Cook of the 2/10th Australian Field Ambulance from Sydney, who had been wearing a Red Cross armband when he and other Australians, without arms, surrendered to the Japanese at Tol plantation. A Japanese officer asked them if they would prefer to be shot or killed by bayonet. They replied 'shot'. The Japanese soldiers returned and called 'Next!' and three medics were taken into the bush. They were attacked from behind. Cook was stabbed several times in the middle of the back. He held his breath to feign death as his attacker was about to walk away. But he couldn't hold his breath any longer and the Japanese heard breathing. He was stabbed with six more bayonet thrusts:

The last thrust went through my ear, face and into my mouth, severing an artery which caused the blood to gush out of my mouth. He then placed coconut fronds and vines over the three of us. I lay there and heard the last two men being shot.

Private Cook was able to struggle to his feet after about an hour and make it down to the beach, where he bathed his wounds in salt water. He staggered away through the bush and the following day saw campfire smoke and came across a group of Australian officers, including the Lark Force commander, Colonel John Scanlan, who dressed his wounds. Australia was stunned and then outraged. First news of the Japanese atrocities reached the Australian public through the arrival of evacuees at Townsville in North Queensland, as the *Townsville Daily Bulletin* reported:

They tell of the cold-blooded slaughter, shooting and bayoneting of helpless Australian service personnel who, as a result of starvation and lack of arms, were forced to surrender to the enemy at Tol plantation in the Gasmata region early in February.

The newspaper was told that most of the Australians who were sent to their deaths cursed the Japanese and one typically said, 'You'll be sorry for this when our chaps get you.' The Board of Information at Japan's Foreign Office in Tokyo in April said the allegations of a massacre were 'utterly unfounded propaganda'.

Queensland's chief justice, Sir William Webb, would later conduct an inquiry for the government. He found that the Australians were killed one by one practically in the presence of each other. The atrocities, he said, were 'outrageously cruel and wicked and carried out with savage brutality'. Detailed accounts of the massacre were published in Australian newspapers from early April 1942. The news was disturbing for the families and friends of well over 1000 Australians who had been in Rabaul in January 1942 and whose fate was as yet unknown.

The suffering of the men from Rabaul was far from over. The Japanese interned 836 Australians from Rabaul as prisoners of war. One of them was the Lark Force commander, Colonel Scanlan, who had surrendered. According to a survivor, he capitulated 'in a blaze of glory', complete with summer-weight uniform, collar and tie, red tabs and red cap band alongside his men dressed in rags. Scanlan spent the war as a prisoner at Rabaul and later in Japan, where he was shipped with other officers and nurses in June 1942. Vunapope Sacred Heart Catholic Mission near Kokopo became an internment camp for a group of seventeen captured Australian nurses from the Australian Army Nursing Service, the Australian Government Hospital in Rabaul and the Methodist Mission. It also housed male and female missionaries from various faiths who also became 'hostages to fortune' under Japanese guard. After six months' internment at the mission hospital, the nurses were shipped under appalling conditions to Japan, where they remained in various camps until after war's end.

*

On the night before Curtin's departure by train from Perth he took part in a revealing broadcast on local station 6KY from his house at Cottesloe, clearly aimed at the local audience. Curtin stressed how imperative it was for him to have defence consultations on the spot in Western Australia to obtain first-hand knowledge. He and Don Rodgers were still attempting to disguise his ill-health and his need for rest. But towards the end of the broadcast, Curtin briefly mentioned his health when he thanked the many people in the state who had expressed the hope that he would have 'the health and strength to continue in the prime ministership', which was a rather strange thing to admit given that he was covering up his illness. Curtin finished his broadcast with some telling introspection:

> Whatever be my fate, it will always be a source of great pride to me that in this great crisis which our country faces it has been my supreme privilege to be its humble servant.

An old friend and Labor Party colleague went to see Curtin around this time. John Tonkin had been the member for North-East Fremantle in Western Australia's Legislative Assembly since 1933 and later became premier. Tonkin was a sergeant in 11th Battalion:

> I went to see him, I was in the Army and our situation for equipment was deplorable.

Tonkin told Curtin that soldiers in Western Australia were drilling with broomsticks and Curtin alerted Army Minister Forde of the great shortage of rifles:

> in the event of hostilities it would be impossible to supply this weapon to the local troops who normally would be armed with it.

Forde admitted that Western Australia alone was short 2000 rifles. The national rifle shortage was 18,000, he said, with First World War Lee-Enfield .303 bolt-action rifles being reconditioned to fill the gap.

*

John Curtin feels the strain.
Bitterness and animosity
between prime ministers
Curtin and Churchill
began soon after Curtin's
appointment as Prime Minister
in October 1941. Their key
disagreement concerned
the allocation of significant
resources to stopping the
Japanese thrust. Churchill
wanted to defeat Hitler first.

The John Curtin Prime Ministerial Library

Capt. Horton/ IWM via Getty Images

Prime Minister Winston Churchill outside 10 Downing Street, London.
In 1942, Churchill secretly described the fight against Japan as the 'lesser
war', while publicly stating the war in the Pacific was not a 'secondary
operation'. Privately he believed that Japan would try to establish bases in
Australia.

US National Archives

The beginning of the attack on the battleships at Ford Island, Pearl Harbor, on 7 December 1941. Taken from a Japanese aircraft.

US National Archives

Pacific shock. The battleship USS *West Virginia* settles in Pearl Harbor after being hit by seven Japanese torpedoes. A naval boat approaches, rescuing seamen from the water. The following day, the US declared war on Japan.

US Office of War Information, Library of Congress

America at war. President Roosevelt signs a declaration of war against Japan in Washington on 8 December 1941. Despite the Japanese attack in the Pacific, Roosevelt supported Churchill's 'Beat Hitler First' policy.

The John Curtin Prime Ministerial Library

John Curtin watching Governor-General Lord Gowrie signing the Australian declaration of war on Japan, December 1941.

Records of Frederick McLaughlin/ The John Curtin Prime Ministerial Library

Curtin's agony. The defence chiefs advised Curtin that the 1400 soldiers and airmen in Rabaul must be abandoned. Curtin is pictured in late 1941 with the Chief of the Air Force, Sir Charles Burnett, the Chief of the Navy, Sir Guy Royle, the Chief of the Army, Sir Vernon Sturdee and, standing, Defence department head Frederick Shedden.

The John Curtin Prime Ministerial Library

Breaking point. Prime Minister Curtin is having breakfast with a secretary, Mary McGuire, in the splendour of his luxury carriage travelling between Melbourne and Perth. Rabaul was being invaded and Malaya and Singapore were in danger of being lost.

The John Curtin Prime Ministerial Library

January 1942, Prime Minister John Curtin arrived at Cottesloe, Perth. Looking tired, he poses with his family: son John, daughter Elsie and wife Elsie. Fearing a health breakdown, he had abandoned Australian defence headquarters in Melbourne as Rabaul was invaded.

AWM H10395

Mechanics work on a Zero at Lakunai airfield at the great Japanese stronghold of Rabaul, with Mount Tavurvur smoking in the background. Rabaul's occupation was a serious blow to Curtin, who saw it as a stepping stone to Australia.

The Sydney Morning Herald/Fairfax

Greatest crisis. Curtin on 17 February 1942 forcefully tells a war rally in Martin Place, Sydney, that the fall of Singapore two days earlier had opened the Battle for Australia. Within hours Curtin collapsed and was hospitalised.

News Ltd/Newspix

Darwin ablaze. Oil storage tanks at Stokes Hill hit by Japanese bombs in the first enemy attack on Darwin, 19 February 1942. Prime Minister Curtin declared Australia needed to provide 'resistance to an enemy threatening to invade our own shore'.

National Archives of Australia

The bombing of Darwin. Cashman's store and the Bank of New South
Wales in Smith Street were badly damaged in the first Japanese air raid on
Darwin. The massive raid prompted a wild flight of residents and some
Australian servicemen from the town.

The Courier Mail, 20 February 1942

The first bombing raids on Darwin followed just days after the fall of
Singapore. On 20 February, amid the avalanche of bad war news, the
Curtin government censored news reports.

World War Two Database

Controversial leader. General Gordon Bennett thought the British command in Singapore was 'panicky' and lacking in the offensive spirit. He was especially critical of the lack of air cover for Allied troops. After Singapore fell, Bennett controversially escaped to Australia as thousands of Australian expats became prisoners of the Japanese.

Aggressive leader. Prime Minister General Hideki Tojo reportedly said in early 1942: 'I think we will have few problems occupying not only Java but Sumatra and also Australia if things go on like this.' Before his execution for war crimes, Tojo denied that he ever had an interest in invading Australia.

AWM 150818

Major General 'Tubby' Allen (right) near the start of the Kokoda Track with generals MacArthur and Blamey in October 1942. Within weeks MacArthur, surrounded by jumpy US officers, ordered Allen to attack 'the weaker enemy'. Allen's staff convinced him not to send a reply through Blamey that said, 'If you think you can do any better come up here and bloody well try.'

AWM 13645

Grim work. Soldiers of the AIF 7th Division, who had been engaged in bitter hand to hand fighting with the Japanese, have just buried their enemy, placing helmets over the common grave. The Australians in November 1942 had pushed the Japanese from Gorari, beyond Kokoda, towards Sanananda on the Papuan north coast. Horrific fighting was still to come.

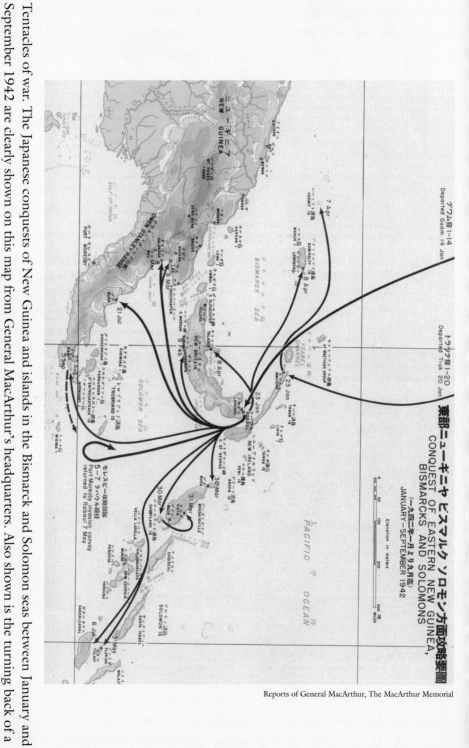

Tentacles of war. The Japanese conquests of New Guinea and islands in the Bismarck and Solomon seas between January and September 1942 are clearly shown on this map from General MacArthur's headquarters. Also shown is the turning back of a convoy, headed from Rabaul to Port Moresby, as a result of the Battle of the Coral Sea.

Reports of General MacArthur, The MacArthur Memorial

Reports of General MacArthur, The MacArthur Memorial

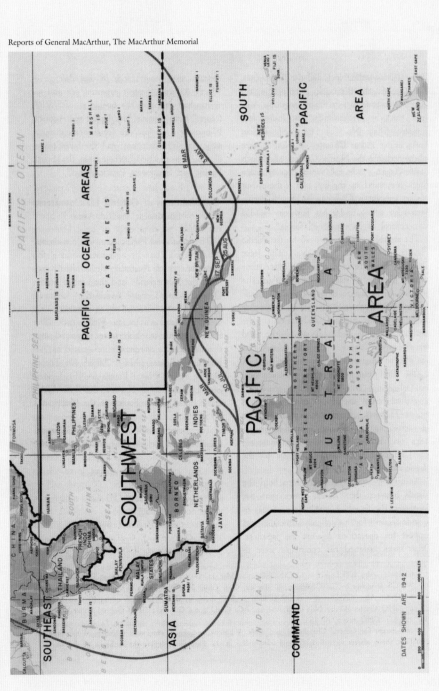

Southward conquest. The red lines above Australia indicated the extent of the Japanese ground advance in 1942. The Japanese planned to isolate Australia by capturing New Caledonia, Samoa and Fiji, but the Allies reinforced the islands.

Records of Frederick McLaughlin/ The John Curtin Prime Ministerial Library

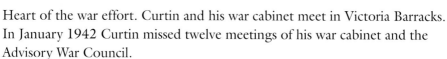

Heart of the war effort. Curtin and his war cabinet meet in Victoria Barracks. In January 1942 Curtin missed twelve meetings of his war cabinet and the Advisory War Council.

West Australian News Ltd

Thundering speech. Prime Minister Curtin, surrounded by Diggers, demands that civilian workers show the same 'inextinguishable spirit' as the fighting forces. He is speaking at a patriotic rally at Caulfield on 8 March 1943, attended by 20,000 people.

The John Curtin Prime Ministerial Library

The turning point. Curtin emerges from a conference on war leadership with Supreme Commander General MacArthur, Governor-General Lord Gowrie and army minister Frank Forde, 8 June 1943.

Records of the Curtin Family/The John Curtin Prime Ministerial Library

Catastrophe passes. Curtin and MacArthur shake hands in Sydney on 8 June 1943. Curtin soon announced, 'I do not think the enemy can now invade this country.'

Yomiuri Shimbun, Hijime Muratani

Advance or retreat? This Japanese wartime propaganda photo shows troops 'about to attack the enemy' in New Guinea. The date given is 15 September 1943. The following day the town of Lae was recaptured by Australian troops.

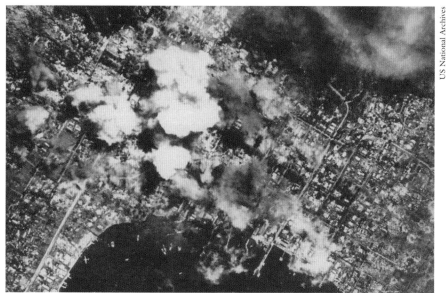

US National Archives

Saturation bombing. As the war progressed, the once powerful Japanese base of Rabaul was attacked by Allied bombers. This raid took place on 22 March 1944. Eventually Japan was forced to withdraw almost all her fighting aircraft.

Center of Military History, US Army

Relief at last. Australian and US troops wounded in Buna–Gona region wait to be evacuated by the Papuans they called the 'Fuzzy Wuzzy Angels'. Total Australian casualties on the coast and along the Kokoda Track were 2165 dead and 3533 wounded. The Americans lost 798 in the Buna–Gona area.

Records of Frederick McLaughlin/The John Curtin Prime Ministerial Library

Restored relations. John Curtin is pictured with Winston Churchill and King George at Buckingham Palace in 1944. By this time the two prime ministers had patched up their differences following acerbic cables to each other earlier in the war about Empire defence policy, especially in relation to the Japanese threat.

The John Curtin Prime Ministerial Library

Curtin, sick yet again, poses with wife Elsie in the grounds of the Lodge on 27 April 1945. It is their last photograph together. Three days later Curtin was admitted to hospital. He died at the Lodge on 5 July 1945.

US National Archives

General Douglas MacArthur at the Japanese signing of the surrender aboard USS *Missouri* in Tokyo Bay, 2 September 1945. Behind him, second from left, is Australia's General Sir Thomas Blamey.

On Thursday 29 January Curtin boarded the Westland express to start his long journey back over the Nullarbor. He had seen his son John but wasn't present for his twenty-first birthday. Prime minister and son wouldn't see each other for another twelve months and even then it would be a transitory meeting on a railway platform in Perth before young John headed off to a posting in Darwin. The impression given by Curtin's son in later interviews, although not proven, was that Curtin and his son might not have been all that close as a result of Curtin's long absences. But John Curtin the son did speak about his father in an oral history interview in 2004:

> I don't know that Dad had any sense of humour. He was too concerned about the way things were going and all that sort of thing. He was a real worrying type. I didn't get any humour from him . . . Oh I didn't have a great deal to do with Dad you know because he was seldom home. He'd come home for Christmas and I'd be playing pennant cricket. He'd come up if we were playing at home and sit there with a few of his cronies . . . If an umpire failed to turn up, well he'd go out and umpire . . .

While the prime minister upheld the sense of dignity associated with his office, and exuded a rather 'formal' persona to many, he was motivated by a sense of propriety and duty. Whether the father felt a sense of guilt over his long absences is not recorded. On balance, it's likely that there was an element of guilt. The son suffered in a different way, not fully experiencing the company of a father. None of this, of course, was unusual in wartime.

The prime minister had enjoyed little rest at home that January, according to Richard Hughes from Perth in the Sydney *Daily Telegraph*:

> He went home to read and to potter in the garden in the short hours he snatched from his long desk in the Commonwealth offices.

Despite his war efforts while in Perth, and his emotive speeches to the people, Curtin unusually was criticised in the *West Australian* in Perth for what the editors saw as his unseemly clashes with Churchill. The newspaper had editorialised that there should be 'dignity and cool resolution' and 'less talk of what others should do to help us'. Richard Hughes commented on the local criticism:

> They didn't think, after all, that a Westralian ought to be taking a crack at Whitehall as John Curtin was, arguing that Britain ought to do this, demanding that Winston Churchill ought to do the other . . . They've got a higher proportion of enlistments than any other State, but they still tend to look at the world through British rather than Australian glasses.

*

At this time RAAF personnel in Britain were beginning to express their disquiet at fighting in Europe while Australia was so threatened. The secretary for dominion affairs, Lord Cranborne, asked the the Defence Operations Committee in London whether it was proposed to send any of the Australian or New Zealand squadrons back to defend their own countries. He understood that 'there was some unrest among the personnel over here who felt that they should be taking part in the battle nearer home'. Air Chief Marshall Sir Charles Portal said he had not received any official request. The need for Australia was for aircraft, not personnel, he said. Cranborne added the justification:

> it would be wise to explain to the Australians at what sacrifice elsewhere we were finding resources for the Far Eastern theatre and for Australia and New Zealand.

The secretary for foreign affairs, Anthony Eden, said he was disturbed at the extent to which Britain was spreading its resources all over the world. The committee agreed to a proposal to provide 125 US P-40 Kittyhawks to Australia and eighteen to New Zealand.

Portal added that he would like to look further into the possibility of providing some long-range fighters, though he felt 'very doubtful whether anything could be done in the near future'.

Government sources in Whitehall now were actively down-playing the possibility of an invasion of Australia. Australian Associated Press in London cabled Australian newspapers a long, detailed interview with an unnamed British 'authoritative source' giving the reasons why it was unlikely that Australia would be invaded, including the shortages of Japanese ships and aircraft. Deputy Prime Minister Forde responded angrily:

> The Government regards an attempt by Japan to invade Australia as a logical possibility of the military situation which is developing in the Pacific . . . The advantage to Japan of a successful invasion is so obvious that we must most gravely assume that an attempt may be made.

Navy Minister Norman Makin said that to 'write down the possibility of invasion of this country was sheer nonsense'.

*

As Curtin was trundling east across the Nullarbor Plain, a new disaster befell the defence of Australia. On the night of 30 January three battalions of Japanese infantry and a battalion of marines landed on the small island of Ambon in the Molucca Islands, west of the New Guinea mainland and north-west of Timor. Ambon's position – 562 miles (905 kilometres) north of Darwin – made the island an important air and sea link between Australia, New Guinea and the Dutch East Indies. The 2/21st Battalion had been sent from Darwin to Ambon five days after war had broken out with Japan. The battalion joined an Australian anti-tank battery and other supporting units comprising Gull Force. The commanding officer of the 2/21st, Lieutenant Colonel Leonard Roach, told Melbourne headquarters of his difficulties in holding the island. Cooperation with the Dutch forces was problematic and there were many short-ages, including of transport, air and artillery support and reserves of rations and ammunition. Roach said the combined Australian and Dutch force of 3700 troops was likely to be overwhelmed by larger Japanese forces and the defence of the island was untenable. He was soon replaced by Lieutenant Colonel William Scott, who found himself in the same predicament.

When the Japanese landed, the Dutch surrendered within a day and the 2/21st couldn't hold back the Japanese troops despite fierce fighting. The Japanese were supported by heavy air and sea bombardments. About 300 Australians from Gull Force defending the airfield at Laha fought strongly but eventually were overwhelmed and killed or captured. Four separate mass executions of Australians, ordered by Rear Admiral Koichiro Hatakeyama, took place at Laha. Some of the victims were beheaded with swords, others bayoneted or clubbed to death. All of the executioners were volunteers apparently taking revenge for the deaths of their comrades in battle. The massacres were not discovered until Ambon was reoccupied in 1945 and mass graves were discovered, making the tragedy even more agonising for loved ones in Australia, who had hoped that the men had been in captivity.

The vast majority of the Australians taken as prisoners of war on Ambon would die from sickness and injury before the end of hostilities. After the war, four Japanese were executed for their war crimes on Ambon, including Commander Kunito Hatakeyama, the officer who supervised the executions. Rear Admiral Koichiro Hatakeyama died before his trial. Ambon was yet another place where small forces of Australian troops were posted to withstand invasions by much larger Japanese forces. These desperate postings were fraught with disaster.

*

Malaya was now all but lost. On 28 January the Australian commander, General Bennett, attended a conference with the British commander, General Percival, at which it was announced that the Allies would evacuate mainland Malaya to the Singapore island on the night of 30–31 January. Bennett knew the situation was hopeless and was already planning his escape from

Singapore. He called on his friend the Sultan of Johore to thank him for his kindnesses while the Australians were based in the Sultan's state. He mentioned that he might escape and hoped the monarch could help him obtain a boat. Bennett met with the commander-in-chief of ABDA Command, General Wavell, on 30 January as the withdrawal from the mainland in Malaya was about to begin. Bennett, writing in his diary, now held fears for the security of Singapore:

> Not only was Malaya now on the point of going the same way as Hong Kong, but there had been retreat in Borneo, Celebes, everywhere. The position in Singapore, to which we are to withdraw tomorrow, was discussed in detail. That was not particularly reassuring, because there are not enough troops to defend it.

Bennett drove slowly through the small town of Johore Bahru just over the strait from Singapore. He passed retreating troops, burning cars and buildings and saw crowds of desperate Chinese and Malays:

> It was a funeral march. I have never felt so sad. Words fail me. This defeat should not have been. The whole thing is fantastic. There seems no justification for it.

Early the next morning Bennett went to the causeway to see the last of the AIF – the 22nd Brigade – crossing. After them, with pipers playing at the head of the battalion, came all that remained of the 2nd Argylls, who had suffered greatly in the fighting. Then Indian sappers and miners fired a charge that demolished a part of the causeway with a terrific explosion. 'That's the end of the British Empire!' a Chinese student and first-aid assistant at Singapore's Raffles College, Lee Kuan Yew, said to a fellow student. Lee would narrowly avoid execution by the Japanese and eventually would become Singapore's prime minister.

*

At the end of January operational planners in Admiral Yamamoto's Combined Fleet Headquarters on the Inland Sea at Hashirajima were well advanced with their invasion planning. They submitted a new plan to Navy General Staff in Tokyo, listing priorities:

> One, invade Ceylon at the end of May/June; establish contact with the German forces; mission accomplished, Combined Fleet will turn toward the east.
> Two, Port Darwin must be taken.
> Three, Fiji and Samoa need not be taken, only destroyed.
> Four, we should like to take Hawaii, if possible.

The proposals would provoke more debate in Tokyo. Admiral Yamamoto's staff officers aboard the battleship the *Nagato* had come out in favour of an invasion of Darwin, and Yamamoto's chief of staff, Ugaki, recommended the proposal to the Operations Bureau of the General Staff. But as Ugaki wrote in his diary on 5 February, the General Staff had other plans, which involved massive air raids on Darwin:

> The high command in Tokyo is against an invasion of Port Darwin. In order to destroy it [Darwin] thoroughly we are to capture Dili as well as Koupan [Kupang] at the same time.

As a result, planning for the invasion of Timor via Dili and Kupang was initiated, together with a plan for a major carrier raid on Darwin as the first big attack on the Australian mainland.

At this time the British Joint Intelligence Committee in London estimated that a limited invasion of Australia, namely at Darwin, was a distinct possibility. The intelligence chiefs said that before any major attack on Australia and New Zealand, the Japanese probably would need to meet a number of conditions, including the occupation of Singapore, Java, Sumatra, the Philippines and control of the South China Sea. They said Japan also would need to occupy Timor, the islands of New Guinea and others including New Caledonia, Fiji and Samoa. Many of these conditions in fact were being accomplished at this time by the Japanese. The British intelligence chiefs said that before attempting any major operation against Australia and New Zealand, the Japanese were likely to deny the Allies the only possible bases in northern Australia. They said that due to its isolated position Darwin was an attractive target for capture before it was strengthened and while Allied military strength in the region was comparatively weak:

> If and when Japanese decided to develop major operations against Australia and New Zealand operations likely to take form of simultaneous landings at, or in vicinity of, important ports, with a view to gaining stranglehold on key points and communications.

The Joint Intelligence Committee report, presented to the Combined British-US Chiefs of Staff Committee in Washington on 31 January 1942, said that as soon as Port Darwin was captured, the Japanese could establish additional airstrips and fly in additional land-based aircraft:

> Assuming operations in Malaya and Philippines successfully concluded, they might make available some 400 of such aircraft and possibly in addition some 30 long range flying boats.

The British intelligence chiefs concluded:

> It seems likely that Japan will at this stage be content with endeavouring to isolate Australia and New Zealand without embarking on major operations to southwards except for capture of Darwin. Attack on Darwin likely in any event.

*

Curtin's train arrived in Melbourne on a sunny Sunday, 1 February, to news of disloyal conduct in his cabinet. He went straight to Victoria Barracks where the war cabinet met into the night. The following morning *The Courier-Mail* in Brisbane came out with an editorial warning the prime minister that he must grasp the reins when he got back to Canberra. The newspaper said Curtin's 'large and difficult team was getting out of hand'. It reported that some ministers had been talking as though they had forgotten they were members of one team sharing collective responsibility in Australia's hour of gravest danger:

It is not the Japanese who are making many Australians afraid. It is despair of leadership which will not even at this eleventh hour put country before part and oppose the enemy with a united front . . .

While Curtin addressed the issue of recalcitrants who had enjoyed more freedom of expression during his absence, he was also receiving fearsome reports from the commander-in-chief of Australia's Home Forces, Lieutenant General Iven Mackay, about courses of attack on Australia open to the enemy. The possible scenarios included the most controversial: the government abandoning regions outside the major capital to their fate:

Considering the extensive coastline to be watched and guarded, and since our forces are so small and distances so great, we must make up our minds that we cannot successfully defend the whole of the Australian coast . . . This policy will mean leaving many portions of the Australian coast (even important towns) without troops.

Mackay insisted that the defence of Australia must be confined to the portion of the country that would enable the major part of the war effort to carry on. A few days later, in a memo to the minister for army, Frank Forde, General Mackay went even further:

In reality most of the Australian coast and many important towns must be left without troops, whilst other troops are likely to be withdrawn from dispositions in which they are now temporarily placed.

Curtin was being asked to face possibility of deserting parts of Australia to Japan. At the end of a long report, Mackay astonished the Curtin Government in words that provide an insight into Curtin's dispirited thinking:

> It may be necessary to submit to the occupation of certain areas of Australia by the enemy should local resistance be overcome, and I remind the Government that it may be necessary to accept such a possibility.

Curtin and Mackay weren't the only ones taking stock of the grim prospect. At this stage the National Bank began to take urgent action to protect its interests if its branches were bombed by the Japanese. The chief manager of the bank, Sir Leslie McConnan, on 2 February ordered the manager of the Thursday Island branch to destroy banknotes by fire and take action to ensure the bank's firearms would not fall into the hands of the enemy. Further, all branches north of Bundaberg in Queensland were told to send duplicate records of all accounts south so that if branches were bombed customers' accounts could be reconstructed. National Bank branches in southern states were planning to carry on in the inland of Australia if the big cities were bombed. McConnan wrote to his managers:

> Without, I hope, laying myself open to the charge of being alarmist, I say that obviously the speed with which the Japanese are working southward make one feel that North Queensland is now definitely in the danger zone and ordinary prudence demands that we consider the possibility of the enemy reaching our shores.

*

While three weeks earlier Prime Minister Churchill had asked Curtin rhetorically, 'Do you think you are in immediate danger of invasion in force?', a senior US officer had doubted that Australia could be held. Brigadier General Leonard T. Gerow, assistant chief of staff of the War Department in Washington, began his own assessment to the Board of Economic Warfare with the unsettling words:

it is not practicable to state how long Australia will remain in friendly hands.

Gerow didn't think the Japanese would try to conquer all of Australia, but acknowledged that the enemy could occupy portions of the country, bomb any cities with carrier-based aircraft and, if they seized New Guinea and New Caledonia, bomb northern Australia using long-range bombers.

*

In Tokyo, the Australia debate continued. The army's chief of military operations, Major General Shinichi Tanaka, feared that Japan was becoming 'blinded by victory' and believed 'our onslaught in the Pacific is getting dangerous'. Tanaka wrote in his diary, 'We must realise our limits in the Pacific offensive.' After the war Tanaka would tell US interrogators:

The Navy wanted to take Port Darwin in northern Australia. They insisted that we take it because the American Navy would use it as a base from which to attack Moresby and the Bismarcks . . . I absolutely refused to agree to the operation.

Infighting between navy war planners, led by Baron Captain Sadatoshi Tomioka, and his army counterpart, Colonel Takushiro Hattori, was continuing. Hattori now branded the navy's plans for a large landing expedition to Australia as 'reckless' because it would 'exceed the war strength of Japan' and require twelve divisions for land operations, in addition to a tremendous amount of shipping. Hattori, later interviewed by US officers, spoke of navy 'plans', rather than proposals or ideas:

The Army disagreed with the plans to invade Australia and strongly opposed their implementation.

But the navy planners would persist doggedly. Colonel Hattori said the navy and the army did, however, soon agree to other operations close to Australia:

Towards the end of January 1942 the Army and Navy departments of Imperial General Staff agreed to invade Port Moresby and Tulagi [in the Solomon Islands]. Later the Fiji, Samoa and New Caledonia invasion plans to sever the line of communication between the United States and Australia came to the fore . . . and Imperial General headquarters approved these plans . . .

The Imperial Navy would see this as a workable interim plan.

*

Australian militia troops from the 39th and 53rd Battalions, and units of the 30th Brigade had been sent north to take part in Port Moresby's defence. They had arrived on the liner the *Aquitania* on 3 January. They included 104 teenagers who had only recently been called up for duty. Some of these young conscripts had been given a leave pass for one night, embarking on the *Aquitania* in Sydney the very next day. Others were selected the day the *Aquitania* sailed and did not even get a chance to say goodbye to family. The average age of the raw and largely untrained reinforcements, excluding officers, was estimated at eighteen years and six months. It would be an understatement to say that Australia's initial defence of Port Moresby, the coastline and the wild hinterland was meagre and precarious.

Port Moresby, the administrative capital of Papua – only 320 miles (515 kilometres) from Cape York Peninsula in Queensland – soon became the new Japanese focus of attention. The first phase was the Japanese navy's air offensive campaign against the town and port. Port Moresby was bombed on 3 and 5 February. The bombing created great panic, especially among the local Papuans, who naturally feared for their lives. An outbreak of lawlessness followed and among the most unruly were undisciplined Australian troops. The bombings and the panic soon forced the civil administration to hand over control to the military.

The Japanese built an airstrip at Gasmata, on New Britain's southern coast on the Solomon Sea and from 24 February, twenty-seven fighters and a similar number of bombers from the 4th Air Corps joined the bombing of Port Moresby. Inexperienced anti-aircraft gunners did their best. The Japanese also flew sorties from Rabaul. From February 1942 until July 1944, a war of attrition was fought by the air forces of the United States, Australia and Japan in Papua, New Guinea, the Bismarck Archipelago and the Solomon Islands. Initially, Allied forces had precious few suitable aircraft to meet the powerful Japanese attacks.

Australian militiamen in Moresby soon became accustomed to the raids, according to Private Jack Boland, of the 39th Battalion, who personally experienced some eighty Japanese raids. He recalled that after each raid the officers would go down to the captain's tent and have a snifter of whisky:

> we had nothing, so after a certain bombing raid Burns Philp store got the side blown out of it, our truck went in – just happened to be going into town – and he come back with a truck load of grog of all sorts, whisky and spirits and all sorts of things. So after that we used to have a little snort too after the raids.

Eleven Squadron, RAAF, had been at Port Moresby since the outbreak of war. The squadron's Catalina, Seagull and Empire flying boats from Moresby carried out bombing attacks against Japanese shipping at Rabaul and other targets on Japanese-occupied islands. They patrolled as far afield as Thursday Island, Tulagi, New Zealand and Bougainville. Later, with Japanese naval and air attacks on Port Moresby escalating, the squadron was in danger of being wiped out and was forced to withdraw to Bowen in Queensland.

The reality was that Port Moresby, the gateway to northern Australia, was hopelessly exposed. The Australian chiefs of staff determined that any seaborne assault on Port Moresby from

Rabaul would be a distinctly hazardous operation for the enemy. But at the same time they knew that the Allied land-based forces, mostly Australian, were much below strength and could offer little meaningful resistance. The chiefs decided not to increase the strength of the army garrison from the existing brigade group, primarily because supply operations from the south were already operating at their maximum. Port Moresby then existed tenuously on just a hope that US carrier-borne aircraft might be available to block any invasion of the gateway to Australia.

Curtin saw Port Moresby in the north as a stepping stone to Australia. The Japanese navy and army had different reasons for planning its capture. The navy saw Moresby as strengthening its position at Rabaul. The army sought it to prevent Allied counter-offensives from Australia and to expel any Allied forces from New Guinea in preparation for a possible advance on Australia.

Chapter 8

MOUNTING DISASTERS

In Malaya there were many casualties in the desperate fighting on the withdrawal south through the jungle and plantations of Johore and the crossing of the straits to Singapore island. The Singapore situation was now critical. Private Henry Ritchie, who had written from Mersing of his A Company of the 2/20th as 'a likely crowd', now found them defending the rugged, waterlogged west coast of Singapore in impossible conditions.

A Company was trying to patrol the west bank of the Kranji River overlooking Johore Bahru town. The boys had expected to find well-prepared and fortified defensive positions looking across the strait. Instead they were surrounded by a mire of swamps and mangroves and often had to place men out in boats to act as forward sentries. Some of the defenders were non-swimmers who drowned while moving about, especially at night. The gap between their individual defensive posts was so wide that they were highly vulnerable. The Australians were poorly armed and often short of ammunition. Lieutenant Frank Gaven, second-in-command of A Company, 2/20th Battalion, was startled when he first saw the terrain his men were expected to defend:

I remember going down to the water front which A Company was going to hold. And when I saw it, it was like walking to the edge of a mangrove swamp . . . it was impenetrable with all these little bits of streams coming in. I've never felt such a feeling of desperation and despair in all my life. And I realised this was, you know, an impossible situation. There were no fortifications, nothing done.

So much for the oft-quoted phrase 'Fortress Singapore'. During the night of 8–9 February, 13,000 Japanese troops attacked the shores of Singapore island, which was guarded by two Australian battalions. The enemy came in waves of armoured landing craft during the night, supported by artillery fire. Tanks would soon follow. Beach lights set up by the Australians were quickly shot out. The Australians poured machine-gun fire into the landing troops and fought fiercely. Many of the first landing craft were sunk or beaten off, but many more kept coming. The Japanese seemed to have an endless supply of troops and armoured barges. The defenders inflicted heavy casualties but suffered grievously themselves. Eventually they were overwhelmed by sheer weight of numbers and firepower, according to war correspondent and historian Frank Legg. The forward posts were mostly overrun, the minority of survivors scrambling to safety any way they could.

A Company of the 2/20th, the 'likely crowd', pulled back inland and crossed the Tengah fighter strip after the Japanese attacked. The strip was soon in Japanese hands. British, Indian and Australian troops were retreating elsewhere. There were heavy casualties on both sides, especially among the Australians. Much now depended on holding the Japanese at the Jurong-Kranji line. If the Japanese could not be held there, the British commander, General Percival, had a plan to form a defensive arc on the outskirts of Singapore's city area. This would involve abandoning most of the island and, unless they could be destroyed, large ammunition dumps and stores. Typed copies of Percival's proposed plan were distributed to his generals and commanders.

As the historian Lionel Wigmore commented, the proposal 'acted to some extent as a magnet to their thoughts' about further retreats.

Percival and his officers had no real idea of the strength of the enemy. But Percival knew the situation was 'undoubtedly serious', as he cabled the ABDA commander-in-chief, General Wavell. Early on 10 February, Wavell flew in from Batavia and went with Percival to see Bennett at his forward headquarters. While they were meeting, Japanese aircraft dropped bombs on the headquarters, showering the generals and staff with debris as they dived for cover. There were some casualties, but the generals were unharmed. By this time two Australian brigades had withdrawn from their fronts. General Percival found Bennett 'not quite so confident as he had been up-country':

> He had always been very certain that his Australians would never let the Japanese through and the penetration of his defences had upset him. As always, we were fighting this battle in the dark, and I do not think any of us realised at that time the strength of the enemy's attack.

Prime Minister Churchill was astounded to hear of the reverses on Singapore island, firing off a cable to Wavell:

> Percival has over 100,000 men, of whom 33,000 are British and 17,000 Australian. It is doubtful whether the Japanese have as many in the whole Malay Peninsula . . . In these circumstances the defenders must greatly outnumber Japanese forces who have crossed the straits, and in a well-contested battle they should destroy them.

Churchill told Wavell that the newly arrived British 18th Division, which included many raw recruits, had a chance to make its name in history in Singapore:

> Commanders and senior officers should die with their troops. The honour of the British Empire and of the British Army is at stake. I rely on you to show no mercy to weakness in any form.

Spurred on by Churchill, Wavell engaged in his own rhetoric in an order of the day late on 10 February, just before flying back to the relative safety of the Dutch East Indies. He urged that there be no surrender:

> It will be disgraceful if we yield our boasted fortress of Singapore to inferior enemy forces. There must be no thought of sparing the troops or the civil population and no mercy must be shown to weakness in any shape or form . . .

Japanese troops reached a large British ammunition magazine at Kranji before British engineers arrived to destroy it, and much of the ammunition, reserved for a prolonged resistance, fell into enemy hands. General Bennett issued instructions for a counter-attack, but it was hopeless.

Australian soldiers were being overrun by the enemy and sometimes shot at from both flanks and even from the rear. Some Australians retreated without orders. The Australian Diggers generally were disgusted at events after their bravery and dash in the fight in mainland Malaya. Lieutenant Frank Gaven of A Company, 2/20th received his order from a brigadier amid confusion and contradiction:

> From the time the battalion pulled out at Kranji . . . there was a schmozzle, a general schmozzle, perhaps with individual acts of great heroism, between that time and the time we gathered together back at Tengah Aerodrome . . . but by that stage, appar-ently, it was realised that we weren't in any position to counter attack.

Gaven confronted General Bennett about the effect of disor-ganisation on the morale of his men:

> Within that week that we were on Singapore desperately trying to do something, the series of silly bloody instructions we got from the Army made me realise this was just a fantasy.

Between actions, which at times included hand-to-hand fighting, Lieutenant Gaven received bizarre orders for arrangements made to give his troops recreation leave in Singapore. Other orders concerned details for the laundering of troops' clothing. A Company had received the worst of it in its forward position. The officer in charge, Major Ron Merrett, estimated that of 145 men in A Company, fifty-seven were killed, twenty-two wounded, with less than half surviving the Japanese assaults. The 2/20th sustained 334 killed and 214 wounded in one night out of a total of 1000 men. Private Henry Ritchie died of his wounds in one of the ferocious battles on that critical day, 10 February 1942, as Churchill and Wavell were demanding fights to the death.

The remnants of 2/20th Battalion withdrew to the Singapore Botanic Gardens where they snatched some rest. The troops were now within close marching distance of the built-up inner town area, where one million people, the majority of them Malays and Chinese, were enduring appalling conditions. The town area was being bombed and shelled.

*

General Percival moved his Combined Operations Headquarters to an underground concrete bombproof command centre alongside the British barracks at Fort Canning, located at the top of a small hill overlooking the sea. The increasing, muffled explosions and shudder of bombs brought the war above starkly home. At its peak around 500 mostly British officers and men crowded into the underground concrete labyrinth. Men worked, ate and slept there. The recycled air was thick and foul and the humidity always high. In one large room RAF personnel, relying on telephone calls from the narrowing ring of the defenders, plotted on a large table waves of Japanese bombers and fighters descending on Singapore. In the end they might not have bothered.

In the earlier stages the plotting exercise was invaluable in getting fighters into the air. But towards the end there wasn't much point, as Japanese bombers and fighters were now coming over whenever they wanted, mostly unchallenged, apart from the efforts of a diminishing number of anti-aircraft guns. On General Wavell's orders, the last of the serviceable British and Australian aircraft and the remaining airmen on Singapore had been withdrawn to Java. The big table with the aircraft plotting maps, the lines of now silent telephones and the charts are still there today much as they had been in 1942. What you have difficulty in imagining at Fort Canning is the last, hopeless and inevitable meetings and the subsequent dishonour and the stink of fear. Willie Phua, a Singaporean Chinese, saw that fear in the average defending soldier as teenager:

> I saw a small soldier sitting in the gutter in a back lane and I still remember the sight of him. He was all on his own and his mates had gone. I don't know if he was Australian or British. But there were no other soldiers around. He was young. He didn't look that much older than me, only a boy of seventeen or eighteen. He was sitting down at the edge of the lane and crying and shaking. He had his head in his hands. He was in uniform and had a rifle on the ground next to him.

Air raid shelters for many Chinese in Singapore were stormwater drains, as Phua recalled:

> I was curled up in there with my mother. There were lots of other people huddled in the drain. You could hear the shelling and then one shell exploded just opposite, killing a man, who was an Indian.

*

Heavy bomb blasts repeatedly shook Fort Canning. A short distance away, Japanese bombs and artillery shells smashed rows of buildings and created havoc in the town's main commercial area. Some Europeans, not on duty, gathered resignedly in pubs and gentlemen's clubs. Firemen were having difficulty controlling the blazes and rescuing people from the rubble.

Japanese guns near Johore Bahru were able to fire into the commercial business areas, and the great white colonial dwelling, Government House, home of the British governor of the Singapore Straits Settlements, Sir Shenton Thomas, became a target. Governor Thomas advised immediate surrender, given the suffering now being inflicted on the civilian population. But the commander, General Percival, initially felt that surrender was premature.

By Friday 13 February the Australian defenders were falling back along the Bukit Timah Road and in from the direction of Changi, all heading towards the town area. That afternoon deep in the bowels of the Battle Box at Fort Canning, Governor Thomas, General Percival, General Bennett and other chiefs were deep in conference. Water supply in Singapore that day had broken down in the AIF-held area, and the supply to the whole of Singapore was now tenuous as the Japanese neared taking control of the island's reservoirs. Each commander gave his opinion on the situation and all agreed that further resistance was hopeless. When this was put to the commander-in-chief, General Wavell, on Java, he ordered Percival to fight on. Evacuees on small ships and craft of all types were now urgently fleeing Singapore. After making his way back to his own Australian headquarters that day, Bennett wrote in his diary of the utter devastation he had witnessed on his drive from Fort Canning. He saw an old Chinese man digging frantically into a bombed shelter, sweat streaming from his body, until the top of the shelter was uncovered:

> Beneath lay a crushed mass of old men, women – young and old – and young children, some still living, others dead. The little Oriental never stopped his work and his sallow face showed signs of deepest anguish. His wife and four children were there. One by one he unearthed them – all dead, but for one daughter.

The following day Japanese troops with bayonets fixed stormed Singapore's Alexandra Military Hospital, which was flying a Red Cross flag. They began randomly shooting and bayoneting patients and hospital staff, including nurses and doctors. Soon scores of others, including the walking wounded, were lined up and shot.

The official Australian representative in Singapore, Vivian Bowden, now a member of Britain's Far Eastern War Council, decided to make his escape. On 9 February the minister for external affairs, Doc Evatt, had cabled Bowden as shells crashed near Bowden's office, suggesting that he shouldn't attempt to escape:

> We appreciate your difficulties but think you should stick to your post. Otherwise we shall be deprived of independent information and effect on morale would be bad.

Evatt had assured Bowden that if captured he would be included in exchanges of diplomats with the enemy. After an unnecessary delay, Bowden fled on 14 February. As the white-haired gent boarded a launch, a party of some twenty Australian soldiers threatened to open fire unless they too were taken. When the overcrowded launch pulled away from the harbour steps it had thirty-eight people aboard. It was soon apprehended by a Japanese patrol boat. The Australians were taken to Muntok (now Mentok), on Bangka Island in Sumatra. A colleague who escaped with Bowden, A. N. Wootton, later testified that he saw a guard punch Bowden and make passes with his bayonet at Bowden's throat while attempting to remove his gold watch and gold identity bracelet. Bowden apparently argued. Two guards took Bowden outside. Later Wootton heard two shots. Other prisoners saw two Japanese guards kicking the Australian representative in the stomach and striking him with rifle butts. They said Bowden was forced to dig a shallow grave and was then shot.

*

On this same day army minister Franke Ford received another 'shocker' from the commander-in-chief of Home Forces in Australia, General Mackay, emphasising in capitals the difficulties home defence troops in Australia would experience in repelling Japanese invaders:

> men will fight with the greatest vigour and tenacity, BUT . . . There are NO TANKS OR (TROOP) CARRIERS. The Australian Military Force is an army without armoured fighting vehicles.

Frank Forde now fully realised the weakness of Australia's position. On the eve of the fall of Singapore on 14 February he told Curtin that an attack on Australia was likely 'in the very near future'. He said the Military Board had recommended that another 60,000 men be called up for service in Australia and he strongly advised the prime minister to urgently request 100,000 well-equipped troops from the United States:

> With the realisation of the loss of Rabaul and the imminent attack upon Port Moresby and Darwin, and in view of the comparatively untrained condition of our Australian Militia Forces, it is wise to take early steps to try to increase our strength, not only in the Air Force, but also in the Army.

Forde also suggested that Australia should try Canada for assistance. Any troops sent must bring their own equipment, he said, because Australia was having great difficulties equipping its own militia.

Astoundingly at this time, Curtin was busy personally intervening to head off and settle serious industrial stoppages, including those in essential industries. His minister for labour, Eddie Ward, was disinclined or unable to bring many of the worst disputes to an end. The coalmining industry was the worst affected by random stoppages. Strikes in northern New South Wales coalmines in the week to 12 February caused the loss of some 22,000 tons of urgently needed coal. Men at two idle mines went back to work while another four went on strike over seniority and methods of work. Curtin called in leaders of the Miners' Federation. On 13 February they issued a statement:

In view of the grave menace facing the country we direct members now on strike to resume work pending a full working out of matters now in dispute.

Germany was now gloating over the Japanese success. A report by the commander of the German navy, Grand Admiral Erich Raeder, to Adolf Hitler on 13 February saw excellent opportunities for the German ally in the Far East:

Rangoon, Singapore and, most likely, also Port Darwin will be in Japanese hands within a few weeks. Only weak resistance is expected on Sumatra, while Java will be able to hold out longer. Japan plans to protect this front in the Indian Ocean by capturing the key position of Ceylon . . .

Tokyo Radio said Japanese forces had occupied Singapore's high point, Bukit Timah, and were only 5½ miles (8.9 kilometres) from the city.

After attending a brief communion service, General Percival called another conference of generals on Sunday 15 February in the underground headquarters at Fort Canning. From Java, General Wavell had ordered that Singapore must fight on, but he gave General Percival an outlet to surrender:

Time gained and damage to enemy of vital importance at this crisis. When you are fully satisfied that this is no longer possible I give you discretion to cease resistance.

The Japanese in Singapore soon demanded unconditional surrender. General Bennett that memorable Sunday wrote in his diary:

Each of us at that conference urged a termination of the hopeless struggle . . . The civil hospital had been without water for twenty-four hours. The civilians were in a similar plight . . . Food supplies were almost depleted, the army having less than three days' food on hand. Ammunition, artillery ammunition particularly, was exhausted . . .

The conference decided to surrender. Bennett advocated capitulation to save the population of the city from disaster, since there were fears that if Japanese troops entered, there would be horrific scenes, as had occurred in Chinese cities where Japanese troops had gone on murderous rampages.

Leaving the meeting General Bennett now put own his plan of escape into action. The subsequent controversy would follow Bennett all his life:

> My decision was fortified by the resolve that I must at all costs return to Australia to tell our people the story of our conflict with the Japanese, to warn them of the danger to Australia and to advise them of the best means of defeating the Japanese tactics.

At 3.45 pm on 15 February the British flew a large Japanese flag from the top of the Cathay Building skyscraper, a sign to the Japanese that the British had given up. General Percival with British officers drove and then marched towards the Ford Motor factory at Bukit Timah, which had become headquarters of the commander of the 25th Army, General Tomoyuki Yamashita. British officers carried a large white flag and a large Union Jack and were taken to meet Yamashita, later known as the Tiger of Malaya, who insisted on unconditional surrender. Percival briefly haggled about the timing of the formal surrender but quickly gave way. His men had already laid down their arms anyway. The formal surrender was to be 8.30 pm. Yamashita warned that he planned to launch a major, final attack at 10 pm that night. At 6.15 pm Percival signed the terms of surrender and prevented an immediate bloodbath in Singapore.

*

Japan wildly celebrated the capture of Singapore at home with marches, flag-waving and patriotic speeches. Prime Minister

General Hideki Tojo spoke in the diet in Tokyo of crushing the main body of the American fleet, taking Hong Kong in eighteen days, Manila in twenty-six days and now Singapore in seventy days. He had a warning for regions further south:

> Australia and New Zealand also should avoid a useless war with their reliance upon the United States and Britain which are not worth any dependence. Whether the peoples of these regions will or will not enjoy happiness and welfare depends entirely upon whether or not their Governments understand the real intentions of Japan and take a fair and just attitude.

The fall of Singapore was a triumphant landmark in world history, according to the *Japan Times*, paving the way for the future of Greater East Asia and 'a better life for Asians freed from the colonial yoke':

> At last the inhabitants of this entire area will be able to work as free men to build a happier and more prosperous Greater East Asia of their own . . . We have passed a landmark in history. We have altered the face of the earth.

Japan's Foreign Office issued a statement saying Prime Minister Curtin could 'no longer mislead the innocent people of Australia' that war materials were on their war from Britain and America.

Singapore's rapid fall was a great shock to Churchill and it soon awakened the sleeping black dog. He called the fall of Singapore 'the worst disaster and largest capitulation in British history'. In a broadcast on the fall of Singapore Churchill said:

> I have nothing to offer except a hard and adverse war for many months . . . I speak under the shadow of a heavy and far-reaching British and Imperial military defeat. Other dangers gather around us in the Far East and none of the dangers we have hitherto faced at home and in the Middle East have diminished.

As Singapore was overcome, sections of the press in Australia, Britain and the United States began to question directly the leadership of Prime Minister Churchill and members of his war cabinet. Some British parliamentarians began clamouring for a cabinet reshuffle. The *Daily Mail* editorialised that Churchill had blamed his predecessors for every war reversal for at least a year, but the disaster of Singapore was not allowed to be placed on the shoulders of Churchill or his ministers. 'Why does almost complete absence of air support persist?' On 16 February many members of the House of Commons were adamant that war reverses demanded a searching inquiry. While *The Times* and the *Daily Telegraph* in London supported Churchill, they too insisted that there must be an inquiry into the circumstances of war reverses. The day after the fall of Singapore, 16 February 1942, *The Argus* in Melbourne blamed the 'Beat Hitler First' strategy:

> A policy which envisaged the Japanese menace as a secondary one, to be dealt with when the older perils had been disposed of, has certainly proved disastrous.

Churchill said his government would persist through bad times and cruel vexations and 'come out at the top of the hill'. In fact Churchill was 'stupefied' by the fall of Singapore, according to his doctor, Sir Charles Wilson. He recalled that in the middle of January he had found Churchill 'in a positively spectacular temper' over events in Singapore:

> He had just learnt from [General] Wavell that the defences of Singapore – the work of many years – were built only to meet attacks from the sea. Many of the guns could only fire seaward. It had never entered his head, he complained, that the rear of the fortress was quite unprotected against an attack from the land. 'Why didn't they tell me about this? Oh no; it is my own fault. I ought to have known'.

Wilson said Churchill, deeply dejected, couldn't comprehend how 100,000 men, half of them of British stock, could surrender to an inferior number of Japanese:

He felt it was a disgrace. It left a scar on his mind. One evening, months later, when he was sitting in his bathroom enveloped in a towel, he stopped drying himself and gloomily surveyed the floor: 'I cannot get over Singapore', he said sadly.

In London, the British foreign affairs secretary, Anthony Eden, had drinks with Churchill, who was dejected, as Eden recalled in his diary:

Winston was tired and depressed, for him. His cold is heavy on him. He was inclined to be fatalistic . . . that he had done all he could and . . . that Malaya, Australian Government's intransigence and 'nagging' in House was more than any man could expect to endure.

Wilson noted:

He had to school himself not to think about things when they went wrong, for he found that he could not live with his mistakes and keep his balance.

The loss of Singapore stunned most Australians. Suddenly Australia had lost touch with a vast number of Diggers, with particular impact on friends and family of those now missing. There were 18,231 Australian troops in Malaya around the end of January. Army Minister Forde had no official advice as to whether any Australian had escaped, but he believed that comparatively few had got away. Prime Minister Curtin faced the defeat of Singapore with great trepidation, calling it 'Australia's Dunkirk':

The fall of Singapore opens the Battle for Australia. On its issue depends not merely the fate of this Commonwealth but the frontier of the United States of America and, indeed, all the Americas, and therefore, in large measure, the fate of the British-speaking world.

Australia must defend herself, Curtin said, knowing that rein-forcements from the United States were painfully slow in coming and that Britain had other priorities:

> Our honeymoon has finished. It is now work or fight as we have never worked or fought before and there must not be a man or a woman in this Commonwealth who goes to bed to-night without having related his or her period of wakefulness to the purposes of war.

Curtin worried that Australians were still idly enjoying a lazy summer, carrying on their lives almost as normal with sport, leisure activities and industrial strikes. It galled Curtin when unflagging toil and resistance was needed to prevent Australians becoming 'a people governed by others':

> All of us are now obligated by fate to a more salutary way of life. Whatever criticism that direction may evoke, I tell this nation that, as things stand to-day in Australia, brains and brawn are better than either bets or beer.

The *Sydney Morning Herald*, three days after the fall, said Australians in their easygoing democracy had been consumed by 'sloth and faction', but now must not panic nor despair:

> The war that, to Australia, hitherto has been a red glow on the horizon is now very close to our shores. In the glare of its approaching flames we see much that is wrong with our country, much that is weak, woefully much that has been left undone.

On the day Singapore fell, coalminers in New South Wales passed resolutions recognising the necessity of uninterrupted coal production. Curtin had successfully encouraged leaders of the Miners' Federation to recommend that all strikes be abandoned. But then miners at the pits continued to stage rolling strikes. The following evening, in a thundering sermon, the bishop of Bendigo, the Right Reverend C.L. Riley, lashed out at strikers, including those who had demanded danger money:

> Is there no expression of public opinion on such matters? Our men continuously for nine months at Tobruk did not ask for danger money but here in Australia people on urgent war work want to sit down and argue about their rights.

A week later the Curtin Government gazetted regulations to be used to deal with any further stoppages in the coal industry. Curtin warned striking miners that unless they returned to work the government would intervene directly. On the same day Victorian Railways said they were drawing on dwindling coal reserves because promised coal from New South Wales had not arrived to meet the state's railway demands.

*

General Gordon Bennett was determined not to be captured. After the surrender he made his escape bid at night with several other officers and a company commander, boarding a traditional timber sailing vessel and sailing through the low islands away from Singapore.

Bennett wasn't the only one who had been trying desperately to leave the island. Just before the surrender, Prime Minister Churchill sent a cable to General Wavell with a message about leaving escape to the general's discretion:

> Also just before final cessation of fighting opportunity should be given to any determined bodies of men or individuals to try and effect escape by any means possible.

Most of the Allied servicemen, exhausted and sometimes leader-less, were resigned to their fate. But after the surrender hundreds of British and Australian troops did make determined efforts to escape. Some used their weapons to force passage on boats. Others had made careful plans to buy their ticket to freedom by purchasing or stealing boats. Lieutenant Arthur Tranter of the Australian 2/29th Battalion, who had fought at Muar River, and a few others commandeered a boat with a small motor and took off through the maze of islands towards Sumatra. For five days they headed up the remote winding Kampar River, eventually making it to Padang on Sumatra's west coast. But they were soon captured by the Japanese.

In Singapore, Australian army nursing sisters who were in Malaya with the 8th Division AIF had been evacuated in two groups a few days before the fall of the island. One ship, the *Empire Star*, although attacked by Japanese bombers, reached Batavia. The second group of sixty-five nursing sisters had been ordered during an air raid to leave Singapore. According to one, Sister Betty Jeffrey, the sisters had refused to leave because their hospital was grossly overcrowded, with more wounded soldiers constantly arriving. But they were given no say and were driven by side roads to the wharves, which were a scene of chaos. Hundreds of people were trying to get ships or boats to escape. The whole of Singapore seemed ablaze. The nurses boarded a small ship, the *Vyner Brooke*, which was carrying 600 evacuees. The following day at sea six Japanese aircraft dive-bombed the vessel. One bomb hit the bridge. Another went straight down the funnel. The ship soon was sinking and everyone took to the lifeboats, which were strafed.

After drifting for some time the survivors, including a number of men and many of the nursing sisters, made it to tropical Bangka Island south of Singapore, off Sumatra. In time the group agreed they must surrender, so a naval officer walked off to find the Japanese. He returned with Japanese soldiers who immediately marched the men down the beautiful tropical palm-fringed beach and around a bluff out of sight. The Japanese soldiers returned, wiping blood from their bayonets. The shocked nurses were told to line up and walk into the sea. As they did so a machine gun cut them down from behind. Nursing sister Captain Vivian Bullwinkel was shot in her left side. She fell and floated among the bodies, but she regained consciousness and found herself washed ashore and lying on her back, while Japanese were running away up the beach in the distance, laughing. After a further period of unconsciousness she found herself on the beach surrounded by bodies:

> I was so cold that my only thought was to find some warm spot to die. I dragged myself up to the edge of the jungle and lay in the sun where I must have slept for hours. When I woke the sun was almost setting. I spent the night huddled under some bamboos only a few yards from my dead colleagues, too dazed and shocked for anything to register. Next morning I examined my wound and realised I had been shot through the diaphragm and that it would not prove fatal.

Captain Bullwinkel was the only survivor from her group of twenty-two Australian nurses. She found an English soldier who had been bayoneted while lying on a stretcher. He was still alive, but soon died. About ten days later Bullwinkel was captured again and became a prisoner of war.

On Tuesday 17 February New Zealand's prime minister, Peter Fraser, sent a rather anxious cable to Churchill and Roosevelt on Japan's next intentions:

> We think there are strong reasons for supposing that the conquest of India by military force is not practically realisable in the near future. The invasion of Australia appears more immediately advantageous to the Japanese.

Fraser begged both leaders to help overcome the severe shortages of equipment in the Pacific and in New Zealand. Roosevelt had been giving much thought to Japan in the Pacific and sparked debate in Washington, especially among younger high-ranking officers who spoke their mind about halting the Japanese advance. The president said the Allies must 'at all costs' maintain the two great flanks: 'The right hand based on Australia and New Zealand and the left in Burma, India and China.' He said Britain should take the left flank and reinforce Burma and India while the United States could best reinforce the right flank:

> ... I think that the United States should take the primary responsibility for that immediate reinforcement and maintenance using Australia as the main base.

Roosevelt was also thinking about putting an American commander-in-chief in Australia. General Douglas MacArthur, then in his besieged command headquarters of the Malinta tunnel on Corregidor Island in Manila Bay, was in the president's mind. Ironically, MacArthur had been mentioned by American newspapers as a possible replacement for Roosevelt. Curtin believed that Churchill was interested in preserving India but not Australia. Under considerable pressure and anxiety, Churchill willingly agreed with Roosevelt's suggestion, but he and his war cabinet continued to be parsimonious and reluctant when it came to extending much assistance to Australia. Churchill revealed his state to Roosevelt a few days later:

> I do not like these days of personal stress and I have found it difficult to keep my eye on the ball. We are however in fullest accord in all main things ...

With the news of Singapore's surrender hot off the presses, it was a highly charged atmosphere on Tuesday 17 February when one of the biggest crowds ever seen in Martin Place in Sydney gathered for the opening of the Australian Government's drive for subscriptions to its latest Liberty Loan. Fifteen minutes before the prime minister mounted the dais he was in his Martin Place Commonwealth office in complete agony. It was one of his old maladies, gastritis, which can cause acute abdominal pain accompanied by nausea. In the street below, the lunchtime crowds were gathering rapidly and the military bands were playing rousing tunes. Only Curtin's closest colleagues knew what he was going through. As the time for his appearance drew near, Curtin insisted on attending and went down in the lift. He paced quickly with head held high through the big crowd. Proceedings began with the crash of marching feet down Martin Place from Macquarie Street as units of the Australian army, navy and air force, followed by a pageant representing foreign Allies, came by. Curtin was joined on the covered podium in Martin Place by the opposition leader, Arthur Fadden, senior defence officers and dignitaries. He had been in Sydney for two days of intense meetings with his cabinet and the Advisory War Council. Curtin rose to speak to a receptive audience. He quickly got to the point:

> Men and women of Australia – for I am speaking now to everybody in this Commonwealth, wherever he or she may be – I speak surrounded by representatives of the fighting forces; those forces upon whose gallantry, supported by the maximum equipment that we can give to them, stand between us and the invasion of our country.

With one thumb in a vest pocket, Curtin was now shouting at the throng, ramming home his words, saying that the full cabinet that very day had directed the gazettal of regulations for the complete mobilisation of the nation by galvanising all resources, human and material. Everyone in Australia, he said, whether they liked it or not, was now at the service of the government to work in the defence of Australia. Every material thing in the country, including money, machinery, plant and buildings, could be diverted by the government for war purposes. Curtin took it that an attack on Australia now was a *fait accompli*. Australian life itself, he warned, was at stake. 'Fill the loan!' Curtin bellowed, while trying to mask his pain:

> . . . I ask you Australians to fill this loan as a complete and immediate indication to the enemy that Australia will meet him inch by inch, foot by foot, yard by yard, and that he shall not enter

upon our country – that all the advancing that will be done will be done by Australians.

Curtin was close to collapse with the pain. What play Japanese propaganda would have given to an enemy leader who collapsed at a war rally? Curtin made it through to rousing applause. His office was just across the street. He made it. A waiting doctor thought he might have appendicitis and sent him immediately to St Vincent's Hospital in nearby Darlinghurst, where gastritis was diagnosed. Press secretary Don Rodgers wanted a 24-hour news ban put on any press coverage of Curtin's illness, but this was soon lifted because Curtin was too ill to chair the war cabinet or the Advisory War Council, a fact that would quickly become public. Some newspapers associated the prime minister's ailment with stress. 'CURTIN ILL' headlined the *Daily News* in Perth on Wednesday 18 February:

> Sydney, Tuesday – Overcome temporarily by the weight of war responsibility, Prime Minister Curtin is in St. Vincent's Hospital. He was taken there yesterday suffering from gastritis resulting from prolonged nervous strain.

Political reporters in Canberra knew what really ailed the prime minister. They had been informed on 17 February that all Australian forces would abandon the Dutch East Indies. Joe Alexander was told in confidence that the government view was that 'it would be throwing away our men and material to send them to Java'. It was an epic decision for Curtin. The following day Alexander, noting that Curtin had been hospitalised, wrote in his diary: 'He is overcome by the weight of the decisions he has made.'

*

On Thursday 19 February a group of Tiwi islanders and a Catholic missionary on Bathurst Island, north-west of Darwin, spotted a large number of high-flying aircraft heading in the direction of Darwin. Father John McGrath turned his radio transceiver to an emergency frequency:

Eight-S-E to V.I.D. I have an urgent message. An unusually large air formation bearing down on us from the north-west. Identity suspect. Visibility not clear. Over.

McGrath was asked to stand by. Within minutes Japanese aircraft strafed his village on the island. The message was received by the wireless station at Darwin at 9.35 am and passed on to RAAF operations within two minutes. But no general alarm was given in Darwin until just before 10 am. Communication with the southern capitals was broken. The landline to Perth had been cut by a recent cyclone. A Department of Civil Aviation operator at Parap airfield in Darwin, Bruce Acland, saw anti-aircraft guns open up on waves of approaching aircraft. He dashed off a coded message and ran outside, diving into a trench. Morse code burst into life at cattle stations across the Northern Territory with the message 'QQQ QQQ QQQ DE VZDN'. It was code for an air raid in progress at Darwin. Mainland Australia was being attacked for the first time. The cattle stations quickly relayed the astounding news to the south.

The Japanese fleet that attacked Darwin was an overwhelming force. It comprised 188 aircraft, commanded by Captain Mitsuo Fuchida, from the carriers the *Akagi*, the *Kaga*, the *Soryu* and the *Hiryu*, supported by two battleships, three cruisers and nine destroyers. Had the fleet had accompanying crowded troopships, landings would easily have been affected. The big Nagumo Force was out to smash, not invade, Darwin. It had left Palau Island, east of Bougainville, on 15 February, the day Singapore surrendered. Fuchida was dismissive of the need for such a strike force to cripple Darwin:

As at Rabaul, the job to be done seemed hardly worthy of the Nagumo Force. The harbour, it is true, was crowded with all kinds of ships, but a single pier and a few waterfront buildings appeared to be the only port installations. The airfield on the outskirts of the town, though fairly large, had no more than three small hangars and in all there were only twenty-odd planes of various types scattered about the field. No planes were in the air. A few attempted to take off as we came over but were quickly shot down, and the rest were destroyed where they stood.

Fuchida said Admiral Yamamoto and his Combined Fleet planners were most concerned over probable Allied use of north-west Australia as a base from which to impede the Japanese seizure of the Dutch East Indies:

Proposals for mounting an amphibious invasion of Port Darwin met a flat rebuff by the Naval General Staff [in Tokyo] and the Army, so [Yamamoto's] Combined Fleet decided upon the next best alternative, a carrier air strike to completely wreck base installations in the area.

In the first raid, which lasted some forty minutes, Japanese heavy bombers pattern-bombed the harbour and town while dive-bombers escorted by Zero fighters attacked shipping in the harbour and military and civil airfields. Bombs were falling before air raid sirens began sounding. They struck Darwin's major wharf, demolishing a long section of it. Some twenty-one wharf labourers, trapped on the open wharf, were killed. Eight ships were sunk, including two US transport vessels and a US destroyer.

The USS *Peary*, an old and battered four-funnel destroyer, had escaped from the Japanese at Manila Bay. Refuelling from the *British Motorist* when the attack began, she was unable to slip her anchor quickly and had barely got underway when she was hit by five bombs. Even as she was sinking, men continued to fire a machine gun on the afterdeck house and another on the galley deck house. While the water rose, the last unknown gunner was still at the gun controls and firing continued as the *Peary* went down stern first. Eighty-nine officers and men from the destroyer were killed and fifty-seven survived, twenty of them wounded.

An Australian cargo ship carrying explosives, the *Neptuna*, went up in a giant mushroom cloud, killing forty-five aboard. The modern passenger liner the *Manunda*, which had seen war service in the Middle East, was clearly identified as a hospital ship. She was painted white and had large white crosses on her funnel and deck facing skywards. There was a broad red band running around the entire ship interspersed at intervals with large painted red crosses. Yet a bomb crashed through a skylight, exploding at B and C decks, causing great damage. It was possible that the airmen were trying to hit a US destroyer close by. The *Manunda* death toll, including patients and those taken from the sea, would increase to thirty-four the following day.

As bombs began falling, the administrator of the Northern Territory, Charles Abbott, his wife and staff sought shelter under the concrete floor of his office in the grounds of Government House overlooking the harbour. Almost immediately there was a huge blast:

I could see the concrete floor above us lift as the reinforced pillars snapped like dry sticks; then it settled down, and there was a crash and rumble of falling masonry and grey dust everywhere . . . The office walls and floor were blown in and a huge block of concrete fell on the little half-caste girl, Daisy, burying her from the head to the waist and killing her instantly . . .

Abbott could hear the incessant scream of Japanese dive-bombers as they zoomed along the foreshores, machine-gunning the wharf and the men struggling in the water. The Zeros paid particular attention to the flagstaff flying the Australian flag on the lawn of Government House, returning to strafe it repeatedly. Japan had excellent knowledge of Government House and the port of Darwin. Japan's Consul General to Australia, Masatoshi Akiyama and Chancellor Mitsumi Yanase, both spies based in Sydney, had stayed at Government House as Abbott's guests in 1940.

For years Japanese agents, including members of the Japanese population living in Darwin, had sent home intelligence and had photographed and mapped the Northern Territory coastline, especially near Darwin. A member of the 21st Battalion AIF had this letter intercepted by army censors:

We had a bit of a stink with the Japs up here a while ago. We had to shoot one b . . . in the leg to get him. They were off a Jap fishing boat and were . . . about in our defensive areas. The coast patrol got their ship and brought it in. It had on board a hell of a lot of ammunition and service revolvers, a short wave wireless which could send and receive, and a few hand bombs about the weight of a grenade.

A bomb hit the main Darwin post office, killing the postmaster and his family plus six young women telegraphists sheltering in a slit-trench outside. Many buildings in the town were destroyed, including those in residential areas. But the first raid did little damage to Darwin's oil tanks, floating dock or water supply, a fact that suggested implications of a 'grave threat' of later enemy intentions, according to Justice Charles J. Lowe, who conducted an immediate on-the-spot inquiry. There was a good deal of panic in the town as people feared an imminent Japanese invasion. Every available transport was used to head south and the evacuation became an unruly shambles. Law and order broke down. Some civilian and military personnel began looting abandoned businesses and houses.

Nineteen-year-old Victorian trooper, Rex Ruwoldt of 19th Machine Gun Battalion, was among some 5000 troops that had arrived in the Top End in January 1942 to defend Darwin. He didn't think the troops would have had a chance if the Japanese had landed in force:

A lot of us didn't have rifles or bayonets, the equipment was absolutely disgusting. We knew something was going to happen because the Japs were moving south through the isles in New Guinea and Malaya and Singapore. We were next in line.

The rest of the infantry only had five rounds of ammunition per man and that doesn't last very long. The machine-gun regiment had 30,000 rounds, which for a machine gun would last a five-minute battle. That's what made us nervous.

Jack Mulholland was the commander of an anti-aircraft gun set up on Darwin Oval when the enemy planes came over. He said the shells had been tested just a few days earlier and the fuses were faulty. So his gun fired ammunition that was of no use:

You see, we'd never actually fired the guns. We weren't allowed to fire the guns because it might upset the local population. So the first time our guns went off – and they were big guns – was on the 19th of February when we went into action. It was a shame. With a couple of shoots, we could have found the errors, which would have made a complete difference to the attack.

Even before Fuchida's massive fleet of carrier aircraft had reached Darwin, heavy bombers were taking off with the specific aim of bombing the RAAF base at Parap, Darwin, Australia's forward air base. The new attackers were in two separate groups, each comprising twenty-seven twin-engined bombers. Mitsubishi 'Kate' bombers had taken off from Ambon in the Moluccas while the second group of Mitsubishi 'Betty' bombers roared off a dirt strip to the cheers of ground crew at Kandari in the Celebes, well west of Ambon. It was a typical sunny tropical day with scattered high cumulus cloud. Both groups of heavy bombers began converging on Darwin. Japanese archival footage shows intense young air crewmen in heavy clothing in the 'Betty' bombers eating a morning meal from tin cans as they near northern Australia. No fighters rose to challenge the fifty-four bombers. The bombers made the flight from the islands to Australia's coast without fighter escorts. At around 11 am the town of Darwin came into view. The archival footage shows bombs exploding as clustered puffs of smoke that grow wider and more intense.

The RAAF station at Parap was unprepared to meet hostile attack and was promptly deserted. The total Allied air strength at Darwin that day consisted of nine Hudson bombers, six of which had just arrived from the East Indies, ten Kittyhawks and five unserviceable Wirraways.

The second raid smashed the RAAF station. Australian anti-aircraft crews fought back but, as Air Commander Fuchida said, the anti-aircraft fire 'was intense but largely ineffectual'. The station was unprepared to meet any hostile attack and was promptly deserted. The acting station commander had ordered his men to go down the road and gather in the bush. Many men on the base simply took off into the bush or joined the wild civilian evacuation southwards. Some men from the air station got as far as Batchelor, Adelaide River and Daly Waters. One RAAF man actually reached Melbourne thirteen days later.

Hugh Bonython was an RAAF pilot but could do nothing about the attack because he was in hospital with dengue fever. In later life he remembered that fateful day:

We heard the drone of many aircraft and we thought 'Oh good, the Yanks have arrived' but it was shortly followed by the all too familiar sound of the whistling of bombs as they fell and we realised it wasn't the Yanks at all. It was the first raid on Darwin . . . we were all fairly convinced that come the dawn the Japanese would be landing in Darwin.

The Administrator, Charles Abbott, sent a report to Canberra eight days after the attack:

The confusion which followed the raid was very bad and was greatly accentuated by unauthorized actions by various service sections, including the Provost Corps. Discipline there was very bad, men were drunk, and salutary action including the arrest of an Officer and a Non-Commissioned Officer had to be taken. The worst feature was that soldiers, entirely without orders, kept advising civilians to leave the town. This resulted in a stream of cars, cyclists and pedestrians making down the road . . .

Abbott's own behavior immediately after the first raid did not do him proud. He admitted to securing the services of two police sergeants to rescue valuable crockery, wine and spirits from the cellar of Government House and carry them to cars. The services of the policemen were keenly needed at the time to help restore order.

Darwin was not put out of action, although its capacity to operate was much reduced. Ships now had to load and offload cargo using lighters. Darwin would be bombed sixty-four times before the war finished. Subsequent raids in April, June, July and November 1942, and March 1943 would involve thirty to forty fighters and bombers in each raid. Between the large raids there were numerous smaller attacks involving a dozen or less aircraft.

'Darwin Bombed' screamed the headline across the front page of Perth's afternoon newspaper the *Daily News* on the same day as the bombing:

First bombs ever to hit Australia fell on Darwin this morning as Japanese raiders struck their most southerly blow of the war. It has not yet been revealed how heavy the bombing was or what damage resulted.

Curtin received the news from the Air Ministry in bed at St Vincent's Hospital in the early afternoon of the raid. He had not been well enough to attend a meeting of the Advisory War Council. Members of the council were taking part in a practice air raid exercise in Martin Place when they received the startling news from Darwin. Curtin and Don Rodgers put together a brief press statement designed to thwart public panic. The prime minister said Australia had now experienced physical attack:

The statement of Darwin's bombing is official. Nothing has been hidden and there is no call for any rumour. If rumours circulate, take no notice of them. The Government has told you the truth. Face it as Australians.

Later that night Curtin said damage was considerable and a severe blow had been struck:

In this first battle on Australian soil, it will be a source of pride to the public to know that the Armed Forces and the civilians comported themselves with the gallantry that is traditional in the people of our stock.

He reminded the people that 'we too, in every other city, can face these assaults' and the nature of Australia's war had now changed:

The protection of this country is no longer that of a contribution to a world at war but the resistance to an enemy threatening to invade our own shore.

Much was hidden from the Australian public. Newspapers two days later were reporting the death toll as seventeen. The two raids on 19 February 1942 killed at least 243 people and wounded between 300 and 400. Twenty military aircraft were destroyed, eight ships at anchor in the harbour were sunk, and civil and military facilities in Darwin were damaged beyond repair. Newspapers had been restricted from immediately publishing the true death toll, although the Melbourne *Herald* on 30 March got away with a minute three paragraphs in which the death toll was given as less than 240. At that time Curtin told the press that 'the interests of security prevented me from stating previously the number who were killed or drowned at the harbour and on the wharves'. Not until 29 September 1942 would Curtin reveal to the media, in a confidential briefing, that 'some months ago' Darwin had been 'bashed to pieces' by Japanese bombers. 'At any time,' he said, the Japanese 'had reached a position where they would have been able to establish a bridgehead on Australian soil.'

Curtin's close adviser, the secretary of the Department of Defence, Sir Frederick Shedden, was present in the Cabinet Room in Martin Place when the Darwin attack was announced. Much later, war historian Sir Paul Hasluck quoted Shedden's observations:

Shedden told me of a pitiful scene in the Cabinet room at Sydney when ministers were told of the bombing of Darwin. He spoke of agitated ministers running around like a lot of startled chooks.

*

'NAVY BOMBS PORT DARWIN; NIPPON LANDS IN TIMOR', the *Japan Times* in Tokyo joyfully announced:

> The Imperial Navy Air Corps on February 19 carried out extensive raids in large formations on Port Darwin, the greatest enemy naval air base on the northern coast of Australia, and smashed the enemy's air strength and destroyed enemy warships and shipping in the port . . . No attack was made on a hospital ship which lay at anchor in the port.

Japanese propagandists portrayed the severe Darwin bombing as the end for Australia. The *Tokyo Nichi Nichi* newspaper said the fate of Australia had become quite clear. The *Chugai Shogyo* had gratuitous advice:

> Australia without doubt should be included in the Greater East Asia Co-Prosperity Sphere . . . we can hardly comprehend why Australia is continuing its resistance against Japan.

The *Miyako Shinbun* in Tokyo emphasised Australian anxiety:

> Now the most important strategic point in Australia is about to be captured. It is little wonder that the enemy should now be completely depressed with all hope gone for regaining lost ground.

The *Yomiuri Shinbun* said Australia had been abandoned:

> Australian Premier John Curtin declared recently that Australia has lost its hope for American and British aid completely . . . The worst stage is thus confronting Australia now.

The great first raid on Darwin was not intended as a precursor to a Japanese invasion as so many Australians at the time thought, although the Imperial Navy Combined Fleet wanted it. On 16 February, the day after the fall of Singapore, Japanese army and navy war planning section heads had confronted each other again in Tokyo. A navy ministry official advocated a clean sweep of Australia's forward bases by invading forces. The army objected. Colonel Etsuo Kotani, an intelligence specialist, drew attention to the significant extent of Japan's theatre of operations and the demands on manpower and shipping. 'It is too difficult. We have no reserves,' he said bluntly. But aggressive Naval Staff war planner Baron Captain Sadatoshi Tomioka had been adamant:

But if we take Australia now, we can bring about the defeat of Great Britain. With only a token force we can reach our aim!

The Combined Fleet chief of staff, Admiral Ugaki, accepted the planned aerial destruction of Darwin but he and other senior navy officers would not abandon the idea of an invasion at some later stage. After the Darwin raid, Ugaki recorded his elation in his diary:

The task force surprise-attacked Port Darwin on a large scale up to 0800 and sank three destroyers, one sub chaser, and eight merchant ships. All of twenty eight planes were also destroyed and installations too. I am sure all the Australians were shocked and scared stiff.

Indeed they were, if *The Age* was any indication:

This attack dissipates the last vestiges of doubt about Japan's intentions and designs against ourselves and our country ... The unique event must strike home to the consciousness of every dweller in Australia a vivid realisation of how the war has begun to surge over our own shores.

Chapter 9

'THEY'RE COMING HOME!'

Curtin was dismayed at Australia's precarious situation after the fall of Singapore and the massive raid on Darwin. While large numbers of experienced AIF infantrymen were fighting in the Middle East, Australia at home had been weakened by the loss of so many fighting men in Singapore. An estimated 85,000 servicemen had surrendered to inferior numbers of Japanese in Malaya and Singapore. The Australian military death toll would be 1789, while the almost 15,000 Australians taken prisoner would go on to suffer appallingly brutal and degrading forms of captivity, which would kill many of their number. The total British, Australian, Indian and local volunteer manpower lost as a result of battle casualties and by the surrender amounted to 138,708, according to official figures, a disaster on an enormous scale.

Curtin cabled General Wavell on 18 February 1942 saying that Australia still had scant air support. The RAAF at home could muster only about fifty bombers and reconnaissance planes, most of them outmoded, and no fighters to match the impressive air power of the Japanese.

Promises of aircraft for Australia from the United States to date had resulted in the arrival of only a trickle. Many of the US aircraft required assembly from crates, often parts were missing and there were insufficient trained personnel to do the assembling. The war cabinet tried to help by approving the production of 100 new Wirraway Boomerangs to assist the critical fighter shortage. While a big improvement on the original Wirraway, now relegated to a training role, the Boomerang was a lemon; it had reasonable maneuverability, but lacked speed and range, and was no match for Japanese Zeros.

The only bright news on the horizon was that the 6th and 7th divisions AIF had been relieved at Tobruk and had departed from the Mediterranean theatre for Australia in five convoys to prepare for the war against Japan.

*

Alarmingly, there still was talk in Washington among high officials in the defence forces and in the Roosevelt Administration of letting Australia fall to the Japanese because of the resources it would take to keep Australia free. The earlier undisclosed agreement by the British and Americans to declare the war with Japan a secondary theatre of operations and put the defeat of Germany first had now left Australia grievously exposed.

General George C. Kenney, commanding general of the 4th US air force on the West Coast, was appointed Allied air chief in the South West Pacific, to be based in Australia. On his appointment Kenney detected an apparent neglect of the war against Japan. He took his concerns to the US chief of the army, General George C. Marshall and US chief of the army air force, General Henry 'Hap' Arnold. The Pacific, Kenney was told by the generals, would have to wait until Germany was disposed of. General Kenney's private recollections starkly underlined Curtin's deepest fears:

The thing that worried me most, however, was the casual way that everyone seemed to look at the Pacific part of the war. The possibility that the Japs would soon land in Australia itself was freely admitted and I sensed that, even if that country were taken over by the Nipponese, the real effort would still be made against Germany. I gathered that they thought there was already enough strength in the Pacific, particularly in Australia, to maintain a sort of 'strategic defensive', which was all that was expected for the time being.

General Arnold told Kenney that he had sent 'a lot of airplanes over there and a lot of supplies', but Arnold read reports indicating that 'most of the airplanes were out of commission' and that 'there didn't seem to be much flying going on'. Kenney was told that some 600 aircraft had been sent to South West Pacific areas. The US chiefs said they would do what they could to help Kenney out when he reached Australia, but 'they just had to build up the European show first'. Roosevelt had told the secretary of the treasury, Henry Morgenthau: 'I would rather lose New Zealand, Australia or anything else than have the Russians collapse.'

The British Government now said openly that it thought Darwin would be attacked as the so-called Malay Barrier crumbled. The British Dominions Office at the start of March gave a hint, though, in a message to Curtin, that the capture of Darwin might not be critical to the future recovery:

Port Darwin is principally of value while we retain any hold on the Malayan Barrier, but is not strategically essential for the eventual offensive. The remainder of Australia, in particular the east and southwest, will be one of the main bases from which the offensive against Japan will eventually be launched. Australia is insecure at present but, as we have not the forces available, United States must be largely responsible for reinforcing this area.

The inference appeared to be that if Darwin was captured, it could be retaken later. Curtin soon told Churchill that there had been 'a rapid deteriorating in the strategic situation'. He put forward proposals for the higher direction of policy and operations in the ANZAC area. He warned that Darwin, Port Moresby, New Caledonia and Fiji were immediate threatened:

> The loss of Australia and New Zealand would mean the loss of the only bases for offensive action by the Allied nations against the Japanese from the Anzac area.

*

The island of Timor north-west of Darwin was clearly doomed in the ongoing Japanese onslaught, with an invasion on 20 February. The 2/2nd Independent Company – trained Australian commandos who operated behind enemy lines in the island's east – withdrew to the hills as Japanese carrier planes destroyed the few Australian aircraft on the island. Two Japanese battalions, complete with light tanks, landed south of Kupang in west Timor, and Japanese paratroopers landed east of the town. The 2/40th Battalion group of Australians put up a spirited defence and took a high toll on the invaders, especially the para-troops, but control of the sea and the air gave the Japanese the advantage. A Japanese force of about 4000 soldiers had also been sent against Dili, the Portuguese capital, where it faced only limited resistance. More than half of the Australian defenders had been stricken with malaria even before the Japanese landed. On 23 February the Australian group, short of ammunition and food, surrendered near Kupang. From then onwards it was left to the Australian commando force to conduct a prolonged and successful guerrilla campaign, aided by the local Timorese, in the rugged interior from the Portuguese side of the island. The Australian consul in Dili, David Ross, who had been under house arrest but otherwise treated well by the Japanese, was allowed to trek inland to make contact with the Australians and present them with a Japanese request to surrender, which they rejected. Ross was amazed to find the commandos fighting fit, well fed and well supplied by aircraft drops from Australia. Further, Australian authorities had been in constant wireless contact with them. The Australians were in good spirits and were content to continue their guerrilla activities provided mail and supplies from Australia continued.

*

In Singapore, one million or so people, mostly Asian civilians, were now hemmed in to the town area and waterfront awaiting their fate at the hands of the victors. Many British, Australian and Indian soldiers wandered the area. Some were deserters; others had simply become separated from their units. Evacuation ships trying to escape through the islands were being bombed. Local services had broken down. Hospitals couldn't cope with the injured and sick. Food and water was running short.

After the bombing and shelling had stopped, the Chinese living in Singapore, or Shonan as the Japanese now called the island, faced a new terror. The Chinese called it 'Sook Ching', or 'Purge through Purification'. The Japanese created twenty-eight temporary concentration camps all over Singapore, which were mass screening centres for the locals. Many thousands of Chinese, mostly men, were rounded up into public squares or sporting venues. They had little food and water and most were exposed to the glare of the tropical sun. Healthy males from the mid-teens up were ordered to one side if they were thought to be agitators, had supported the British or simply had the potential to be a threat to the Japanese because of their age and stamina. Small boys and old men were among those allowed to go free. The Japanese aim was to secure Singapore employing the least number of troops, as every available soldier was needed in future operations.

To gain freedom Chinese men had to pass before a table at which sat a Japanese Kempeitai officer surrounded by armed soldiers. Those allowed to pass to freedom left with an 'examined' chop or stamp on the arm, face or clothing. Chan Cheng Yean, who had served in the Malacca Volunteer Corps, who was arrested, was one of the rare survivors of the massacres that followed. He was crammed into a truck with many others, all with hands tied behind their backs. They were taken to Bedok and pushed down into a broad trench, as Chan recalled:

The order came and then they just shoot. Bang! The second time they shot, bang! Up to about three times. So all those who died would fall down. I was hit on my knee. Suddenly, I remember that I am still alive. So when the first man dropped dead, I followed him. Then the third man covered me on top.

The mass murders were spread over at least eleven massacre sites. Changi Beach was a major site for execution. Chinese men were constantly herded into the sea and cut down by machine-gun fire. In some cases Japanese officers encouraged young soldiers to use the Chinese prisoners for bayonet or target practice. A small number were tied up and buried alive. Others were beheaded with swords or taken offshore, weighted down and dropped overboard. Singapore's resort island, now called Sentosa, was a major killing field. For many days the bodies of the murdered Chinese washed up on Singapore's shores. The Japanese army later admitted to a preconceived plan to eliminate many thousands of Chinese men on Singapore. The Chinese in Singapore subsequently estimated that somewhere between 50,000 and 100,000 of their people were massacred by the Japanese, mostly between 18 February and 3 March 1942.

The bald-headed staff officer Colonel Masanobu Tsuji, a bellicose petty tyrant, was later named as the man who issued the orders for the Sook Ching massacres in Singapore, as well as for other significant war crimes elsewhere, including the Philippines. He often falsely used the names of more senior officers to carry out his purges. Tsuji would pose as a Buddhist monk to escape punishment after the war.

*

The Japanese, by taking Timor and effectively neutralising Darwin, ensured that no Allied reinforcements could reach Java from the south. The so-called Malay Barrier across south-east Asia down to northern Australia was rapidly disappearing. Many civilian and military escapees from Singapore and Sumatra had made their way to Batavia (now Jakarta) on Java. But Sumatra and Java were being bombed and were clearly next on the Japanese invasion list. Two days after Singapore surrendered, some of the Australian troops returning from the Middle East – including the 2/2nd and 2/3rd Machine Gun Battalion and 2/6th Field Company – arrived in Sumatra before going on to Batavia. The Australian troops, as well as a battery of American artillery and a squadron from the 3rd King's Own Hussars, combined to defend the huge island of Java. They became known as Black Force under Brigadier Arthur Blackburn, who had won the Victoria Cross at Pozières, France, in 1916. There were also some 25,000 Dutch troops in Java, many of them indigenous soldiers, who were well equipped but poorly trained and ineffective.

General Wavell, in the hill country well inland from Batavia, recommended to his chiefs of staff in London that the ABDA Command now be dissolved and removed from the East Indies, given the rapid Japanese expansion. The chiefs agreed and Wavell and his headquarters staff were ordered to leave Java for India, where he would become commander-in-chief. Before Wavell flew out, he instructed that Java be defended to the last man.

A motley fleet of naval ships from the Netherlands, the United States, Britain and Australia, under a Dutchman who had never commanded a fleet before, Rear Admiral K.W. Doorman, had been hastily fashioned to challenge any Japanese invasion convoy heading to the East Indies. Soon two such convoys were approaching Java, one close to Batavia and the other 400 miles (644 kilometres) away approaching the north coast. Doorman had taken out his eastern force, comprising the Dutch cruisers the *De Ruyter* and the *Java*, the American cruiser the *Houston*, the British cruiser the *Exeter*, and the Australian cruiser HMAS *Perth*. They were escorted by nine destroyers and had never before operated together as a fleet. Most ships had no radar and communications between them was poor. They reached the Japanese convoy and escorts on 27 February and a fierce battle ensued, with the Dutch cruisers, the *De Ruyter* and the *Java*, being sunk.

After the battle, on the night of 28 February, the *Houston* and the *Perth* unexpectedly came across the Japanese convoy landing its troops. A fierce exchange of prolonged firepower followed in what became known as the Battle of the Sunda Strait. The two Allied cruisers were heavily outgunned by the larger Japanese fleet. Japanese destroyers attacked from all directions, firing torpedoes. Little damage was done to the *Perth* until the very end of the action. Around midnight the *Perth*'s gunnery officer, Lieutenant Commander P. S. Hancox, of Hobart, told Captain Hec Waller on the bridge that very few six-inch (15-centimetre) shells remained. Waller decided to force a passage through Sunda Strait and ordered full speed ahead. He was hunted by the Japanese destroyers. The *Perth* had barely steadied on the course when, at five minutes past midnight, a torpedo slammed into the cruiser's starboard side. The report came to the captain: 'Forward engine room out . . . speed reduced.' Waller merely said 'Very good!' as the *Perth* ploughed on. A few minutes later Hancox told Waller that ammunition was almost expended. The turrets now were firing useless practice shells and the four-inch (10-centimetre) guns were equally reduced to star shells. Waller again said, 'Very good.' Then a second torpedo hit under the bridge, also on the starboard side. Waller exclaimed 'Christ! That's torn it . . . Abandon ship.' Hancox asked, '*Prepare* to abandon ship?'

'No! Abandon ship!'

The *Perth* was repeatedly smashed by shells while the men abandoned ship. Able seaman Frank McGovern, twenty-three, of Sydney, felt a torpedo almost lift the ship out of the water. He was thrown off his feet and recalled the heat from the torpedo blast feeling like opening a furnace door. The ship was in a pathetic state. Lots of men on the signal deck were killed or wounded. Wearing a Mae West life jacket, McGovern went over the side:

The next minute I was sucked under the ship because one of the screws was still slowly turning and as I came down under the stern of the ship I could see these huge blades coming down, then I was dragged in and tumbled about, like in a giant washing machine . . .

McGovern was expelled from the wash and somehow made it to a lifeboat. He was eventually picked up with other seamen by a Japanese destroyer.

Many on the *Perth* were killed or wounded in the water by exploding shells, and by the third and fourth torpedoes that crashed into the *Perth*, causing her to roll over. Waller and Hancox were among those who went down with the ship. The *Perth* lost 357 men. Of the estimated 320 who survived and became prisoners of war of the Japanese, 106 died in captivity. McGovern and many others from the *Perth* worked on the infamous Thai–Burma railway and were eventually sent to Japan. En route, the ship he was on was torpedoed causing a great loss of life among Allied prisoners. McGovern survived, but was forced into slave labour. The American cruiser the *Houston* was also sunk. Of the ship's complement of 1061 men, 368 survived the sinking. Captain Albert H. Rooks went down with his ship. The heavy cruiser HMS *Exeter* was sunk in the Java Sea on 1 March after coming under attack from the overwhelming forces.

A few days later the sloop HMAS *Yarra* was ordered to escort the depot ship the *Anking*, the tanker the *Francol* and a minesweeper convoy from Tjilatjap on Java's south coast to Fremantle. Dawn on 4 March revealed the topmasts of Japanese ships steaming in from the north-east. The squadron consisted of three heavy cruisers, each armed with ten eight-inch (20-centimetre) guns, plus two destroyers. Commander Robert Rankin on the small sloop made a sighting report, ordered the other ships to scatter and laid smoke in a vain attempt to escape. He then daringly turned the *Yarra* towards the three cruisers and prepared to engage.

The *Yarra*'s small guns were no match for three of the most powerful ships in the Japanese fleet. The cruisers opened fire while remaining outside the *Yarra*'s range and their shells quickly destroyed the sloop's engine room and steering. The ships that the *Yarra* had been escorting were sunk. The *Yarra* continued firing, despite listing heavily to port and drifting helplessly. Just minutes after Rankin gave the order to abandon ship he was killed when a salvo destroyed the bridge. The *Yarra* sank following a further barrage of close-range fire from the destroyers. In a final act of defiance, leading seaman Ronald Taylor ignored Rankin's order, manned a four-inch gun mount and continued firing as the ship went under. Survivors of HMS *Stronghold*, sunk two days earlier in the same area, looked on as prisoners aboard the Japanese cruiser the *Maya*. Much later they reported:

> We were taken on deck and shown, as they tried to impress us, the might of Japan's navy. The *Yarra* was the only ship left afloat, and we could see flames and a great deal of smoke. The two destroyers were circling *Yarra* which appeared stationary, and were pouring fire into her. She was still firing back as we could see odd gun flashes.

Navy signallers tried to make contact with the *Perth* and the *Yarra* for over a week without success. Prime Minister Curtin, rocked by the disappearances, finally made a statement:

> In view of the circumstances surrounding operations in that area, it is with deep regret that I announce that those two ships must be presumed lost . . .

*

Japanese forces began large-scale landings from the sea on the island of Sumatra in the Dutch East Indies and were soon advancing towards the significant oil production centre of Palembang, in southern Sumatra. The Japanese had already captured oil fields on Borneo.

The enemy's Western Force landed in Java in three places closer to Batavia and advanced quickly on the city. The remnants of the Dutch, British and Australian air forces tried to oppose the Japanese landings, but suffered severe losses against stronger numbers.

Black Force, consisting of 3000 Australians, had been intended to protect and defend airfields. But it was seen that they would be quickly overrun, so Brigadier Blackburn formed them into offensive fighting forces. Initially Blackburn concentrated his meagre force in the cool mountainous country about Bandung. But, acting partly on medical advice about the effects on his troops of fighting in the hills without shelter from chill wind and downpours, he moved his force to Tjikadjang, covering the roads leading to the island's south coast. Superior numbers of Japanese quickly began overrunning Java. Black Force faced shortages of munitions, medicines and food, and in time Brigadier Blackburn felt compelled to surrender to the Japanese, who had swept into Bandung on 12 March. Thirty-six of his men had been killed and sixty wounded. Blackburn was sent to Singapore as a prisoner of war. Dutch resistance to the Japanese quickly crumbled, and the long Netherlands rule of the great islands of what is now Indonesia came to an end on March 8. The Dutch East Indies campaign, with the small exception of the Australian and Dutch guerrillas holding out in places like Timor, had come to an end.

At home Army Minister Frank Forde announced that casualties in the AIF campaign in Malaya and Singapore were higher than the total casualties suffered by the AIF in the Middle East. Although the figures were preliminary, Forde estimated that the casualty figure, which included prisoners of war, was more than 17,000. Casualties in the Middle East had been over 13,000.

A more realistic picture of the number of Australians initially captured by the Japanese would emerge later. The capture of Java in March 1942 had left an army of Allied prisoners, including many Australians. About 15,000 Australians had been captured in Singapore, 2736 in Java, 1137 in Timor, 1075 in Ambon and 1049 in New Britain after fleeing Rabaul. The effect on the Australian nation and the government of all the Australians missing in Japanese-occupied areas was tremendous. People clamoured to get news of their loved ones. Every city, countless towns and families on remote properties were swept up in the great tragedy.

After the fall of Singapore most Australian prisoners had been force-marched to Changi, on the north-eastern tip of the Singapore island, to the large barracks, formerly occupied by the British garrison and partly destroyed by Japanese bombing, and to the jail there. Quarters were grossly overcrowded. Life at first was relatively calm in comparison to the slave labour of many prisoners in the jungles of Asia. There were few fences and the prisoners could wander about, sometimes growing their own food to supplement a poor diet and occasionally setting fishing traps. But as the number of prisoners increased, amenities broke down and food became short. In the tropical heat flies fed by Singapore's corpses, offal, rotting garbage and unprotected latrines, bred in their thousands. Outbreaks of diarrhoea and dysentery began within a fortnight of the arrival of the Australians at Changi. Gunner Russell Braddon, captured after the Muar Battle, described Changi as 'a holiday camp' in comparison with what he and thousands of others were to experience in the living hell of the primitive death camps in the jungle along the infamous Thai–Burma railway. But Changi was no holiday camp once conditions deteriorated and the brutality of the Japanese began to be felt.

*

Burma had been a theatre of war neglected by Britain. The Japanese had begun their assault on southern Burma through Thailand from mid-January. No adequate steps had been taken to build up the forces required to repel a comparatively small Japanese force on the Thai border. Further, there were no fewer than six changes to the British command structure in charge of Burma operations over a short period.

Prior to the fall of Singapore, when Lieutenant General Sir Henry Pownall had been chief of staff to Wavell, Pownall wrote in his diary that the British should abandon Burma:

> there's no doubt that Burma is very thinly held and it should be packed up as soon as possible. We have no resources to give them and don't propose to direct anything from a Malayan convoy where the danger is much more pressing.

But a few weeks later Churchill suddenly elevated Burma to paramount importance at a new Pacific War Council established in London. On 20 January Churchill had told his chief military assistant and staff officer, General Hastings Ismay, that as a strategic object he regarded keeping the Burma Road open as 'more important than the retention of Singapore'.

The battle for Burma, according to Churchill, produced 'a painful episode in our relations with the Australian Government and their refusal of our requests for aid'. Churchill feared that the capture of Burma would give the Japanese a gateway to India. He was also most anxious to react to the wishes of President Roosevelt to maintain the American supply line over the Burma Road to the Chinese Nationalist forces of Chiang Kai-shek that were fighting the Japanese in China. The Far Eastern supreme commander, General Sir Archibald Wavell, had formed two scratch British divisions, the 1st Burma and 17th Indian, to stop Japanese advances in Burma. In the second week of February, Wavell, after visiting the Burma front, wrote that 'all commanders expressed themselves to me as confident of their ability to deal with the Japanese advance'.

The new British forces in Burma, like the British 18th Division sent too late to Singapore, were raw, lacked combat experience and were mostly inadequately trained and equipped. Apart from two experienced light tank regiments and an infantry battalion brought in from the Middle East, no other reinforcements were likely to reach Burma. With this in mind Churchill turned to Australia's manpower resources once more. The Australian 6th and 7th divisions AIF, comprising 17,800 battle-hardened troops, had been withdrawn from the Middle East on various ships between late January and early March. Plans changed with Japanese advances while the men were at sea. The 6th Division was intended to go to central Java while the 7th was meant to go to southern Sumatra. But when the East Indies archipelago was in immediate danger of collapse, Australia wanted the majority of the 17,800 servicemen back in Australia for jungle training and redeployment, especially to New Guinea. Churchill in his memoirs lays claim to proposing the withdrawal from the Middle East of what he called 'the best Australian divisions'. During his war cabinet meeting of 27 January 1942 at Whitehall, Churchill had supported the return of these troops as being necessary for the defence of Australia, as the war cabinet minutes record:

The prime minister said that it went without saying that the Australian troops and air squadrons serving overseas must move homewards to the defence of their own country, now that danger threatened it.

But Churchill rapidly changed his mind about the seriousness of the danger threatening Australia. The Burma situation was deteriorating quickly and Churchill had new priorities. On the night of 18 February 1942, Australia's special envoy to Britain, Sir Earle Page, reported that the newly formed Pacific War Council in London had decided to ask the Australian Government to agree to the 7th Division being diverted to Burma. Page said that apart from the 7th, the remainder of the Australians returning from the Middle East could proceed to Australia. Prime Minister Churchill, Page said, had assured him that 'very substantial air reinforcements' would be sent to Australia.

Churchill cabled Curtin on 20 February. It was an inopportune time – the day after the first major attack on Darwin:

> I suppose you realise that your leading division, the head of which is sailing south of Colombo to the Netherlands East Indies at this moment in our scanty British and American shipping, is the only force that can reach Rangoon in time to prevent its loss and the severance of communications with China. It can begin to disembark at Rangoon about 26th or 27th. There is nothing else in the world that can fill the gap.

Churchill now told Curtin that 'we are all entirely in favour of all Australian troops returning home', but a vital war emergency could not be ignored. Churchill even bluntly warned Curtin that Roosevelt would not be pleased with a refusal:

> I am quite sure that if you refuse to allow your troops which are actually passing to stop this gap . . . a very grave effect will be produced upon the president and the Washington circle, on whom you are so largely dependent.

Churchill immediately sought and got Roosevelt's support for this reinforcement plan using Australian troops, adding the words 'in view of your offer of American troops to help defend Australia'. Roosevelt subsequently informed Curtin that if Burma went, it would seem that the whole position, including Australia, would be in extreme peril. Curtin responded that if his government allowed one division to go to Burma, the 7th Division AIF, inevitably there would be calls for the extra support from the whole Australian army corps returning from the Middle East. Because Japan had control of the sea and air in the region, Australia considered that Churchill's request was not a reasonable hazard of war. With that Curtin turned down the request. Churchill then took an extraordinary decision without consultation, as Churchill blandly states in his memoirs: 'Meanwhile, assuming a favourable response, I had diverted the Australian convoy to Rangoon.' He told Curtin on 22 February:

> We could not contemplate that you would refuse our request, and that of the president of the United States, for the diversion of the leading Australian division to save the situation in Burma.

Curtin, still ill, was outraged because he keenly felt that Australia's survival was at stake. If ever there was an example of Churchill dismissing Australia as little more than a subservient colony, it was this. As Curtin saw it, Australia's outer defences were quickly crumbling. Malaya, Singapore and Java were gone or going, and now Churchill contemplated using the AIF to save Burma. All this had to be done, as in Greece and Crete, without adequate air support. Curtin responded curtly to Churchill:

> It appears that you have diverted the convoy towards Rangoon and had treated our approval to this vital diversion as merely a matter of form . . . We feel a primary obligation to save Australia not only for itself, but to preserve it as a base for the development of the war against Japan. In the circumstances it is quite

impossible to reverse a decision which we made with the utmost care, and which we have affirmed and reaffirmed.

In a cable to Australia's General Sir Thomas Blamey, then Allied deputy commander-in-chief in the Middle East, Curtin explained his actions:

Briefly put, as Malaya and Singapore have gone and the Netherlands East Indies is indefensible, both the bastion of Empire defence in the south-western Pacific and the outer screen to Australia leave Australia bare.

The issue of what to do about Churchill diverting the Australian division to Burma at the last minute divided members of the Advisory War Council, which included opposition members who wavered and even Australia's defence chiefs of staff, both groups recommending differing and confusing courses of action. The conservatives on the council felt the need to assist Britain once more. The decision eventually fell to Curtin alone. At this critical time the *Sun Pictorial*'s political reporter in Canberra, Harold Cox, bumped into Curtin late one night crossing the almost deserted King's Hall in Parliament House, as Cox recalled:

Curtin looked the picture of a complete physical wreck and I said to him 'You're overdoing it. You look dreadful. I've never seen you look worse and I think you ought to go home and get a good sleep tonight.'

Curtin made it plain that he was desperate about the returning 7th Division. According to Cox, the prime minister replied:

I'm not going to get any sleep tonight . . . I can't get any unanimity of opinion on what we should do, but by six o'clock in the morning they will have reached the point of no return. I've got to go home and between now and six o'clock I've got to decide the message I'm going to send.

Curtin walked towards the government lobby, stopped and called to Cox, 'Harold! What would you do if you knew their equipment was on another convoy two days behind them?' He didn't wait for an answer and disappeared into the lobby. Cox said that by coincidence, he met Curtin again in much the same circumstances the next night:

> He was a changed man. I said 'You look a lot better tonight.' He said 'Yes, I feel a lot better too. They're coming home!'

Curtin's relief was cautious and brief. He now feared for the safety of the thousands of Australian AIF soldiers in troopships heading home. At this time the prime minister's driver, Ray Tracey, also was deeply worried about Curtin's health and wellbeing. They played billiards together at the Lodge. Tracey had quietly spoken with the clerk of the House of Representatives, Frank Green, an old friend of Curtin's from Perth:

> . . . Ray Tracey came to me to express his concern that Curtin had not been to bed for some days and spent each night walking about the grounds of the Lodge.

Green said the 7th Division was still at sea on its way from the Bay of Bengal to Fremantle. Curtin agonised at the thought of the Australian troops without adequate escort protection passing through dangerous seas with the enemy lurking. Frank Green described Curtin as 'living on his nerves':

> That night the House sat until midnight, and on my way home I entered the grounds of the Lodge and walked round until I met Curtin face to face. I asked him what was the matter, but he did not answer me. We stood in silence in the darkness for some minutes, and then he said: 'How can I sleep with our men in the Indian Ocean among enemy submarines?' I tried to talk him into getting some sleep, but the best I could achieve was to walk with him up to the kitchen of the Lodge where I made some tea.

When Stanley Bruce, Australia's High Commissioner in London, saw a copy of Churchill's cable to Curtin, he told Curtin that it was 'arrogant and offensive' and contradicted assurances given to Australia's special envoy, Sir Earle Page, that the convoy of Australian AIF troops would not be diverted. Nevertheless, Bruce in fact supported Churchill in the diversion of Australian troops to Burma. To Curtin he now urged restraint, citing Churchill's current anxiety after discussing the Burma issue with the British lord privy seal, Sir Stafford Cripps:

> He stressed the fact that at the moment the prime minister is so near the end of his tether owing to the strain of the war situation – the work involved in the Cabinet reconstruction and the preparation for Tuesday's critical [parliamentary] debate – that allowance must be made for the tone of his telegram.

Reinforced by Cripps's view, Bruce urged that despite Churchill's provocation, Curtin should maintain his usual 'admirable tone and reasoned argument' on the Burma issue.

Roosevelt contacted Curtin to say that he fully understood his position in relation to the Australian troops, even though he didn't wholly agree with it. He said he thought the main thrust at the moment was against the left flank, Burma, 'and that we can safely hold the Australian or right flank'. He therefore hoped Curtin would divert the second returning division to India or Burma. But as Churchill himself later admitted, 'no troops in our control could reach Rangoon in time to save it'. The Burmese capital Rangoon (now Yangon), north-west of Bangkok in Thailand, would fall to the Japanese on 7 March.

Curtin's special envoy in London, Page, also had supported Churchill's sudden diversion of Australian troops to Burma on the spurious grounds that it would 'strengthen our demands for similar action to meet Australia's own important requirements'. Churchill had put much pressure on Page over relief for Burma, which included sending a colonel around to him at the Dorchester with copies of his cables to and from President Roosevelt. Page in his memoirs would later claim that 'bold action through Burma could conceivably have relieved the agonies of thousands of Australian and British prisoners of war' and rescued Australian and British prestige. This was pure wishful thinking. Australian official war historian Lionel Wigmore said it would have been astonishing if the 7th Australian Division could have landed a brigade at Rangoon and successfully counterattacked against two seasoned Japanese divisions:

> It is even more doubtful whether, had the 7th Division done this, the success could have been maintained in the face of increasing Japanese air power and Japanese naval control of the eastern part of the Bay of Bengal and beyond.

The reason was that the Australians' supplies of fighting equipment had not been tactically loaded aboard the same ships as the troops, as Curtin had said. According to Lieutenant General Sir John Lavarack this meant that it would have taken about three weeks to re-sort and rearm the units once they had arrived in Burma, by which time it would have been way too late. The British war historian Major General S. Woodburn Kirby estimated that in any case only one Australian brigade could have reached Rangoon before the port had to be abandoned. The last British commander in Burma before the fall of Rangoon, Lieutenant General Thomas Hutton, had warned British authorities that to send large convoys to Rangoon at that late hour would incur a 'very considerable risk' from a well-established enemy air force. According to Kirby, Hutton 'could not promise that the presence of part or all of the Australian division would in fact change the course of events at the last moment.'

General Sir Henry Pownall, chief of staff ABDA Command, would soon leave General Wavell's headquarters at Lembang near Bandung, south-east of Batavia, to command in Ceylon (now Sri Lanka.) Even Pownall, who was close to Churchill and who disliked Curtin, wrote in his diary on 25 February that he also doubted the Australians could ever have saved Burma, despite all of Churchill's fulminations:

Three or four days ago Winston diverted the 7th Division convoy northwards, whilst the argument went on, and in so daring Curtin to demand them back. However, Curtin dared and back they have been turned. I don't know if they would have arrived in time to save Rangoon. I rather doubt it now for things have gone very badly there in the last few days, but Winston has certainly got a big stick to beat the Australian with now, and he'll do it.

If the Australians weren't so damn well pleased with themselves all the time, and so highly critical of everyone else, it would be a bit better. But they are the most egotistical conceited people imaginable. I sincerely hope I shall have nothing further to do with them.

His petulance aside, on Pownall's reckoning the Australians, if landed at Rangoon, stood an excellent chance of being killed or captured. The likelihood of them being rescued would have been slight. As Curtin had indicated, once the first disorganised shiploads of Australians had come under intense attack, many in Australia would have felt obliged to divert more and more AIF ships to Burma to assist the Diggers in trouble. By any measure, Curtin's decision was correct.

On the eve of his own escape from the Dutch East Indies to Ceylon, Pownall demonstrated his own and Churchill's antagonism towards the Curtin Government's insistence on having the final say on Australian troop movements. He was outraged that the Australians wanted to evacuate from Java as the Japanese were overwhelming the Allies:

To the last the Australian Government kept up their damnable attitude, practically demanding that these [troops] should be removed. Wavell sent a pretty warm telegram back saying that his instructions were that fighting troops were to remain here to fight . . .

How the Australians have shown up in their true colours. Not so much the troops and commanders themselves (though some of the latter have very distinct signs of 'separatism') as their Government, actuated presumably by a mixture of public opinion in Australia and common funk. Winston had little enough use for them before,

especially after they demanded to be relieved at Tobruk, to everyone's great inconvenience. He'll be madder still now.

General Pownall said the Curtin Government's problem was
that it was 'in actual terror of being invaded themselves', although
he admitted that Darwin might be taken:

The Japs are a long way from bringing that on yet anywhere that
matters, though they might have a crack at Darwin, a sufficiently
useless place for them.

He added another sniping comment: 'As for the soldiers, they
don't fight as much as they talk about fighting.'

*

Curtin might well have been in a state of 'funk' – a state of fright
or terror – to use Pownall's word, in reaction to the Japanese
threat. Curtin personally had no doubt that Australia was in the
most imminent peril of invasion. The senior political reporter of
the Melbourne *Herald*, Joe Alexander, and his senior colleagues in
Canberra, met with the prime minister almost daily and received
secret intelligence from him, not for publication:

Curtin summonsed the 'travelling circus' to his office and ...
produced this great pile of cables between himself and Churchill
and although we were staggered at the idea of Curtin opposing the
will of a man like Churchill at a time like this, we all felt, I think,
proud of him, because he was determined to put Australia first.

While Curtin called for public calm and no panic, he worried
anxiously about the troops fighting for Australia and the population generally. But this dread, according to his daughter Elsie,
extended to his family and his own fate:

... I suppose really he probably could see what would happen
if the Japanese had won, then they would have crucified him.

I don't think Dad would have ever pretended to be the greatest hero in the world. The Irish are either devil-may-care or they're the other way. I think it was a big worry to him, a worry in all respects I think with his nature, that didn't help him . . .

The 7th Division arrived intact in Adelaide in March and quickly went into training for jungle warfare in Queensland, before being posted to Port Moresby in September 1942.

*

With Japan on the rampage in the Pacific, in Washington Brigadier General Dwight D. Eisenhower of the War Plans Division had begun to have regrets about large scale military involvements that did not involve the war in Europe. At the direction of President Roosevelt, Eisenhower had sent a message to the besieged General Douglas MacArthur on Corregidor Island in Manila Bay, directing the general to start south to take command of the Australian area. But Eisenhower had 'always been fearful of this plan' which would draw the United States into the south-west Pacific. He wrote in his diary that the United States had 'dilly dallied' about Burma, India and China. Now, with Singapore gone and the East Indies practically gone, 'and the Japs free to move as they please, we're getting scared':

Circumstances are going to pull us too strongly to the Australian area. We've got to keep Russia in the war and hold India. Then we can get ready to crack Germany through England.

Eisenhower's plan by the end of February was very much a 'holding war' in the Pacific so the United States could 'devote its major offensive effort across the Atlantic'. As 1942 went on, Eisenhower would conform even further to the 'Beat Hitler First' policy. In May he would even flick back over the pages of his diary and insert the following words under his entry for 22 January 1942, at a time when his views were quite different:

We've got to go to Europe and fight, and we've got to quit wasting resources all over the world, and still worse, wasting time . . .

Prime Minister Churchill's mind, too, was always concentrating on limiting the need for reinforcements in the Far East and the Pacific in order to focus fully on Germany. Churchill would always draw a line between *invasion in force*, and *raids* on Australia. Despite his remonstrations to Curtin and in public, Churchill's private statements in February 1942 began to reveal that he himself had genuine cause for worry about Australia's safety from the Japanese. In fact it is clear that he believed the Japanese would probably establish bases in northern Australia, a belief based on British defence assessments. The first of these private admissions came when the prime minister had his weekly lunch with King George VI to report on the war's progress. The King at Buckingham Palace received copies of all of the major war communications read by Churchill, including some of those to and from Curtin. On 24 February Churchill, in a despondent mood, told the King:

Burma, Ceylon, Calcutta and Madras in India, and part of Australia, may fall in to enemy hands.

The sovereign recorded these words in his diary, which is now in the archives in Windsor Castle. It was a private admission that Churchill had never intimated to Curtin. King George stated that he responded:

Can we stick together in the face of all this adversity? We must somehow.

Then four days later King George wrote in his diary:

I cannot help feeling depressed at the future outlook. Anything can happen, and it will be wonderful if we can be lucky anywhere.

The British monarch's representative in Australia, Governor-General Lord Gowrie wrote a concerned letter from Canberra to King George on 27 February 1942 saying that at the opening of the war the great majority of the people had been fully convinced that Japan would not dare go to war and that Australia would never be seriously attacked:

> but events in Hong Kong, Malaya, Borneo, New Guinea and the loss of Singapore and the air raid on Darwin have had a very steadying effect, and people are realising at last that attack, or invasion of Australia, is a possibility that may occur in the near future.

Lord Gowrie said the increased threat had enabled the Australian Government to take measures they 'could not have contemplated' before. Curtin knew he must go further. He was talking in particular about military conscription. Gowrie saw the proposals as drastic but wise measures that only a Labor government could enforce, given the history of the conscription debate during the First World War:

> The Government have taken power to transfer workers from one industry to another, which virtually means conscription of labour, and although the word 'conscription' has to be studiously avoided, as it would revive an old and very bitter controversy, conscription in effect though not in name, is being gradually introduced, both in war industries and the Defence Forces.

The political activist who fought tooth and nail against conscription in the First World War was now manoeuvring to introduce military conscription. According to the Defence Act the CMF could not be employed outside Australian territory, but, as Gowrie explained, if the necessity arose Curtin planned to proclaim certain areas such as Java and the Pacific islands part of the defence zone of Australia and issue regulations enabling the militia to occupy those areas without requiring a special act of parliament. Curtin felt it was preposterous that Australia would rely on conscripted American troops to fight the Japanese in places that could threaten Australia, while Australian conscripts could not be used.

*

Prime Minister Curtin had genuine cause for his anxiety about Japan and continued his forceful calls for assistance from Australia's allies. By late February 1942 his views on the extent of the threat were shared by Australia's three defence chiefs of staff – General Sir Sydney Rowell, Air Chief Marshall Charles Burnett and Admiral Sir Guy Royle – as well as the governor-general, Lord Gowrie. Soon General Sir Thomas Blamey and General Douglas MacArthur would also share Curtin's apprehension, regardless of British opinion. Australia's army, navy and air force were in a woeful state to meet the enemy.

Chapter 10

THE LAST BASTION

After rapid successes in first stage operations Japanese war planners debated the possibilities of further expeditions. The Imperial Navy planning staff once again sought to press for more aggressive action across the Pacific. On 27 February 1942 an important two-day meeting that would affect the future of Australia and many other regions in the Pacific began at the ornately baroque three-storey mansion the *Suikosha*, or Navy Officers' Club in Tokyo. The club, occasionally visited by the Emperor, had a rich history. It staged its own sumo wrestling competitions, was the site for many naval officers' wedding receptions and had its own adjoining Shinto shrine.

The conference involved senior officers of the war operations sections of the Imperial Navy and the Imperial Army. On the first day, army and navy representatives clashed in lengthy debate about Japan's war aims for the second stage of offensive operations. The debate opened with discussion about the proposed invasion of Hawaii, originally instigated by the planners in Admiral Yamamoto's Combined Fleet. Without agreement on Hawaii, the conversation soon moved to the issue of Australia. Planners with Yamamoto's seaborne Combined Fleet were now supported by Navy General Staff operational planners, based in Tokyo, to consider an invasion of Australia somewhere along the northern portion of the east coast. The aim was to eliminate Australia as a potential springboard for a counteroffensive by the Allies. But Army General Staff representatives argued strongly that an invasion of Australia was foolhardy and could bog down Japanese forces in a war of attrition on the Australian continent. According to minutes, the army representatives this time were adamant that the invasion should not proceed:

This operation is not an absolute imperative for prosecuting the war. It is an effective step, but it will not decide the fate of U.K. or the U.S. Neither does it have particularly great value in bringing the Empire to a position of self-sufficiency and self-reliance.

According to investigations into the feasibility of the operation, it will require at least 10 divisions, but these cannot be spared. At present, Australia is judged to have 300,000 (Caucasian) troops, and can mobilise 600,000. As a comparison with recent operations, there were 130,000 Japanese troops to 70,000 enemy troops in the Malaya campaign; 75,000 Japanese to 100,000 in the Philippines campaign; and 50,000 Japanese to 70,000 in the Netherlands East Indies campaign.

It is not possible to field sufficient troops to face 600,000 Australian troops. If we do field enough troops to Australia, Japan will be threatened to the north. We will also need 2,000,000 tons of shipping. Because of the long distances involved, the operation would probably require more shipping than even this.

The Japanese estimates were excessive. At the end of 1941 the total number in the Australian armed forces, including 64,000 men overseas in the 6th and 7th Divisions, was 431,300. Not until the end of 1942 would there be some 160,000 US personnel in Australia and New Guinea. Australia's army chief of staff, General Sturdee, had described troops in Australia generally as 'untrained and ill-equipped', while the country's three chiefs of staff had said that if Japan had invaded, it was 'clearly beyond Australia's capacity' to meet an attack of the size the Japanese could mount. Many of those servicemen in Australia were still undergoing training. The likelihood was that if the Japanese had landed in force in northern Australia, they could have established themselves in sufficient time, before the overwhelming build-up of American forces and aircraft in Australia. From Darwin the Japanese could have staged successful bombing raids on key targets in the south. The United States in such a scenario might have accelerated the despatch of bombers to Australia. At the minimum, successful landings would have delayed the Allies' eventual push northwards through New Guinea.

Australia's future was on the agenda again in Tokyo on the following day, 28 February 1942, when navy and army officers together with ministry officials gathered for the 90th liaison conference in Tokyo. On this occasion the Prime Minister General Hideki Tojo was present. The meeting heard that oil production in both Malaya and Brunei on Borneo was now almost completely restored and production quotas were looking promising. The isolation of Australia and India from America and England, as the Japanese called Britain, was one of the main issues on the agenda. A research paper pointed out that although Australia traditionally relied on England, it had gradually become very close to America. Australia's industry, the research showed, consisted largely of 'primitive things', and its defence industry now depended entirely on America. The relationship between England and Australia was said to be relatively weak and the loss of India and Australia would be 'a big psychological blow to England'. Listening to the report was the Imperial Navy's senior representative, a man with close cropped hair and a semi-permanent supercilious look on his face, the chief of the Naval Affairs Bureau of the Navy Ministry, Rear Admiral Takasumi Oka. He had taken a strong role in formulating Japan's aggressive war policy in China. Oka wondered if merely quarantining Australia was sufficient. He made a suggestion:

To the extent of destroying commerce, complete isolation would be quite difficult if we did not completely occupy Australia.

The meeting went on to discuss Japan's various new and proposed domains and which should be allocated into defence spheres, co-prosperity spheres and resource spheres, ranging from occupation of foreign lands to enforced economic cooperation. Lieutenant General Akira Muto was the army's chief of the Military Affairs Bureau. Muto had taken part in the Rape of Nanking in 1937. He was keen to see Australia brought under Japan's influence:

> National defence spheres ought to be clearly decided. Once that is done Australia and India ought to be strategic spheres, and we should make a move when necessary.

Prime Minister Tojo urged the group to research what areas should fall into what spheres:

> we must start to realise that if we have a shortage in resources we should cover it somehow within the sphere.

It was agreed that more research must be undertaken, but some decisions were made, including this agreement:

> The Imperial resources sphere will be Japan, Manchuria and China and the South Pacific territories, and Australia and India will be supplementary spheres.

Tojo expressed uneasiness about navy proposals to invade Australia because of the enormous resources required, which would detract from other operations. But navy minister, Admiral Shigetaro Shimada, did not want to exclude capturing Australia as an important resource sphere:

> Because the construction of the new order in East Asia starts from the psychology of liberation for the peoples of East Asia, it would not be pertinent to exclude India and Australia; it is not possible to agree to the proposition of excluding territories that we could

take in to our hands now when we cannot see how the war situation will develop.

Shimada was under considerable pressure from his fiery operational planning staff to invade Australia. Captain Toshikazu Ohmae was an officer in charge of missions and movements of ships within the Naval Affairs Bureau. He served as a staff officer on several of Japan's important fleets. Ohmae thought the Imperial Navy's plans to invade Australia had little to do with gaining further natural resources, as he much later would explain:

It was thought that such key areas as Darwin in the north and Townsville, Brisbane and Sydney on the east coast should be occupied. The Navy was responsible for New Guinea, New Britain and the Solomons and Australia figured heavily in its plans ... By invading Australia the supply of war materials, particularly airplanes, gas and oil which had already begun to flow from the United States, would be stopped.

*

In late February 1942 the Governor-General Lord Gowrie wrote to King George VI pinning his hopes on reinforcements from America:

a large quantity of men, munitions and aeroplanes will before long reach these shores and even one month's grace would make a great deal of difference to our powers of resistance, and by the beginning of May we should be a good deal stronger still, and should be in a position to hit back with considerable force.

The question was, could Australia hold out until May? Gowrie was by no means sure. He told the King he had no doubt that every effort would be made to 'render Australia unserviceable' by aerial attacks on the great industrial centres, docks and harbours:

And although invasion with the object of occupation of the whole of Australia might not be undertaken, landings in certain portions of the Northern Territory or Queensland may occur and land attacks on vital points carried out from these areas. But should invasion of Australia occur, Your Majesty may be assured that the Australian people will fight it out to the bitter end . . .

There was much debate and hesitancy by America before US reinforcements in strength would be authorised for Australia. In Washington on 28 February, the US army's assistant chief of staff, Brigadier General Eisenhower, sent off recommendations for 'strategic conceptions' for the south-west Pacific to his boss, the chief of staff, General George C. Marshall. To summarise the nine-page document, it is sufficient to say that the security of Australia was a long way down his list of priorities. Worse, Eisenhower said the collapse of the defences in Malaya and productive parts of the Dutch East Indies meant that one of the reasons for the original US decision to support the south-west Pacific had disappeared:

We must now face the fact that Japan controls ample sources of oil and tin and practically the entire rubber resources of the world. Thus, reasons for expanding our forces into the far south west Pacific are, in this respect, less compelling than they were two months ago.

Eisenhower wanted the United States to maintain safe lines of communication to Australia but he thought there were many higher priorities. He was trying to minimalise the role of American forces in Australia and he recommended as much to General Marshall:

Limit Army commitments to Southwest Pacific to [US] forces already arrived or planned for that area.

*

When the Rabaul survivors, among them men from Victoria in the 2/22nd Battalion, reached Port Moresby, they were allowed to send brief messages home to their loved ones. Private Charles Cummins was brief: 'Left Rabaul 23-2-42 and am still running, CHC August 1942.' He would die from wounds in fighting in the Aitape region of New Guinea in December 1944. Private Val Glynn wrote simply, 'The man who raced the Japs from Rabaul and won easily, Stidger.' Sergeant Eric Blaby escaped the Rabaul area late, writing, 'Walked 300 miles. Little food. Lots of fun at times. Best of luck to those left.' Private Austin Judd had few words to say other than 'Happy days are here again.' Private Bill Witnish: 'Walked, Rode and Sailed 350 miles. Little food, many rivers, crocs and plenty rice. All the best to those left behind. Bill.' Private Hugh Webster: 'I'll tell you no'er of what I saw. Nipper, August 1942. Wounded twice by Japs.' Many, like Private Doug Yensch, were thinking of their mates who hadn't yet made it: 'Walked and staggered 400 miles. Sailed 50. Food little but enough. Best of luck to those left behind.'

In early March 1942 a group of five survivors from Lark Force, who had successfully escaped the Japanese at Rabaul, shuffled silently into the lounge room of a house in Port Moresby, some thirty-seven days after escaping from the Japanese. Waiting was a group of war correspondents who had set up a table with glasses and bottles of beer. Osmar White, from the Melbourne *Herald*, later an author, poured them a drink. The men looked ravaged. Only after a few beers did they feel comfortable enough to tell of their experiences during their trek over New Britain, which was followed by a boat journey to the mainland. Escaping through jungle, their clothes and boots became rotten with the unending mud and rain. Their feet got spongy and bled. Mosquitoes could be tolerated but the sand flies made them scratch until they couldn't stop, creating terrible sores. They said some of the Australians trying to flee were killed in crocodile and shark attacks while crossing estuaries:

There were always Japs on your heels. Often the sound men ended up as bad as their sick mates. A lot got malaria. They had to travel with it until they were raving. Then they'd lie up in a native village . . . The Japs took plenty of them that way. If you didn't like the idea you could always rig up a string between the trigger of your rifle and your big toe. One or two went out that way, poor devils.

Other stories of escape from Rabaul emerged. Lieutenant Bob Emery of the New Guinea Volunteer Rifles, who was almost killed in the bombing of Madang, had embarked on a journey with others from the mainland to find Australians who had escaped from Rabaul. They took a motor boat east over the Bismarck Sea through rough conditions and steamed down the remote north coast of New Britain:

When we went ashore we found there was about three or four hundred men, refugees, who had got this far from Rabaul . . . A lot of these army fellows were in very poor physical condition and some of them hardly had any clothes. They had left in such a hurry and they had come through some terrible country from Rabaul.

Emery met a fiery red-haired Irishman who would be much honoured for his daring and bravery, John McCarthy, a government officer, now coastwatcher, based at Talasea. McCarthy had prepared an escape route for the ragged bands of Australians, according to his boss, Commander Eric Feldt:

Though sufficiently fed, they were suffering from malaria and sores and were feeling hopeless, helpless and dispirited. Their ignorance of the country was their worst enemy . . . It was difficult to rouse the men out of their languid stupor. Most had given up and were prepared for anything except to make an effort on their own behalf.

McCarthy and Emery bullied, threatened and cajoled the escapees. They found a trading steamer, the *Lakatoi*, abandoned on a nearby island, and after a voyage through Japanese-patrolled waters, remarkably arrived safely in northern Australia.

*

Another escapee from the Japanese arrived in Melbourne. On 2 March Prime Minister Curtin welcomed the AIF commander in Malaya, Major General Gordon Bennett, into a meeting of the war cabinet at which the defence chiefs were also present. Bennett said that if there had been a greater number of AIF troops and more artillery available, Malaya might have been held. The AIF was otherwise well equipped. In his opinion, if Indian troops had been up to standard, the strength of forces would have been adequate. Bennett claimed the leadership of the British troops was poor:

Senior officers had a retreat complex and when they reached one position they looked to the next one back. The destruction of dumps in accordance with the scorched earth policy also affected the morale of troops.

Bennett said no attempt had been made to fortify Singapore. Curtin later publicly expressed confidence in Bennett. Knowing the controversy brewing around Bennett's departure from Singapore, he said:

He remained with his men until the end, completed all formalities in connection with the surrender, and then took the opportunity and risk of escaping.

Yet Bennett in leaving his men in Singapore did not have the confidence of the service chiefs, even though he was later posted to command in Western Australia. Before Bennett addressed the war cabinet he had gone to the office the chief of staff, General Sturdee, who carried on with his work at his desk, leaving Bennett to stand aside in his room like a schoolboy. Then, after a few minutes of formal conversation, Sturdee told Bennett his escape was 'ill-advised.'

*

Japanese aircraft attacked the north-west coast of Western Australia on Tuesday 3 March. The pearl-diving centre of Broome had become an entry port for thousands of evacuees, including women and children, fleeing the Japanese, who were in the process of capturing all of Java. Zero fighters from Timor fitted with long-range fuel tanks swooped down on the crowded Broome airstrip and on nearby Roebuck Bay. Once again lessons of dispersal had not been learned. An evacuation fleet of seaplanes had gathered, including 16 Dutch and Australian flying boats. In a short time many of the flying boats were on fire and sinking. An American Liberator with thirty-three sick and wounded servicemen was attacked flying near Broome. It exploded, broke in half and crashed into the bay. It was a scene of carnage. The Zeros swooped down on the flying boats, some of them crowded with refugees and about to take off, and attacked them with little opposition. The screams of the injured and drowning filled the air. Two Qantas men in a rowboat pulled aboard two Dutch aviators supporting a young woman. They then rescued another Dutch serviceman swimming on his back supporting a baby on his chest. An estimated seventy people were killed in the first raid on Broome and many others were injured in what became Australia's worst air raid after the initial attack on Darwin. The raid on Broome destroyed twenty-four aircraft, including sixteen flying boats.

A simultaneous raid was carried out on Wyndham, closer to Darwin, on the same day. A Department of Civil Aviation radio operator at the airstrip, Rod Torrington, was in his radio shack when he saw an RAAF man run past into the bush. He went outside and saw a line of Zeros coming straight for him so he too bolted, afraid that his white shirt, shorts and socks would give him away. Looking back, he saw a big stack of fuel drums on fire. The hangar and an RAAF Dragon biplane were also burning. He later found his radio equipment intact.

The Australians fought back with wherever they could with whatever aircraft they had. Lumbering RAAF Catalina flying boats performed extraordinary work, owing to their resilience and ability to stay in the air so long. Flying Officer Cliff Hull of 42 Squadron recalls dropping bombs on Japanese airfields at night. Over New Guinea, they dropped bombs and for the heck of it threw over the side beer bottles filled with old razor blades, which made a terrifying scream as they fell and were aimed at frightening the Japanese, if not hitting them. On another mission Hull dropped his first mine at night near a Japanese base at Makassar on the western side of the Celebes (Sulawesi) when his aircraft was hit:

> WHAM, we got hit in the starboard engine, and the navigator went on counting and we let the second mine go and then the flight engineer said again in a quiet voice, 'We've been hit, Cliff, and there's petrol streaming down inside.' And we were only about 200 feet above the water ...

The Catalina lost an engine and the plane was forced down, crash-landing on the surface, springing leaks. Next day they were rescued by a Catalina from 43 Squadron and flown to the base at Darwin, arriving home from their mission thirteen hours late, as Hull recalled:

> At that time this rescue was the longest air-sea rescue in the Pacific war and probably remains so. But it was a brilliant rescue.

*

In New Guinea, the situation for the Australians deteriorated rapidly. Bombing attacks were increasing on Port Moresby. Some 124 bombs were dropped in one air raid on the Seven Mile airfield on 28 February. Another attack on the harbour sank two RAAF Catalinas. Australian anti-aircraft gunners – barely trained youths – shot down a Japanese fighter on this day and the pilot was taken prisoner by the 39th Battalion. A war correspondent for the *Sydney Morning Herald* later described some of these anti-aircraft militia gunners as 'windy':

They will tell you now how one of the regular sergeants, who has been the backbone of this battery from the beginning, used to cuff the youngsters on the ears when some of them showed signs of taking shelter until they were more afraid of him than the Japanese.

Another war correspondent, Osmar White, found the 'youngsters' of the 39th in a poor state of health:

They were scrawny, yellow, wild eyed and listless in their movements. Their skins were pocked by inflected insect bites. I shall never forget one boy who thumbed a ride from the airfield to town . . . His knees and lower legs were encased in scabs that oozed serum and pus.

The first effective air reinforcements would not arrive until 21 March 1942, when Kittyhawk fighters of 75 Squadron RAAF became the sole fighter defence of Port Moresby for the next forty-four days. The 75 Squadron downed thirty-nine Japanese planes but lost twenty-four aircraft and twelve pilots.

Japanese aircraft next raided the port of Lae, capital of New Guinea and gateway to the hinterland. But Lae was almost empty of people. The following day Lae and the nearby coastal centre of Salamaua to the south-east were invaded by Japanese troops landing by ship. Both centres were guarded by small contingents of the New Guinea Volunteer Rifles, mostly expatriate Australians with some indigenous New Guineans, together with a few men of the 2/22nd Battalion who had escaped from Rabaul. With invasion ships in sight, troops from Lae were sent inland to destroy a petrol dump and a fleet of cars. The remainder escaped in the early hours when they heard the Japanese troops coming ashore. At Salamaua, the bulk of the New Guinea Volunteer Rifles fell back to a bridge they destroyed when the Japanese approached.

It was a close call. As the Japanese advanced Lance Corporal Thomas Brannelly of the 2/22nd Battalion shot a Japanese soldier at point-blank range – probably the only Japanese casualty from the initial land action at that time at Salamaua or Lae. Many in the European population since January had fled to the inland goldmining town of Wau. But soon it too was being bombed and Australian aircraft were making hazardous mercy flights out to Moresby. On 10 March the Americans struck back. A group of 104 aircraft, including torpedo bombers, took off from the USS *Lexington* near the southern shore of Papua, flew over the Owen Stanley Range and headed for Lae and Salamaua. The Americans sank a light cruiser, a troopship and a minesweeper and plastered the town with bombs, briefly retarding the enemy's advance.

During March and April the Japanese landed small parties on Bougainville, hunting out and at times killing small batches of Europeans, including planters in hiding. Soon most of Bougainville was effectively in Japanese hands, although volunteer Australian coastwatchers, living in remote native villages or in the bush, continued to send reports on their radios about Japanese movements.

*

Key officers from the Imperial Army and navy General Staff and relevant ministries met again in Tokyo on 4 March 1942 to consider Japan's future operations. It was more than a mere discussion by a few middle-ranking staff officers. Present at this meeting were Rear Admiral Takasumi Oka, and Lieutenant General Akira Muto, respective chiefs of the Navy and Army ministries and Major General Shinichi Tanaka and Rear Admiral Shigeru Fukudome from the Army and Navy General Staff operations sections.

After much debate a final compromise was reached. The navy committed itself to eliminating British forces in the Indian Ocean and undertook not to launch any major campaign beyond the Pacific perimeter of Fiji, Samoa or Hawaii. The army, in turn, acquiesced to tactical operations by the navy beyond the Pacific perimeter 'as opportunities arise', but details were left vague.

The army committed itself to making feasibility studies of invasions of Hawaii, Australia and Ceylon that might be put into practice 'at some time in the future'. Three days later at the next liaison conference, Rear Admiral Oka would not let the subject of an invasion of Australia drop. Oka was concerned about the Allies using Hawaii and Australia to launch counterattacks. He told the conference that the navy felt it important to remain on the offensive and make the enemy act defensively. He said there was a need to 'actively move our forces to Australia and Hawaii' and 'decimate our enemies' bases for counter attack'. The navy minister, Admiral Shigetaro Shimada, supported by the commander-in-chief of the Navy General Staff, Admiral Osami Nagano, again demonstrated the Imperial Navy's aggressiveness, asking:

Have we tried to give adequate consideration to the issue of actively going to Australia?

But the army wasn't moved and dismissed the debate. Deputy chief of staff of the Supreme Command, General Hajime Sugiyama, responded:

Supreme command has adequately considered Australia, India, Hawaii and Ceylon. To go to Australia would require a force of ten divisions and two to 300,000 tons in terms of ships. It is impossible to carry out however you look at it.

On 6 March Japan's Foreign Office sneered at Britain's failure to assist Australia:

Now that Singapore has fallen and the defence of Java and Australia become hopeless, Britain thought the defence of Burma and India means more. So Britain finds it more convenient to desert her comrades-in-arms by dissolving the Supreme Command and leaving Java and Australia to fight alone.

In Tokyo on 11 March another liaison conference convened and formally ratified the 'fundamental outline' of the army–navy agreement. The document was presented to the Emperor on 13 March by Prime Minister Tojo, Army Chief of Staff Sugiyama, and Navy Chief of Staff Nagano. On the same day, the Board of Information at the Foreign Office in Tokyo issued a statement on 'the Salvation of Australia' that said Britain had abandoned the Dutch East Indies and Australia in their most critical hour:

We wonder, for whom and for what purpose the Australian Government continue their useless and hopeless resistance at the expense of the innocent population, whose untold suffering and misery are the only rewards for the folly of their Government.

*

Senior US officers in Australia in March were convinced that Darwin would be invaded and captured before long. Major General George Brett, the US commander, rated the threat to north-eastern Australia as serious, although not so immediate as the menace to Darwin. Brett thought the enemy's first objective would be Port Moresby or the southern Solomons. But he had no doubts that Australia's north-west would be invaded, as he told the War Department in Washington:

Conclusion inescapable that enemy will make an attack in force on north western coast Australia within a comparatively short period.

Raising the tension on 8 March, General Gordon Bennett made a national broadcast saying it was 'wishful thinking' for Australians to believe that the Japanese would not attack northern Australia in force. He predicted the capture of Broome, Wyndham and most of North Queensland. From those positions the Japanese would expand from base to base, as they had done in Malaya. *The Times* of London had made a similar prediction two weeks earlier, calling for no effort to be spared in reinforcing Australia.

*

Prime Minister Curtin broadcast directly to the American people on 14 March on the eve of sending his external affairs minister, Doc Evatt, to Washington:

> He will go to tell you that we are fighting mad . . . that we Australians are a people who, while somewhat inexperienced and uncertain as to what war on their own soil may mean, are nevertheless ready for anything, and will trade punches, giving odds if needs be, until we rock the enemy back on his heels.

Curtin said that with the loss of Java, Japan had moved one step further in her speedy march southwards. He said that in the countless islands of the Pacific the tide of war now flowed 'madly and badly' for Australia and America. The Americans 'must be our leader', Curtin declared:

> We never regarded the Pacific as a segment of the great struggle. We did not insist that it was the primary theatre of war, but we did say, and events have so far, unhappily, proved us right, that the loss of the Pacific can be disastrous.

Curtin now was quite aware that the Pacific was considered a secondary theatre of war in British and American eyes, although Australia had not been formally informed that this status had been reconfirmed during the Washington talks. Curtin took a new tack, saying that he understood that Britain, with all her commitments, 'could not go all out in the Pacific', so had turned to the United States. But he now wanted US citizens to realise the implications:

> . . . I give you this warning: Australia is the last bastion between the West Coast of America and the Japanese. If Australia goes, the Americas are wide open. It is said that the Japanese will by-pass Australia and that they can be met and routed in India. I say to you that the saving of Australia is the saving of America's west coast.

Curtin feared that if the Japanese became established in northern Australia, their hitting power against the larger centres of Australian population and economic activity would become all the more hostile. General Sir Thomas Blamey returned from the Middle East on 23 March. In addition to his duties as the Australian army Commander-in-Chief, Blamey would become commander of Allied land forces, South West Pacific. In the early stages of the war Blamey had not doubted Japan's ability to capture Curtin's home state:

> Had the Japanese wished to seize it, Western Australia, with its vast potential wealth, might have fallen an easy prey to them in 1942. While it would have extended their commitment to a tremendous degree, it would have given them great advantages.

*

General Douglas MacArthur's command on Corregidor Island was crumbling. The fortress, partly underground, with big guns just off the Bataan Peninsula, was undergoing intense bombardment. On nearby Bataan thousands of Americans and Filipinos were struggling but failing to hold back the Japanese advance. President Roosevelt's signal, through General Eisenhower, for MacArthur to go to Mindanao in the southern Philippines presented the general with a conundrum. He initially told his officers that he would not leave and if necessary he would resign his commission and fight on as a 'simple volunteer'. Roosevelt wanted MacArthur as the South West Pacific's supreme commander, based in Australia, with agreement of the Australian and British governments. It was Curtin who had recommended MacArthur for the post. MacArthur's senior staff agreed:

> They felt that the concentration of men, arms, and transport which they believed was being massed in Australia would enable me almost at once to return at the head of an effective rescue operation.

MacArthur delayed a few days on Corregidor but eventually left on 11 March with some of his senior officers, his wife, son and their Chinese amah. They took a hazardous escape route at night through enemy shipping in fast, wooden torpedo boats, eventually arriving at Mindanao Island, where they waited for a bomber sent from Australia. MacArthur rejected the first battered US bomber sent to collect him for Australia. His party finally left the southern Philippines at midnight on 17 March. On reaching Australia the pilot avoided Darwin, where an air raid was in progress, and flew inland to Batchelor airfield. Another plane then took MacArthur's party to Alice Springs further south. Ten minutes after MacArthur departed Batchelor, Japanese dive-bombers and fighters roared in for an attack. From Alice Springs on Wednesday morning, 18 March, MacArthur and his group took a slow train journey in searing heat in an old carriage devoid of luxuries, further south towards Adelaide. At Terowie, a one-horse town in the mid-north of South Australia, 137 miles (220 kilometres) north of Adelaide, MacArthur was met by a horde of Australian and American pressmen who had travelled up the line. The reporters surrounded MacArthur seeking a statement, and the showman famously obliged:

> The president of the United States ordered me to break through the Japanese lines and proceed from Corregidor to Australia for the purpose, as I understand it, of organising the American offensive against Japan, a primary object of which is the relief of the Philippines. I came through and I shall return.

As well as the reporters, a small crowd of local residents at the tiny Terowie station cheered and called 'Welcome to Australia!' when they spotted the general. MacArthur, smiling, walked towards his new admirers and saluted. MacArthur's party were in the whistle stop only a few minutes, but he had time to inspect a guard of honour of Australian troops and chat with the major in charge. MacArthur was determined that he would return to rescue the Philippines. Prime Minister Curtin immediately commented in Canberra:

What General MacArthur has said is the truth. We hold that which we have got and we take back that which has been lost.

General MacArthur would soon be shocked at Australia's defences. His Allied air force commander in Australia, General George Brett, described conditions in Australia just before MacArthur's arrival:

The situation was, to put it mildly, muddled and unhappy. Australia's defences were weak and Australia expected an invasion. There were no better fighting men in the world than the hard-bitten soldiers of the island continent, but there were far too few of them. The RAAF was equipped with almost obsolete planes and was lacking in engines and spare parts, as well as personnel. We had only one American infantry division and that was incompletely trained. When General MacArthur arrived he was extremely disappointed in what he found.

A wave of relief and appreciation quickly spread across Australia with the arrival of the new supreme commander. 'MacArthur to begin offensive on Japanese' was one of the many welcoming headlines. It was a measure of the anxiety and desperation of the Australian people and Government that when MacArthur arrived in Australia, he was not seen as the flawed general who had botched his preparations to meet the first Japanese attack in the Philippines, nor as a general who had been defeated on the ground. For Australians MacArthur was the first bright hope of stemming the Japanese southward advance. By the time MacArthur's train arrived at Adelaide station on Friday night, 20 March, word had quickly spread and a cheering crowd was waiting. Much larger crowds lined Melbourne streets and Spencer Street station on the Saturday morning when the Overland arrived. MacArthur himself described it as 'a tumultuous welcome', yet he harboured great concern about the morale of the Australian people.

The Argus said that when MacArthur stepped on to the platform at Melbourne he looked younger than his sixty-two years.

His bearing and manner suggested 'complete confidence and ease'. He shook hands with Army Minister Frank Forde, who told reporters that MacArthur's presence 'would give Australia and Allied fighting services great heart'. *The Argus* reported the defeated general's arrival with the gushing headline 'Magician MacArthur'. International analyst Professor Stephen Roberts would soon write that after the first emotional enthusiasm, Australians would begin to appreciate the situation in a more realistic fashion:

> Australia is facing the fact that she is still in imminent danger of invasion, and that a considerable time must elapse before vast numbers of Americans can pour into the continent.

En route to Melbourne MacArthur had been startled to discover that he had less than 25,000 American troops at his disposal in Australia. Most had been assigned to duty with air units. At first glance on paper, the strength of the US air units in Australia seemed impressive, with forty-seven bombers, twenty-seven dive-bombers and more than 500 fighters of various types, but barely a dozen of the key B-17 Flying Fortress bombers were operational. Most of the aircraft were long overdue for repairs or overhaul. Of the fighters, 125 had already been shot down or destroyed on the ground and another 175 were awaiting assembly or repairs. More importantly, most of the American fighters in service were old types that were inferior to the Japanese Zero, especially at higher altitudes. MacArthur had almost no experienced infantry of real value, no tanks and no navy. Advised of these realities, he reportedly said, 'God have mercy on us!'

Crowds lined the way up Melbourne's Bourke Street and people leaned from the windows of buildings for a glimpse of the general. Some stood on the roofs of cars. A huge crowd thronged outside the Menzies Hotel and gave MacArthur a grand ovation when he arrived. As he turned to wave to the crowd, shouts of 'Good old Mac' and 'Now we shan't be long' could be heard. More than 1000 people cheered again an hour later when the general left the hotel to pay his respects to the governor of Victoria, Sir Winston Dugan. But MacArthur's warm welcome did nothing to mask his anxiety about Australia:

> Its actual military situation had become almost desperate. Its forces were weak to an extreme. The bulk of its ground troops were in the Middle East, while the United States had only one division present, and that but partially trained. Its air force was equipped with almost obsolete planes and was lacking not only in engines and spare parts, but in personnel. Its navy had no carriers or battleships. The outlook was bleak.

The Japanese already possessed superiority in air, sea and ground forces. It seemed evident that the Japanese march from Burma to Australia could not be long delayed. The Japanese were hastening the battle to Australia's northern approaches in what the American command thought would be an attempt to secure air bases from which to strike further south. As if to underline MacArthur's apprehensions, a medium force of heavy bombers attacked Darwin's residential areas on Friday 20 March in the fifth assault on the town. Some fifty bombs were dropped. Two people were killed and several injured. Broome was hit again on 20 March, while bombs were also dropped on Derby, to the north-east. Horn Island near Thursday Island was hit on 14 March and again later. Thursday Island and adjacent sites on the tip of Cape York Peninsula were raided for the fifth time. Port Moresby was bombed and machine-gunned in two raids on the same day, the fifteenth and sixteenth raids on the town. An enemy raid also took place in the Solomons. The Japanese were showing signs of closing in on Port Moresby, according to analysts. They were advancing without opposition through the Markham Valley in New Guinea, newspapers said on 21 March, and an invasion fleet had landed troops at Salamaua and Lae in New Guinea. Analysts said raids from Darwin and Torres Strait to the Solomons revealed Japan's wider designs.

Curtin worried about the widening attacks, especially as they seemed to presage raids further south, down both the east and west coastlines:

As time passes, the enemy comes ever nearer. Darwin, Wyndham and Broome are three important strategical posts in the security of Australia as a whole. I have been impressed by the menace to the populations of our larger capitals which this part of Australia would constitute if the enemy were to use it as a base.

*

In the midst of all this, prime ministers Curtin and Churchill had another major row, which further soured their relationship. Churchill quietly secured the appointment of Australia's effective and well-placed minister to the United States, Richard Casey, as Britain's minister of state resident in the Middle East. It was a surprise and disappointment to Curtin, as Casey had an excellent working relationship with President Roosevelt and senior US officials.

Hero worship of MacArthur might have given some passing satisfaction to civilians and others, but it unwittingly disguised Australia's dire situation. A feature writer for Adelaide's newspaper *The Advertiser*, who attended an 'off-the-record' meeting of sixty American and Australian newsmen with General MacArthur in Melbourne, wrote about what it was like being in the presence of the man 'who held Bataan Peninsula with the greatest weapons of all, moral courage'. It wasn't held for long. Bataan would surrender on 9 April. About 2000 American and Filipino troops would escape in small boats to the island fortress, leaving behind 76,000 men to be captured by the Japanese, who showed no mercy in the infamous 'death march of Bataan', which claimed the lives of somewhere between 7000 and 10,000. If a man fell, it was certain death by bayonet or bullet unless another could pick him up and support him. When MacArthur later heard of the horrific Bataan death march, he told the story to the press for publication, but Washington the same day forbade the release of any details of prisoner-of-war atrocities. MacArthur later commented:

> Perhaps the Administration, which was committed to a Europe-first effort, feared American public opinion would demand a greater reaction against the Japanese.

MacArthur had arrived in Australia with deep concerns about the established US and British 'Beat Hitler First' policy that had been reconfirmed in Washington. In the *Reports of General MacArthur*, prepared by MacArthur's staff in Tokyo after the war, it was clear that MacArthur regarded the policy as a serious hindrance to his work.

MacArthur's besieged Corregidor Island fortress would surrender in early May. His chief immediate concern was the insufficient US and Australian forces available to protect the vast continent, as his reports later indicated:

> by the middle of March the Japanese were approaching the doorstep of Australia ... With each passing day the Japanese were forging new links in their chain of encirclement and preparing new strikes against Australia and her life line to the outside world.

On the east coast three minor raids would be made on Townsville in late July. Other small Japanese air raids would be made in northern Australia during the war on Drysdale, Exmouth Gulf, Katherine, Milingimbi, Mossman, Onslow, Port Hedland, Port Patterson and Cairns.

*

Prime Minister Curtin arranged for a dinner for General MacArthur at Parliament House in Canberra on 26 March after they attended a meeting of the Advisory War Council. The new supreme commander said his reception in Australia had far exceeded anything he could have anticipated. His emotional message for Australians was brief:

We shall win or we shall die, and to this end I pledge you the full resources of all the mighty power of my country and all the blood of my countrymen.

MacArthur didn't have the authority to make such a pledge, but he certainly did everything in his power to secure arms and reinforcements. Curtin was buoyed by the possibility of a large US army forming in Australia to join forces with Australians for assaults on the Japanese across New Guinea and the islands. In March 1942 only the beginnings of this powerful force existed in Australia. But there was hope.

The day after the dinner at Parliament House for MacArthur, a new Australian military team flew from Adelaide to Darwin. Major General Sir Edmund (Ned) Herring, who had returned a few days earlier from the Middle East where he had been commander of the 6th Division, had taken command in Darwin. Herring was a man who exuded the sort of quiet confidence needed in panicky Darwin, where Japanese bombing raids were frequent. Indeed the port was becoming untenable but was essential to the defence of Australia. The war cabinet had placed the whole area north of Alice Springs under military control. Herring's total strength on arrival in Darwin was 14,000 in the Australian army, 1000 in the RAN, 857 in the RAAF and 3200 in the US forces.

Some progress was beginning to be made in the defence of Australia's remote north. Lines of possible Japanese approach were being explored and mapped, new airfields were developed south of Darwin and new roads cut through bush while existing major roads were upgraded. Herring's Australian and American forces were building, slowly at first, but then steadily. Herring had been assured that Australian troops would be increased by another 10,000 and US forces by a further 3000. With McArthur's arrival, Curtin announced that 'a substantial number' of American armed forces, with their equipment, had arrived on Australian shores. He told parliament hopefully that the calamitous trend of events since the invasion of Malaya might well have reached a turning point, but added 'let us not exaggerate the speed with which we can reach it'. The first Americans had arrived in Brisbane on 22 December 1941 and there was great anticipation that on 1 April 1942, 41,000 AIF troops from the Middle East would disembark from ships at Adelaide. By mid-1942 the number in Australia was expected to rise to 150,000, of which 90,000 were in the army. The largest initial concentrations would be in Queensland.

*

The protection of India now became a key British priority. Despite Curtin's momentous clash with Prime Minister Churchill over Burma, the Curtin Government now permitted elements of the 6th Division AIF returning from the Middle East to be sent to Ceylon. With the Japanese advancing in Burma, British strategists were concerned about an invasion of India from Burma and from the south of Ceylon. The Japanese navy at the time had complete control of the Bay of Bengal. The 2/6th Battalion of the 6th Division had taken part in withdrawals in Greece and Crete in another of Churchill's disastrous plans. It now landed in Ceylon with the rest of the 16th and 17th brigades AIF and immediately discovered a serious shortage of stores and equipment. Trained in desert warfare, they were thrown into jungle warfare training.

*

Japanese historian on the war in New Guinea, Professor Hiromi Tanaka, could never understand why John Curtin surrendered Australia's sovereign power to General MacArthur:

> If he had the choice of the whole US Army in the South Pacific, Curtin's handing over of all his forces might have been a natural decision. But MacArthur had almost nothing to begin with . . . it makes no sense, because he was a defeated general and his political situation was very unstable. He was almost politically defeated. There is no rational explanation.

Fortunately for Australia, Curtin's decision proved a sound one. Prime Minister Curtin and General MacArthur had a common yearning: they were obsessed with the need to use Australia to launch an offensive against Japan to the north and to convince Washington and Whitehall that the war against Japan could not await the defeat of Hitler. When MacArthur arrived in Australia he said he found Australians were not thinking of taking the offensive:

> The concept was purely one of passive defense and I felt it would only result in eventual defeat. Even if so restrictive a scheme were tactically successful, its result would be to trap us indefinitely on an island continent ringed by conquered territories and hostile ocean, bereft of all hope of ever assuming the offensive.

MacArthur and Curtin had promptly found a sense of mutual trust and cooperation, according to the general:

> He was the kind of a man that Australians called 'fair dinkum'. As I rose to leave, I put my arm about his strong shoulder, 'Mr Prime Minister,' I said 'we two, you and I, will see this thing through together . . . you take care of the rear and I will handle the front.' He shook me by both hands and said 'I knew I was not wrong in selecting you as Supreme Commander.'

*

Haunted by the spectre of a Japanese occupation of parts of Australia, Curtin's first day back at work in Melbourne, after returning from Perth across the Nullarbor on 2 February, had been to instigate directions for a scorched-earth policy in Australia. Curtin knew full well that the chance of stopping multiple divisions of veteran Japanese fighters from advancing towards the main population centres of Australia would be minimal. A policy of denial and destruction was needed in case Australian forces on the mainland were obliged to evacuate under Japanese pressure. He had encouraged the war cabinet to discuss the issue at length. Details were publicised, mostly in

Queensland. State governments were involved and newspapers across Australia's north, in particular, carried detailed reports on what was required of the people. The *Cairns Post* on 2 February reported that army authorities were ready to put into operation at a moment's notice secret plans 'to ensure that Australia would not be caught napping'.

But the scorched-earth policy was poorly explained and soon created alarm and confusion. A meeting of the war cabinet in Canberra on 4 February agreed that undue emphasis should not be placed on evacuation measures 'as it would be to the detriment to morale and to the maintenance of essential production'.

Curtin personally signed confidential letters to the state governments and local authorities, but insisted that the policy didn't mean a lack of fighting spirit:

You will realise that such preparations are part of the general defence scheme and are not in any way inconsistent with the government's resolve to defend Australia to the limit of our capacity.

By late April the 17th Field Engineers had arrived in Cairns, buoying the spirits of many Cairns people who felt beleaguered. But the men weren't there to defend the place. They were the 'demolition boys' and they mined the Kuranda Range Road and other main transport links including railway and wharf facilities. Australians in Far North Queensland understandably had the jitters. Many women and children were evacuated to the south. The policy for the denial of resources to the enemy would be dropped on 26 May 1943 in all areas except those north of the Tropic of Capricorn.

When General MacArthur had first arrived in Australia, amid the cheering he had clearly detected a whiff of national despair, as he later summarised:

heartening as the welcome was, it did not disguise the fact that a sense of dangerous defeatism had seized upon a large segment of Australia's seven million people. The primary problem was to replace the pessimism of failure with the inspiration of success. What Australians needed was a strategy that held out the promise of victory.

Chapter 11

CHURCHILL'S 'LESSER WAR'

At the start of April 1942, General MacArthur's senior officers believed that Australian military forces were preparing to abandon much of Australia to the Japanese if it became necessary. MacArthur's General Staff, including his intelligence chief, General Charles Willoughby, reported to Washington:

> The Australian chiefs of staff would be virtually compelled to yield the northern part of the continent to the Japanese should they attempt an invasion.

They said that if it came down to it the Australians would make their defence against the Japanese at Brisbane. Defence by Australian units north of Townsville was not even contemplated, and sufficient forces were not available to secure Fremantle in the west and Darwin in the north against determined enemy assault. The American report was close to the truth. Minimal or no reinforcements were planned for the more remote northern outposts, perhaps with the exception of Darwin, which were expected to fight to the last should the Japanese land, along the lines of what happened at Rabaul. Withdrawal of forces was considered bad for morale. While Brisbane would be defended, protecting Australia's southern manufacturing capitals of Sydney and Melbourne, as well as the great steel plants at Newcastle and Port Kembla, had priority.

At this time Prime Minister Curtin heard the most worrying assessment of the Japanese threat to Australia from his defence chiefs, Air Chief Marshall Burnett, Admiral Royle and General Rowell. Their report was jointly signed by the US deputy supreme commander, South West Pacific, General George Brett. Their assessment said:

> Attacks in force against Australia and Australian lines of communication are likely at an early date.

The senior Australian and American officers noted that the Japanese had virtually undisputed control of both sea and air in the south-west Pacific and 'could be expected to undertake an offensive in great strength against Australia's supply line and against Australia itself' in the very near future.

MacArthur and the Australian chiefs believed the 'critical point' that controlled the enemy's access to the vast Australian coastline was Port Moresby, against which 'a major offensive could be expected at almost any time':

> If Port Moresby fell to the Japanese, its loss would put in immediate jeopardy the safety of Australia's 'all important area' – the Brisbane-Melbourne coastal belt.

Curtin immediately sent the latest assessment to External Affairs Minister Evatt in Washington and to High Commissioner Bruce in London for the attention of President Roosevelt and Prime Minister Churchill. Curtin told the Advisory War Council that General MacArthur was 'in entire agreement' with the defence appreciation. Further, MacArthur was sending the report to the US army chief of staff, General George C. Marshall, 'urging the provision of the Naval Forces and aircraft recommended in the appreciation as being the minimum essential . . .'

Curtin knew Australia could expect no practical assistance from British forces. Churchill had given him an assurance on 30 March and again on 1 April that Britain would support Australia in the event of 'an invasion in force'. He now promised the assistance of the 2nd British Infantry Division and artillery units, which were rounding the Cape of Good Hope en route to the Far East in late April or early May:

> If, by that time, Australia is being heavily invaded, I should certainly divert it to your aid. This would not apply in the case of localised attacks in the north or mere raids elsewhere. But I wish to let you know that you could count on this help should invasion by, say, eight or ten Japanese divisions occur.

Curtin and the Australian defence chiefs were highly sceptical about Churchill's promise, because it suggested there might be no British assistance in a 'limited invasion' of Darwin, Fremantle or other remote locations outside Australia's key industrial east-coast centres. Curtin and MacArthur had privately agreed that the Allied forces in the Australia region must immediately to go on the offensive. Depressed, Curtin met confidentially in his Parliament House office in April 1942 with Gavin Long, then a senior journalist with the *Sydney Morning Herald*.

Curtin said he and MacArthur had strongly supported a major offensive proposal developed by the chief of the Australian Naval Staff, Admiral Royle, on secondment from Britain, who had been emphatic that his own superior officers in London were wrong in opposing the possibility of an offensive from Australia. The Americans, nevertheless, with vital intelligence about a massive build-up of forces in Rabaul, were beginning to see the benefits of unexpectedly striking at the so-far victorious Japanese fleet. The governor-general in Canberra, Lord Gowrie, gave King George VI a frank assessment of the situation in Australia:

We are, as you will gather, having rather an anxious time out here at the present, and things are moving pretty quickly.

Gowrie wrote that the fall of Singapore and Java had created a serious situation:

But a great deal has happened in the last month or so and provided we can have another month or so immune from serious attack, we ought to be secure, but this next month will be critical and I shall be glad when it is safely over.

Gowrie said Australians now realised that they 'may be invaded at any moment'. Parts of Australia were already being bombed and it was likely that more bombing would take place before long. Gowrie assured the King that the industrial troubles, inspired by 'a few ignorant and short-sighted people' would not affect Australia's war effort. The governor-general noted that 'a lot of stuff, men, aeroplanes, material etc', was 'coming into this part of the world from America'. General MacArthur had impressed him as a 'very live man, full of energy and thoroughly inspired with the offensive spirit'. Gowrie had words of praise for the work of John Curtin, but added a jarring note of alarm for the King about the prime minister's health:

He is thoroughly sound, honest and clear-headed and has made no mistakes up to now. But he has rather a difficult team to drive and I should be anxious at what might happen if his health gave way. He is not strong and I am almost afraid that he might crack up.

MacArthur was getting no support in Washington for his plan to go on the offensive. In London, the chief of the Imperial General Staff, General Sir Alan Brooke, was in a gloomy mood. The Japanese fleet now was in the Indian Ocean and the British eastern fleet was retiring westward. He wrote in his diary in early April that the Empire had never been in such a precarious position:

We were fighting for our lives to stop gaps. Cairo was none too safe. Persia was threatened with its precious oil by German advance in South Russia, India's eastern flank was threatened, vital communications through Indian Ocean might be cut at any moment, and Australia and New Zealand even open to attack.

Churchill soon stressed in a letter to Australian High Commissioner Stanley Bruce that Australia would need to be more than 'in deadly peril' for Britain to come to its aid. The phrase he had used was 'if Australia was being heavily invaded'. Churchill soon told a war cabinet defence meeting in London that he did not want to divert forces to points in Australia and the South West Pacific. His defence chiefs 'entirely agreed'. Churchill thankfully said the United States 'seemed to indicate' that the US navy was 'not thinking of pressing matters on a large scale in the Pacific' although US public opinion appeared to be in favour.

Journalist and historian Gavin Long met with Curtin and took down the transcript of an interview that was not for publication but intended as a briefing. In the secret interview Curtin said Admiral Royle's plan for a large-scale naval and air offensive against Japan was being opposed in both London and Washington. Curtin said the plan had involved sending big US and British naval forces against Japan:

The time to carry out this offensive, according to Royle, MacArthur and myself is now while there is stability in Europe. We believe that the present deadlock in the two European theatres may last until the end of June, and that this would give us time to push Japan out of her conquered territories.

Curtin said two million men were tied up in England yet Churchill opposed the plan:

He does not believe that Australia is seriously threatened, though he is very much alive to the threat to India and the importance of India. He offers Australia, in the place of [our] plan, an assurance that, if Australia is seriously attacked, a British infantry division and a British armoured division ... will be diverted to Australia. My reply to this is that the Australian army leaders consider that twenty five divisions would be needed to hold Australia against attack if she lacked naval and air superiority.

Curtin said the nation's army leaders considered that Australia's population could not maintain more than fifteen divisions without straining manpower resources beyond reason:

Thus, at the best, Churchill is offering too little too late as he did at Singapore. On the other hand a sea-air offensive now would stun Japan.

If Australia was lost, Curtin said, apart from 'seven million white British people being lost to the Empire', South Africa, with its strong pro-German party, would abandon the Empire:

I do not say that Churchill is more concerned about the black Empire than the white, but he is more alive to the danger to India than to Australia. He would not abandon Australia. He would send help, but he does not consider Australia is seriously threatened.

Curtin said that for years he had seen the present situation coming. He had 'felt it in his bones' that Singapore could not stand.

*

Japanese navy and army war planners had now activated their plan to invade Port Moresby. The operation would also include capturing the island of Tulagi and nearby islands in the Solomons as bases to support the Moresby operation. Operation MO, the plan to invade Port Moresby, was an Imperial Navy proposal, intended partly to strengthen the major Japanese base in Rabaul. The Japanese army believed that the capture of Port Moresby and the southern coastline of the great New Guinea 'tail' would help prevent expected counteroffensives from Australia. The invasion was also intended to 'expel any Allied forces from New Guinea in preparation for a possible advance on Australia', according to historian Professor Hiromi Tanaka.

A number of senior Japanese officers in early 1942 were keen for an invasion of Australia. They weren't all naval men. Having taken Singapore, the 25th Army commander, General Tomoyuki Yamashita, who became known in Japan as the 'Tiger of Malaya', strongly advocated capturing Australia and, with staff officers, worked on his own invasion plan. Yamashita's work was separate to plans by the operations section of Navy General Staff in Tokyo and Combined Fleet Headquarters aboard Admiral Yamamoto's new flagship, the *Yamato*, the world's largest and most powerful battleship. Research continued through late February and into early March, further delaying the conclusion of the debate about whether to invade Australia, or at least part of the continent. With the fall of Singapore and most of the Dutch East Indies all the way south to Bali, deliberation and argument in Japan among senior planners and political leaders still raged about where to invade next. General Yamashita's plan, which he put to Prime Minister Tojo, was similar to his successful campaign in Malaya. He planned to land on each side of major Australian cities and cut them off, after first making a series of dummy landings to draw off Australian troops. Speaking to his British biographer, John Deane Potter, at New Bilibid prison near Manila during a break in his war crimes trial in 1945, Yamashita said there had been hardly enough Australians to have organised an effective resistance to the Japanese in early 1942:

All they could ever hope to do was make a guerrilla resistance in the bush. With only Sydney and Brisbane in my hands it would have been comparatively simple to subdue Australia. I never visualised occupying it entirely. It was too large. With its coastline anyone can always land there exactly as they want.

But it is a long way from anywhere and I could have poured in enough troops to resist effectively any Anglo-American invasions.

Although the Japanese General Staff felt my supply lines would have been too long, so would the American or British lines. They might never have been able to reach the place at all. We could have been safe from there for ever.

Despite reportedly telling army general Prince Naruhiko Higashikuni, uncle to Emperor Hirohito, earlier in the war that Australia might even be occupied, after the war's end Prime Minister Tojo denied any desire to invade the continent. Before he went to his death on 23 December 1948 at the conclusion of the international war trials in Tokyo, Tojo gave a final interview at Sugamo prison, saying:

We never had enough troops to do so. We had already far out-stretched our lines of communication. We did not have the armed strength or the supply facilities to mount such a terrific exten-sion of our already over-strained and too thinly spread forces. We expected to occupy all New Guinea, to maintain Rabaul as a holding base, and to raid Northern Australia by air. But actual physical invasion – no, at no time.

It is clear that various Japanese in positions of real power supported an invasion of Australia in early 1942. But none were given final approval. The Japanese army and navy could only agree on aerial attacks on Australia and a blockade of the conti-nent. A Japanese diplomat who became wartime foreign minister in 1943, Mamoru Shigemitsu, wrote after the war that 'in order to cross from Timor to Port Darwin in North Australia, it was necessary to have a firm grip on Papua', for this would not only provide a useful base, but would prevent the enemy counter-attacking from Australia. Shigemitsu believed that Darwin would have fallen easily in February 1942:

Port Darwin had already been twice attacked by bombers and as a military station had been abandoned by the Australians.

Although after the first raid Darwin might have had the appearance of being abandoned altogether, it was never the case. Indeed, within two months of the first major attack the garrison had almost doubled in strength.

*

People living in the north of Australia in particular had genuine apprehensions about their safety. Many in the United States could not fathom Australia's defence priorities, as the *Washington Post* demonstrated:

> The gallantry of Australia on other fronts has weakened her defences in her hour of need. Today, when she needs them most, more than 170,000 Australians are manning the battle lines in Libya, Burma, Java, Britain and the Middle East. At home there is an army of only 250,000 — which includes 50,000 veterans of the last war.

With bombs regularly falling on Darwin and Port Moresby, Curtin was handed a letter and a small box on Friday 20 March. The letter was from a Mareeba resident on the Atherton Tablelands in Far North Queensland. Curtin opened the tiny box from Mrs E. Cronin and took up her letter:

> I am sending you my keeper and wedding rings as a small contribution to the War Effort.

Mrs Cronin's letter documented the fear and consequences for many in North Queensland:

> It has been heartbreaking to know of hundreds of families shifting from the North lately to what they consider safer places, as they were panic stricken at the thought of the Japanese invading the North. Some left their furniture in their homes, others sold it for a mere trifle, one man selling his home and furniture for twenty pounds to let his wife and child to go South.

The Mareeba housewife thanked Curtin for his untiring efforts in persuading President Roosevelt to send General MacArthur and American aid to Australia. It had 'given Northerners fresh hope', she said, 'so I am sure these peoples will return to the North'. She thanked Curtin and his ministers for their 'spirit and determination to keep the enemy from our shores'. Curtin was surprised and humbled. His private secretary Eric Tonkin responded:

> Mr Curtin very much appreciates the spirit which prompted you to donate these rings but feels that, as your wedding ring is of such sentimental value, he would not like to deprive you of it. I am therefore returning the rings to you.

Soon Mrs Cronin at Mareeba would see the effects of the cooperation between Curtin and General MacArthur when it took only eight days to build a new Mareeba airfield for US air force B-17 Flying Fortresses and RAAF Beaufort bombers.

*

Apart from his concerns about Burma, Ceylon and India, Prime Minister Churchill at this time was content to leave the main thrust of the war against Japan, including the defence of Australia and New Guinea, to the Americans, provided southern operations didn't consume too many American resources. We know this because Churchill secretly declared in April 1942 that the war against Japan was a secondary and less important one. The details of what Churchill said were not released until 1946. He was speaking at a time when the Nazi pressure on Britain at home had eased. In Germany, Hitler had given orders for the cancellation of the long-term plans for the invasion of England, called Operation Sealion, in September 1940.

Prime Minister Churchill had declared in parliament, on 27 January 1942, 'there is no question of regarding the war in the Pacific as a secondary operation'. Yet less than three months later that precisely is what he did. In London on Friday April 23, 1942,

Churchill rose to his feet in the Hoare Memorial Hall of the Church House Annex in Westminster, which had become the temporary House of Commons after the parliament buildings were bombed. He spoke of the 'dark panorama of ruin', both actual and prospective, in the Far East. His address was not released in any form during wartime.

Members of parliament were sworn to secrecy, under Britain's Defence of the Realm Act. The chamber was guarded by a heavy detail of special police. Churchill himself kept the only copy of his speech. He was unequivocal about how he regarded the war in the Far East and the Pacific:

> I now leave the lesser war – for such I must regard this fearful struggle against the Japanese – and come to the major war against Germany and Italy.

In Churchill's handwritten notes, he actually took an even stronger line in downplaying the war against Japan. He wrote, and then crossed out, reference to the minor war, replacing the word 'minor' with 'lesser'. He had always sent his secret speeches out for comment by senior military officers before delivery, which might explain the replacement of the word 'minor' with 'lesser'. He insisted that simply defeating Japan's overseas forces wasn't sufficient because the future depended on beating Hitler:

> The war cannot be ended by driving Japan back to her own bounds and defeating her overseas forces. The war can only be ended through the defeat in Europe of the German armies, or through internal convulsions in Germany produced by the unfavourable course of the war, economic privations, and the Allied bombing offensive.

In his speech notes, Churchill heavily scored out as potentially embarrassing the leading paragraph on page three where he appeared to welcome Japan's entry into the war at Pearl Harbor. He said he could not pretend to be discouraged or alarmed by Japan entering the war.

Before the Japanese entered the war, Churchill said, Britain was already fully extended in the North Sea, Atlantic and Mediterranean:

> But in spite of all we could do and the risks we ran and are running, we have been and are at present outnumbered by the sea, land and air forces of Japan throughout the Eastern theatre. This fact must be faced by all who wish to understand what has happened and what is going to happen.

Churchill said he had always hoped for the entry of the United States into the war. He bluntly indicated that he had under-estimated Japan:

> . . . I did not think that the injuries Japan would certainly inflict upon us in our ill-guarded and even denuded Eastern theatre would be too heavy a price to pay for having the immense resources and power of the United States bound indissolubly to our side and our cause. That is still my feeling. But I frankly admit that the violence, fury, skill, and might of Japan has far exceeded anything that we had been led to expect.

Churchill could not mask his pleasure at the Roosevelt Admin-istration agreeing to the defeat of Germany before Japan. He expected to find the United States' efforts concentrated on the war with Japan, and was prepared to argue that the defeat of Japan would not necessarily lead to the defeat of Hitler, but the defeat of Hitler meant finishing off Japan was 'merely a matter of time and trouble'. Churchill and his government were relieved to find that their concept of war was shared by the government of the United States.

In his secret speech to parliament Churchill was critical of the defence of the Singapore islands, saying 100,000 troops had surrendered to 30,000 Japanese:

After five or six days of confused but not very severe fighting, the army and fortress surrendered. The Japanese have not stated the number of prisoners they have taken, but it does not seem that there was very much bloodshed. This episode and all that led up to it seems to be out of harmony with anything that we have experienced or performed in the present war . . .

Australian accounts reflect upon the Indian troops. Other credible witnesses disparage the Australians. The lack of any effective counterattack by the [British] 18th Division, which arrived in such high spirits and good order, and never seem to have had their chance, is criticised. The generalship is criticised. There is endless field for recrimination.

The 18th Division did not arrive in good order. The main body landed very late in the battle on 29 January, with its machine-gun and reconnaissance battalions arriving on 5 February just ten days before the surrender. Churchill told the secret session of parliament that that the Japanese had established in just four months their vast Asiatic Co-Prosperity Sphere with largely superior forces. He then turned his attention to Australia:

Australia naturally fears immediate invasion, and the United States, which has accepted responsibility for everything east of a line drawn west of Australia, has sent and is sending continuous strong reinforcements. We have transported back to Australia a large part of the Australian Imperial Forces from the Middle East. We do not see here that the Japanese would get great advantages by invading Australia in force.

The prime minister's words 'in force' should be noted. He did not suggest that Australia, or certain parts of the continent, might not be invaded. Churchill correctly surmised that if Japan did invade Australia 'in force', the Japanese would be committing themselves to a very formidable campaign at a great distance from home. It was here in his speech that Churchill considered a real threat to northern Australia, and this included a belief that Japan would try to establish Japanese bases in the north:

> No doubt the Japanese will do their utmost to threaten and alarm Australia and to establish lodgements and bases on the northern part of Australia in order to procure the greatest locking up of Allied forces in that continent.

Churchill had never admitted this to Curtin. He repeated the previous promise that he had made to Curtin that Britain would come to Australia's aid if the worst happened: 'We have done and will continue to do everything in our power to sustain our kith and kin.'

The promise now had a hollow ring. At this stage of the war, it was probably not within Britain's power to come to Australia's timely aid if Japan had established bases in northern Australia. Churchill went on to speak of the danger of having too many troops based in Australia, New Zealand and the nearby Pacific islands, when they could be better used against the Germans and Italians:

> But neither Great Britain nor the United States must be drawn into immobilising in Australasia undue numbers of the limited forces which they can transport across the sea within any given period.

He concluded with an uplifting prediction of deliverance: '. . . I am frank to say that I feel better about the war than at any time in the past two years.' His gamble was still that even though much would be lost in the early years to Japanese domination, it could be regained later. Had this speech been revealed to the Government of Australia during the war, it would have caused outrage.

John Curtin had, however, accurately interpreted Churchill's thinking. Just a few days before Churchill's secret speech, Curtin had sensed the need to take Australia's plight and plans directly to the people of Britain over the head of its prime minister. In a broadcast to the United Kingdom, rebroadcast in Australia on the ABC, Curtin compared the current spirit in Australia to that of the people of Britain after Dunkirk:

Men and women of Britain! I speak to you from Australia, a land that is preparing to meet an invasion . . . Dangerous days lie ahead of us but under this threat the Empire is more united than ever before.

Curtin stressed that Australians were serving in every continent in the world and on every ocean. Now, faced with the threat of an invasion, Australia's armies, with American help, were preparing to take the offensive:

Australia is a great bastion of Empire. From a securely held Australia the strategy and forces essential to free the Pacific Ocean, to hold firmly the Indian Ocean, and to liberate the enemy occupied places threatening these oceans, can go forward to the offensive . . . This is Australia's resolve. On our people and the people of New Zealand now falls the burden of the Empire in the South Pacific.

*

The so-called 'lesser war' soon flared in the Coral Sea, the vast expanse of ocean that touches the tropical shores of north-eastern Australia, parts of Papua New Guinea and the southern Solomon Islands down to New Caledonia. It covers an area of some 1.8 million square miles (4.7 million square kilometres). How serious was the threat to Australia in late April 1942? The commander-in-chief of the US fleet and chief of naval operations, Admiral Ernest J. King, later summarised the situation in an official report:

the Japanese had established bases in the New Guinea–New Britain–Solomon Islands area, which put them in a position to threaten all Melanesia and Australia itself, and they were moving their forces through the mandates in preparation for an extension of their offensive to the south east. Our available forces at that time were eager and ready for battle, but they were not any too strong for effective defense against major enemy concentrations, much less adequate to carry out a large-scale offensive operation.

Increasingly in April, Japanese intelligence gained evidence of the small but growing numbers of American aircraft, ships and submarines operating in parts of the vast region that Japan mostly controlled. To date Japan had operated with relative freedom in the South Seas. But General MacArthur was making every effort to send as many American aircraft as possible, including B-17 bombers, north from Queensland to Port Moresby. The bombers, with RAAF aircraft, were now making regular raids on Rabaul.

Japanese plans were completed for the invasion by sea of Australia's administrative centre in Papua, the bustling town of Port Moresby, and for the protection of the large base at Rabaul. Its occupation would lead to Japanese dominance over north-eastern Australia. After occupying Rabaul and Port Moresby, together with the capture of Lae and Salamaua, the Japanese would have a mesh of mutually supporting air bases that could concentrate large numbers of land-based aircraft on any Allied naval force that tried to challenge the new Japanese southern perimeter.

The MO operation involving the capture of Port Moresby was conceived by the Japanese navy but, unlike many of the navy's aggressive and risky propositions, this one was deemed by the army to be 'quite simple' and was thus approved. The capture of Moresby would have important implications for Australia. Apart from taking Port Moresby, MO also would include the invasion of the southern Solomon Islands to establish a seaplane base on Tulagi Island, tentatively held by Australians. The MO operational order considered other initiatives:

We will establish air bases and strengthen air operations in the Australian area. Successively, an element will carry out a sudden attack against Nauru and Ocean islands and secure the phosphorus resources located there.

The MO operation, if all went well, included the capture of the New Hebrides (Vanuatu) and New Caledonia. Japanese carriers would finally launch a massive air attack on Townsville in North Queensland, with raids on Cooktown and Thursday Island.

In the Philippines, General MacArthur's deputy, General Jonathan Wainwright, and his American and Filipino forces, were under sustained attack on Corregidor Island. Surrender now was only a matter of weeks away. In Burma, British and Indian forces were being pushed back into India and would withdraw from Burma on 20 May.

In the southern Solomons, Japanese air attacks on the island of Tulagi were intensifying, reaching a climax on 2 May with eight heavy air raids on that one day. Australian coastwatchers on other islands tipped off the small AIF and RAAF contingent on Tulagi that Japanese ships were approaching. The Australians calmly went about burning and demolishing anything that might be of use to the enemy. As fires lit up the night sky, the Australians escaped in a boat to Vila. The next day the Japanese began their occupation of Tulagi.

*

American and Australian intelligence knew that strong Japanese forces were on their way generally southwards and would swing around the 'tail' of the great New Guinea island en route to Port Moresby on the southern coast of Papua.

Allied intelligence indicated that ships and aircraft were being assembled for an invasion and the target was likely to be Port Moresby. The build-up of intelligence had ensured that the Americans were ready for action by early May. Rear Admiral Frank J. Fletcher of the US navy brought a carrier force to a rendezvous south of the Solomons with Rear Admiral Aubrey W. Fitch. Fletcher's force included the aircraft carrier the *Yorktown*; the heavy cruisers the *Astoria*, the *Chester* and the *Portland*; plus six destroyers and the oil tanker the *Neosho*. Fitch had the carrier, the *Lexington*, heavy cruisers, the *Minneapolis* and the *New Orleans*, plus five destroyers.

A cruiser squadron from Sydney, under Australian Rear Admiral John Crace, was next to rendezvous near the carriers in a support role. It comprised the heavy cruisers HMAS *Australia* and USS *Chicago* plus the light cruiser HMAS *Hobart*. The *Yorktown* headed to Tulagi and immediately attacked the island and Japanese boats there. Fletcher steamed westwards. He was unaware that two large Japanese carriers, the *Shokaku* and the *Zuikaku*, were just 200 nautical miles (370 kilometres) to the east. Japanese aircraft searching to the south found the *Neosho* and the American destroyer the *Sims*, and attacked both vessels, which were sunk. Japanese pilots had reported the *Neosho* as a carrier.

Admiral Crace in HMAS *Australia* assumed anti-aircraft formation, with HMAS *Hobart* and USS *Chicago* respectively on *Australia*'s port and starboard quarters with a destroyer stationed ahead of the three cruisers. Shortly after three in the afternoon the first attack on the force was made by twelve land-based bombers of the Japanese navy. It was 'most determined but fortunately badly delivered', according to Crace. Torpedoes were dropped, after which the aircraft flew on to fire on the ships with cannon. Timely and skilful handling enabled the *Australia* to avoid two torpedoes which passed particularly close by. The *Chicago* also cleverly avoided three well-aimed torpedoes. Five of the enemy aircraft were shot down.

Australian naval war history records that a few minutes later nineteen heavy bombers attacked HMAS *Australia* from astern at a height of about 5500 metres. The bombing was accurate, but not quite good enough. Some twenty 500-lb (227-kilogram) bombs and several smaller, were dropped. The flagship was straddled in all directions, her upper decks drenched with spray, though she suffered only superficial bomb damage. Two men were fatally wounded on the *Chicago* and seven slightly injured. These aircraft had only just gone when three more dropped bombs close to the destroyer USS *Perkins*. Crace later reported with some disgust on the episode:

It was subsequently discovered that these aircraft were US Army B-26 from Townsville, and they were good enough to photograph [the] Task Group a few seconds after 'bomb release', thus proving beyond all doubt that they had attacked their own ships. Fortunately their bombing, in comparison with that of the Japanese formation a few moments earlier, was disgraceful!

Captain Harry Howden, master of the cruiser HMAS *Hobart*, had served in the waters around Malaya and the Dutch East Indies and was a hero to the men who served under him. Captain Howden became the recognised master at dodging bombs dropped by enemy aircraft while they were in the air, a technique he employed with great skill during the Coral Sea battle. Howden would order everyone on the bridge and even those below deck to lie prone. He often had his stretcher on the bridge and lying on it he would train his glasses on the attacking aircraft and visualise where falling bombs would land. He and the helmsman would be the only two left standing on the bridge. Then, at a direct command, even the helmsman would lie flat. Howden would spin the helm over and then lie flat himself as the bombs fell harmlessly into the ocean. According to those who served with him, Howden knew no fear as he violently manoeuvred his ship. Those in the engine room coping with the dramatic movements of the cruiser likened Howden to a younger, dashing, carefree destroyer captain. A leading stoker once said, 'We had so much faith in the grand gentleman's judgment that we just knew he would get us out of bother, which he so often did.'

On 7 May the Battle of the Coral Sea between the carriers and their aircraft began in earnest. Patrolling aircraft from the carrier USS *Yorktown* discovered the Japanese light carrier the *Shoho* by chance near the Jomard Passage connecting the Solomon Sea with the Coral Sea. The *Shoho* was accompanied by four cruiser escorts. The first American dive on the carrier scored no hits, but near misses blew five planes over the side of the *Shoho*'s flight deck. Then she was hit by two bombs and burst into flames before going dead in the water. American planes swarmed in. Hit by thirteen bombs, up to seven torpedoes and a crashed US Dauntless dive-bomber, the *Shoho* sank at 11.35 am on 7 May with a loss of

638 Japanese. 'Scratch one flattop!' an elated flyer radioed to the big carrier, the *Lexington*. The commander of the Japanese Task Force, Vice Admiral Takeo Takagi, knew his principal role was the safe arrival off Port Moresby of the invasion troops and their equipment aboard eleven following transport ships, which were protected by a destroyer squadron. He now proceeded with great caution.

Aboard the *Lexington* Admiral Fletcher still had no contact with the big enemy carriers, the *Shokaku* and the *Zuikaku*, which he now knew were in the vicinity. The following morning thirty-nine aircraft from the *Yorktown* sighted the *Zuikaku* and the *Shokaku* with their escort vessels. The two carriers were about 10 miles (17 kilometres) apart. The Americans turned their attention to the *Shokaku* and bombed and strafed her, setting the carrier on fire. She was badly damaged but the fires were brought under control as the *Shokaku* headed for home.

Next day Japanese bombers attacked the *Yorktown* and the *Lexington*. Torpedo bombers came in from both sides of the bow of the *Lexington* at low range, releasing torpedoes. The captain made great efforts to steer between parallel tracks of the torpedoes but two hit the port side of the carrier. Dive-bombers made direct hits on the carrier as she tried to escape. It was all over within nineteen minutes. The *Yorktown* was damaged but her flight operations continued. The USS *Lexington*, or 'Lady Lex' as her crew called her, now had three boiler rooms flooded and fires burning elsewhere. As the crew struggled to get the carrier on an even keel, petrol vapours ignited, followed by violent eruptions. Remarkably, flight operations continued, even though the carrier was critically damaged as the fires spread and more explosions rocked the ship. Finally the aircraft were flown off and the order was given to abandon ship. The majority of the crew escaped down lines to a waiting destroyer. The big carrier sank amid massive explosions, one of which formed a huge mushroom cloud. American aircraft losses were small in comparison to the Japanese.

Snippets of news were received in Canberra on 8 May. In the House of Representatives, Prime Minister Curtin stood to deliver what would become a famous rallying speech at a critical turning point. He had received brief messages about a great naval battle that had begun in the Coral Sea but had no idea of the eventual outcome:

> The events that are taking place to-day are of crucial importance to the conduct of the war in this theatre.

Curtin began to speak with exceptional emotion before a small audience in a mostly empty chamber. He spoke with such passion and gravity that members of parliament and reporters began hurrying into the house and press gallery to hear his words. Curtin said nobody could tell what the result might be of the battle underway:

> If it should go advantageously, we shall have cause for great gratitude and our position will then be a little clearer. But if we should not have the advantages from this battle for which we hope, all that confronts us is a sterner ordeal, a greater and graver responsibility ... As I speak, those who are participating in the engagement are conforming to the sternest discipline and are subjecting themselves with all that they have – it may be for many of them the 'last full measure of their devotion' – to accomplish the increased safety and security of this territory ...

Curtin's press secretary Don Rodgers was there:

> He made a great speech and I saw tears on both sides of the House and even among hardened members of the Press Gallery. It was a very moving speech; I think one of his greatest speeches.

Under enormous pressure from US aircraft, Japanese commander Vice Admiral Shigeyoshi Inoue, rocked by the loss of the *Shoho*, called off the invasion of Port Moresby. Inoue was not prepared to risk further attacks, even though the commander-in-chief of the Combined Fleet, Admiral Yamamoto, had radioed orders to 'annihilate remaining enemy forces'. Inoue briefly turned back to re-engage, but soon thought the better of it and retreated towards Rabaul. Yamamoto's chief of staff, Admiral Ugaki, was unimpressed with his officers in the battle, as his diary noted:

> Not only did they not reply to our inquiry, they postponed the invasion of Port Moresby indefinitely ... Thereupon our staff officers became very angry and demanded that we send a strongly worded telegram to the [Inoue's] Chief of Staff. They charged that the Fourth Fleet had fallen into defeatism after losing *Shoho* ...

Ugaki thought Admiral Inoue had overestimated his losses. He said Imperial Headquarters subsequently made the battle out as 'the most significant gift to the nation'.

The Battle of the Coral Sea was a tactical victory for Japan, with the loss of a light carrier compared with the American's loss of a heavy carrier. But US shipbuilders were becoming far more capable of quickly replacing lost ships than the Japanese. More importantly, the strategic victory for the Allies was in turning back of the invasion fleet heading for Port Moresby. Tiny Nauru and Ocean, the phosphate-rich islands north-east of the Solomons, would be occupied by the Japanese in August 1942 after the initial unsuccessful attempt. New Caledonia and the New Hebrides would never be occupied by the Japanese.

*

Another benefit for the Americans in the historic carrier clash was that the big carrier the *Shokaku* was so badly damaged she would not be able to take part in another great battle, which was about to focus on the tiny and isolated US-held island of Midway, deep in the Pacific, between Hawaii and Tokyo. The Battle of Midway was now in the final stages of Japanese planning based on a proposal by Yamamoto. The commander-in-chief of the Combined Fleet planned to draw out the American carriers in a bigger clash, his long-awaited 'great decisive battle', intended to secure Japan's total victory in the war and force the United States to sue for peace.

Townsville, being built up as a US bomber base, was never smashed by a mass carrier attack after the Battle of the Coral Sea, as Japan's foreign minister from 1943, Mamoru Shigemitsu, later wrote:

> The plan to attack Northern Australia was thwarted and, to make matters worse, the rear of our Solomon Island expeditionary force was harassed by the American counter-attack that developed.

The Japanese knew that preparations for a major Australian–American counterattack were being made in Australia. According to Shigemitsu, ports on the Pacific coast served as subsidiary bases for the Australian and American forces 'that were being equipped and trained' by General MacArthur. That is why the Japanese navy's plan of campaign had to be extended to cut communications between the United States and Australia.

The commander-in-chief of the US fleet, Admiral Ernest J. King, much later wrote a summary report in Washington to the secretary for the navy, Frank Knox. He said the Battle of the Coral Sea had marked the end of the period of the US navy being totally on the defensive. It had, King reported, great implications for Australia in stemming a major assault:

> Such an attack was likely because of the prospect of success in the immediate operation, and because, if successful, the advance to Australia and the islands in the south Pacific could be accomplished in due course with comparative ease, once the enemy had cut our lines of communication.

In Canberra, Governor-General Lord Gowrie noted in a letter to the King on 19 May that the Battle of the Coral Sea was only a temporary setback for the Japanese. Gowrie thought the capture of Port Moresby would have been followed up by a further landing in force, probably on the northern coast of Queensland or in the Solomon Islands. While Japan's attempt had been frustrated, it would, no doubt, soon be resumed:

This lull was only a calm before the storm, and in the meantime the Japanese were vigorously reorganising and re-equipping their forces after the fighting in Malaya and Java, preparatory to a large scale attack against this country . . . It has given us time to build up a force which should be capable of putting up a determined resistance, by reinforcements from America and the arrival of the AIF from the Middle East, and the military situation today is very different from what it was two months ago.

*

John Curtin was severely rattled by how near Port Moresby came to capture. He was aghast at how much had gone wrong for the Allies in the major naval battle, despite the Allies being in possession of vital intelligence about Japanese naval movements. This data was provided by American- and Australian-based signals intelligence units. As early as 25 April the Combined Operational Intelligence Centre in Melbourne had issued an assessment that a Japanese operation to occupy Port Moresby was imminent. Aerial reconnaissance was flown from Australia and Port Moresby by USAAF and RAAF aircraft. Curtin's anxiety for reinforcements was demonstrated in a cable to External Affairs Minister Doc Evatt in London on 13 May:

> I hope there is full realisation in London and Washington of the grave threat with which we were confronted last week. We knew the strength of the enemy concentration, we knew his intentions, and we knew the prospective date of his attack, yet we were unable to marshal the superior strength to deal him a heavy blow and the whole of his convoy of twenty four transports fell back on Rabaul unscathed.

Curtin's rising anger, given Australia's past sacrifices for the Motherland, becomes clear in his cable to Evatt:

> If Japan should move in force against Australia and obtain a foothold, as threatened to occur last week with the Coral Sea action, it may be too late to send assistance. Possibly in the long run the

territory might be recovered but the country may have been ravished and the people largely decimated. History would gravely indict such a happening to a nation which sacrificed 60,000 of its men on overseas battlefields in the last war and, at its peril, has sent its naval, military and air forces to fight overseas in this one.

Curtin's angst had been fired up by General MacArthur the previous day when he told the prime minister there were in the South West Pacific Area 'all the elements that have produced disaster in the western Pacific since the beginning of the war'. MacArthur had asked his superior, General Marshall in Washington, for two aircraft carriers, a corps of three divisions and enough first-line aircraft to bring his strength to 1000. Churchill, appalled, suggested to Roosevelt that MacArthur was exceeding his authority.

*

While all of this was going on, industrial disputes continued unabated in Australia. The demands on Curtin were enormous. He couldn't rely on his labour minister but didn't want the party upheaval that would come from sacking him at this critical time, so when striking workers asked him to intervene in disputes, like the one in Melbourne, the prime minister, with all his pressing duties, did so.

In May the *Sydney Morning Herald* called for an end to the 'criminally irresponsible minority of miners' who had deprived the nation of more than 300,000 tons of coal since the beginning of the year by precipitating petty strikes 'often on absurdly trivial pretexts'. The action of militant coalminers in Australia, which had recorded a strike almost daily, was 'hardly short of treason', the *Herald* said. The *Canberra Times* on 14 May was similarly outraged:

Who is to rule Australia? That is the issue which the Prime Minister (Mr. Curtin) has brought fundamentally to the miners in his stirring appeal for continuous work by every miner on the coalfields . . .

Curtin reportedly 'worried himself sick' over these strikes. There was a public expectation that a prime minister with his trade union background might be able to control strikes as the Japanese 'thundered at the gates'. Addressing parliament in May, Curtin threatened to force striking coalminers into the army or labour corps, which didn't happen. Coal production overall, though, was steadily increasing. Curtin took time out to meet all parties in the industry over two days of discussions. He told parliament on 30 May that all had agreed on a standard code of rules and procedures to be observed in local disputes.

*

In five months the Japanese had conquered the Far East colonies of Britain, France, the United States and the Netherlands and had taken Australian possessions. The Greater East Asia Co-Prosperity Sphere had gained more than 100 million people. The Japanese had severely damaged the main US Pacific Fleet of battleships, sinking one large carrier, and had sunk many sizeable British, American and Dutch warships in East Indian seas or the western Pacific. In comparison the Japanese had lost very few naval ships. They had taken the surrender of about 250,000 enemy troops, mostly Asian, but also an Australian division, a British division and, in the Philippines, the equivalent of a division of Americans. Only remnants of the defending air forces survived and had made their way to Australia or India. Japan was ecstatic because this had been achieved with the loss of about 15,000 killed and wounded. The Japanese forces now had a vast perimeter that stretched through the central Pacific to New Guinea, and embraced the East Indies, Malaya, Thailand and Burma. In the west they were on the border of India. To the south, within easy range of their aircraft, lay Australia.

*

In late May the minister for external affairs, Doc Evatt, who had travelled from Washington to London, insisted on receiving a copy of the 'grand strategy' agreement between Britain and the

United States. The agreement included grandiose clauses about the need to ensure Australia's security but asserted that a full-scale invasion of Australia was unlikely. The strategy revealed what Evatt and Curtin had suspected:

> The strategy defined in it was primarily defensive in character. The offensive was to take place in the future.

This went against every conceivable notion of Curtin and MacArthur. At the Advisory War Council in Canberra only two days before Evatt's cable, MacArthur had clearly outlined his most secret plans:

> The immediate problem is to make Australia secure. After this has been accomplished the next step is to organise Australia as a base for a counter-stroke towards the Philippines and from there to attack Formosa [Taiwan].

MacArthur had doubted the Japanese would invade Australia as the spoils were not worth the risk. Although it would not be a good plan from a strategic point of view, he said, 'there may be other factors which would influence the Japanese to launch such an attack'. He said Australia's anti-aircraft defences were 'very poor' and he proposed to reorganise adequate defences for the main cities and air bases.

Evatt and Curtin were further infuriated by the fact that the two former conservative politicians – the Australian minister in Washington, Richard Casey, and Australia's special envoy in London, Sir Earle Page – had known the latest details of the 'Beat Hitler First' arrangement between Britain and the United States, but had failed to report to the government that the policy had continued without alteration even after Japan had entered the war. Evatt had just come from a meeting with Churchill and his defence chiefs and was buoyed by their words, even though they had said it was 'very unwise to divert large land forces to Australia until it is reasonably clear that the enemy will strike heavily against Australia'. Evatt seemed content with a promise to return two Australian brigades currently in Ceylon to Australia and send some British troops if required in an emergency. What satisfied Evatt most, though, was Churchill's promise to send three fully equipped Spitfire squadrons – two RAAF and one RAF – from Britain to Australia 'in the near future':

This wing is being despatched with the utmost secrecy and the prime minister is extremely keen on Australia regarding it as a special gesture in the present emergency. As you see, it will involve the immediate provision of forty-eight of the best fighters in the world and a flow of 180 machines per annum.

However, the 'special gesture' Spitfires would not arrive for the intended defence of Darwin until January 1943, when the emergency of a Japanese invasion had significantly diminished. At Government House in Canberra, Lord Gowrie wrote to a colleague saying that the more he saw of Curtin, the greater his respect for the man. But the governor-general had mounting concerns:

He is handling a difficult crew with firmness and courage and as long as he is at the helm things will go right – but his health is not good and I can see no satisfactory alternative if anything should happen to him.

Chapter 12

PACIFIC TURNING POINT

It was early in the morning on Saturday 30 May 1942 when the powerful and well-armed Japanese submarine the *I-21* broke the surface of a heavy swell off Sydney and ratings rushed to bring out a Yokosuka E14Y float plane from its small waterproof hangar on the dripping deck. They quickly assembled the wings and tail and it soon stood ready for take-off. The captain of the submarine brought the big sub into the wind. The young pilot, Warrant Officer Susumu Ito, confident and extremely resourceful, swung into the little aircraft's cockpit and was followed by his co-pilot, Iwasaki. They knew Sydney Harbour well from charts and photographs. Ito's job now was to plot the main targets of a raid to take place the next day by three midget submarines, each with a crew of two, which currently were underwater moving towards Sydney Harbour. Each was attached to the deck of one of three big mother submarines. The midget subs had many technical defects and had been used without success in the attack on Pearl Harbor. Ito waited for the bow of the *I–21* to dip just before rising and then hit the launch button, catapulting his plane into the air into a strong headwind. It was 2.45 am and the pilot turned west, flying at 500 metres. Encountering cloud, he descended over

Sydney to just 150 metres and lower. The city looked beautiful under twinkling lights.

Sixty-five years later Susumu Ito sat opposite me in the board-room of his office supply company at Iwakuni, south-west of Hiroshima. He looked more like a sixty-year-old and had lost none of his verve and brashness:

> I am the only person left alive in Japan who participated in the war at Pearl Harbor and was on the submarines there. I saw the battleship *Yamato* being built. It was prohibited to fly over the top, but I did.

The defence of Sydney at this time was deplorable and it would get worse. Lieutenant Ito had flown unmolested by gunfire over Sydney Harbour. There had been earlier Japanese reconnaissance flights. The aircraft were seen by many, including armed servicemen on duty, and were targeted by searchlights, but no one below thought it remotely possible that a Japanese navy float plane could be operating so far south. Only a day earlier a New Zealand forces aircraft had spotted a large submarine 40 nautical miles (74 kilometres) east-south-east of Sydney. The Navy Office in Melbourne had later responded, remarkably, that there had been 'no reported submarine activity on the east coast of Australia' since 16 May, which was enough to dismiss the confirmed New Zealanders' sighting. On 16 May a Soviet steamer, the *Wellen*, had been unsuccessfully attacked by a submarine off Newcastle firing its deck gun from only 100 metres. The steamer replied with machine-gun fire and the submarine had submerged. A search for the sub had failed to find anything.

Ito's flight over Sydney Harbour was a success, as he recalled:

> For the midget subs to go to the harbour that morning they needed to have some sort of target. I did find a target. It was something good.

There were many warships in the harbour but one appeared to Ito to be a battleship. It was in fact a heavy cruiser, the USS *Chicago*, moored off Garden Island. The *Chicago* had come to Sydney after participating in the Battle of the Coral Sea. Returning to land on the sea near the mother submarine, Ito crash-landed in a heavy swell. Despite being an accomplished swimmer, Ito began to sink, owing to a pistol and three small cases of bullets in his clothing:

> I was choking on the seawater . . . splashing around in the sea and
> I was about to drown and was pulled out.

The wrecked aircraft had to be smashed with hammers until it sank. Ito went below and apologised to the captain for the loss of the aircraft. By now there were five large Japanese submarines submerged off Sydney, three of them carrying the highly unreliable midget submarines, each armed with two large torpedoes. The six crewmen were making preparations, writing final farewell letters and placing locks of hair and fingernail clippings in envelopes for loved ones. None of them believed they would survive.

On Sunday evening, 31 May, all the Japanese submarines were submerged. The two crewmen for each of the three midget subs moved from their respective mother subs through watertight hatches to their tiny, cramped vessels and the midget subs were mechanically released. Just after 8 pm the first midget submarine, the *M-27*, manned by Lieutenant Kenshi Chuman, the commander of the three midgets, and his petty officer, Takeshi Omori, entered Sydney Harbour. Low cloud covered a full moon. As with all three midgets, the leading submarine was registered by an RAN surveillance system at South Head. The system worked on indicator loops under the harbour that recorded the movement of vessels passing over them. But those on duty at South Head did not report the 'signature', which was scratched out on paper like a seismic recording. 'There was a good deal of traffic on the night of the attack, and the confusion was, to some extent, understandable,' the Navy Office later said in explanation of the blunder.

The *M-27* followed a large fishing boat heading for the eastern gate of a wide boom net stretched across the harbour and held by floating buoys on the surface. Disaster came quickly. Chuman for some reason, perhaps a technical fault with the sub, made a sudden change of course and his midget sub mounted part of the steel net strung across the harbour. The *M-27* was trapped and with the tide falling the midget would become increasingly exposed. A Maritime Services Board watchman, James Cargill, rowed over to an old pleasure cruiser, the *Yarroma*, now pressed into navy service. 'There's something in the net,' called Cargill to the vessel. The watchman thought it might be a submarine. The crew of the *Yarroma*, without communications or even a decent torch, tried to contact the RAN office at Garden Island without success. The men aboard *Yarroma* thought the object on the net was too large to be a mine but too small to be a submarine. Their investigation wasted precious time. In the meantime another old pleasure cruiser in RAN service, the *Lolita*, raced towards the object in the net and fired three depth charges, but none exploded because the water was too shallow. Sydney's naval officer-in-charge, Rear Admiral Gerard Muirhead-Gould, on secondment from the Royal Navy, was reluctantly called away from entertaining visiting American officers from the *Chicago* in the RAN's mansion at Elizabeth Bay. Just before 10.30 pm Muirhead-Gould belatedly sounded the general alarm. Inside the midget, the boyish skipper with the child's face took his pistol, pointed it at the head of his crewmate Takeshi Omori and pulled the trigger. He then put the pistol to his head and simultaneously pulled the trigger and detonated a demolition charge. A great ball of fire rose above the harbour into the night air, lifting the midget submarine off the net.

At about 9.50 pm the second midget, the *M-24,* crewed by Sublieutenant Katsuhisa Ban and his petty officer, Mamoru Ashibe, had made it safely over the indicator loops near the harbour entrance and gained access to the inner harbour by following a vessel, probably a Manly ferry, through the boom net opening. The *M-24* headed up-harbour towards the naval base at Garden Island. It steered towards the Harbour Bridge, passed about 200 metres off Garden Island in the path of a dockyard motor boat, the *Nestor*, which was urgently forced to alter course to avoid the midget. An observer on Garden Island ferry wharf saw the midget sub caught in the searchlight of the US cruiser the *Chicago*. Quick-firing 'pom pom' rounds with red tracers began streaking across the water, landing 'all around the submarine', a witness said. At 10.45 pm the navy in Sydney belatedly alerted the RAAF that 'Midget submarines number unknown' were at the 'entrance to Port Jackson [Sydney Harbour]' with 'possibility of some being in harbour'. A naval officer ran around the big dockyard trying to get night workmen to turn bright lights off. Soon after, the *Chicago* spotted the conning tower of Ban and Ashibe's *M-24* midget and opened fire. The Australian heavy cruiser HMAS *Canberra*, moored near Bennelong Point, also opened fire. Smaller vessels joined in with whatever weapons they had. About thirty minutes after midnight Ban fired a torpedo at the *Chicago*. The torpedo missed the cruiser and passed under a Dutch submarine, the *K-9*, before exploding under the *Kuttabul*, an old ferry boat being used to accommodate men of the RAN. The ferry lifted in an enormous explosion. Able seaman Neil Roberts found himself swimming underwater out through the side of the sinking ferry. Twenty-one sleeping men were killed on the *Kuttabul*. Ban had fired a second torpedo, which ran on to the rocks on the eastern side of Garden Island and failed to explode. The governor-general, Lord Gowrie, who was relaxing with Lady Gowrie at their official Sydney residence, Admiralty House, at Kirribilli Point on the northern side of the harbour, later told King George VI:

Zara and I took up our positions on the balcony and had a good view of the proceedings. We couldn't actually see the submarines, but we could see the small craft buzzing about dropping depth charges and searchlights moving all over the surface of the water.

The *Chicago* began firing five-inch (13-centimetre) shells at the midget *M-24*. They didn't hit the midget but one struck a glancing blow to Fort Denison, on 'Pinchgut' island, in the harbour between Kirribilli and Garden Island. Other shells landed in Cremorne and Mosman. The moon came out and searchlights played all over the harbour. People living around the harbour foreshores were now highly alarmed at the war coming to Sydney. Ships were firing shells and machine guns, and bullets were glancing off the small conning tower of the *M-24*.

Only two minutes after the *Kuttabul* exploded, the third midget submarine the *M-22*, crewed by Lieutenant Keiu Matsuo and his petty officer, Masao Tsuzuku, was sighted down harbour by the small anti-submarine ship HMAS *Yandra,* which spotted a conning tower well ahead. Increasing speed it pursued the submarine towards the eastern channel and rammed it, striking the *M-22* a glancing blow, damaging a protective cage around its torpedo tubes and preventing it from firing its two torpedoes. The ship reversed and pressed home a depth charge attack, sustaining damage due to her closeness to the explosion.

In the early hours of the morning, a trawler, the *San Michele*, reported sighting a submarine off Cronulla, a southern Sydney beach. It was one of the five mother submarines positioned in a line stretching seaward from a point about 6 kilometres from Port Hacking. The mother subs were waiting to recover any of the crew from the three midgets who might escape. But none did.

At dawn on Monday 1 June, as the first rays of the sun broke through the clouds, the Sydney ferry timetable was not greatly altered by the midget submarine attack. Rear Admiral Muirhead-Gould had ordered the ferries to continue to operate in the hope that harbour traffic would 'keep the midgets down'. Bullets and shells were still being fired around the harbour in a great commotion. At one stage a ferry with twenty-seven early morning commuters aboard was on course to cross through the gunfire. The ferry master had to throw the ferry into hard astern at the last moment. At five in the morning the patrol boat the *Sea Mist* discovered a midget submarine on the surface in Taylors Bay, Mosman, and saw it crash-dive. The *Sea Mist* dropped a depth charge, which made an enormous explosion that damaged the attacking boat. Another passing ferry had a ringside view. More patrol boats arrived and dropped more explosives. In the *M-22* lying on the bottom of the bay on an even keel, the young skipper Keiu Matsuo had been unable to fire either of his torpedoes. The submarine, with its motor still running, was found a little later by a diver. When the bodies of the two submariners were recovered, both had been shot in the head. The navigator Masao Tsuzuku was found with his boots off; RAN investigators conjectured he had wanted to escape when the sub was on the surface. Strangely, Matsuo was slumped in the navigator's seat while Tsuzuku had fallen dead on the floor. Regardless, it would seem that Tsuzuku had been shot by Matsuo before the skipper had shot himself in the head. The third midget sub, the *M-24*, the only one to fire her torpedoes, simply disappeared. The disappearance would remain a mystery for sixty-four years.

On that Monday Defence Headquarters at Victoria Barracks issued a communique that said all three enemy midget submarines were believed to have been destroyed:

The enemy's attack was completely unsuccessful. Damage was confined to one small harbour vessel of no military value.

The *Sydney Morning Herald* speculated that a ship standing well to seaward might have brought the submarines to Sydney. The newspaper, like the government, tended to play down the attack:

Harbour-side residents had an exciting experience when they saw searchlights try to pick up the raiders and heard guns fired when the periscope of one of the submarines was spotted. The din was added to by the dropping of depth charges. The detonations shook houses and broke windows.

In federal parliament on 2 June the minister for the navy, Norman Makin, heavily gilded the lily by ignoring the many alarming failures on the night and commended the defence forces for their preparations to meet a raid designed to cause havoc on Sydney Harbour. He said the harbour raid was 'instantly detected', and that counter measures were 'prompt and effective':

The attempt was unsuccessful. Its failure was due to the preparedness of our defences for such an attempt, and the prompt
counter-attack carried out by harbour defence vessels and other
warships in the harbour.

*

On the day Makin was speaking in Canberra, a Japanese aircraft
was taking special interest in the idyllic tropical black-sand and
coconut-palm fringed coastline around the villages of Buna and
Gona in Papua. The reconnaissance aircraft was circling Buna,
which had a government station, and Gona, where there was a
small Anglican mission. The villages were east of the inland
Kokoda station and plantation and on the north coast of the
'tail' of New Guinea, directly over the massive, rugged Owen
Stanley mountain range from the major centre of Port Moresby
on the south coast, where the Australians and some newly arrived
American servicemen were building up a major base. Having
failed to secure Moresby directly by sea after the Battle of the
Coral Sea, Japanese navy planners had investigated other means.
On the night of the midget sub raid, Allied bombers attacked
Rabaul and dropped incendiaries on Lae on the way back to
Moresby. On 1 June, eighteen Japanese bombers with a screen of
ten Zeros made another heavy raid on Port Moresby, destroying
houses. Surveillance aircraft had been told to pay particular attention to the difficult rough track, which the Japanese called a road,
running over the Owen Stanley Range linking Port Moresby to
the other side. But they could see little though the dense foliage.

*

Japanese submarine activity around Australia now stretched
around the east coast. Just before dawn on 4 June, a small
steamer, the *Barwon*, heading from Melbourne to Port Kembla,
was attacked by gunfire and torpedo near Gabo Island, off
the coast of Victoria near the New South Wales border. She
suffered no damage or casualties, although fragments from the
torpedo, which exploded close alongside, came on board the ship.

At 7 am that day a bigger coastal passenger steamer, the *Canberra*, reported sighting a 'suspicious object probably submarine' off Cape Moreton near Brisbane. The *Canberra* luckily would outrun her prey and survive to carry Australian troops to New Guinea.

When it became clear that none of the midget submariners was going to return from the Sydney attack, the mother subs waiting off the coast of Sydney were ordered to sink Allied commercial shipping instead. They headed in different directions but on 6 June the *I-24* was still lurking off Sydney in the diminishing, forlorn hope of recovering Ban and Ashibe. In a desperate act of defiance and revenge, the *I-24* began to shell the Sydney Harbour area. Sydney was not fully blacked out when the shelling began. Switches were thrown and the city was at last was in blackness as air raid sirens wailed. Some people headed for backyard or community shelters. The sound of shells fired from the sea could be heard across the eastern suburbs of Bondi, Bellevue Hill, Rose Bay, Bronte, Coogee and Randwick. The *I-24* fired ten shells at Sydney but only four exploded. Three caused minor damage, partly demolishing two houses, and one exploded harmlessly. Other shells landed in the harbour. Sydney's coastal batteries opened up on the distant flashes at sea, but the *I-24* soon safely submerged. One Japanese shell gave a Sydney woman a great shock. The shell had failed to explode after tearing through flats in Manion Avenue, 'Woollahra' (actually Rose Bay). Miss M. Lanham was staying with friends:

> I heard some whistling sounds overhead. I tried to be calm and tell myself it was only practice. Then I felt the building shake and saw some debris. I took the baby and went out to a shelter room. I felt very nervous as I passed the shell [unexploded] on the stairs on my way down.

On 7 June Prime Minister Curtin told the House of Representatives that Japanese submarines were being destroyed quickly off the coast of Australia. He read a brief statement from Defence Headquarters that exaggerated the truth:

An Allied plane bombed and destroyed an enemy submarine. This brings the enemy's losses in his submarine drive in this sector to seven with a probable eight.

The Japanese recorded the loss of the three midget submarines only.

*

Lieutenant Susumu Ito, who had flown over Sydney Harbour, scrambled up into the dripping conning tower of the *I-21* as soon as the big sub surfaced in Stockton Bight off Newcastle in the darkness of Monday 8 June. Gunners raced to the sub's 5.5-inch (14-centimetre) deck gun and began firing the first of thirty-four rounds towards Newcastle, aiming at the shipyards at Carrington and at the steelworks at Kooragang Island. Some of the shells failed to explode, but twenty-four fell in the area of Newcastle's power station and customs house, causing minor damage. After an unexplained delay of thirteen minutes, the gunners on the coastal hilltop at Fort Scratchley eventually fired on the enemy vessel with only four rounds from one of the six-inch (15-centimetre) guns. Gunners at the fort could not see the sub but could see occasional flashes at sea. Pilot Ito was on the conning tower of the *I-21*. At age ninety-two, he clearly recalled the fort's response and confirmed that the Australian shells came dangerously close:

> We wanted to cause concern for the people and make them feel uncomfortable. I was on the bridge watching the gunfire. The enemy shells hit the water with a splash. That was scary. If they hit us we were dead. Even one would sink us. Usually if a sub comes up to fire guns, you don't expect return fire . . . I was thinking . . . we should get out of there.

Eventually the *I-21* submerged without damage.

The remains of the four submariners killed in the Sydney raid were given a formal funeral service by the RAN, which attracted a good deal of adverse public comment, given that twenty-one RAN personnel had been killed in the Japanese raid. The submariners' coffins were placed in a crematorium chapel, each draped with a Japanese flag. The RAN escort, which included a firing party, bearers and a bugler, stood at attention. As the last coffin disappeared from view, three volleys were fired. Sailors presented arms with fixed bayonets while a bugler sounded 'The Last Post'. The ashes of the four were given to the Japanese minister to Australia, Tatsuo Kawai, who was under house arrest at his home in Melbourne. He took the remains back to Japan when he left on a diplomatic exchange in October 1942. When Kawai arrived at Yokohama port, the submariners were confirmed as 'Hero Gods' and their feats were hailed in Japanese newspapers in an extraordinary flurry of nationalistic publicity.

The mystery of the missing *M-24* challenged Australians for decades. The midget sub was the only one of the three that did escape from Sydney Harbour. On leaving the heads, the midget had turned north, not south where the mother sub was waiting. Lieutenant Katsuhisa Ban and Petty Officer Mamoru Ashibe had expected death and would not risk the safety of the mother sub *I-24*. In November 2006 a team of Sydney amateur divers discovered the *M-24* in fifty-four metres of water off Bungan Head near Newport Beach. There was clear damage to the sub from heavy machine-gun bullets and shrapnel. The bow was crumpled. The hatch was locked down and the ladder was in the stowed position, meaning Ban and Ashibe never left the sub. Ban almost certainly shot Ashibe and then himself, which was standard procedure in emergencies. But the hatch of the *M-24* will never be opened. Australian authorities declared the site a heritage zone and after the initial discovery divers were strictly forbidden from going near the wreck. The submariners' relatives in Japan wanted it that way.

During the period of the midget submarine attacks and the subsequent shelling of Sydney and Newcastle, coalminers stunned the rest of Australia with a series of new strikes despite, as *The Argus* in Melbourne put it, John Curtin's 'honest and patient efforts' to prevent the industrial disruption. 'In the face of such a menace, internal squabbling becomes sheer insanity,' *The Argus* cried, calling on the government to quell the stoppages with 'stern measures'.

*

One of the great secrets of the war was that American and Australian cryptanalysts were able to learn a great deal about Japan's future war plans. After the arrival of General Douglas MacArthur in Australia as Supreme Commander, a Combined Operational Intelligence Centre (COIC) was established in Melbourne involving intelligence experts from the United States and the three branches of the services in Australia. It followed the establishment of the Special Intelligence Organisation in Sydney in November 1941. The new, highly secretive, intelligence operation had monitoring posts at various centres, including Melbourne, Canberra, Townsville and Darwin. It worked in close cooperation with US intelligence services overseas and was aided by MacArthur's experienced intelligence operatives, who had flown in from the Philippines. The Allied interception and decoding of Japan's secret radio messages was to become one of the significant success stories of the Allies in the Pacific. MacArthur's intelligence chief, General Charles Willoughby, would later claim that signals intelligence, as it was termed, 'chopped two years off the war in the Pacific'.

The British had created Ultra, a highly successful machine to decode German messages. The Allies used the name to classify its most secret messages. The Americans created a machine of their own design comprising selectors and relays and operated by a keyboard. It was the exact mirror image of the Japanese code machine and it originally enabled them to read Japanese diplomatic messages. That machine was called Purple and the information extracted was referred to by those in the know as 'Magic'. By mid-1941 the US navy had been operating a forward intercept unit and code-breaking group on Corregidor Island in the Philippines. The information gathered by both the British and the Americans was shared. The Americans had been reading Japanese diplomatic messages from September 1941 and earlier had been aware of the Japanese preparations for war. The various branches of the Australian services began training intercept operators before Japan went to war. Allied code-breakers, especially just before the outbreak of the war, had to contend with the Japanese navy frequently changing their codes, each of which had to be unravelled with great haste. But the rewards were enormous. Some three weeks before the Battle of the Coral Sea, defence officials in Washington and Australia, including General MacArthur, had been advised of the names of the Japanese carriers that were expected to arrive in Truk, and of large numbers of aircraft heading for Rabaul. The intercepted intelligence allowed them to predict the meaning of the moves:

> The indications of Carrier Div 5 moving to Truk, following other indications of heavy air reinforcements proceeding to Rabaul, and the maintenance of extensive and regular air patrols all support and suggest an early enemy offensive against Port Moresby before the end of April.

Thus American and Australian ships had been able to scramble to their battle stations. It was almost too much to hope that the Japanese navy would guide enemy ships to their intended invasion fleet. But that's precisely what occurred in the enormously important Battle of Midway, with Australian code-breakers playing a role. The following message in Australian intelligence archival files landed on the desks of the most senior officers in the United States and Australia:

> TOP SECRET – ULTRA. 14th May. C-in-C Combined Fleet [Admiral Yamamoto] informed 2nd and 4th Fleets that bombs and ammunition for the 'forthcoming campaign' will be supplied. They are asked to supply their own transport and to requisition on Kure [major naval base on the Inland Sea].

On 15 May a supply ship requisitioned by the Imperial Navy, the *Goshu Maru*, requested various charts for voyages from Midway

Island to Hawaii and the seas around the Hawaiian islands. Admiral Yamamoto had thoughts about winning his great 'decisive victory' over the Americans at Midway and contemplated following that up with an invasion of Hawaii. The Allied intelligence experts also correctly guessed other battles were being planned, given the direction of the Japanese 1st and 5th Fleets:

> It is suggested the first force may operate in the Aleutians [islands at the extreme western end of Alaska] and the second force may make another attempt on Hawaii or attack other islands in the Central Pacific.

Details soon became clearer when the chief of staff of the 1st Air Fleet, Rear Admiral Ryunosuke Kusaka, stated in a signal on 18 May that 'on the day of attack' he would be in position 50 nautical miles (93 kilometres) off 'AF', which the Allies knew was Japanese naval code for Midway Island. Kusaka said he would 'fly off aircraft as quickly as possible'. A signal from the commander-in-chief, Admiral Yamamoto, was picked up the next day talking about an unnamed ship or ships that would be 'included in the invasion force' and would soon sail for Truk. The names of aircraft carriers to be used and in some cases the aircraft they were carrying were mentioned, all valuable pieces of the jigsaw. By 1 June the amazed code-breakers reported:

> There is considerable volume of traffic being broadcast for units in the Midway operation forces, but no traffic being originated by them. The operation has apparently begun and forces at sea are keeping radio silence.

The Midway Island operation had been approved by Imperial General Headquarters and largely planned by staff officers aboard Yamamoto's flagship, the *Yamato*. The work was super-vised by Yamamoto's aggressive chief of staff of the Combined Fleet, Rear Admiral Ugaki. But the key protagonist was Yamamoto himself. According to his air commander, Captain

Mitsuo Fuchida, his chief made 'a hasty and uncompromising insistence on the Midway operation' in the face of cogent arguments against it. Fuchida believed that Yamamoto's judgement was 'warped by his obsession' to keep Tokyo immune from air attack and by his sense of injured pride after a US B-25 bomber raid from an aircraft carrier, led by Lieutenant Colonel James Doolittle, on Tokyo on 18 April. The raid was partly inspired by President Roosevelt's wish to boost the morale of the American people. That it did, but the raid caused little significant damage. Of the eighty airmen who participated, three were killed bailing out of their aircraft and eight were captured, of which three were executed and one died as a prisoner.

Yamamoto's Combined Fleet Headquarters wanted to seize tiny Midway Island partly as an advance base that could detect enemy forces operating westward from Hawaii. A broader objective, according to Fuchida, was to draw out the US Pacific fleet's remaining strength so that it could be engaged and destroyed in the grand decisive battle that had long been part of the Imperial Navy's strategy. Apart from the large Midway operation comprising some 200 Japanese ships, the Combined Fleet also planned to capture key points in the remote US Aleutians. The aim of this operation was to protect Japan's northern flank and to act as a diversion from Midway. It was thought that the invasion of the Aleutians might throw US forces off balance. Admiral Yamamoto said Japan's first-phase operations had already established an invincible strategic position:

> This position, however, cannot be maintained if we go on the defensive. In order to secure it tenaciously, we must keep on striking offensively at the enemy's weak points one after another. This will be the central aim of our second-phase operations.

When the time to prepare for the Midway battle arrived, the extraordinary intelligence gathered about Japan's plans allowed the Pacific fleet commander, Admiral Chester W. Nimitz, to establish an ambush. His carriers would be waiting for the Japanese.

The converging Japanese fleets ran into heavy seas and poor visibility from heavy fog. Vice Admiral Chuichi Nagumo, in the aircraft carrier the *Akagi*, was desperate to get information of enemy fleet movements, but even Admiral Yamamoto, in the flagship the *Yamato*, 600 nautical miles (1110 kilometres) to the rear, was maintaining radio silence.

US Task Force Sixteen, commanded by Rear Admiral Raymond A. Spruance and formed around the big carriers USS *Enterprise* and USS *Hornet*, had departed Pearl Harbor on 28 May to take up a position north-east of Midway. Two days later, Task Force Seventeen, commanded by Rear Admiral Frank Fletcher, formed around the now repaired *Yorktown*, and sailed to join the task force already north-east of Midway. The three American carriers, augmented by cruiser-launched float planes, provided 234 aircraft heading to Midway. They were supported by 110 fighters, bombers and patrol planes based on Midway Island. The United States also deployed twenty-five submarines around Midway.

On 2 June, at this crucial time, Prime Minister Curtin came out with a surprisingly buoyant statement while speaking in support of Australia's second Liberty loan. He claimed Japan's war program of constant expansion had at last reached a stalemate:

> today I speak with you with a spirit of confidence born of a knowledge of how the war is proceeding. I defy the enemy to land large forces in Australia.

On 3 June US aircraft from Midway located and attacked Japanese transports about 600 nautical miles west of Midway Island. But the army air force Flying Fortresses inflicted little damage. After midnight on 4 June, Admiral Nimitz, based on patrol plane reports, advised the two task forces of the course and speed of the Japanese main body of ships located 574 nautical miles (1063 kilometres) from Midway. Shortly after dawn, a patrol plane spotted two Japanese carriers and their escorts and reported 'many planes' heading to Midway. Four night-flying Catalinas attacked the Japanese transports, sinking the fleet tanker *Akebono Maru*.

Thirty minutes before sunrise on 5 June cheers rang out aboard the four aircraft carriers, the *Akagi*, the *Kaga*, the *Hiryu* and the *Soryu*, as aircraft after aircraft thundered off the decks and headed for Midway, the US base of two small, heavily defended atolls. When the last attacking aircraft lifted off there were 108 bombers and fighters in the air. Slower US Grumman Wildcats and Brewster Buffalos were no match for the Zeros, and the dogfights quickly became a slaughter. Of the defending twenty-six US Marine Corps Buffalo and Grumman fighters, seventeen were shot down, although damage to the Midway base was only slight. Word was radioed back to the Japanese carriers that another attack was necessary. The decks of each carrier were now packed with aircraft armed with torpedos in case of US carrier attacks. But another mass raid on Midway required rearming with bombs, which took a superhuman effort by Japanese crews. In another twist of fate, a reconnaissance aircraft reported sighting US ships 200 nautical miles (370 kilometres) to the east. Admiral Nagumo had assumed there were no aircraft carriers in the vicinity as scout planes sent up earlier had found none. But a reconnaissance pilot, nearly an hour into the rearming, reported that the enemy fleet included an aircraft carrier. This created pandemonium. Many aircraft had to be sent down to their hangars yet again to exchange bombs intended for Midway for torpedoes to be used against the US carriers. In the rush, bombs were abandoned in hangars and on decks, along with the torpedoes waiting to be fitted.

In the turmoil American dive-bombers pounced on the *Akagi* and the *Soryu* and scored direct hits. The air commander, Captain Mitsuo Fuchida, was on the *Akagi*'s flight deck as Zero fighters began to take off, but they did not have time to gain sufficient height to engage the Americans:

I looked up to see three black enemy planes plummeting towards our ship. Some of our machine guns managed to fire a few frantic bursts at them, but it was too late. Dauntless dive bombers quickly grew larger, and then a number of black objects suddenly floated eerily from their wings. Bombs! Down they came straight towards me! I fell intuitively to the deck and crawled behind a command post mantelet. The terrifying scream of the dive bombers reached me first, followed by the crashing explosion of a direct hit.

At 11 am, the one Japanese carrier that escaped destruction that morning, the *Hiryu*, launched 'Val' dive-bombers that temporarily disabled *Yorktown* around noon, dropping bombs on the flight deck, killing many and causing serious fires below. But the fires in five of the ship's boilers were snuffed out. Admiral Fletcher transferred his flag to the cruiser, the *Astoria*. A medical officer, Lieutenant Joseph P. Pollard, was on the *Yorktown*'s flight deck when, as he put it, all hell broke loose:

I saw a burst of fire, heard a terrific explosion and in less than ten seconds was overwhelmed by a mass of men descending from the gun mounts and flight deck into the Dressing Station ... I was overwhelmed with work. Wounded were everywhere. Some men had one foot or leg off, others had both off; some were dying – some dead. Everywhere there was need for morphine, tourniquets, blankets and first aid.

On the flight deck Pollard saw men cut in half at their anti-aircraft posts. There were dead men, or portions of them, everywhere. The carrier slowed and finally came to a stop. Remarkably, the boilers were repaired and relit and the *Yorktown* got underway again. Three and a half hours later, the *Hiryu*'s 'Kate' torpedo planes struck a second massive blow, attacking from four different angles at masthead height or lower. The *Yorktown* manoeuvred violently to dodge two torpedoes but two others hit and exploded, causing fuel tanks to erupt and jamming the ship's rudder. All power connections were cut and the ship took on an immediate list of seventeen degrees. Captain Elliott Buckmaster called for abandon ship and four destroyers closed in to take off crew or pick them up from the water. Injured men were lowered by rope, but many wouldn't make it, as medical officer Pollard in a dressing station recalled:

A man lying beside me with one foot shot away and a severe chest wound turned his head towards me and asked, 'What does this mean for us?' and turned his head away. He knew that he would have no chance in the water.

Pollard was told by Captain Buckmaster to leave the ship and the doctor went over the side on a rope into oily water as the carrier seemed ready to roll over:

As each wave broke over our heads the oil burned our eyes and noses like liquid fire. It was impossible to keep from swallowing some of it. Someone would swim alongside and say 'hold me up a minute please' and proceed to vomit the oil and then swim on.

The sea was smooth and some sailors on the water showed they were not defeated by calling 'Taxi! Taxi!' and thumbing imaginary rides at floating debris. Meanwhile scout bombers returning to the *Yorktown*, not knowing her fate, saw the carrier the *Hiryu*, two battleships, three cruisers and four destroyers steaming north about 110 nautical miles (200 kilometres) from the *Yorktown*. Hearing this report, the *Enterprise* turned into the wind and launched twenty-four Dauntless dive-bombers, ten of which had flown in from the crippled USS *Yorktown*. A straddle of bombs landed along the *Kaga*, starting raging fires. American bombs and exploding fuel tanks of aircraft on the decks of the *Akagi* started disastrous fires. Fuchida recalled the mayhem on board:

We had been caught flatfooted in the most vulnerable condition possible – decks loaded with planes armed and fuelled for attack. Looking about, I was horrified at the destruction that had been wrought in a matter of seconds. There was a huge hole in the flight deck ... deck plates reeled upwards in grotesque configurations. Planes stood tail up, belching livid flame and jet-black smoke. Reluctant tears streamed down my cheeks as I watched the fires spread.

The hangar area of the *Akagi* was a blazing inferno and the flames were moving up towards the bridge. The order was soon given to abandon the carrier. Admiral Yamamoto aboard the *Yamato*, now 400 nautical miles (740 kilometres) away, received a report that the *Kaga*, the *Soryu* and the *Akagi* were ablaze. He ordered the invasion transports to withdraw. The *Hiryu* launched her aircraft against the enemy carriers. The carrier the *Yorktown* and the destroyer, the *Hammann*, were the only two American ships lost. US aircraft from Midway and the carriers continued their attacks during the day. By late afternoon the *Hiryu* had been hit by scores of bombs and some twenty-four torpedoes. Yamamoto ordered all ships to retreat. It had been a disaster.

The Navy General Staff in Tokyo received increasingly grim signals on the progress of the battle. When the report came in that the *Hiryu* had suffered the same fate as the *Akagi*, the *Kaga* and the *Soryu*, they knew that the operation was doomed. As Mitsuo Fuchida put it:

> Our four finest fleet carriers were lost. Enemy air strength on Midway was not destroyed.

Midway was the second of five great Pacific battles primarily involving aircraft carriers and their planes. As historian Samuel Morison said, it established the vital role of carrier-borne air power in naval warfare. Moreover, Midway was a victory of the use of intelligence, as acknowledged by the commander-in-chief of the US Pacific fleet, Admiral Chester W. Nimitz:

> Had we lacked early information of the Japanese movements, and had we been caught with carrier forces dispersed . . . the battle of Midway would have ended differently.

The destruction of the Carrier Strike Force compelled Admiral Yamamoto to abandon his Midway invasion plans, his interest in capturing Hawaii and other cavalier proposals being discussed by his naval war planners. The Midway battle, with the loss of four Japanese aircraft carriers and one heavy cruiser, helped to change the course of the war. Although the Imperial Navy still had an impressive fleet, the United States technically had regained naval supremacy in the Pacific almost six months after Pearl Harbor.

News of the battle was suppressed in Japan. Survivors returning to Japan, including Captain Fuchida, who broke both ankles jumping to safety from the *Akagi*, would be hidden away from the Japanese people. Propagandists turned their attention to the unimportant capture of two small US-controlled towns in the remote Aleutians, which were recaptured by US troops just a year later. On 8 June 1942, six months after Hirohito had declared war, the Japanese Government launched a campaign of self-praise and nationalistic fervour. The *Japan Times* reported that Japan had occupied 3.8 million square kilometres of territory and captured abundant quantities of raw materials. Her forces had claimed 290,000 captives in the South Seas and had shot down or disabled 1800 enemy planes for the loss of 9000 Japanese dead. All of this was true, but Japan's position was now in jeopardy as the United States significantly increased its mass production of aircraft and ships of all types as well as numerous other armaments of war. Japan's production could not hope to keep pace.

*

Soon after the great battle in the Pacific, Curtin astonishingly disclosed to senior Australian political journalists just how the US fleets had managed to be near Midway at the right time to engage the Japanese invasion fleet. According to the diary of Joe Alexander from the *Herald* in Melbourne:

> The Nip Naval concentration was discovered ten days ago by means of an intercepted signal. He thought now was the time for us to open an offensive of limited targets and Evatt was discussing this with Roosevelt now. It might mean an attack on Rabaul or some similar objective.

The reporters never outwardly disclosed one of the most important Allied intelligence secrets of the war. However, some stories in Australian newspapers would make broad hints about the depth of knowledge of Japan's intentions. Curtin's reckless disclosure of how the enemy information was discovered was the result of his trust in the senior journalists. With these he shared his anxieties and deepest fears and told them who was saying what behind closed doors.

The US navy's success at Midway led MacArthur, when meeting with Curtin in Melbourne on 11 June, to say that 'the security of Australia has now been assured'. According to historian Professor David Black, as it transpired, MacArthur's relief was somewhat premature. Curtin was afraid that talk of the significant Midway victory could detract from the war efforts of Australians and felt obliged to assert that what had so far occurred was 'by no means decisive', although history would prove that it was. Australia, Curtin knew, was still in a dangerous position, with the Japanese controlling much of the territory across a vast island arc north of Australia. Curtin's dread still haunted him. In a national broadcast on Wednesday night, 17 June 1942, he insisted that Australians 'face invasion and the horrors that accompany it'.

In his broadcast Curtin for the first time openly challenged the British concept of Australia being in a 'secondary theatre of war' to be dealt with 'when other more pressing matters have been adjusted':

> I say flatly it is possible that Australia can be lost. And if that happens, then Hawaii and the whole North American coast, from Alaska to Canada down to Mexico, will be open to Japanese attack free of any threat from any base in the Japanese rear. Had the outcome of the Coral Sea battle been adverse who could give guarantees as to the consequences for Australia? That battle was crucial with fate.

Many years later at least one Australian historian would accuse Curtin of 'whipping up of the fear of invasion'. Curtin's ongoing fears might be more readily understood when considering the opinion of General Sydney Rowell, who found the despatch of a brigade of half-trained and poorly equipped militia to Port Moresby in June 1942 unforgivable, when the whole of the trained and seasoned 7th Australian Division, returned from the Middle East, was then available in Queensland. Historian Professor David Horner has said that although Curtin and his military advisers could be excused for expecting an invasion between February and June 1942, after the Battle of Midway, 'it was clear that it would not eventuate'.

The situation in the Pacific, however, remained tenuous. Japan had 355,000 troops in the Dutch East Indies and part of New Guinea, with negligible air opposition so far. In a review of the early air campaigns of the Pacific war, the Military Analysis Division of the US Strategic Bombing Survey recorded that around this time Rabaul formed a pivotal Japanese base for supply and reinforcement of the whole New Guinea–Solomons area. While the 5th US Air Force had helped to establish local air superiority over Darwin, and were rebuilding the base, Japanese forces had captured massive territory to Australia's north:

> By July 1942, Japanese conquest of the Netherlands East Indies was virtually complete. Sumatra, Java, Borneo, the Celebes and the north-east coast of New Guinea were securely in enemy hands.

The record shows that publicly Curtin probably prolonged the concept of the threat of an invasion of Australia by a few months. He and his own defence chiefs still believed it possible, though. Australia was still badly underarmed and vulnerable. Northern Australia was being bombed.

Curtin's war cabinet colleagues also genuinely feared a Japanese invasion through 1942. His minister for war organisation of industry, John Dedman, initially thought the invasion threat had ended with the Battle of Midway. But later Dedman wrote that 'this was a retrospective judgement':

At the time it appeared to members of the war cabinet that the danger persisted until well into 1943.

Dedman thought that MacArthur's briefings to Curtin were responsible for the prime minister's belief in a continuing invasion threat into 1943:

> At the end of the month [August 1942] the prime minister advised that in a talk he had had with General MacArthur in Brisbane, the latter had said that critical times lay ahead of us.

*

Curtin's openness in sharing secret Allied information with his trusted journalists dismayed US navy officials. Soon after the Battle of the Coral Sea, Curtin made the public comment that there would be plenty of warning of any future invasion attempts. Then the *Canberra Times* dropped this clanger:

> No secret is made of the fact that the Japanese invasion preparations have been known to the Allied High Command and the action by Allied forces is hailed as a well-timed and perfectly executed intervention.

In his later memoirs, a US naval intelligence chief, Rear Admiral Edwin T. Layton, was scathing of Curtin's recklessness. He said the Chief of the US Fleet, Admiral King, had ordered that daily Ultra intelligence bulletins be sent to the navy boards of Australia and New Zealand:

> This was against the better judgement of Admiral King who was increasingly disturbed about how they were being used by Australia's prime minister.

Admiral Layton feared that the Ultra radio intercept operation could have been compromised.

Chapter 13

TRAGEDY AND RETREAT

The Japanese occupation of Rabaul had a terrible sequel in mid-1942. The greatest single maritime tragedy in Australia's history went publicly unknown during the war although thousands of Australians across the country felt the agony of not knowing the fate of their loved ones, whom they suspected might have gone into Japanese captivity. Many families of prisoners of war occasionally received a brief card through the Red Cross, but the families of those men who boarded the Japanese cargo–passenger ship the *Montevideo Maru* heard nothing for the duration of the war. In June 1942 the ship of the OSK Line had been in Simpson Harbour, Rabaul, for almost a fortnight and had avoided serious damage from Allied bombing raids. On 22 June just over 1050 prisoners of war, mostly Australian, were marched from their slave labour camps in Rabaul and elsewhere on New Britain to the docks, where many had been forced to work daily. The men were being transferred to Japan on the *Montevideo Maru* and were bound for further slave labour, to work mostly in Japanese mines. They were not accompanied by any Australian officers and were crammed into the ship's holds in Simpson Harbour.

Not long after midnight on 1 July the captain of the submarine USS *Sturgeon*, Lieutenant Commander William L. Wright, spotted the *Montevideo Maru* close to Luzon in the Philippines on a westward course. Wright followed the ship at top speed and managed to get close enough to fire two torpedoes, which found their mark. The ensuing mayhem can only be imagined. There were no Australian survivors. Many probably never made it out of the holds. While the exact number and identity of all of the men who died has never been confirmed, Japanese and Australian sources suggest an estimated 845 military personnel, mostly from Lark Force and the New Guinea Volunteer Rifles, plus up to 208 civilians, including Australian government officers, planters and missionaries. Most of the lifeboats were wrecked and a small number of the Japanese crew made it to shore, where some of them were killed by Filipino guerillas.

Despite later evidence that the Japanese navy forwarded information about the loss of the vessel to Japan's Prisoner of War Information Bureau as early as January 1943, Australian authorities were not provided with a list of casualties until October 1945, when Major H. S. Williams of the Recovered Personnel Division in Tokyo began investigations into the loss of the *Montevideo Maru*. Williams said that during the war seven fruitless efforts were made through the Swiss Legation in Tokyo on behalf of Australian authorities.

Walter James Ryan, formerly of Ireland, had worked on New Britain for a local trading company since 1931. He was looking forward to taking long service leave in 1942 to be with his English wife Frances, who had transferred to Sydney to settle their children into schooling. Ryan was captured by the Japanese and went down on the *Montevideo Maru*. Throughout the war Frances Ryan struggled to support her family. She wrote to the government after the war seeking pension benefits from the time of her husband's death in July 1942. Her poignant letter revealed the plight of those who waited:

we women were kept in ignorance of our men's fate far too long. To us has been the years of anxiety, loneliness and sadness, and to many, including myself, it has been years of hard work and separation from my children, having had one room to live in and go out to work.

A former Japanese merchant seaman, Yoshiaki Yamaji, was one of the few crew members of the *Montevideo Maru* who escaped the sinking:

When I got up on deck, the ship was leaning to starboard. People were jumping into the water.

Thick oil was spreading across the sea. There were loud noises . . . metal wrenching, furniture crashing, people screaming. I have not been able to forget the death cries.

There were more POWs in the water than crew members. The POWs were holding pieces of wood and using bigger pieces as rafts. They were in groups of 20 to 30 people, probably 100 people in all. They were singing songs. I was particularly impressed when they began singing *Auld Lang Syne* as a tribute to their dead colleagues. Watching that, I learnt that Australians have big hearts.

Yamaji, interviewed by the ABC in Tokyo in 2003, said he had been told that some Australians prisoners of war were picked up by a destroyer, but Australian historians could find no evidence that any of these Australians made it to Japan.

*

On the day 1050 prisoners from Rabaul went to a horrible death aboard the *Montevideo Maru*, Prime Minister Curtin in Canberra was fuming in a secret meeting with senior political reporters about the British and American neglect, as he saw it, of the war in New Guinea. His anger was directed at Churchill and Roosevelt:

Two men thousands of miles from here are inclined to think that Australia is in no great danger.

Curtin unburdened himself to reporters about what he called his 'bitter disappointment'. He bemoaned the fact that Australia was now looking to a harder and more drawn-out war. He felt he would have to commence his fight for military strength in the Pacific all over again. As a result of the German advance in the Middle East, the British Government had requested that the delivery of three squadrons of Spitfire fighters promised to Australia – a total of forty-two planes – be postponed. Curtin's distress was the result of Churchill's not unusual procedure of making promises of material assistance, and then reneging when other theatres of war excited greater interest and demand than Australia. Curtin argued that Australia's needs were no less urgent than those in the Middle East. Churchill declined to accept Curtin's argument. The previous day Curtin had privately told the reporters of his hopes:

> If we could get some Spitfires we could bash the enemy in New Guinea. The Spitfires could fly higher than the Zeros and force them down to the Kittyhawks which could deal with them.

It took until February 1943 for the first Spitfires and their pilots to begin operations attacking Japanese aircraft over Australia's north-west and beyond.

Curtin was also in a funk about statements in Washington describing Australia's war strength in overoptimistic terms. Curtin worried that 'the feeling may get abroad in America that supplies which would have been sent to Australia could better be employed elsewhere' and he regretted statements about General MacArthur putting a positive spin on the Pacific war effort.

Curtin's fears were well directed. Australia at this time was the 'neglected stepchild', as verified by the man who would become MacArthur's air chief, Major General George C. Kenney.

*

The Owen Stanley Range is the huge, soaring backbone that runs down the centre of what is now called Papua New Guinea and divides the mainland neatly in two. It rises in places along its long spine to more than 4000 metres. Planter Bert Kienzle remembers standing on the balcony of Mamba Estate – his homestead near the start of the Kokoda Track – and hearing, then seeing, the swarm of Japanese aircraft coming from the coast and heading over the range:

> The Japanese started raids into Moresby. I was able to report via pedal radio these fellows going over. I'll never forget one raid when about 60 of them went over to Moresby. They dropped four sticks at Kokoda.

On 31 March 1942 Kienzle had received a wireless signal delivered by a Papuan policeman from Kokoda. It said 'close down the mines and plantations and report Moresby immediately':

> We cleaned up the plantations and paid off the labour, leaving a skeleton staff to maintain the place. I had to take all the gold in. I had 50 or 60 deserters with me who had fled plantations from around Moresby. It took me five days to reach Moresby.

Kienzle had initially been made a private and he supervised the labour on a rubber plantation. He later returned to his Mamba Estate and on 9 July received another signal via Kokoda to come to Port Moresby on a patrol boat being sent for him:

> I was told to take charge of lines of communication between Moresby and Kokoda in charge of 1000 native carriers and to build a road to Kokoda in twenty-eight days.

Kienzle recalls, 'The orders were well meant but impossible.' Clearly the Australian authorities in Moresby had no idea of conditions along what became known as the Kokoda Track or, to the Americans, the Kokoda Trail. There is no such road even today. Kienzle received a quick promotion to lieutenant (later captain) in the Australian New Guinea Administrative Unit (ANGAU).

With his vast experience in the region he quickly organised Papuan carriers, who would become known to the Australians as the Fuzzy Wuzzy Angels.

*

In Australia, the supreme commander South West Pacific, General MacArthur, was coming to grips with British demands on Australian forces. Curtin had invited the general to speak at one of his secret off-the-record conferences with political reporters in Canberra. Some of the prime minister's views about Churchill and his demands on the Australians had no doubt rubbed off on MacArthur when he spoke:

> This war would be a lesson to Australia. She must never again engage in valiant, cavalier expeditions overseas, leaving herself unprepared for the shock of battle on her own shores.

MacArthur moved his headquarters from Melbourne to Brisbane in July to be closer to the action and increasing numbers of Americans. At this time, Japanese troopships carrying 14,000 men sailed from Rabaul in another effort to take Port Moresby, which was aborted earlier in the Battle of the Coral Sea. The new invasion attempt was to take the Papuan capital by the 'back door' on the north coast and then cross the mountain range. MacArthur's new air chief, General George Kenney, flew into Brisbane in August to take up the role, noting:

> It didn't take long for me to learn what a terrible state the Air Forces out here were in.

Kenney found an angry and tired MacArthur on the fifth floor of his requisitioned offices in the AMP Insurance building on the corner of Edward and Queen streets in Brisbane. For the next half-hour MacArthur paced back and forth telling Kenney of his plans and woes:

He wanted to get going but he had nothing to go with. He felt Washington had let him down and he was afraid they would continue to do so. He had two American infantry divisions, the 32nd and the 41st, but they still needed training. The Australian militia troops up in New Guinea were having a rough time and they were not considered first-class combat troops anyhow. The 7th Australian Division was back from the Middle East and they were about the only veteran trained fighting unit that the general could figure on for immediate action.

Kenney said MacArthur's available shipping was barely enough to supply the existing garrisons in New Guinea:

His Allied Air Force of Australian and American squadrons were not only small but what there was had not impressed him very favourably to date. No wonder he looked a little depressed.

Australian military resources everywhere were stretched to the limit. The last surviving Australian general who served in the Second World War, Royal New South Wales Regiment historian Major General Gordon Maitland, recalls the situation:

Where did Australia stand? We had virtually no troops, the shattered Militia didn't know what was happening, whether it was about to be attacked, and believed that it would be attacked. The Japanese as a preliminary to isolating America wanted to capture New Guinea and their other target was Port Moresby.

*

On 13 June 1942 Prince Tsuneyoshi Takeda, an army major and first cousin to Emperor Hirohito, had shown the staff of the 17th Army in Rabaul an account of an English explorer indicating that there was a road, or at least a horse trail, linking the northern side of Papua to the southern side and providing access to the Australian base at Port Moresby. The only barrier to this administrative centre of Papua was the Owen Stanley Range, but the reported 'road' or track now provided the Japanese with a new opportunity to capture Moresby after their failure following the Battle of the Coral Sea. As a result the RI Operation Study began. It quickly developed into an invasion plan involving the 8th Base Force and the South Seas Force at Rabaul. Soon the plan was presented to Imperial Headquarters in Tokyo. A reconnaissance aircraft confirmed that there was a motor road from the coastal region of Buna to the Australian government station inland at Kokoda in the foothills of the mountain range. On 18 July orders were issued by the 17th Army Headquarters for the Commander of the South Seas Force, Major General Tomitaro Horii, to prepare for an invasion of Port Moresby. Horii was told his force, in cooperation with the navy, would land near Buna and quickly advance along the roads and over the mountain range to eventually attack airfields in the Port Moresby area. The key planner was the army staff officer Colonel Masanobu Tsuji, who was directly responsible for mass Japanese atrocities against Allied servicemen and civilians in Malaya, Singapore, the Philippines and elsewhere. Japan's postwar war history, *Senshi sosho*, hailed Tsuji's planning work:

> The mobilisation of the overland offensive was a credit to the positive and prompt leadership of staff officer Tsuji.

The invasion convoy of ships left Rabaul on 20 July. Land-based planes and Zeros plastered Port Moresby for several days while others protected the convoy as it neared Papua. On Wednesday 22 July some 100 Japanese planes attacked the sleepy tropical coastline between Gona and Buna. Destroyers joined in shelling the coast but there was little of military value to shoot at, at least for the first few days. Moresby's planned capture was 'a prelude to a Japanese occupation of northern Australia', according to US naval historian Professor Paul S. Dull's interpretation of *Senshi Sosho*. The contention is open to debate, but certainly occupation of Moresby would have favoured greater attacks deep into Australian territory.

*

The war erupted on the Papuan beaches on 21 and 22 July with terrible consequences for the local people. When the Japanese troops poured off their landing barges with their guns and heavy packs they despoiled and grossly ill-treated a normally peaceful paradise. Those village people who sided with the Japanese later were similarly ill-treated by the Australians. Local guide Eric Damai, thin and frizzle-haired, survived the invasion. In 1942 he peeked through the trees after the shelling stopped and some 7000 Japanese prepared to storm ashore from their landing craft:

> The big ships were off the beach and at first we were told they were American, but then we realised they were Japanese. We could see the natives [Tolais from Rabaul] doing a dance on the deck of the ship. They were shouting and banging their bamboo poles on the deck. It sounded like great drums.

The sight and sound shocked Damai and his fellow villagers. They melted into the bush and wisely fled as the landing ships disgorged the invaders, who met no opposition.

*

Australian officials had known of the probable Japanese landing on the coast near Gona or Buna as early as March 1942, when the Combined Operations Intelligence Centre in Melbourne had warned of the possibility of a Japanese landing at Buna with a view to an overland crossing of the Owen Stanley Range to capture Port Moresby. General MacArthur, on receiving advice from General Blamey, disregarded these intelligence reports. According to historian Professor David Horner, the decision to send militia rather than AIF troops to New Guinea and the unhurried build-up of the force in Moresby seemed to indicate that neither MacArthur nor Blamey had given the area the priority that it deserved.

As the war expanded, Anglican missionaries in the coastal region, mostly from Australia, had been given the opportunity to leave, but nearly all declined to desert their Christian charges and

the Anglican hierarchy in Australia failed to insist on their departure or at least withdrawal to Port Moresby.

Australian Anglican missionaries Sister May Hayman, thirty-
three, in charge of the tiny hospital at Gona, and teacher Mavis
Parkinson, twenty-one, who ran the village mission school, were
in their small thatched house at Gona when alerted by a trainee
teacher about the approaching Japanese, as she related:

> 'Sister, Sister, are you there? Oh, Sister, come quickly!' [he called]
> as he ran up the path from the beach. I simply could not believe
> my eyes. There were four big ships not far out to sea and another
> two on the skyline. Then the boats farther out opened fire on
> those nearer the beach, burst after burst of shell fire until the
> ground shook with the explosions. Then ensued a most thrilling
> naval battle.

As the missionary women looked on, the transports began to
lower boats and troops disembarked, 'so we decided we'd better
move to a healthier spot', said Mavis Parkinson in her last letter
home. The women quickly dressed and ran away, hiding in the
jungle overnight:

> In the morning the air seemed thick with bombs and shells, the
> planes roared just above our heads, and the air seemed full of
> dog-fights.

The Japanese invasion convoy arrived on the beach at Gona
on 21 July. It was attacked by American bombers, with one transport receiving a direct hit. Buna was occupied by troops on foot. It
became the site of a major Japanese landing a month later.

After the Gona landing, some of the local Papuans, later
convicted of treason, discovered Hayman and Parkinson and
handed the women over to the Japanese. The missionaries were
taken to the Haruru coffee plantation inland near Popondetta.
There several soldiers began digging a shallow hole in the bush, as
the Australian judge who later conducted an inquiry into Japanese

atrocities, Justice William Webb, recounted in his report. One of the soldiers then proceeded to hug Mavis Parkinson:

> She struggled and almost got out of his grip, but the Japanese thrust his bayonet deep into her side. She screamed and fell. At that moment Miss Hayman hid her face in a cloth or towel. The Japanese escorting her then stabbed her through the neck with his bayonet.

The bodies of the two women were thrown into the grave. The Japanese atrocities continued for more than two weeks after the Japanese had established themselves on the coast. Another mixed party of nine was rounded up by hostile Papuans and handed over to the Japanese, who took them to the beach at Buna. Two days later the nine were lined up on the beach near the headquarters of the Sasebo No. 5 Special Naval Landing Party. A Sublieutentant Komai, a company commander, appeared with his samurai sword. The group included two white Anglican priests, Reverend Henry Holland and Reverend Vivian Hedlich; an English lay preacher, John Duffield; an Australian nursing sister, Margaret Brenchley; and two mixed-race men, Louis Artango and Anthony Gore, with his wife and their little six-year-old son. Also on the beach at Buna was Auckland-born Lieutenant Louis Austen, aged fifty, of ANGAU, previously a planter based at Sangara on the road to Kokoda. Austen had not escaped the region, thinking the trek across the mountains to Port Moresby would be too difficult. In an orgy of cruelty, Komai, with the assistance of his soldiers, used his sword to either decapitate or hack the prisoners on the beach. It appears that those not killed by beheading were stabbed or shot. The terrified Gore boy of six saw all other eight victims, including his mother, to whom he tried to cling, brutally murdered before he, the last victim, was pursued along the sand and beheaded. The heads and trunks of nine bodies were thrown into the gently lapping surf. Sir William Webb was appalled at what he termed 'the savage brutality' and described the atrocity, especially the murder of the mother and her small boy, as 'fiendish barbarity'.

Dozens of Papuans were implicated in handing victims over to the Japanese in the region and some were later executed by Australian authorities. Sublieutenant Komai would be killed in action later in the war.

*

In July 1942 Lieutenant Bert Kienzle headed from Moresby over the track with his native bearers, meeting Captain Sam Templeton of the 39th Battalion, which was comprised of mostly young men of eighteen or nineteen who had been called up in the militia for national service. Templeton's men had arrived in Moresby only in January 1942 and had received little military training. Now they were heading over an appallingly difficult track towards their first encounter with superior numbers of well-trained Japanese troops. They were ordered to prepare to oppose the Japanese on their possible lines of advance from the north coast and to save Kokoda, and the track that led up into the massive mountain range.

Kokoda is a good defensive position, being on a slight plateau thrusting into a point above the countryside below. It could be reached by steps built into the side of a steep hill. Looking towards the coast, the wild Mambare River runs past at right angles in the near distance. The administrative centre in those days consisted of a cluster of village houses for the workers of the rubber plantation, through which a track led to the foothills of the Owen Stanley Range. There were a few modest European buildings for the Australian government officers and the plantation manager. The hope was that the defenders could hold off the Japanese here and be reinforced and resupplied by aircraft either landing on the Coastal strip or dropping supplies. At worst, the defenders could retreat across the plateau, through the rubber plantation and into the vast Owen Stanley Range rearing upwards from the rear.

Kienzle established staging posts along the track equipped with enough food to supply the 39th Battalion:

> It took five or six days to reach Kokoda before the Japs attacked ... I got as far as Kagi village when the first evacuees

from Gona and Buna caught up with me saying the Japs had landed.

*

On the afternoon of 23 July a small party of the Papuan Infantry Battalion (PIB), which comprised Australians resident in Papua, including planters and former government officers, plus Papuan soldiers, saw a force of Japanese a kilometre east of Awala, between Buna and Kokoda, heading inland. Many of the Japanese were riding bicycles and appeared to be moving behind a screen of local villagers. The defenders positioned themselves and fired at the Japanese as best they could and the villagers out front fled into the bush. The Japanese returned fire with rifles, mortars and machine guns, forcing the PIB men to retreat. The Australians fell back across the Kumusi River, destroying bridges and stores as they withdrew. On the way they staged several ambushes, including one near the village of Gorari, where fifteen Japanese were killed for the loss of six PIB men missing.

The Japanese forces encountered no serious ground opposition for almost a week on the coastal plains. While Port Moresby was close in terms of distance – 87 miles (140 kilometres) – the Owen Stanley Range was a massive natural barrier to be overcome only on foot.

The Maroubra Force under Colonel William Owen retreated to Kokoda at night. At its strongest the force consisted of members of the Papuan Infantry Battalion, the 39th Battalion and the 53rd Battalion. Owen sent a signal to Moresby including the line 'must have more troops . . .' He wanted two fresh companies to avoid being outflanked. The plan to service Kokoda with fresh troops and supplies was quickly dashed. So serious was the lack of preparation and available war equipment in Moresby that supply to Kokoda was initially a trickle. Many of the aircraft on the ground were unserviceable. Only two transport aircraft got through to Kokoda, on 26 July, each carrying only fifteen reinforcement troops. On the other hand the Japanese were heavily reinforced on 29 July and established a new beachhead at Giruwa near Buna.

In the invasion force's wake came a heavy flow of crack troops and supplies from Rabaul as well as many conscripted Formosan and Korean coolies and Tolai men mostly employed as labourers. The Australians were surprised to encounter tall, fit and heavily armed Japanese soldiers wearing camouflage uniforms, painted faces and steel helmets disguised with foliage. More to the point, the Australians found the Japanese skilled and confident from previous battle experience.

Colonel Owen decided to pull back beyond Kokoda to the higher village in the range of Deniki, where the Australians had built a supply dump. The withdrawal took place, but Owen soon realised that the Japanese had not taken the Kokoda plateau and that he had mistakenly abandoned the chance of further rein-forcements by air from Moresby. He hastened to return to Kokoda with about eighty men, including some twenty Papuan riflemen. The Australians had placed obstacles on the runway and as they worked to remove them, two Allied aircraft bringing relief flew over and then, on instructions from Moresby, flew away without landing or even dropping supplies. At 2 am on 29 July the Japanese South Seas Detachment of about 1500 men opened up on the plateau with mortars and machine guns as a prelude to a major infantry encircling attack up the steep slope of the plateau. In the close fighting the men of Maroubra Force beat back the Japanese with grenades. That was when their commander, Colonel Owen, was killed, as recounted by Private Charlie Pyke:

he was pulling pins out of grenades and tossing them. But they came up – there were hundreds of the buggers.

Owen was shot above the right eye by a sniper. The enemy broke through the defences and confused counterattacks took place. The Japanese eventually overran the Kokoda plateau and the remaining defenders retreated towards the mountains under cover of smoke and mist as the Japanese occupied the government station and airstrip. The Japanese were seen dancing around a flagstaff flying the Australian flag. On the way out two Diggers sprayed the celebration with bullets, killing a number of Japanese. An estimated twelve Australians were killed and five wounded in the attack and retreat. The Japanese had seized Kokoda, their second major objective in the Papuan campaign, within eight days of the initial landing. The exhausted defenders at Deniki enjoyed their first good rest and sleep. In the meantime, Bert Kienzle had discovered a dry lake bed that was ideal for air drops of supplies. He named the place Myola after an officer's wife. US aircraft were soon dropping supplies and, although most were lost in the surrounding bush, the Myola store would temporarily fill an important gap.

*

The news of the Japanese landing and the initial withdrawal of Maroubra Force stunned Prime Minister Curtin. He was sick again with neuritis and rheumatism. At this time he once again turned to Prime Minister Churchill, demanding assistance for Australia, given her unswerving aid to Great Britain:

> Japan is now consolidating her position in New Guinea and the Solomon Islands and has made a landing in Papua which threatens our important advanced base at Port Moresby, which is vital to the defence of the north-eastern coast against landings and the maintenance of the passage through Torres Strait for the support of Darwin. It is imperative to force the enemy back to his bases in the Mandated Islands in the north east and to drive him out of Timor in the north west.

Just when Curtin had thought his country safe, Australia was under direct Japanese threat again. Curtin was appalled that neither he nor General MacArthur could get definite assurances of further significant war supplies from Britain or the United States. Britain had been particularly lax in supplying weapons. Curtin gave Churchill more than a hint that the continuity of part of the 9th Division AIF in the Middle East in the immediate months would depend on Britain assisting Australia to get more much-needed aircraft for the RAAF.

The new lunge at the Australian base at Port Moresby spurred Prime Minister Hideki Tojo, in a broadcast from Osaka, to renew pressure on the Australian people to lay down their arms:

Australia is now completely isolated and is hopelessly awaiting reinforcements from America. If she persists in her useless resistance there is no need to reiterate that Japan will show no mercy in crushing her.

*

In Papua, neither the Japanese nor the Australians in high command fully appreciated the difficulty of attacking and defending the foot track over the Owen Stanley Range. As many fit, young trekkers of the modern day will willingly testify, it is difficult enough to walk the track in peacetime and almost unimaginable to envisage carrying guns and ammunition while fighting along the track in wartime. The weather alternates between the heat of the tropics and frequent lashing torrential rain. Scratches and cuts can quickly turn septic. The narrow track itself is invariably covered in slippery mud. The steep slopes when wet can see a walker crash downhill uncontrollably. The slopes require climbers to have a firm grip on tree roots and branches to haul themselves up or down. Roaring streams are crossed over slippery logs lashed together. In essence, it would be difficult to find a place more inhospitable for battle, where thick foliage of jungle and bush makes for poor visibility. Bert Kienzle knowingly called the track 'some of the roughest country in the world'.

General MacArthur, not unknown for self-aggrandisement, later wrote that he used the Japanese thrust into the Owen Stanley Range to abandon the Australian notion that the country must maintain a concept of passive defence:

I decided to abandon the plan completely, to move the thousand miles forward into eastern Papua, and to stop the Japanese on the rough mountains of the Owen Stanley Range of New Guinea to make the fight for Australia beyond its own borders. If successful this would save Australia from invasion and give me an opportunity to pass from defence to offence, to seize the initiative, move forward, and attack.

This was what exactly what Curtin had wanted. In the Kokoda campaign, however, the heavy lifting would be done by Australian and not American ground forces. The Americans would enter the brutal fray on the ground well after the Japanese had been turned back to the coast. MacArthur said his decision to go on the offensive 'gave Australians an exhilarating lift and they prepared to support me with almost fanatical zeal'.

*

The initial Australian commander in New Guinea, Major General Basil Morris, became concerned at the availability of transport aircraft based at Moresby needed to make air drops to his troops. Morris signalled to Army Headquarters on 3 August the plight of his forces:

> Supply situation Maroubra and Kanga most serious. Must repeat must have transport planes with parachutes stationed here immediately. Failing this operations will be jeopardised and forward troops liable to starvation.

Kanga was an Australian guerrilla force that had joined the campaign. An indication of how pathetic the air supply program was can be gleaned from the fact that on 5 August the only two aircraft available for supply work had returned to Australia and that Allied Air Force Headquarters promised that one aircraft would soon be stationed permanently at Moresby. Morris responded:

> Transport planes previously made available all returned to mainland ... Kanga and Maroubra personnel cannot be fully maintained by native carriers and latter will desert in large numbers if tracks subjected to air attack ... Consider two machines permanently based here is minimum requirement.

On 11 August Lieutenant General Sydney Rowell arrived at Port Moresby from Melbourne and formally took over command in New Guinea from Morris. He brought the promise of reinforcements, including the experienced 7th Division, which had fought in the Middle East and was preparing to move from Queensland to New Guinea.

*

With the Kokoda campaign barely underway, the United States surprisingly launched an offensive campaign against the Japanese on the island of Guadalcanal in the Solomons. In July, the Japanese had landed troops and labourers on Guadalcanal and had begun the construction of an airfield whose planes would greatly imperil the islands to the south-east including the New Hebrides (now Vanuatu) and, even closer to Australia, New Caledonia. Along with General MacArthur's lobbying, Australia can be thankful to the irascible US chief of naval operations, Admiral Ernest J. King, for this swing from the defensive to the offensive in the Pacific. As King later explained, it marked the Allies' change of fortunes:

> Our first really offensive operation was the seizure of Guadalcanal in August 1942. This campaign was followed by a general offensive made possible by increases in our amphibious forces and in our naval forces in general, which has continued to gain momentum on the entire Pacific front.

King had undergone an uphill battle in Washington challenging the might of the 'Beat Hitler First' school, including President Roosevelt. But as the prospects for an early second front in Europe dwindled, Roosevelt's advisers began to mutter among themselves about reconsidering the Europe-first strategy. In fact, some were itching to strike a blow at the vast Japanese occupation of the Pacific and they, at last, also saw it as good American politics. Admiral King fought people like General Eisenhower for the new strategy and won the day with approval for this initial offensive campaign.

US marines landed at Guadalcanal against only token resistance in early August. But a simultaneous landing on Tulagi Island was met with fierce opposition. The ultimate US objective was Rabaul, quickly being built into a Japanese fortress to the north. On Guadalcanal and Tulagi the small Japanese garrisons were overwhelmed by the Americans.

As soon as the Japanese base at Rabaul heard of the landings, every available aircraft was sent south. The Australian cruisers the *Australia*, the *Canberra* and the *Hobart* joined American warships in shelling Japanese positions in the islands. At dusk on 8 August five heavy Japanese cruisers, two light cruisers and a destroyer from Rabaul sailed through the Bougainville Strait and then southwards down through 'The Slot', the narrow seaway between a chain of islands. In the early hours the Japanese saw the American cruiser the *Chicago* and the *Canberra* between Savo Island and Cape Esperance. The heavy Japanese cruiser the *Chokai* fired torpedoes. The Americans lost three cruisers, the *Vincennes*, the *Quincy* and the *Astoria*. The *Chicago*, which had narrowly escaped a torpedo in Sydney Harbour, was severely damaged.

In the Battle of Savo Island HMAS *Canberra* was hit by two torpedoes and twenty-two Japanese shells. Captain F. E. Getting stood on the bridge, slowly and calmly giving orders. Then a shell exploded on the compass platform, killing and wounding many officers and men. The *Canberra*'s torpedo control position was hit and no torpedoes could be fired. The ship was out of the fight. It slowed and was listing, blazing amidships with many fires burning between decks, as related by the surgeon commander, Captain C. A. Downward:

there was a loud explosion in the sick bay flat, followed by screams of the wounded. Almost immediately the first casualty appeared with his left arm shot away.

Some ten minutes into the action, Downward arrived on the bridge to see Captain Getting seriously wounded:

I spoke to the Captain but he refused any attention at all. He told me to look after the others.

The survivors were transferred to US ships. Getting died on board the USS *Barnett* on passage to Noumea and was buried at sea. Of the 819 of those serving on board the *Canberra*, 193 were casualties. The Australian ships lost seventy-eight killed, mostly from the *Canberra*. The Allies lost four cruisers, a destroyer and over 1000 men in all. Two Japanese ships suffered only minor damage. On 18 August Japanese destroyers landed 1500 reinforcements on Guadalcanal but they were swiftly defeated.

The Japanese had underestimated the original American force occupying Guadalcanal, thinking it to be about 2000 when in fact it was 17,000. For the first time in the war the Americans had taken territory from the Japanese and they would hold it, at great cost to both sides. The campaign on Guadalcanal was much in doubt for nearly four months and would not be certain until the Japanese completed a stealthy evacuation of their surviving ground troops in the early hours of 8 February 1943.

*

On the Kokoda Track, the fighting Australian retreat continued, but the defenders, especially the militiamen of the 39th Battalion, who had been so raw and inexperienced just a few weeks before, were beginning to show more confidence in their fighting ability. They also showed improved morale and comradeship, having held off numerous Japanese attacks and killed many of the enemy. Their organisation had improved under Major Alan Cameron, who now commanded Maroubra Force, and supplies were still getting through, although in small quantities. The Australians began to receive some new weapons including light Thompson submachine guns, which proved effective in jungle conditions.

Bert Kienzle walked the Kokoda Track eight times during the war. He was amazed at the work of the boy soldiers:

A lot of the 39th Battalion blokes were only youngsters, not well trained and not well equipped. They stopped the Japs who came in about 2000 strong and were opposed at first by only eighty-five.

He remembered one whole platoon being encircled:

If the Japs had good knowledge of the area, they could have grabbed the lot. They didn't know our strength. Our fellows just weren't skilled. They could have ambushed us from time to time and pushed straight through to Moresby.

On 10 August the Japanese on the track prepared for a major attack and began loud chanting after which a Japanese called out in English, 'You don't fancy that do you?' The young Diggers responded with derision, including, 'Never heard worse!' Attack after attack was beaten off from morning until night, when ammunition began to run short and the Australians were forced to withdraw slowly again. By 13 August they pulled back from the village of Deniki for the two-hour climb to Isurava, perched high in the Eora Valley. As soon as they were established, their patrols launched attacks on an estimated 1000 to 2000 Japanese moving upwards from Kokoda. The Australians numbered about 460. Soon the 39th had another new commander, Colonel Ralph Honner, who joined the defenders at Isurava, where his men were dug in for a day long battle, as Honner recalled:

If Isurava's defenders had wavered in the face of the first onslaughts, or had fought less tigerishly through the succeeding days and nights, the ensuing course of the campaign must inevitably have been radically changed.

Isurava was a good position to delay the Japanese advance. It had creeks to the front and rear, which the Japanese would need to cross, and the enemy could be seen from above. Small rectangular weapons pits were dug at strategic locations in which men would stand to fire down on the enemy. Filled with earth and leaf matter, the outline of these pits could still be seen clearly decades later. Here the Australians fought in searing tropical heat during much of the day, with lashings of tropical rain most afternoons and cold conditions at night.

Soon Colonel Honner could plainly see that his 39th 'young warriors', as he called them, were in poor physical shape, worn out by almost continuous action with a lack of good food, sleep and shelter. Many were suffering from malaria. Despite the lads' strong spirit, Honner realised he didn't have enough fighters to hold the perimeter at Isurava. So they were made to research counterattacks and cooperative fire between neighbouring companies in preparation for the enemy breaking through their ranks. Honner saw the men's confidence begin to grow. He placed B Company, some of whom had earlier run from the enemy, in the most dangerous sector and personally told them they now had 'the place of honour'. When the time came, they held on doggedly. Honner's orders were simple: hold the enemy on the northern side of the Owen Stanley Range until the 21st Brigade AIF, which had fought in the Middle East, could arrive to relieve them.

The experienced 7th Division men arrived in Port Moresby on 13 August and were on the Kokoda Track heading for action by 16 August. The Australians fighting on the Kokoda Track suffered an indirect blow the next day. The new commander in New Guinea, Lieutenant General Sydney Rowell, in Port Moresby, had driven past rows of American aircraft, including bombers, parked wing-tip to wing-tip at Jackson's strip at Seven Mile. Rowell contacted US Brigadier General Ennis Whitehead with the warning:

There are too many aircraft stacked at the end of the runway. Few things are more capable of demoralising an army than seeing their aircraft smashed on the ground.

At ten o'clock the next morning Japanese bombers attacked the strip and dropped their bombs across the double line of parked aircraft, which had not been moved. Three Flying Fortress bombers and two Dakota transports were destroyed while another five Fortresses and five Dakotas were damaged. The supply of the Australians by air, always deficient, was now critical. Lieutenant Bert Kienzle expanded the recruitment of carriers needed to keep up a flow of food and munitions while bringing out the wounded along the track. The Australians mounted mostly defensive actions and kept gradually withdrawing along the track to shorten supply lines from Moresby.

On 21 August two reinforcement battalions of the Japanese 41st Regiment landed at Buna from Rabaul, together with supporting arms, including a regimental gun unit, a mountain battery, a quick firing gun detachment, an additional 100 troops of the 5th Sasebo, 175 labourers from Rabaul and 230 horses. General Horii now headed a major force ashore of 15,000 men, including 10,000 fighting forces. The rear echelon of the South Seas Force and another battalion were still to come.

The Japanese orders were simple: block the Australian withdrawal from Isurava and 'annihilate them'. They surged forward in many attacks and were frequently repulsed in counterattacks. The close fighting took place in the most appalling conditions. By this time some of the Australian defenders were without shirts. Almost all suffered from exhaustion, malaria, cuts, rashes and often bloodied feet. Casualties mounted on both sides, the Japanese seemingly taking the worst of it, but their suffering did not stop them from mounting new assaults, including frontal attacks. The arrival of the fresh 21st Brigade at Isurava now allowed the Australians to ambush effectively, creating killing grounds and taking high causalities. But the Japanese kept coming. Towards the end of August the brigade headquarters at Isurava was in danger of being cutoff. A desperate counterattack was ordered. The Japanese were then poised for a final assault. Corporal Lindsay Bear – 'Teddy' to his mates – was wounded three times in one attack and couldn't go any further. So he handed his Bren gun to Private Bruce Kingsbury, aged twenty-four, who rushed forward, firing from the hip, clearing a path through the enemy as his patrol followed. Lieutenant Alan Avery saw Kingsbury, his childhood mate, turn the Japanese back as they were about to make their final charge on the battalion headquarters:

> He was an inspiration to everybody else around him. There were clumps of Japs here and there and he just mowed them down. He just went straight into 'em as if . . . bullets didn't mean anything . . . when you see a thing like that you sort of follow the leader, don't you?

A Japanese soldier appeared above a rock, fired one shot and vanished. Kingsbury was killed instantly on 29 August. He would be awarded the Victoria Cross posthumously. The Japanese renewed their attacks along the line and defences began to yield. Eventually the Japanese were able to secure the high ground on both flanks of the Australians. Elements of the 2/14th Battalion from the 7th Division and companies of the 39th Battalion were having trouble holding the line near Isurava. The Japanese were launching attacks from various quarters and the situation became desperate. Further inland at Alola, men of the 53rd Battalion were resting. After having been cut off for several days, they hurried back down the track to help their comrades, despite most being hungry and sick. War historian Dudley McCarthy quotes an eyewitness who was there on 29 August:

> When I saw those poor bastards, tottering on their bleeding, swollen feet, turn round and go straight back to Isurava, I knew they were good.

Lieutenant Stewart Johnston, a farmer from Dardanup, Western Australia, led forward a party of physically unfit volunteers from the 2/16th Battalion and told Colonel Honner simply, 'We heard the battalion was in trouble so we came back.' Elsewhere the defences were yielding. Some of the Australian companies had repulsed eleven separate Japanese attacks that day, each of about company strength. One company calculated that it had taken about 200 Japanese casualties out of an estimated 550 enemy casualties that day. With the withdrawal to the native rest house on the track between Isurava and Alola, the first phase of the campaign of the 21st Brigade, part of the 7th Division, came to an end in temporary defeat. Well-trained, aggressive and hardy Japanese closely watched the withdrawing Australians on 30 August. The Australian withdrawal occurred on parallel tracks – the Kokoda Track on the west and the Abuari track on the east with Eora Creek in the middle. All the time the Japanese were in hot pursuit. Some of the Australians remained in position to cover those withdrawing. In the evening the track to Alola became just a faint mark that merged with the bush on the steep hillside. Some of the Australians lost the track and blundered in circles in the dark. A slippery log bridge over a stream had to be crossed on hands and knees. The result became an often confused fighting retreat from Isurava inland to Alola and then back even further still over the high ridges.

Just two weeks after their arrival the 2/14th had lost ten killed, eighteen wounded and 172 'missing', including many officers who couldn't be accounted for.

War correspondents Osmar White and Chester Wilmot with cameraman Damien Parer found a fearful situation after trekking over the track from Owers' Corner. White quickly assessed the situation as the Australians fell back through Deniki and Isurava:

This means that the Japs were at last getting into the Owen Stanleys themselves and that something was wrong.

White described his own trek across the track being 'depressed, sick and almost dead' to get near the action. The newsmen passed more and more wounded straggling back from the front:

Most of them were walking skeletons. Their eyes were bright with fever. They travelled a few yards in a burst. You could see the loose skin on the sides of their necks palpitating like a lizard's throat. Their greeting was unvaried. They said 'G' day, Dig. Pretty tough, eh?' and grinned . . .

White found a fearsome situation at the Eora Creek camp halfway down the last ridge of the day:

Hundreds of men were standing about in mud that came up to their shins. The whole village, built of pandanas and grass, looked as if it were about to flounder in the sea of mud . . . The men were slimed from head to foot, for weeks unshaven, their shins bootless under their filth.

Lines of exhausted carriers were squatting on the fringes of the congregation eating muddy rice . . . eyes were rolling and bloodshot with the strain of long carrying . . . Machinegun fire was about continuously. A Jap 50 calibre was going *dub-dub-dub* away in the east. They said the Japs were gradually cracking us. The 2nd/16th was moving into position. The 53rd Militia had broken on the right flank and was on the run.

The Australians at the end of August were in real trouble. How serious was this for the future of Australia? The Japanese army embarked on the Kokoda campaign seeking to prevent Allied counteroffensives from Australia and 'to expel any Allied forces from New Guinea in preparation for a possible advance on Australia', to quote Professor Hiromi Tanaka, Japan's foremost historian on the fighting. He has walked the track and doesn't think the Japanese could have made it down to the town of Port Moresby. But if it had been taken, he thinks the Imperial Navy might have pressed for more:

I believe the Navy Headquarters might have wanted to occupy Australia again if they had successfully occupied Port Moresby in this second attempt. But . . . the Army would have said no; they would not support the occupation of Australia. However, throughout the ages in Japanese society, Japanese have been easily swayed by the emotion and the social atmosphere that can be created, such as the taking of one of the enemy's biggest bases in the South Seas – Port Moresby. Such a victory . . . could possibly also influence the Army to go further south.

In short, Japan had no grand strategy. After the successful completion of the first stage operations and the occupation of so many regions, they really had no plan as to what they were going to do. Therefore, anything could have happened . . . It was highly possible that the Navy might have launched some campaign against Australia.

Chapter 14

TAKING THE OFFENSIVE

Despite the crucial victories in the Coral Sea and Midway battles and the successful US invasion of Guadalcanal, by mid-August 1942 the Curtin Government continued to hold genuine fears for the safety of Australia. Curtin was not to know that the Japanese Imperial Navy's strenuous manoeuvring for an invasion of the Australia area had been effectively sidelined by the Imperial Army at General Headquarters and that navy firebrands were biding their time, hoping for a change in fortunes. Even after Midway, the Imperial Navy remained a most formidable opponent. The Japanese temporarily outnumbered the US navy in aircraft carriers, battleships, heavy cruisers, light cruisers and destroyers. The only warship type in which the US Pacific fleet held a current advantage over the Japanese was submarines.

But the US navy was catching up rapidly and was expanding its fleet with remarkable speed. By August 1942, the following warships were on the slipways or awaiting completion in American shipyards: six fleet carriers, eight light carriers, twenty-two escort carriers, five battleships, four heavy cruisers, nine light cruisers, 113 destroyers and twenty-nine submarines.

Australia's external affairs minister Doc Evatt cabled the commander-in-chief of the US Fleet, Admiral Ernest King, on 14 August:

I feel it is probable that the enemy will soon attempt some spectacular counter blow, and probably at the mainland of Australia.

Evatt asked King to reassess the needs of General MacArthur's command 'so as to make vital strategic bases here, at any rate, secure against large scale invasion'. King had more immediate concerns. From August 1942 to February 1943, the United States and its Allies were fighting the brutal battle against the Japanese for possession of Guadalcanal.

*

The second Japanese attempt to capture Port Moresby, with General Tomitaro Horii's forces now halfway across the Kokoda Track, was intended to be a two-pronged assault on the Australian base. While Horii would push over the mountains, the 8th Fleet and the Kawaguchi Force would take Milne Bay with its harbour on the south-eastern tip of Papua. They would build an air base and other facilities. Japanese troops would land at Milne Bay and this would be followed by their coordinated landing near Port Moresby in concert with the forces advancing over the Owen Stanley Range. Together they would capture Moresby.

Milne Bay was 35 kilometres long and 15 kilometres wide and was surrounded by mountains usually covered in rain clouds. The Japanese navy saw Milne Bay as an excellent strategic position from which to attack Port Moresby by briefly flying over the southern tip of the 'tail' of Papua then flying north-west up the undefended coastline to Moresby. But the Allies got there first, American construction troops arriving in June 1942 to build airstrips. An Allied air base there would make any further naval operations in the area hazardous for the Japanese. It would also allow the Allies to attack the Japanese on the north coast of Papua without first making the climb over the Owen Stanley Range.

At the request of General MacArthur, the Americans were protected by two companies of the 55th Australian militia battalion, which had arrived in groups between 22 and 29 May. But two companies of the 2/12th at Milne Bay suffered badly from malaria and tropical diseases and soon had to be replaced. The troops called the Milne Bay district a hellhole. They complained that the sun hardly ever came out and it rained all the time. It was stinking hot, with boggy marsh country abounding.

Australian troops deployed along Milne Bay's northern and western shores. Soon three airfields had been carved out of plantations and swamp with the help of conscripted local labour. They were ready for service by 21 July when the Japanese landed at Gona and Buna. The few roads along the coast were in a frightful, boggy state and required extensive rebuilding with coral and coconut logs, while work proceeded on wharves and other new facilities.

The new Milne Bay airstrips had surfaces of steel Marsden matting to stop the planes from sinking into the mud. The airstrips were primitive, mostly just a swathe cut through coconut plantations. The next day the first US P-40 Kittyhawks arrived after a fight with Japanese aircraft over Gona. The Kittyhawks had been given to Britain and then piloted by Australians and New Zealanders in the Middle East. They later became a key fighter in the south-west Pacific, especially in the earlier stages of the war. They were effective as air-to-air fighters, but also proved their durability in ground-attack operations, carrying 1000 pounds (454 kilograms) of bombs. At last RAAF pilots had an effective fighter. The Kittyhawks from the RAAF's 75 and 76 squadrons arrived, together with Hudson bombers of 6 and 32 squadrons. Soon after arriving in Moresby, two Kittyhawk pilots had shot down a Japanese bomber, and the next day 75 Squadron destroyed twelve enemy aircraft during an attack on Lae airfield.

In mid-August the AIF's 18th Brigade had arrived, commanded by Brigadier George Wootten and included the 2/9th and 2/10th Battalions plus additional men from the 2/12th Battalion. The AIF's battle-hardened 18th Brigade, veterans of the Middle East who had only recently arrived in Milne Bay, were held in reserve. As with the Kokoda campaign, many of the Australians at Milne Bay had never been in combat. One of them was Sergeant Colin Hoy, of the 61st Battalion:

> .... I'd only fired seven shots out of my rifle prior to Milne Bay! I could salute well, I could march well ... you see, it's very hard for people to understand that in those days every round of ammunition had to be accounted for ... we just didn't have much of it.

Major General Cyril Clowes, who had been an officer at Gallipoli and on the Western Front in the First World War, arrived in Milne Bay from Moresby on 13 August after a hazardous flight piloted by an American airman who lost his way in thick cloud and rain. Clowes, a quietly spoken man, became known as 'Silent Cyril'. He decided to spread the bulk of his defensive forces on the beaches either side of a plantation at Gili Gili with its wharf located in the centre. The Australians covered the approaches with machine guns, Bofors 40-millimetre guns and a few 25-pounder field guns. American maintenance units were also allotted beach defence roles. However, there were no naval or coastal guns capable of engaging Japanese warships and no searchlights. Hostile Japanese aircraft occasionally flew over. On 24 August a coastwatcher reported Japanese troops travelling in seven barges east of the Australians at Milne Bay. The next day RAAF aircraft sighted a Japanese naval force of three cruisers, two transports, two tankers and two minesweepers heading for the bay. Clowes knew invasion was imminent. RAAF Kittyhawks had no luck attacking the Japanese convoy. Colin Lindeman, later Wing Commander, in 1942 was one of the raw and inexperienced Kittyhawk pilots who attacked the invasion fleet:

> Both squadrons, 75 and 76, went out to bomb and strafe the transports and the weather was not the best and the bombing was bloody awful. I don't think we had any hits at all and did a bit [of] strafing but did very little damage to those four transports.

It was the wet season and as the airstrips at Milne Bay got more use, the steel matting began to sink and the surface became muddy, making take-offs and landings hazardous. Col Lindeman was taking off one day and his Kittyhawk started to slide like a car skidding on an icy road. The plane crashed into a Hudson bomber parked on the side of the strip. Two RAAF ground crewmen were killed. Other Kittyhawk pilots found and bombed seven Japanese landing barges beached at Goodenough Island to the north of Milne Bay.

Soon men of the Australian 61st Battalion at Milne Bay were engaging the Japanese to the east near Koebele Mission, or K. B. Mission as the Australians called it. There was a brief skirmish on the beaches as about 100 Japanese advanced. Casualties occurred in the darkness on both sides. As the Australians began withdrawing to a more secure position, a Japanese tank approached, firing into the bush on both sides and then dropping back to allow infantry to move forward again. The Australians pulled back to their main company area as the tank nudged forward. But the tank commander pushed his luck in trying to negotiate a log bridge. He stood up in his turret and was shot. The tank fell into the creek and disappeared.

In the morning Japanese ships leaving the bay were attacked by Allied aircraft. Australian Kittyhawk fighters were also attacking Japanese barge landing points along the beaches. With the help of the aircraft, the Australians were able to push the Japanese troops back along the coastal track. But as night came on, the Japanese massed for another attack with more tanks. The Australians had no anti-tank guns and were forced to withdraw again. Further fierce and confused fighting continued during the night with the Japanese at one stage using flamethrowers. One group of Australian defenders retreated and another took over from the exhausted troops and pressed forward. The Japanese withdrew beyond the K. B. Mission. Japanese bombers and fighters were also active, attacking the newly built airfields. On the night of 27 August the Japanese launched another attack, led by two tanks that moved backwards and forwards through the Australian lines to pave the way for Japanese infantry who rushed forward. At the same time Australian artillerymen back near Gili Gili fired 25-pounders whose shells screamed overhead. Strong attacking groups were fighting the Australians from many points inside their own defences. By midnight four separate attacks by chanting Japanese soldiers had been beaten back. RAAF Kittyhawks taking off were under fire, according to Flight Lieutenant Arthur Gould, a Queenslander:

> The Japs landed and in the end they took one end of the strip and we had the other. So we'd take off over them, crouched down under the armoured plating. They shot at you when you pulled your wheels up, which is not recommended.

Defence Headquarters in Melbourne was feeling increasing concern about the chances of holding Milne Bay. The Australian commander General Blamey urged on General Rowell in Moresby the need for offensive action by Major General Clowes and his men. Rowell's reply to Melbourne, sent days later, was sympathetic to Clowes, saying in part:

> Feel sure that complete freedom sea movement enjoyed by enemy compelled Clowes retain considerable portion forces in hand to meet landing south coast of bay.

MacArthur was worried and demanded that Clowes be instructed to 'clear the north shore of Milne Bay without delay' and report by the following morning. The deputy chief of the Australian General Staff, General George Vasey, told Rowell that 'a wrong impression of our troops had already been created in the minds of the great'. He said MacArthur's concern about Clowes was driven by a lack of information on the Milne Bay operation. Vasey said MacArthur was planning to send the US 25th Brigade to Milne Bay. As official war historian Dudley McCarthy put it, MacArthur's staff lacked experience in war, especially at the tactical level:

They almost completely lacked knowledge of the terrain over which the fighting was taking place and could therefore make no proper appreciation of the conditions at Milne Bay.

A turning point at Milne Bay came when the Japanese launched a major attack across the number three airstrip in the early hours of Monday 31 August. A big Japanese force had formed up on the eastern end of the strip. When the enemy was discovered a flare was sent up and every available Australian and American opened fire. The assault, which might have taken the strip and its defenders, was repulsed by the 25th and 61st battalions together with Australian artillery and American engineers effectively using every weapon at their disposal. On three occasions the Japanese reformed to attack only to be cut down. In the morning Lieutenant General Clowes counterattacked and the 2/12th Battalion drove forward as the Japanese were withdrawing. At dawn that morning Japanese bodies lay everywhere in a terrible scene of carnage. The Japanese would lose an estimated two-thirds of their men in the Milne Bay campaign.

That same day men of the 2/12th Battalion made their way along the coast from Gama to the K. B. Mission, where Captain Angus Suthers of Brisbane had his headquarters. Getting there meant overcoming numerous ambushes of Japanese waiting in the bush with snipers in coconut trees. Japanese feigning death opened fire as the Australians passed. As a result the Australians were merciless in ensuring that every Japanese they encountered really was dead.

From 2 September onwards, the Diggers of the 2/12th Battalion, supported by the 2/9th Battalion, steadily advanced along the north shore of Milne Bay, pushing the Japanese back. Japanese ships shelled the shore but caused few casualties. On 4 September the Australians made attack after attack on the Japanese, who were fighting back fiercely. The advance of the section commanded by Corporal John French of the 2/9th Battalion, was held up by fire from three enemy machine-gun posts. French ordered his section to take cover. He successfully assaulted two positions with grenades, then a third with a submachine gun. He finally fell dead in front of the enemy gun pit. French was posthumously awarded the Victoria Cross for most conspicuous bravery.

The Japanese had miscalculated the strength of the Australian Milne Force. In late August–early September 1942 there were some 9500 defenders, including 7500 Australian soldiers, at Milne Bay. The rest included 1300 men of the US 43rd Engineer Regiment sent to construct the airstrips, and RAAF personnel. By comparison the Japanese sent only 2800 men of the Special Naval Landing Forces to take Milne Bay. Although the Japanese high command had advocated reinforcement of its force at Milne Bay, its commander, noting increasing sickness and exhaustion among his troops, recommended an immediate withdrawal. Between 4 and 7 September the Japanese evacuated at night.

The fighting for Milne Bay and the Japanese retreat were marked by unforgivable Japanese atrocities towards both local Papuans and Australian soldiers. If the local people did not readily give assistance to the Japanese, even if they couldn't understand what was being asked of them, they were quickly slaughtered. At Point King, near the mission, Captain Angus Suthers found a native boy who had been shockingly mutilated. The Japanese had tied the boy up with signal wire, performed sadistic and depraved acts with a bayonet and then burnt half the boy's head off with a flamethrower. A Papuan woman pegged to the ground had also been horribly mutilated by a debauched soldier with a bayonet. Both had been dead about six hours. Judge Sir William Webb later found that well over sixty atrocities were committed by the Japanese against Milne Bay natives, including two nuns. Many victims were tied to coconut trees and repeatedly bayoneted. Judge Webb noted the case of native girl of only thirteen or fourteen who was stripped on the ground and 'whose hands and legs they tied to stakes, through whose chest and into the ground they drove a bamboo stake'. The little girl was then further outraged. Webb found widespread barbarism committed by Japanese officers and soldiers:

It was an atrocity, seeing that in every case the killing was carried out with savage brutality. The women staked out were, no doubt, raped and then had their breasts cut off by sadists.

Near the K. B. Mission, six Australian soldiers were tied up with signal wire and tortured then finished off with bayonet thrusts in the stomach. One Australian had his head slashed open from temple to temple and was left to die. After the Japanese fled, two Diggers were found in a clearing, one tied to a tree and the other on the ground. The soldier on the ground had his hands tied in front of his chest and had obviously tried to fend off bayonet thrusts. His arms were badly slashed. His buttocks and genitals were cut to ribbons. The tops of his ears were cut off. His eyes were missing from their sockets and he had about twenty knife or bayonet wounds in his body. As Judge Webb commented: 'Only fiends could use men for bayonet practice.'

Much later, during the Japanese War Crimes Trials in Tokyo, evidence would be given that fear of defeat and surrender had prompted sadistic Japanese officers to order the torture of captives. Officers allegedly told their men that a similar fate awaited them if they dared surrender. After the war Australia accused 924 Japanese of war crimes. They appeared before 296 separate trials. The hearings acquitted 280 Japanese and ordered the executions of 148, with the remainder imprisoned.

None of the thirty-six Australians captured by the Japanese in the course of the Milne Bay battle survived. All were killed, and some were badly mutilated. After the battle, Brigadier John Field wrote in his diary, 'The yellow devils show no mercy and have since had none from us.' Flight Lieutenant Arthur Gould, twenty-one, had taken part in the unsuccessful attack on the Japanese invasion fleet. Much later he recalled a Japanese 'Val' bomber being shot down and crash-landing on a beach. Papuans brought the Japanese into a camp at Milne Bay. The pilot was carried by two native men with his arms and legs tied roughly to a pole like a pig:

His wrists were nearly cut through from the vines. They dumped him to the army. They took the thing off him. He was on the ground there and they were going to talk to him. And an Air Force cook came up and said 'my first bloody Jap' and pulled out his gun and shot him. There and then. Whatever happened to the cook, he was in serious trouble after that. He was going to kill a Jap before he finished the war.

After the short battle for Milne Bay, of the 2800 Japanese who landed, only 1318 left the area. An estimated 750 were killed around Milne Bay and the majority of the remainder died while trying to escape overland to the Japanese base at Buna. Allied deaths included 167 Australians and fourteen Americans. The Battle of Milne Bay in August–September 1942 was the first significant defeat of the Japanese forces on land during the Second World War. It was also the most southerly point on land reached by Japanese battle forces in the Pacific war.

*

As the Milne Bay battle was raging during the first half of August, Curtin was sick with neuritis and rheumatism. His illness coincided with a bruising conference involving state premiers in Melbourne. The United States had invaded Guadalcanal in the Solomons on 7 August. It was the fighting in the Solomons that really worried the prime minister. At one stage in an emotional speech he told the premiers:

> The portents indicate that we are engaged in a life and death struggle for survival.

Curtin was ordered to bed by his doctor, but official engagements always intervened. After speaking at another Melbourne function, he was found by a staffer later in the day 'wrapped in a rug, brooding in the dark in his room' at the Victoria Palace Hotel. He bounced back after receiving news of heartening progress in the Solomons.

On Thursday evening, 3 September 1942, on the eve of the Japanese evacuation of Milne Bay, Australians gathered around their wireless sets for an important national broadcast. The prime minister grabbed his listeners' attention:

> To-day, Port Moresby and Darwin are the Singapores of Australia. If those two places fall, then, inevitably, we are faced with a bloody struggle on our soil when we will be forced to fight grimly, city by city, village by village, until our fair land may become a blackened ruin.

Curtin added, 'our fate is in the balance as I speak to you'. He referred primarily to the threat from the Battle for the Solomons:

> it represents a phase of the Japanese drive in which is wrapped up invasion of Australia.

Was Curtin gilding the lily? Perhaps a little. A few days earlier he had privately told political reporters that Australian forces were capable of dealing with the Japanese landing at Milne Bay, based on Australian defence assessments, which were at odds with MacArthur's headquarters. He was receiving sharply conflicting predictions about Port Moresby from MacArthur, who was most jittery and was being advised by his inexperienced staff officers. Curtin's advice came from his own Australian defence chiefs, who weren't jittery. His dramatic words on 3 September were used to introduce his government's new austerity rules. Australians, he said, must strip themselves of 'every selfish, comfortable habit, every luxurious impulse, every act, word or deed that retards the victory march'. He introduced restrictions on all forms of horse racing and announced new taxes on entertainment, alcohol and tobacco. Prepared meals served to the public could no longer have three courses. Expensive dishes at restaurants were out. The black market would be severely punished. Newspapers were even encouraged not to honour sporting heroes as this was considered 'out of place' in wartime when the nation's soldiers were fighting and dying. Such were the times and Curtin's standing that Australians reluctantly accepted the restrictions.

The Milne Bay experience starkly demonstrated what the Australian forces could do in the tropics. It showed that the RAAF was capable of great feats of courage with good fighter aircraft like the Kittyhawks rather than the underpowered and clapped-out Wirraways. Nevertheless, the Japanese were still advancing over the Kokoda Track, inching towards Port Moresby.

There is evidence at this time that General MacArthur and his chief of staff, General Richard Sutherland, were deeply concerned about the potential fall of Moresby. On 6 September MacArthur said in a radio message to the US army chief of staff, General George Marshall, 'If New Guinea goes the results will be disastrous.' MacArthur wanted Marshall to support him in his urgent bid for many transport ships and escorts to enable him to send more US ground forces to Papua, a move that the fighting in the Solomons had to date severely curtailed. A week earlier Australia's deputy chief of the General Staff in Melbourne, General George Vasey, had told the Australian commander in Moresby, General Rowell, that the US General Headquarters in Brisbane was 'like a bloody barometer in a cyclone – up and down every two minutes' and that 'they needed to be blooded'. For his part, Rowell later said that at no time had he considered that the capture of Moresby from the north was possible. Had he had his way, he would have allowed the Japanese to cross over most of the track unassailed before intercepting and beating them, so that they would experience the hardships and supply problems the Australians had suffered on the Owen Stanleys.

The further the Japanese went, the longer their supply lines and the worse their food and munition shortages grew. The Japanese also harboured an unrealistic and callous expectation that when their advancing troops ran out of food they would simply live off the land or capture Australians supplies to survive.

MacArthur was losing faith in the Australians along the Kokoda Track despite the victory at Milne Bay. On 6 September, MacArthur told General Marshall in Washington:

The Australians have proven themselves unable to match the enemy in jungle fighting. Aggressive leadership is lacking.

Behind the scenes at this time, Prime Minister Curtin was worried and disenchanted with Washington's promises of reinforcements. He had long ago dismissed thoughts of Britain coming to Australia's aid if the country was invaded. The arrival of American weapons and men in Australia and in New Guinea had been painfully slow and of insufficient quantity. Lack of available US shipping was a factor. The prime minister was coming to realise that he could not count on the United States to provide the ships, planes and troops in anything like the strength Australia envisaged. Without these, Curtin reasoned, Australia would remain vulnerable to every new Japanese thrust. At a further off-the-record briefing for senior political reporters in Canberra on 9 September, Curtin was asked about a visit by the commander-in-chief of the US fleet, Admiral Ernest King, to London. 'It doesn't auger much good for us,' he replied bitterly. King was in London, according to Curtin, 'to see how much better Hitler could be fought'. Curtin commented, 'It is going to be a long struggle for us to hold this place [Australia] . . . we might have a 100 years' war.' Admiral King, as it eventuated, was one of the strongest US proponents of aid to Australia and the Pacific. Curtin continued to lobby Roosevelt hard for divisions of reinforcements. The president, influenced by Churchill, replied bluntly that the United States was unable to provide a Pacific fleet or many more troops:

> your present armed forces, assuming that they are fully equipped and effectively trained, are sufficient to defeat the present Japanese force in New Guinea and provide for the security of Australia against invasion . . .

Curtin ruminated in the coming weeks about the refusal of the United States and Britain to add significantly to the protection of the Australian homeland while Australians fought in the Middle East. His close military adviser, the secretary of the Defence

Department, Sir Frederick Shedden, counselled Curtin that he wouldn't alter the views of Churchill or Roosevelt on defeating Hitler first. Having pressed the point, Shedden advised that it was better to accept decisions 'with good grace and an expression of agreement'. Curtin seemed to begrudgingly agree. He told parliament in early October that Australia had a commitment that simply exceeded its defensive capability. But he now realised he had no option but to accept that 'so much depends on ourselves', while understanding that 'we do not lack allies and support, and that we fight under guarantees of greater aid should worse befall us'. Nevertheless, while Curtin believed that the recent Coral Sea and Midway battles had prevented an invasion of Australia, he still thought that from now on 'we do not know where the blows will fall'. But he considered it imperative that the AIF should return to Australia and that Australia's limited naval forces should be concentrated in home waters.

*

When the dispirited Diggers along the Kokoda Track heard about what had happened in Milne Bay, it gave them a nice boost, especially the more inexperienced troops among those who had been constantly falling back towards Port Moresby. They now began to understand that the Japanese were not the invincible warriors they were cracked up to be; despicable, hated and excellent fighters they were, but not unbeatable. The knowledge did not immediately improve their dire retreat across the muddy and precipitous track towards Moresby. Japanese patrols now were constantly infiltrating Australian lines, as war correspondent Osmar White witnessed:

> Our men were not prepared for such tactics. The bulk of them were troops trained for desert warfare. They were more than half afraid of the country.

Three hours out from Eora, White learned that the Japanese had been firing mortar shells into the brigade headquarters position. There were wild fights along the track at night. One party of

Australians travelled just under the crest of a steep ridge, parallel to a party of Japanese. Neither side was willing to show a head, so they fought it out by tossing grenades at the each other as they went. It was, in fact, seldom that anyone got a glimpse of the enemy:

> Most of the wounded were very indignant about it. I must have heard the remark 'You can't *see* the little bastards!' hundreds of times. Some of the men said it with tears in their eyes and clenched fists. They were humiliated beyond endurance by the fact that they had been put out of action before even seeing a Japanese.

White had passed a Digger at night on the track whose leg had been blown off below the knee by a mortar bomb after the Australian withdrawal from Alola village on 30 August. The soldier had applied a ligature to the stump, dressed then wrapped the remainder of the leg in an old copra sack. He crawled and hopped along the track. Two days later White passed him on the hill above Eora Creek. White offered to get the man a stretcher party. 'If you can get bearers,' he responded fiercely, 'get them for some other poor bastard! There are plenty worse off than me!' As White staggered along the track, he heard that the enemy had broken through and was making an enveloping movement:

> The 53rd Battalion, on the right, had folded up completely across the river and machine guns duels were going on ... but I was deadly weary and deadly discouraged – appalled by the sense of being a partisan spectator to a disaster ...

Practically the whole available Australian force had been thrown into the battle and one by one their positions had been overwhelmed:

> Stragglers from a dozen different units were making their way back, like sheep, on the trail. The wounded were coming onto the trail from both sides of the river.

AIF signalman Norm Ensor wondered how the Australians succeeded:

I reckon we went close to losing the war at that stage. I lost a few of my mates. It was an interesting exercise. A few times I wanted to dig a hole and bury myself.

A month earlier a Japanese convoy had landed some 1000 fresh Japanese troops at Basabua village near Gona on the north coast. They immediately went forward to join their comrades on the Kokoda Track. Battle casualties and sickness had reduced the Japanese overall strength to about 5000 fighting men. But the Australians soon received strong reinforcements too. The experienced 2/25th Battalion of the 7th Division had fought bitterly, sustaining heavy casualties, in Lebanon. After returning to Australia, the men had arrived in Moresby on 9 September to reinforce battered Australian units on the Kokoda Track. They were on the track the day after disembarking and they entered the fray at Ioribaiwa on 15 September. Terrible fighting had occurred on the ridges near Efogi beforehand and less than half of the Australians who fought there were able to participate in the key battle of Ioribaiwa. Some men had now fought for over three weeks with little rest in the most appalling conditions. The Australians had retreated over the track, fighting all the way through the villages of Kagi, Menari and Naoro to a high point of Ioribaiwa, a trek of about a day and a half from Owers' Corner where the road down to Port Moresby began. The Japanese had eight effective mountain guns, including their three most powerful 75-millimetre guns, on a ridge north of Ioribaiwa. From there they pounded the Australian positions. The casualties mounted with every shell fired. Sergeant Dudley Warhurst saw a Digger, Sid Johnston, hit by a shell:

He was a band sergeant – shouldn't have been there at all. Sid had a hole the size of your hand near his collarbone . . . Sid said to me, 'Dud, save me'. He was talking through the hole, not through his mouth – he was breathing through there. We got him out . . . but he didn't survive.

Sergeant Eric Williams of 2/16th Infantry Battalion saw one of the Japanese shells strike a tree and instantly kill three Australians. He went back and reported that the three had been killed, along with Captain Bill Grayden of Perth:

> about a quarter of an hour later who should come lurching up the track but Bill Grayden. Silly as a weirdo, he had been knocked out. Of course I felt dreadful I had left him. I thought he was dead, same as the other blokes.

Maroubra Force, comprising the Australians who had fought along the track, received a new commander, Brigadier Ken Eather. On 16 September he reported to Moresby that the enemy was pressing forward and he didn't think he could hold them. He requested permission to withdraw to the next great peak, Imita Ridge, which could be seen from the heights near Ioribaiwa. Major General Arthur 'Tubby' Allen stressed the importance of holding Ioribaiwa, but let Eather make his own final decision on withdrawal. Eather knew that if he continued to hold his current position he would have no freedom of movement and that his force, the key protector of the Port Moresby base, could be overwhelmed. So the Australians withdrew towards Imita Ridge. Just as the Australians departed Ioribaiwa, the Japanese swarmed up the slope. Apart from their keenness to come to grips with the Australians, they were desperate for any food left behind. Every one of the Japanese forward companies had been reduced to half strength through sickness, injuries and lack of food.

The bulk of Maroubra Force withdrew into the darkness towards Imita Ridge, leaving men of the 2/25th along the track guarding the withdrawal. Torrential rain fell. The 2/25th soon followed. General Rowell, ordered that Brigadier Eather must not retreat beyond Imita Ridge:

Stress the fact that however many troops the enemy has they must all have walked from Buna. We are now so far back that any further withdrawal is out of the question and Eather must fight it out at all costs.

General Allen passed the message to Eather saying there could be no withdrawal beyond Imita. Allen said, 'You'll die where you stand,' and Eather replied, 'Don't worry, Tubby; the only people who will die will be the Japs.' Rowell's warning wasn't necessary. Imita Ridge – about 30 miles (48 kilometres) from Port Moresby as the crow flies and the second-last great natural obstacle on the Kokoda Track before the road to Moresby – was about to become the last bastion for the Australians. The battle there would become the turning point for the whole campaign and there would be no more retreats.

It would have been exceptionally difficult for the Japanese to take the steep and narrow ridge. From here the Diggers watched with great satisfaction as Australian artillerymen began firing two 25-pounder artillery pieces, first from Owers' Corner and then, after a stupendous effort in hauling the guns forward up hazardous slopes, from points close to the high Imita Ridge itself. The shells began crashing into the jungle surrounding the heights of Ioribaiwa, to the great satisfaction of the battle-wearied Diggers.

*

On the Port Moresby side of Imita Ridge was the sudden descent of the Golden Staircase, a treacherous steep and winding track of thousands of slats of timber hammered into the earth and mud by Australian engineering units to form a stairway down a timbered mountainside. It led down to several creek crossings, full of leeches, then eventually Uberi village and, after a trek of some three hours from Imita Ridge, the welcoming wide, cold and shallow Goldie River. From there was the last long steep haul, with many false summits, up to Owers' Corner and the road to Moresby.

The supreme commander, General MacArthur, told Prime Minister Curtin on 17 September that he had the utmost confidence in the Australian commanders in Papua to deal with the situation. But after the order to withdraw to Imita, MacArthur had asked Curtin to send the commander of Allied Land Forces, the Australian General Sir Thomas Blamey, to Port Moresby.

Curtin kept a record of this conversation about the Kokoda campaign with General MacArthur. He noted that MacArthur was disturbed at the situation in New Guinea. The general's view as to 'the real reason for the present unsatisfactory position' was 'the lack of efficiency of the Australian troops', as Curtin recorded:

He feels quite convinced that we have superiority in numbers, but the report this morning is that once again we are withdrawing, although no casualties are reported. As at the beginning, our troops are constantly pulling back and this is the cause of the Commander-in-Chief's uneasiness.

MacArthur was rattled. He believed the situation was a duplication of what took place under Britain's General Percival in Malaya. MacArthur was arranging to despatch American troops to New Guinea by air or by sea, in order to do 'everything possible to stem the attack'. Blamey arrived in Port Moresby, in no great haste, on 23 September. After a bitter quarrel, he removed Lieutenant General Sydney Rowell and sent him back to Australia. MacArthur had requested permission from Curtin to withdraw Rowell and replace him with General Ned Herring, which the prime minister had agreed to. Blamey was indirectly responsible for the transfer to other commands of Major General Tubby Allen and Brigadier Arnold Potts.

*

Prime Minister Curtin in Canberra on 18 September initially seemed to recognise that the position in New Guinea had stabilised and that the Australians were in stronger position. He thought then that Australia as a nation facing the Japanese 'should be able to hold on until we are ready for an offensive'. Some months later, according to General George Vasey, Curtin confessed to being an inexperienced participant in MacArthur's Australian command fiasco:

> In my ignorance [of military affairs], I thought that the Commander-in-Chief [Blamey] should be in New Guinea.

But his black dog of depression came back barking, urged on by General MacArthur. What really galled Curtin was that the United States and Britain had rejected Australia's further appeals for aid for the next six months. He now said Australia 'shall have to manage with what we have'. Curtin unburdened himself on the senior political reporters, who could not make what he was saying public. He was 'profoundly disturbed' at the replies received from Prime Minister Churchill and President Roosevelt, which referred to the 'Beat Hitler First' policy:

> They mean, in effect, that it is vain to appeal for these places to be made a major theatre. I am not surprised. You were told all this when I was in Opposition. The bloody country was told what would happen before the war came.

Curtin believed the British and American chiefs of staff were 'preoccupied with another matter' and did not want to divert anything from it. He said the major strategy decision allocating war priorities the previous December had not been communicated to his government until May 1942:

> Germany was the major enemy and anything sent elsewhere was regarded as diverted from the main objective.

Curtin confirmed that the United States would not send an extra three divisions of troops as requested, although some US troops were on their way to New Guinea from Australia. As Fred Smith from the news agency Australian United Press noted on 9 September:

> Curtin said it meant that this country had a six months' menace to survive. That period would take us to the European spring. We had to do it ourselves with blood and sweat and hard work.

His nerves on edge, Curtin reasoned that if the Japanese got 30,000 men over the Owen Stanley Range an attempt might be made on Port Moresby, 'but we would be able to hold them'. Curtin was now plagued with 'what ifs'. He worried that the Japanese might launch an invasion from another quarter:

> The Japs may discover that they could make an attempt to take Australia from Timor and Java, instead of from New Guinea. That would bring them down the west coast. They might base on the Kimberleys and cross overland . . . They may bypass Perth and come diagonally across in this direction on the other hand they might be satisfied to take West Australia because it is good country.

Curtin reiterated that he was 'profoundly disturbed' and, said Smith, 'he seemed glad to talk about his troubles'. His scenario of the Japanese landing near the Kimberleys in remote north-east Western Australia and crossing to the east through the inland was somewhat far-fetched given the unforgiving outback territory troops would need to conquer. Curtin was now sounding disturbed and even a little irrational. It was a measure of his state of mind.

*

The expected last great battle on Imita Ridge never came. Advancing patrols heading north from Imita Ridge in ensuing days were surprised to discover only scattered Japanese outposts forward of Ioribaiwa. A marked lack of activity by the Japanese had encouraged General Eather to begin a cautious advance in the direction of Ioribaiwa on 22 September. By nightfall on 27 September the Australians were in a position to attack the Japanese high up at Ioribaiwa. The 2/25th Battalion would keep the Japanese focused on their front, with the 2/33rd and 2/31st attacking from the right and left flanks. But when the Diggers went forward the next morning the Japanese were found to have withdrawn during the night.

The Japanese troops, on their last legs, had been ordered to withdraw from Ioribaiwa and the Kokoda Track itself all the way to the north coast where they had landed. There, they would assume a powerful defence near the beaches. *Asahi Shimbun* war correspondent Seizo Okada had been outside the tent of the commander of the South Sea Detached Force, General Tomitaro Horii, when the commander received an urgent radio message. Horii, he said, was looking elderly, sitting solemnly upright, his face emaciated, his grey hair reflecting the dim light of a candle:

It was an order from the Area Army Commander at Rabaul instructing the Horii detachment to withdraw completely from the Owen Stanleys and concentrate on the coast at Buna . . . It was now beyond doubt that the order had been authorised by the Emperor himself.

General Horii had already lost 80 per cent of his men killed, wounded or sick. Okada recalled that when the retreat order went out, despite dire food shortages, it crushed the spirit of the troops. Once in retreat, though, they 'fled for dear life'. Others described it as a 'fighting withdrawal'.

*

General MacArthur on 1 October ordered that that Japanese be driven northwards towards the Kumusi River with the aim of eventually securing the Gona–Buna area where the Japanese had first landed. The Japanese retreat was already in full progress when the order was issued. MacArthur visited Papua for the first time on 2 October. He is pictured on that day with Army Minister Forde and General Blamey. MacArthur was driven by jeep to Owers' Corner where the road ends, and he spent an hour there looking out across the nearest village of Uberi and the mountains of the Owen Stanley Range in the background. He flew back to Brisbane two days later.

Soon Curtin's own deputy and army minister, Frank Forde, would put his leader's mind at rest on the situation in New Guinea. Forde addressed the war cabinet on 6 October after returning from Port Moresby:

> Notwithstanding the hardships, the morale of the Australian troops was extraordinarily high and they were confident of their ability to drive out the Japanese.

Forde reported that there were now over 29,000 Australian army and 16,203 US army personnel in Port Moresby and on the Kokoda Track. The death toll among the Australians had been 464 with another 567 wounded. He told the war cabinet that General MacArthur now thought there was little chance of the Japanese taking Moresby via the Kokoda Track 'in view of the difficulty in maintaining their supply line across the ranges'. But MacArthur would soon be in an unaccountable panic about the Japanese resistance.

*

The Maroubra Force patrols had moved forward from Imita Ridge cautiously, conserving energy, carriers and supplies, passing through Ioribaiwa and then on through Naoro, Menari, Efogi and Kagi with little opposition. On 9 October they had reached the dry lake bed of Myola, where they encountered the first Japanese opposition.

Following the initial exploratory patrols on the Kokoda Track, men of the 25th Brigade with the 3rd Battalion advanced quickly. Significantly, the Japanese had abandoned equipment all along the track. An estimated 2000 troops were retreating with little food. On 17 October Major General Tubby Allen, on the track near Myola, received a signal from General Blamey passing on a message from General MacArthur. MacArthur said 'extremely light casualties indicate no serious effort yet made to displace the enemy' and ordered Allen to attack 'with energy and speed at each point of resistance'. MacArthur's complaints were baseless, born of ignorance of conditions along the track. They were also superfluous, given the enemy's unexpected retreat. Allen replied to Blamey that fifty of his men had been killed in the pursuit of the Japanese with 133 wounded and 730 evacuated owing to illness. Another two messages for Allen from MacArthur through Blamey arrived on 21 October saying that progress was 'NOT REPEAT NOT SATISFACTORY' and the tactical handling of the troops was faulty. Another message said Allen and his men had made no progress against a weaker enemy and that greater boldness was needed. Allen drafted a response:

> If you think you can do any better come up here and bloody well try.

Allen's senior staff officer persuaded the general not to send that response. Although his forces had broken through at Eora Creek on 28 October, opening the way for the recapture of Kokoda and its airstrip, he was relieved of his command the following day. American ignorance of the track wasn't new. In August MacArthur's chief of staff, General Richard Sutherland, had suggested that parts of the Kokoda Track be demolished by explosives to block the enemy – a ludicrous proposition in such terrain.

*

As the Japanese withdrew there were signs that the troops were reduced to eating grass, roots and even wood. Combatants on both sides suffered diseases including malaria and dysentery. The track itself was a grossly unhealthy place. It was plastered with mud blended with faeces and sometimes rotting flesh. It would not be until 8 November that the advancing Australians would make contact with the enemy at Templeton's Crossing, en route to Alola. The Japanese were well dug in, but under intense fire they withdrew yet again.

When an Australian patrol retook the Japanese position, they found mutilated bodies of Australian soldiers tied to trees, one with his arms cut off at the shoulders. Their thighs and calves were partially skinned and the flesh wrapped in leaves. Uneaten body parts were stored, half-cooked, in the haversacks of dead Japanese soldiers. Cannibalism involving Australians was mentioned in the diaries of Japanese soldiers, including Yasuoka Fumitoshi, who wrote:

> No provisions. Some men are said to be eating the flesh of Tori [an abbreviation for captive]. It is said to have good flavour.

The Japanese retreated to Oivi-Gorari, beyond Kokoda. The village, airstrip and plantation on the plateau of Kokoda fell into Australian hands once more when occupied by the 25th Brigade on 2 November and within a few days transport aircraft were flying in much-needed supplies and equipment. In a fitting ceremony, the new commander of Maroubra Force, Major General George Vasey, assembled hundreds of Papuan carriers and thanked them for their efforts, awarding loyal service medals. The Papuans promptly returned to work supporting the 16th Brigade's attack on Oivi-Gorari.

Rather than continue with a difficult and potentially costly uphill attack against the Japanese at Oivi, Vasey ordered encirclement by the 25th Brigade, which had rested briefly at Kokoda. On 11 November 1942, two battalions broke into the Japanese stronghold and within two days it was overrun. Fighting was fierce, with Australian patrols frequently clashing with groups of Japanese attempting to break out. Small numbers of retreating Japanese reached Buna but most died at Oivi-Gorari or in the jungle.

*

Captain Bert Kienzle, the organiser of the Papuan carriers, was home at Kokoda with his memories of the Fuzzy Wuzzy Angels thirty-five years after the Japanese retreated from the Kokoda plateau:

> Well, there were those who deserted, because they knew in the early stages that the Japanese were on top. When the Japanese took over there were Papuans who looted and raped and they were later strung up when we recaptured this place. But there were some mighty good blokes among those who helped us. We even lost some carriers through sheer exhaustion. Australia would have gone if this campaign was not won and we could not have won the campaign without the carriers.

Later controversy surrounded village executions of many Papuans by ANGAU officials, who employed Australian martial law provisions during the war. Some Papuan men were alleged to have taken part in killing Australian citizens. The contentious swift justice included the execution of seventeen men in one day in 1943. They were hanged on roughly constructed gallows in Higaturu village near Popondetta. It was a grisly business and many Papuan relatives claimed that their menfolk had been forced by the Japanese to take part in crimes. Others claimed innocence and in some cases it was argued that the wrong men were hanged. Executions took place before large crowds of villagers, including classes of schoolchildren brought in for the occasion. One small boy witnessed his father being hanged. A few days later, the boy's mother committed suicide in her grief. An Australian *kiap*, or government official, in Papua after the war, John Fowke, wrote that those punished were often village officials acting as facilitators and spies in the pay of the Japanese. They were convicted on a wide range of charges including murder.

*

John Curtin took his second trip home to Western Australia since becoming prime minister in late October 1942. 'Leave Curtin alone' was the headline in *The Mirror* in Perth on 25 October:

Mr Curtin needs some rest. Those who have never had the affairs of a Nation with them both day and night cannot understand the strain, the drain on a man's physical and mental energy such a task entails. It is well to remember this.

Curtin did get some rest and attended an ABC opera with wife Elsie, but he had many full working days. On the way back to the east by train, Curtin was sick again at Adelaide, receiving diathermy, a heat treatment for the relief of stiff joints and to relax muscles. He was given a reserved sitting compartment for the trip to Melbourne. There were no sleeping compartments on the train as an austerity measure. Passengers boarding the train at an intermediate station crowded into Curtin's private sitting compartment. No railway official attempted to stop or remove them. Arguments broke out among passengers. It seems that Curtin made no fuss, but as a result, the prime minister had no sleep during the night in the crowded compartment. The press and Curtin's colleagues were appalled. His illness recurred. On arriving in Melbourne he cancelled all engagements and went to bed.

*

While the desperate fight was going on along the Kokoda Track in 1942, five coalmines were idle in New South Wales. Some 2400 men were on strike for various reasons, causing a heavy daily loss of coal production. At the South Bulli Colliery on the south coast, 550 miners went on strike because coupons for extra clothes were not issued to colliery surface workers.

The prime minister at this time was dealing with a personal and political dilemma over the divisive issue of conscription, which he knew he must overcome. In Melbourne during the First World War, Curtin had been one of the leaders of the movement against compulsory military service. From November 1942, at a special federal Labor Party conference, Curtin began arguing that conscription for the Australian militia should apply not only for service in Australia and her territories, such as Papua and New

Guinea, but also for islands beyond Australian territory in the whole South West Pacific Area, where Australians might need to fight. Curtin had a dilemma because US conscripts were being called on to fight in Pacific areas Australia had a keen interest in protecting. Some Labor supporters damned Curtin as a traitor. The new conscription bill would become law in February the following year.

The passage of the legislation was hugely wearing on the prime minister. A bitter clash had occurred between then back-bencher Arthur Calwell and Curtin. Calwell, whom the Labor caucus would soon make a minister, openly attacked Curtin at an interstate party conference in early January 1943. Calwell accused Curtin and his government not only of introducing the hated militia conscription, but also of ignoring party policy on social security, and the nationalisation of banks and of the steelmaker Broken Hill Pty Ltd (BHP). Curtin said Calwell's attacks on him were being made inside and outside parliament.

*

On 18 November 1942 the retreating main body of the Japanese South Seas Force reached the Kumusi River, inland from the north coast of Papua. General Horii and a few staff officers went down river on a large raft and reached the mouth of the Kumusi, where they changed to a canoe. They set out down the coast towards Gona but a storm blew up and the canoe overturned. According to the memoirs of the sole survivor, a Major Koiwai, after swimming about 4 kilometres, an exhausted Horii gasped, 'Tell the troops that Horii died here.' The general reportedly put both arms up, shouted 'Banzai' to the Emperor and disappeared at sea somewhere near Gona.

Horii's forces now prepared to defend the swamps and the network of coconut-log redoubts at Buna. Between October and December 1942 they held off repeated Australian and US attacks. The defenders were starving under appalling conditions. Some stood constantly in chest-deep water; most suffered malaria and had a fever. Justice Sir William Webb found that it was beyond doubt that Australian, American and Japanese dead were cut up and eaten by Japanese defenders, although many preferred to starve to death. Webb found that considerable numbers of sick and wounded Japanese in northern Papua had been abandoned by their own along the Kokoda Track without medical assistance or medicines, which was 'a brutally savage atrocity'.

*

Japanese defenders on the coast of Papua between Buna and Gona put up a titanic fight. An American battalion trekking on another trail across the Owen Stanley Range encountered no opposition but described it as 'one green hell', so difficult was the terrain.

Australian forces converged towards occupied Gona and Sanananda. By 14 November 1942 General MacArthur was anxious to finish the Papuan campaign by capturing the beach-heads. The Australians of Maroubra Force were ordered to attack and capture Sanananda and Gona without reinforcements. Through Ultra intelligence intercepts, MacArthur knew that Gona had been reinforced by the Japanese, yet this information had been withheld from the 25th Brigade commander, Brigadier Ken Eather, who wrote in his diary, 'Bastards! Short of everything!' His men were in contact with the Japanese on the outskirts of Gona.

Two regiments of the American 32nd Division attacked Buna a little further down the coast. The Japanese fortifications of the coastal region by elaborate defence systems and redoubts made any advance exceptionally difficult. Dugouts were not always feasible in the Buna area because the water table was too close to the surface, so the Japanese bunkers were built in places almost entirely above ground. The Japanese defenders were not the only ones suffering. Fresh US troops were wracked by disease. According to the US army's historical report of the operation, 'our troops approached Buna completely ignorant of the defences which faced them':

They found the enemy forces established in almost impregnable defensive works, which baffled the earlier attackers and left them uncertain of the exact location of their foes. They first had to find out just where the Japanese were and then solve the problem of how to drive them from their fortifications.

The Americans at the front were perhaps among the most wretched-looking soldiers ever to wear the American uniform, according to one of their number, a warrant officer, E. J. Kahn:

> They were gaunt and thin, with deep black circles under their sunken eyes. They were covered with tropical sores. They were clothed in tattered, stained jackets and pants... Many of them fought for days with fevers and didn't know it...

By late November the fierce Japanese resistance stalled. The Australian 21st and 30th brigades, which had served on the Kokoda Track early in the campaign, relieved the exhausted 16th and 25th brigades. Later, the 18th Brigade was brought from Milne Bay to relieve the Americans attacking Buna.

The first major success for the Australians on the north coast had occurred on 9 December 1942 when the Australian 21st Brigade captured Gona, but because the casualty rate had been extremely high, American tanks and reinforcements were brought into the attacks on Buna. Major General E. Forrest Harding had thought his 32nd Infantry Division would easily take Buna, but his men ran into enormous difficulties. American casualties mounted alarmingly for no gain. In December 1942 General MacArthur in Port Moresby called in Major General Robert L. Eichelberger and ordered him to assume control of the battle at Buna. MacArthur told Eichelberger:

> I'm putting you in command at Buna. Relieve Harding. I am sending you in, Bob, and I want you to remove all officers who won't fight. Relieve regimental and battalion commanders; if necessary, put sergeants in charge of battalions and corporals

in charge of companies – anyone who will fight. Time is of the essence. The Japanese may land reinforcements any night.

Eichelberger said MacArthur strode along the breezy veranda of his Moresby house. The supreme commander, he said, had received reports that American soldiers were throwing away their weapons and running from the enemy. MacArthur then stopped short and spoke with emphasis. 'Bob,' he said, 'I want you to take Buna, or not come back alive.'

On 4 December 1942 John Curtin had received a message from General Blamey in New Guinea:

> It has revealed the fact that the American troops cannot be classified as attack troops. They are definitely not equal to the Australian militia, and from the moment they met opposition sat down and have hardly gone forward a yard . . .

Blamey saw dangers for Australia in the war with Japan as a result. He said that in exchange for the Australian 9th Division serving in the Middle East, Australia had been given two unreliable American divisions:

> You will therefore see that if the 9th Australian Division is not returned for our future operations in this area, we are going to be in a very bad way indeed . . . My faith in the [Australian] Militia is growing, but my faith in the Americans has sunk to zero.

After initial successes, tank losses mounted, but by 3 January 1943 the last positions around Buna fell to the Australians and the Americans. Only fifty Japanese troops survived this action, most becoming prisoners of war. Sanananda was the final Japanese strongpoint on the coast. The Australians and Americans had to advance through swamp, live in it, fight in it and die in it. The Japanese continued to resist under shocking conditions. Poorly trained Australian troops of the 30th Brigade suffered losses of more than half their number in their opening attacks. The exhausted 18th Brigade was brought over from Buna to assist. On 12 January 1943 the Japanese evacuated Sanananda. About 2000 troops escaped by sea or on foot, taking the Allies by surprise. On 22 January, the 18th Brigade finished mopping-up actions and the campaign came to an end the following day.

Total Australian casualties in the campaign between 22 July 1942 and 22 January 1943 were 2165 killed or dead from other causes and 3533 wounded. The American casualities were 798 in the Gona–Buna area. Some 13,000 Japanese died from wounds, starvation or disease. American casualties were far greater than Australian in the final Buna operation. The entire Owen Stanley campaign in Papua saw one of the great victories of Australian arms. It was a major achievement that the Australian army in 1942, with assistance from US infantry towards the end of the campaign on the coast, had established tactical superiority over the Japanese.

*

Deep in the remote mountains 450 Australian commando troops, known as Kanga Force, operated from March until August 1942 along the track between Wau and Japanese-occupied Salamaua on the coast. One of their duties was to guard against a potential Japanese march across the Bulldog track from the western end of the Owen Stanleys to Port Moresby. This was hundreds of kilometres from the Kokoda Track. Down on the north coast the Japanese had 2000 troops at the port of Lae and 500 at nearby Salamaua.

Back in March 1942 a Japanese drive to occupy the settlement of Mubo, only 30 kilometres from Wau, caused the Australians to withdraw behind Wau and set timber buildings in Mubo alight. The Japanese didn't advance beyond Mubo, so it was reoccupied and partially restored. In January 1943, the 17th Brigade arrived at Wau by air to reinforce Kanga Force and ensure the security of the Bulolo Valley. At this time the Japanese moved forward towards Wau and several companies of the 2/6th Battalion were deployed east of the town to engage the enemy.

On the night of 28 January the Japanese force proved too strong for the Australians, who were assisted by attacking fighter aircraft, and came to within 3 kilometres of Wau, which was only lightly defended. Reinforcements were hurriedly flown into Wau as the Japanese neared. With the sloping airfield under fire, the troops went straight into action as they jumped from their transports. The Japanese on 30 January 1943 met fierce resistance and were forced back. This was the turning point of the battle for Wau. The Japanese from New Britain launched strong fighter attacks on Wau, but they were mostly ineffective. With the Australians in pursuit, and reinforcements flying in daily, the Japanese began retreating towards Mubo. The area would be in Australian hands in July 1943.

The failure of the Japanese attempt to take the small town and airstrip of Wau had serious consequences for the Japanese in New Guinea. Not only had some 800 men been expended in futile fighting, but the 18th Army's plans to strengthen the flank defences of the Lae–Salamaua area were seriously disturbed. On top of the Australian–American victories in the Milne Bay and Kokoda campaigns, the new military successes gave Australians at home heart.

*

As 1942 had drawn to a close, Curtin gave a top-secret briefing to senior political reporters in Canberra, including Fred Smith from Australian United Press, who took these notes:

Curtin gave us an end-of-the year summing up of the position which indicated our limitations in disheartening fashion and which included a statement that Australia was Churchill's 'forgotten land'. There is pretty clear evidence that American politics are coming into the question of aid for us. Curtin was asked about the naval position north of New Guinea and he responded by saying that the question of air transport was worrying him, particularly at present.

Promised transport planes had been diverted elsewhere, Curtin said bitterly:

270 planes went over Europe last night, but by Christ you can't get any here. They are over places which could be left alone without it mattering for two months.

Curtin supposed this was the proper fate for a country that 'thought it could fight anybody's war before it made its own position safe'. It was useless addressing questions to Churchill and Roosevelt, he seethed:

They had their minds made up that if the British Empire in the Far East had to go, then it had to go. The only part which had not gone was Australia.

Curtin's invasion fears thus were unrelenting and they would return to haunt him. It was probably Blamey's assessment of the situation and his concern about the efficiency of US troops in Papua that prompted Curtin to force the withdrawal of the 9th Division. The original request for the return of the 9th was made in February 1942, but in view of the situation in the Middle East the troops were allowed to remain there to play a strong role in the Battle of El Alamein. The 9th would finally return to Australia in February 1943.

*

The Australian commander-in-chief, General Sir Thomas Blamey, had many critics. On 9 November 1942 he reportedly told a full parade of men at Koitaki, near the start of the Kokoda Track, that 'soldiers must not be afraid to die' and that 'only running rabbits get shot'. Blamey told officers separately that he doubted the brigade possessed the will to fight. Later historians have said the remarks were taken out of context. War historian Dudley McCarthy wrote that Blamey had demonstrated his greatness almost daily. Historian Professor Hiromi Tanaka agreed:

General Blamey should be accorded much higher recognition for the way the Australian troops performed against the Japanese. Blamey should be highly regarded instead of the Americans who got all the publicity because the Australians under his general leadership were the ones who fought against the Japanese up until October 1943.

*

Early 1943 saw Curtin's morale flag again. According to Fred Smith from the Australian United Press, a disheartened and at times rambling Curtin told political reporters on 2 February that Russia got more planes in a week than Australia got from the Allies in a year and the future of the war worried him:

... Curtin said it would outlast him and a good many other people. He was asked if he meant it would outlast him politically, or in fact. He did not answer directly, but pointed out that he had been leader of a party for seven and a half years, a fact which meant a bit of strain.

Curtin worried about the return to Australia of some 30,000 men of the 9th Division who had served in North Africa. He privately told reporters that the troops were still in grave danger and that he had not slept properly for three weeks. The troops couldn't remain in Western Australia because they would be immobilised for six months by transport difficulties, so they had to sail onwards all the way to Sydney. Their troopships would not arrive in Fremantle until 18 February 1943. Curtin was nervous about reports of Japanese submarines operating off the east coast. Two steamers would be torpedoed off southern New South Wales during February. The last ship of the convoy carrying the 9th Division troops arrived safely in Sydney Harbour on Sunday 28 February.

Many Australian historians believe that the invasion threat to Australia was over after the Battle of Midway, if not earlier. Dudley McCarthy wrote that after early 1943 Australia saw the dark threat of isolation and actual invasion disappear. Australia, he said, had also seen the end of an epoch with the realisation that her strategic destiny lay far outside that of the Motherland, Great Britain, and with the United States.

Prime Minister Curtin had called the campaign on the Kokoda Track and on the Papuan north coast from Gona to Buna a 'complete and utter victory'. But in his caution, he would not readily accept that the Japanese threat to Australia had passed.

After receiving intelligence of massed Japanese troops in Rabaul embarking on eight transports, a big force of US and Australian fighters and bombers was assembled for attack in early March 1943. It was later revealed that the convoy was carrying some 7000 troops to reinforce Lae on the New Guinea mainland. The convoy was attacked by RAAF bomber squadrons from Milne Bay in what became the Battle of the Bismarck Sea. Later in the morning, when cloud lifted, RAAF and USAAF squadrons from Port Moresby flew over the Owen Stanleys to join the attack. By daybreak on 4 March all eight Japanese transports had been sunk and four of their escorting destroyers lost. As many as fifty or sixty escorting Zero fighters had been shot down.

Some 2890 Japanese soldiers and sailors were killed in the battle or later drowned. Thirteen US and RAAF aircrew were killed. The RAAF's 22 Squadron played a major role in the success of the Battle of the Bismarck Sea. Flight Lieutenant Bill Newton, twenty-three, received the Victoria Cross for his constant low-level attacks through heavy flak from the Lae convoy. Newton and one of his crew, Flight Sergeant John Lyon, twenty-seven, survived the battle but within a fortnight were forced down on the sea. They were captured and executed by numerous bayonet thrusts.

Atrocities were not restricted to the Japanese. Through 4 and 5 March Allied aircraft, including RAAF airmen in Beaufighters, were despatched to the Huon Gulf to strafe Japanese life rafts and rescue vessels to prevent Japanese who had escaped their sinking transports from being rescued to fight again. Australian war historian Douglas Gillison wrote:

It was a grim and bloody work for which the crews had little stomach. Some of the men in Beaufighter crews confessed to experiencing acute nausea.

On 16 March 1943, the prime minister's staff took notes of a secret telephone conversation between General MacArthur and Curtin. The previous day the Japanese had conducted a major air raid on Darwin with twenty-four medium bombers and twenty fighters. Two oil storage tanks and four buildings were bombed. RAAF Spitfires intercepted the Japanese formation and nineteen enemy planes were shot down or damaged. Four Spitfires were shot down and two pilots killed.

MacArthur told Curtin there was clear evidence of the enemy's ambitions; they were trying to infiltrate southwards and shove their position nearer to the Torres Strait and in the greatest strength possible. Curtin quoted MacArthur as saying that to meet the situation he had sent generals Kenney and Sutherland to Washington to discuss Australia's defence:

General MacArthur does not think the enemy has sufficient forces to launch a major attack now but that he would require from two to four months to develop the requisite conjunction of forces to make a serious attack. The enemy, however, can be said to be developing what General MacArthur describes as a position of readiness.

The Japanese in early 1943 were developing sixty-seven airfields in the South West Pacific. When completed they could take up to 2000 aircraft, but there were no heavy concentrations of aircraft at that moment. There was, however, evidence of heavy concentrations of ground troops, and the Japanese had at least eight first-class shock divisions. MacArthur said his concern was to deal with the Australian base and to concentrate the whole of his power 'on this weak country'. The notes of the conversation between Curtin and MacArthur concluded with MacArthur's summary:

The enemy has diagnosed the situation pretty well the same as we have. He knows the correct thing in war is to concentrate a superior strength against a weak position. The southwest Pacific is no longer menaced but the northwest approach to the Pacific area and North Australia is.

It would seem that General MacArthur's warnings to Curtin, whether intentional or not, had the effect of stirring up the prime minister's invasion anxieties and maintaining his belief that invasion of Australia was still possible.

Around the time of Curtin's statement in April 1943, Australian army intelligence operators picked up a Japanese signal sent to bases in the New Guinea region detailing the movements of the commander-in-chief of the Combined Fleet, Admiral Yamamoto, for 18 April. It was an extraordinary failure of security on the part of the Japanese. As a result, seventeen US twin-engined P-38 Lightning fighters fitted with long-range tanks took off from Guadalcanal on the morning Yamamoto left Rabaul. At 7.45 am, west of Ballale on the southern tip of Bougainville, the Americans sighted two medium 'Betty' bombers escorted by six Zeros. After a brief skirmish one bomber crashed into the sea. The other bomber, trailing flames and smoke, crashed into dense jungle. When Japanese soldiers found the wreckage, Admiral Yamamoto was sitting in the co-pilot's seat but his head was down among the trees away from the wreckage. His left gloved hand reportedly grasped his sword and his right hand rested on it lightly. His death was another significant blow to the Japanese war effort, which was starting to go badly awry in the South West Pacific.

Chapter 15

DESCENT OF A LEADER

John Curtin was only occasionally seen smiling in public during the long haul of the Pacific war. On 8 June 1943, he emerged from a long conference with General MacArthur. It had been a good conference. The two were pictured on that sunny day shaking hands, both smiling broadly. The Allies had made gains and gradually built up much-needed air power. In January 1943, advanced Spitfire fighters were based around Australia's top end. They were piloted by both British and Australian airmen. No. 1 Fighter Wing, RAF, had moved to the Darwin area with three Spitfire squadrons. The Spitfires had major clashes with the Japanese on 2 and 15 March 1943 and on 20 June 1943 intercepted a formation of twenty-one bombers and twenty-one fighters, shooting down nine bombers and five fighters. This was the most successful encounter by the RAAF over Darwin.

On 9 June the prime minister was most optimistic when privately briefing political reporters in Canberra:

> ... I feel that the pressure on our country, which has so long been continued, is now about to be thrown back and cannot be maintained by the enemy ... The Battle of the Coral Sea was

a deliverance, and the return of the AIF enabled us to stop the Japanese advance in New Guinea just in time.

The following day Curtin released a momentous and much-welcomed public statement: 'I do not think the enemy can now invade this country.'

Curtin had finally said it. The *Sydney Morning Herald* editorialised that the reassuring statement for Australia reflected the determination of the Allied leadership to speed up the war against Japan. Around this time Curtin also felt secure enough to take a public swipe at past conservative governments, which had sent the cream of Australia's defence forces overseas in the service of Britain. He told a national Labor Party conference in Sydney that this had left Australia in a perilous situation:

Before the war with Japan, the primary consideration of the other Governments had been co-operating overseas, with the result that the home defence plan had been defeatist in outlook and preparation. Neither the Menzies Government nor its military advisers provided for the contingency that Singapore might fall or that the British Fleet might not come.

Members of the opposition replied that Curtin's remarks were unworthy of the prime minister and were a slur on the AIF troops who had fought in New Guinea with equipment supplied by Great Britain. Former Prime Minister Menzies pointed out that the Labor Party in opposition had voted against conscription. The jibe was ironic because the same national Labor Party conference now supported Curtin's conscription of Australian men outside Australian territories by a margin of two to one.

*

Curtin's upbeat announcement on the state of the Pacific war coincided with a marked slackening of Japanese submarine attacks off the coast of Australia. During the first half of 1943, after a lull in submarine activity of some five months, sixteen ships had been attacked off New South Wales, with nine ships sunk, while off Queensland in that time four ships had been attacked and two sent to the bottom. Keith Pryor of the merchant navy recalled many of the sinkings being hushed up:

> It wasn't even known by the Australian population that there were numerous ships torpedoed and sunk in Australian waters. There was an ever present danger for ships traversing the coastal waters and that went on for some time.

Of the seventy-six merchant ships that were lost in Australian waters during the war, twenty-nine were Australian. The Seamen's Union estimated that 386 of its members lost their lives.

One of the greatest tragedies off the coast involved an Australian hospital ship, the *Centaur*. She had sailed unescorted from Sydney on 12 May 1943 with her crew and staff, but carried no patients. The white-painted ship, displaying lights and marked with large, illuminated red crosses, was sunk by a torpedo from a Japanese submarine two days into her voyage east-north-east of North Stradbroke Island off Brisbane. Of the 332 on board, sixty-four survived. The survivors spent thirty-five hours on rafts before being rescued. Ellen Savage, the only nursing sister to survive, although injured, helped other survivors. As sharks circled her lifeboat and morale flagged, and ships and planes passed by without seeing the survivors' raft, Savage gave aid and comfort to other survivors, even organising a singalong to keep spirits up. She was awarded the George Medal for her heroism.

*

In an Independence Day broadcast to America on 4 July 1943 (Washington time), Curtin sounded even more buoyant than in his earlier comments to journalists:

> If I liken the Pacific war to a football match, I can say to you that the first half is over, we have kicked off after the interval, and we

are going to carry the ball into enemy territory for a smashing victory.

While Curtin was cheerful about the war news, once again he was not well. It seemed that events constantly conspired to undermine his wellbeing and stamina. The government had introduced an anti-strike code at the end of May 1943, but munitions workers who were against the employment of non-union labour, including previously unemployed women, ignored the provisions because the code was introduced after their industrial dispute had begun. In another dispute on 8 June, as Curtin had been meeting MacArthur in Sydney, miners at a colliery near Cessnock in New South Wales went on strike protesting that the butter ration for their daily sandwiches was insufficient. The *Sydney Morning Herald* was outraged:

The nation must go short of coal because miners dislike going short of butter. Or in the case of the slaughtermen at Homebush, Sydney people must suffer a shortage of meat because the employees will not do a fair day's work.

Curtin called a major government conference with representatives of the nation's trade unions on 19 June to discuss the need for an uninterrupted industrial effort without strikes, but on the eve of the gathering in Melbourne it was announced that the prime minister was ill and couldn't attend. While Curtin's doctor had allowed him to leave his bed, he refused to agree to the prime minister travelling from Canberra to Melbourne because it might cause a recurrence of the throat trouble Curtin had suffered during the previous week. The *Sydney Morning Herald* speculated that with Curtin's absence, the conference could not bring on the 'real showdown' that was needed with the unions.

*

Curtin's sudden dismissal of a Japanese invasion had caught the opposition flat-footed. They accused him of making the war forecast look brighter ahead of an expected federal election, which indeed Curtin would soon call for 21 August 1943. Curtin's Australian Labor Party would win the national poll handsomely, gaining an additional seventeen seats in the House of Representatives. Soon after Curtin's sweeping victory in 1943, Robert Menzies was elected leader of the United Australia Party and leader of the opposition.

*

Curtin later summarised the successes that followed in the New Guinea operations in 1943. The capture of the Trobriands Islands and Woodlark Island in June 1943, he noted, had bridged the gap between the Solomons and New Guinea. The fall of Salamaua and Lae on the New Guinea mainland had occurred in September. General MacArthur had begun employing his highly effective 'leapfrog' tactics pioneered by US navy marines in the Aleutians and in the Solomons. It involved bypassing some key enemy strongholds and leaving them to 'wither on the vine'. One of the largest Japanese air and naval bases was at Rabaul. Taking Rabaul, with its significant fortifications and defences, even if successful, would have resulted in massive Allied losses, so it was allowed to wither while being constantly bombed. MacArthur's New Guinea campaign of 1943 was considered strategically brilliant. A landing by the 9th Division – the 'Rats of Tobruk' – at Finschhafen, east of Lae on the Huon Peninsula, enabled the coast to be cleared. It was part of a twofold manoeuvre to destroy all the important enemy positions, according to General MacArthur:

> Surprised by the swiftness of these movements, the enemy was forced to loosen his hold on New Guinea, with overwhelming loss of irreplaceable troops and supplies.

The threat to Australia had so diminished by October 1943 that the Curtin Government decided to release 20,000 servicemen from the army to be employed in other areas of the war economy where manpower was short. In mid-1943 there would be a limited further release of long-serving servicemen. That same month while opening the fourth Liberty war loan, Curtin told a packed Sydney Town Hall rally that the Allies were gradually capturing the Japanese bases that had been used to launch 'bolts of destruction'. He implied that it had been a near thing:

> they would have come but for the fighting resistance of our forces, could have made some of our capital cities another Rotterdam, could have made certain of our great sites of munitions production another Coventry . . .

While the future peace was yet to be established, Australians could go to sleep at night knowing that no enemy could interrupt their slumbers:

> and that fact alone, if there were no others, has marked you out as indeed a blessed and a fortunate people . . .

In August 1944 the government would reduce the army by another 30,000 men and the RAAF by 15,000.

*

As the war progressed, the test of stamina and endurance was not only on servicemen and women but also the thousands of loved ones, friends and relatives of missing Diggers, many of them captured after the fall of Singapore in February 1942. Some of those waiting received brief postcards of a few simple words through the Red Cross. Others suffered without comforting words of any kind, without knowing whether their son, husband, brother or uncle was alive or dead. So many who were languishing in prisoner-of-war camps, often in frightful and inhumane conditions, were being used and abused by the Japanese as slave labour. Others simply were 'missing'.

Mrs Pat Tranter, of Heathcote in Victoria, thought her husband Arthur, a lieutenant, was in a prison camp in Malaya and sent brief, hopeful postcards through the Red Cross:

ALL WELL. ALWAYS IN THOUGHTS. BRENDA THIRD GRADE SCHOOL. THINKS EVERY DAY OF YOU WITH LONGING FOR YOUR RETURN. DON'T WORRY EVERYTHING GOOD. LOVE PAT.

Lieutenant Tranter's 2/29th Battalion had arrived in Singapore in August 1941 and had fought hard in Malaya, retreating all the way south to the Singapore island. He was actually in a prison camp at Gloegoer (now Glugur, Indonesia) near Medan in steamy northern Sumatra in the Dutch East Indies. Ignoring the horrors of war and his confinement, in June 1943 he sat down and secretly wrote a small book about what he had seen in Malaya and more recently on the island of Sumatra. But he did not write about the horrors that were increasing around him, nor even mention the Japanese. His story about life in the Far East was pleasant, informative, hopeful and vibrant, all the things his life was not:

I will try to tell you about some of the customs of the various races I have had contact with, of their religion and some of their fables, of the work they do and the way they live.

It was written for his little daughter, Brenda, and carried home to her at the end of the war when she was seven. Brenda would not know for many years that her father's beautiful handwriting on a thick note pad had been crafted under worsening conditions. He wrote a covering letter for the book:

Dear Brenda, as you can see I am writing this a long time after I last saw you, but still I can picture you as you were just as though I had seen you a week ago. I still get most of my pleasure from remembering the good times you and Mummy and I had together, and my main regret is that you were probably too young to remember what your old Daddy looked like.

His exotic journal of fifty-six pages was written over six months from June to December 1943. In an extraordinary feat he somehow managed to keep the writing pad safe and in perfect condition for the rest of the war. He was held at the Gloegoer prisoner-of-war camp for a year and nine months. He wrote that to travel as a war prisoner was 'not the best way to see a country', but in spite of the discomfort in moving from Padang to Medan, he saw much in Sumatra that was 'interesting and beautiful', including the local people, the wildlife, the scenery and even the jungle of Sumatra.

From the Gloegoer POW camp Tranter was put to work in March 1944 building a road through mountainous jungle in Aceh, on the northern tip of Sumatra. Dysentery became rife, beatings and bashings a daily event and tropical ulcers common. The road-building had been bad enough, with the men being forced to march great distances, but the Japanese soon had a new project that would claim the lives of thousands of prisoners. Lieutenant Tranter and the remaining Australian prisoners, together with Dutch, British and American captives, were put to work building the Pakan Baroe railway. Survivors and their families now call it the 'forgotten railway'; the stories of horrors along the Thai–Burma railway are much better known. But the Japanese inhumanity on the Sumatran railway was equally atrocious. The Japanese wanted a railway from Moeara to Pakan Baroe, a distance of 137 miles (220 kilometres) through the central inland Sumatran jungle, to exploit coal deposits.

The Romushas – Javanese boys and young men – were forced to do the heaviest labour constructing the embankment for the railway. Yet they received hardly anything to eat and no medical care at all, and they died like flies. Executions of prisoners for a variety of alleged misdemeanours were common. The building of the railway in Sumatra would claim the lives of some 80,000 Javanese men and boys and almost 2500 European prisoners of war. The Paken Baroe–Moeara railway, built over the bodies of so many slaves, was never used and soon sank back into jungle, where a few rusting traces of it can be found today.

*

In 1943 Curtin would receive a personal letter from a man he knew, former conservative Australian minister for defence, Sir Archdale

Parkhill. Lieutenant Robert Parkhill, Parkhill's son, had surrendered in Rabaul with more than fifty other officers and by this time was a known prisoner of war in Japan. What bothered the lieutenant's father was that no realistic inquiry had ever been held into the strange decision to leave Lark Force at Rabaul, as Parkhill put it, 'without the faintest thought that they could hold it against the Japanese' and be 'abandoned to their fate'. Curtin would pass the letter on and would respond 'I shall be glad to look into the aspects you have raised', but the file would show no answer to the gist of Sir Archdale Parkhill's query because there was none.

By late 1943 the Japanese had built Rabaul into a most formidable air and naval base. In October there were some 329 Japanese aircraft, mostly fighters, based at and near Rabaul, using five airstrips. The harbour was crowded with Japanese warships and merchant vessels. The ground at Rabaul bristled with 367 anti-aircraft guns manned by well-trained army and navy crews. Needless to say, intruding Allied airmen considered Rabaul the number one 'hotspot' of the South West Pacific.

*

Despite the easing of the war emergency for Australia in the Pacific, illness and stress had become commonplace for Prime Minister Curtin, who continued to be laid low with various debilitating ailments through 1943. Curtin was hospitalised in Melbourne in November 1943. The press were not allowed to speculate the nature or seriousness of his illness, but he had relinquished his prime ministerial duties to his deputy, Frank Forde. With Curtin bedridden, his two arch party rivals actively campaigned privately and publicly for the introduction of earlier, more extreme political propositions. In late November the *Sydney Morning Herald* editorialised that junior minister Arthur Calwell was 'rapidly taking Mr Ward's place' as the 'enfant terrible' of the cabinet. Calwell, without authority, had declared the government's intention to nationalise Australia's banks, which was not on Curtin's agenda.

In late December 1944 Forde announced that the prime minister would return from Melbourne to Canberra, but would

remain at the Lodge for an indefinite period of rest. The nationalisation of the banks proposal had been deferred. Curtin wanted to
win the war before considering dramatic social change. Not long
after arriving back at the Lodge, Curtin summoned the irascible
Calwell, who was dismissive:

> He was losing his grip. He was sick and contemplating retire-
> ment. He said to me one day: 'When the war is over, I want to
> retire and I think Chifley will retire too.'

Soon after, on 19 January 1945 Curtin, still sick, felt obliged to
again summon Calwell to the Lodge for another dressing down.
Calwell had taken the extraordinary action of publicly criticising
the Australian army for its failure to release information to the
public. Curtin threatened to remove Calwell from the government. Calwell later wrote:

> He said that he was thinking of gazetting me out of the govern-
> ment . . . I put the blame squarely where it belonged: on the army.
> I told him to take things quietly. I said he had been misled.

Calwell said Curtin severely rebuked him, but he retained his
junior ministerial post.

The political correspondent for *The Argus* on 11 December
1943, tired of receiving no comment on questions about the prime
minister's health, asked of Curtin in print, 'What is the trouble?'
Whatever it was, he wrote, the prime minister's illness had
political implications. By the end of the month Curtin took one
of his rare trips home to Cottesloe by train. The *West Australian*
reported that he was going home 'to be with his family and enjoy
a complete rest'. He was home for his 59th birthday on 8 January
1944. In keeping with the nation's austerity drive, his wife Elsie
gave him neither presents, nor baked a cake. Curtin spent the
days happily and quietly at Cottesloe, pottering in the garden or
walking on the beach before dealing with official matters. He was
frequently tired.

The spectre of abandoning Australian troops to the enemy, such as occurred at Rabaul in January 1942, still haunted Curtin. Back in Canberra in 1944, at a conference between Australian and New Zealand ministers, Curtin demonstrated that he had never forgotten the defenders of Rabaul nor their abandonment:

> We wish to avoid a repetition of the experience of the war when the defence of the whole screen collapsed and the outlying island bases with their garrisons became hostages to fortune.

Later that month the *Sydney Morning Herald*'s political correspondent in Canberra, Ross Gollan, reported that the supply minister, Jack Beasley, had collapsed from overwork. Gollan said other senior ministers including Curtin were similarly overworked. The reason was that many other ministers were not pulling their weight, Gollan claimed. Of nineteen ministers in cabinet, he said nearly half 'couldn't be trusted with any but the most simple administrative duties'.

*

The war against Japan, with Australian and US forces now cooperating effectively, was progressing steadily. In New Guinea, the taking of Finschhafen on the coast north-east of Lae initiated a campaign in mainland New Guinea that was successfully concluded in February 1944 when Australian troops were able to link up with American forces. The US troops had landed at Saidor, south of Madang, where the Japanese withdrew inland over the Finisterre Range. The landing of American troops at Cape Gloucester and Arawe on New Britain island in December 1944 completed control of the Huon Gulf and Vitiaz Straits. MacArthur still resisted a full-frontal ground attack on the Rabaul base, where the remaining Japanese had now become 'hostages to fortune' under aerial siege. The American Forces extended their hold of New Britain and also landed in the Admiralty Islands. Parallel with these operations were others in the South West Pacific Area, which had started with the seizure of Guadalcanal and advanced through the New Georgia group to Bougainville. Curtin said the occupation in February 1944 of Green Island at the northern end of the Solomons Archipelago was the culmination of a successful series of flank movements that had gradually enveloped all enemy forces in the Solomons.

*

When John and Elsie Curtin visited Washington at President Roosevelt's invitation in 1944 Curtin was able to say that the Australian people had emerged from a mortal peril, thanks to 'a merciful providence, the aid of great Allies' and Australia's own 'heroic efforts'. For almost two years Curtin had declined invitations from Roosevelt and Churchill to visit them overseas. At the last minute, he rang Elsie and asked her to join him on the unescorted US liner the *Lurline*, crossing the Pacific. There were various reports that Curtin was depressed before and during the voyage; Elsie was ill from the effects of her cholera shot. Curtin at times paced the decks, reportedly carrying a life jacket, presumably worrying about submarines.

In a broadcast in April 1944 he expressed the profound gratitude of the Australia people for American assistance. General MacArthur, he said, had displayed all the qualities of a diplomat and a great military commander. Had Australia been invaded, Curtin said, the process of defeating Japan would have been 'immeasurably lengthened'. What listeners didn't know was that Curtin's broadcast occurred from his bed in Washington. He had taken ill the previous night and been forced to cancel all engagements apart from the broadcast. A White House naval surgeon diagnosed the prime minister as suffering from high blood pressure and a neurotic back condition. One report said Curtin returned from an engagement 'bent nearly double' and complaining of head pains. His departure for London was postponed.

Eventually Elsie Curtin visited Canada while her husband flew on to the Commonwealth Prime Ministers' Conference in London in May. Curtin and Churchill behaved cooperatively and pleasantly towards each other after their earlier stormy relationship.

Curtin even spent most of three weekends with Churchill at the prime minister's official country residence, Chequers. At the close of the conference Curtin claimed that nobody could have 'steered us through these deliberations more graciously, more inspiringly, or more successfully' than Churchill. Churchill responded at a luncheon at the Australia Club by offering the 'right hand of friendship to that most commanding, competent, whole-hearted leader of the Australian people'. Times had certainly changed. Importantly, in England Curtin had reached agreement with Churchill that Australia should be able to reduce its active participation in Britain's overall war effort to increase the supply of fighting forces in the Pacific. After leaving Britain, Curtin joined Elsie in Canada. It was all an enormous strain for him. His press secretary Don Rodgers, who accompanied him to London, later believed that he 'had begun to die during the trip' and had seemed anxious to ensure his early return to Australia. According to Rodgers, 'the Boss' seemed to lose the will to live as time went on. Curtin and Elsie arrived back in Australia in June 1944.

*

There were literally thousands of Australians writing to the prime minister each year asking him to look after them and solve their problems, according to Canberra historian Dr Michael McKernan. The strain, worry and intensity of the pressure might well have led to Curtin's diseases and illnesses, McKernan believed. But it seems likely that Curtin's very humanity contributed towards his workload and stress.

Mrs Lucy Nicholson, of Rutherglen in Scotland, had written to Curtin while he was in London saying that she rarely heard from her two boys who had been sent by the British Government years earlier to the Fairbridge Farm School at Molong, New South Wales. She now had regrets and wished to be near the 'wee ones.' Mrs Nicholson wanted to emigrate to Australia 'to be near my dear boys and make up to them something of the love and joy of life that has not been theirs practically all their life'. Curtin dictated a reply to Mrs Nicholson regretting that he couldn't see the boys personally in Australia, but saying he would endeavour to obtain information about them. In May 1944, Gunner Joseph Nicholson, aged eighteen, received an extraordinary letter from the prime minister's private secretary, Fred McLaughlin, offering personal advice from John Curtin: 'Probably the best course could be for you to write your Mother fully, but if you care to send advice to this office it will be sent to her.'

What is extraordinary in 1944 is that a busy prime minister in wartime could take such personal interest in a mother's regret. The act was not unusual or random for Curtin. The range and extent of his answers to personal correspondence was remarkable, extensive and probably unnecessary given the priorities. But Curtin couldn't help himself, as historian Michael McKernan observed:

> He was the national father of us all . . . John Curtin felt the personal burden for the manifold and manifest sufferings of his people . . .

Pressmen who gathered for their regular background briefing with Curtin on 21 August were surprised to hear him say how ill he had been and still remained. Harold Cox of the Melbourne *Herald* thought he looked remarkably well. But Curtin said his visit abroad, particularly the air travel and the heavy workload had all lowered his powers of resistance. Cox found Don Rodgers 'extraordinarily depressed'. Cox mentioned political debate going on but added:

> He leaves me with a strong impression that Curtin has said something to him about Curtin's future which is worrying him . . .

The prime ministership was now a burden, but it was a duty he couldn't contemplate surrendering. Curtin wrote to his cousin Mollie in Melbourne on 31 August 1944 remembering 'the good old days', but also reflecting on the pressures of his job, as he put it, 'now as we grow old':

Sinking deep into arm chairs is only possible when someone is putting to me some problems. Captaining the government of a nation is a bit more exacting than being captain of a football team. I know for I've done both. But, old girl, thinking of one's self is the worst of misfortunes for then comes self-pity . . . Anyhow I have lots of great interests. Life has given me a pretty good innings.

The governor-general, Lord Gowrie, had developed a deep admiration for Curtin, as had Lady Gowrie. Their only surviving son, Patrick, had been killed in action in 1942. Despite Gowrie's ill-health and their desire to see their grandsons, they had been persuaded to stay on in Australia for another two years. They eventually left Australia on 10 September 1944. Gowrie's appointment continued until he was succeeded by the Duke of Gloucester on 30 January 1945. Gowrie had been governor-general of Australia for nine years. Before leaving Australia, in a farewell letter he worried about John Curtin's health:

I have been filled with admiration for the calmness and courage with which you have tackled your many difficulties and problems in the most critical period of Australia's history. I know what a severe mental and physical strain this must entail, and I do hope your health will not suffer. Take care of yourself as much as you can, for the country's sake as well as your own.

Curtin was so ill between November 1944 and January 1945 that his deputy Frank Forde acted as prime minister. For the following three months Curtin was able to return to work and attend cabinet meetings. He became ill again in June, when there were doubts about his full recovery from a heart condition.

*

In early November 1944 Elsie Curtin received word that her husband was ill in hospital in Melbourne. Mrs Curtin said 'John insisted that he was just feeling a bit knocked up' and wasn't sleeping well, but soon doctors told her that her husband had suffered a heart attack:

> He wouldn't hear of my coming over then as young John was to be married in December, and he wanted one of us to be present at the wedding.

Curtin was forced to miss the wedding. After the wedding Mrs Curtin arrived in Canberra:

> By this time 'Dad' was back on the job, but the strain on his heart was very great. He would make a speech, then have to rest up for a few days, then he would insist on going back to the House again. Even then I didn't know how seriously ill he was. He still said he was just tired. I had planned to return home in April, but when I mentioned it to the doctor he asked me to stay on. I realised then that 'Dad' wasn't just tired.

In early February Curtin didn't give his regular secret background briefing to senior journalists for a week. When he did, the Melbourne *Herald*'s Harold Cox thought he was suffering from the mental disorder then called neurosis, characterised partly by anxious behaviour:

> For the last week he had again looked tired and listless. He improved slightly on the first few days after his return but my impression is that he is looking very sick again although he is not as neurotic as he frequently was before his illness.

Curtin was exhibiting impulsive outbursts. At the end of March, he spoke about wanting to take a holiday at home. On 9 April 1945 he left the Lodge for the first time in more than a week to go to Parliament House. He was increasingly ill and sounded despondent, Cox said: 'he wished he could feel well for a while as there were many things he wanted to do and many things he wanted to say.'

Curtin was admitted to a private hospital in Canberra on 30 April 1945 with what was described as 'congestion on the lungs'. A friend from Perth, the Presbyterian clergyman the Very Reverend Hector Harrison, visited Curtin in hospital. He found the prime minister's health badly run down:

> I went round to see him and he said 'I'm not allowed to read the papers, not allowed to read anything for that matter, and don't know what's going on.'

He would, however, discover that Adolf Hitler, that same day, had shot himself. Germany was all but defeated. For a time it looked as though Curtin had recovered, but on Monday 2 July his office issued an ominous statement to the press:

> Since the last bulletin on the health of the Prime Minister there has been unsatisfactory progress and during the past two weeks a deterioration in his condition has occurred.

Elsie Curtin remembers her husband, after 'another bad attack' in Canberra, wanting to leave the hospital and return to the Lodge:

> [Ray] Tracey drove him home and an ambulance with a stretcher was waiting for him at the Lodge door because 'Dad' wasn't allowed to walk up the stairs. 'Dad' paused for quite a while after he got out of the car and had a good look at the garden, as if he sensed it would be his last opportunity. He was carried upstairs to his room and never came down again alive.
>
> In June he discussed with me his coming death. We both knew he hadn't long to go. He told me he had left a statement that he was to be buried in the Presbyterian portion of the Karrakatta Cemetery, WA, and had had it locked away.

His son John, in Sydney with his RAAF squadron waiting assignment to the islands, was called and visited his father twice, according to Mrs Curtin:

Late on July 4 I had a cup of tea with Dad. You'd better get some sleep, he said. The nurse brought him a sedative. 'Just wait a minute', he said. He was quiet for a moment, then, 'I'm ready now.' I kissed him goodnight and went off to my room. Three or four hours later, when the sister in charge, Sister Shirl, came to my room, I knew before she spoke that it was all over. We rang [daughter] Elsie, just a few hours before the bomber [bringing her from Perth] was to take off, and told her not to come. It was too late.

John Francis Curtin died peacefully on 5 July. He was 'a war casualty if ever there was one', according to biographer Dr Geoffrey Serle. On the Friday 6 July there was a memorial service and a ceremony at Parliament House. After the service Curtin's body was placed aboard a bomber and flown to Perth. An estimated 100,000 people lined the long funeral route, which included Jarrad Street, Cottesloe. Some 25,000 gathered at the gates or attended at the graveside in Karrakatta Cemetery. Mrs Curtin reportedly remained 'remarkably calm', although she was 'deeply moved' when her son Flight Sergeant John Curtin placed a family wreath on the coffin and saluted his father.

*

Curtin lived long enough to know of the American occupation of the strategic island of Okinawa in the Japanese Ryukyu island chain south-west of one of Japan's four main islands, Kyushu, which was achieved after appalling losses on both sides. The fall of Japan was approaching, but came faster than most expected. On 6 August 1945 the United States dropped an atomic bomb on the city of Hiroshima, killing some 70,000 people and injuring 60,000, mostly civilians. When Japan refused to surrender, another atomic bomb was dropped on the city of Nagasaki, killing almost 40,000 Japanese. Both bombs caused a great many shocking, lingering injuries. Emperor Hirohito signed an imperial rescript calling on all Japanese to lay down their arms on 16 August. General MacArthur took the Japanese surrender on behalf of the Allies aboard the battleship USS *Missouri* in Tokyo Bay on 2 September 1945. General Thomas Blamey represented Australia.

There were 14,340 Australian prisoners of war in the hands of the Japanese, the survivors from some 22,400 Australians who had been captured, many at Singapore in February 1942. For three and a half years Allied prisoners of war, along with hundreds of thousands of other, mostly Asian prisoners and internees, had endured injury, disease and grossly brutal treatment at the hands of their Japanese and Korean guards. The prisoners lived on the brink of starvation and many succumbed. Many were taken to Japan and other parts of the Japanese Empire as slave labour, and quite a few were literally worked to death. An estimated 100,000 Asian labourers and the 60,000 Allied prisoners-of-war died building the Thai–Burma railway. One of the heroes and survivors of that 'death railway' was a senior AIF medical officer Colonel Edward Dunlop, known as 'Weary', who took charge of a large number of prisoners transported from Singapore to build the railway. His care for his men and his brave defiance of their captors saved many lives. When finally released at war's end, Dunlop wrote to a colleague about the horrors of the railway:

> That year of 1943 is just a nightmare of starvation, disease and death . . . your lads from Java showed fortitude beyond anything I could have believed possible. I saw them flogged to work reeling with sickness, and I've carried them to the engineer lines when they could no longer stand up, to do some work sitting down . . . I hardly ever saw a man refuse to go out in another man's place nor a man's spirit break until the time came to turn his face to the wall and die.

The Australian officer in captivity who was writing a journal for his little daughter Brenda, Lieutenant Arthur Tranter of the 2/29th Battalion who had escaped Singapore, had suffered enormously with his men in despicable captivity on the island of Sumatra. They were there when Japan surrendered. Tranter had personally experienced dengue fever, dysentery, beri-beri, pellagra, malnutrition and severe headaches. His secret letter and hidden journal would be read by his daughter when she reached the age of fourteen. The tone of the covering letter was more of disappointment and sadness:

> I often wonder if mankind will ever become sensible enough to settle differences without wars – but I very much doubt it. And war in these times is such a horrible thing – not only for the soldiers, but worse still for the women and children who must stay at home. There is little glory in war for anyone – no matter how hard the history books claim there is – and a medal and a piece of ribbon, or some such worthless trinket can never make up to a mother for the loss of her son, or to a wife or a baby for the loss of their husband and father.
>
> And I think it would be better if the history books told us more of the ugliness and destruction and cruelty of war, and less of the so called glory.

*

The end of the war revealed a terrible atrocity committed against Australians in war – the Sandakan death march. Almost 1500 Australian prisoners of war had been moved from Changi prison in Singapore to North Borneo and placed in a Japanese prison camp at Sandakan, on the north-east coast. They were required to build an airstrip. British and Indian prisoners were also sent to the camp. Conditions deteriorated in the second half of 1944, as the prisoners' rice ration was slashed and then abolished altogether. In January 1945 the Japanese began to move groups of prisoners from Sandakan across the rugged, jungle-covered Borneo island to Ranau, about 160 miles (257 kilometres) away. Apart from acute food shortages, all medicines had been withheld from the prisoners. When Australian invasion forces landed at Tarakan to the south, the Japanese destroyed the Sandakan camp and forced the remainder of the prisoners to trek inland. In the wilds of Borneo the prisoners dropped like flies from malnutrition, exhaustion and horrible ill-treatment by the Japanese. Men who dropped out from the march when they became too weak to carry on were immediately shot. Only a paltry six Australians escaped and survived out of the 2500 Australian, British and Indian prisoners who had left Sandakan. Almost 300 prisoners left behind because they were too sick were killed or otherwise died. Even those who reached Ranau were summarily shot by their guards just a month before the formal Japanese surrender. Four senior Japanese officers involved were later executed for war crimes and seven were sentenced to ten years' jail each. Australian nursing sister Joan Crouch, of Sydney, recalled treating some Indian survivors:

> It was Belsen horror camp all over again. It was the saddest and the most frightful thing I've ever seen and of course, they were so weak, so devastatingly ill, that they thought we were the enemy still and they were pushing us away.

*

Around the time of the Japanese surrender there were almost 600,000 Australian men and women in uniform with more than half serving in Australia. But another 224,000 were serving across the Pacific, or were prisoners of war with 20,000 in Britain, mostly in the RAAF. It was only natural that after the Japanese surrender Australian servicemen and -women were anxious to return home. With the sudden end of the war, the Australian Government was faced with the task of finding ships and planes to repatriate and demobilise hundreds of thousands of servicemen and women. Many Australians had to remain at their posts, often guarding Japanese prisoners, well into 1946. The troops became disenchanted and voiced their protest, even with marches and placards.

*

Australia was not without blemish when it came to the treatment of prisoners. When the thousands of Japanese servicemen were rounded up, many were sent to islands off New Guinea and placed under Australian guards, sometimes with disastrous consequences. 'The Japanese know about that but the Australians don't know. We don't mention it,' explained Japan's principal historical expert on the New Guinea campaigns, Professor Hiromi Tanaka. He said Japanese soldiers as of August 1945 were transported to small islands, including Muschu Island off Wewak and Fauro Island off the southern end of Bougainville:

> The Australians tried to send as many of their own troops home as possible at the end of the war. But Australia didn't have enough ships to supply the imprisoned Japanese. Thirteen thousand Japanese soldiers were imprisoned on Muschu island. Only 8000 of the personnel returned. Every day some 200 Japanese soldiers died, many of starvation.
>
> On Fauro island in the Shortland group in the Solomon Sea, 60,000 Japanese were imprisoned there after the war. Six months later only 30,000 had survived. These prisoners were under the Australian jurisdiction. There simply were not enough ships to provide the necessary food and medical supplies to the islands. The Japanese soldiers were starved anyway as of August 1945. They included a Navy unit sent from Nauru island to Fauro . . . Many of the survivors wrote a book about that. No western country will listen to what we say because we lost the war.

Iwao Otsuki, in his book in Japanese *Solomon Prisoner Camps*, writes of Australian cruelty on Fauro Island after the arrival of Japanese from the Nauru Island garrison. Japanese, he wrote, were forced to empty their water bottles and then take part in marches in the heat until they collapsed and often died on Fauro:

> Other Australians watching us along the road threw stones at us like rain and laughed at us running around from them. Our wounded and sick soldiers were also badly stoned. This was the reality for the defeated and I couldn't stomach their behavior.
>
> Australian guards in the boat, naked to the waist, pointed their guns to us and showed off themselves drinking water and Coke. We then realized for the first time that the reason they ordered us to empty our water bottles was to torture us so cruelly . . . If

we stopped walking, then Australian guards hit our backs with their bayonets. It was difficult to catch up with others. We had no energy left to even save our friends, [we] left them behind, made ourselves lighter and kept marching.

Otsuki recalled that Japanese soldiers were on a starvation diet and were forced into labour. They were passing out during a death march. Those who died were carried to a morgue:

One day, I passed through a long queue of patients waiting for their turn at the field hospital and headed to a morgue. There were so many bodies that had died since the previous night at the morgue. More than forty bodies were left on the ground under the strong sun. Among the bodies, I found a dozen of men whom I knew from the Ponape Garrison [now Pohnpei, Micronesia].

Otsuki said that originally 1500 sailors from the 67th Garrison were sent from Nauru Island and six months later only three were still living. The men of the 67th on Nauru had a ruthless reputation and their deeds were known to the Australians. They had refused to surrender on Nauru until eleven days after the official Japanese surrender. In March 1943, five Australians had been beheaded on Nauru by the Japanese. They were the administrator, Colonel Frederick Chalmers, an Australian medical officer, his assistant and two Australian phosphate commissioners. The Japanese navy personnel slaughtered thirty-nine Nauruan lepers in July 1943 by towing them in a boat to sea and then shelling the boat. The Japanese also forced 762 Nauruan natives to work as slaves on Truk Island. At war's end only 461 had survived. Most of the victims had died of starvation and malnutrition.

With the war over, some 830 Australians of the 7th Infantry Battalion AIF were isolated on unhealthy Fauro Island in late 1945 and early 1946 keeping watch over some 25,000 Japanese army and naval personnel who had surrendered. The Japanese were not prisoners of war, having surrendered. Men of both sides were desperate to return to their homelands. But there was a significant difference between the Australians, who generally were fit and healthy, although they had food shortages, and the Japanese, who were in an appalling state of ill-health and often hungry. The Australian army assisted the Japanese with rations and medicines, but the Japanese were expected most of the time to supply their own food and hospitals as well as to labour on numerous projects, including building roads and gardens, and draining swamps. The war diary of the 7th Battalion on Fauro acknowledged the plight of the Japanese:

> Plants are urgently needed, as all [Japanese] areas have ground cleared but not planted [for food].

A week later rations for the Japanese were increased by 20 per cent, with Major T. E. Wilson noting:

> On the present ration scale most of the Japanese troops doing hard manual labour are hungry; and it is therefore considered that with this increase in ration they would be able to do more work.

The battalion's report ending 2 December said the standard of hygiene and building on the island was being improved progressively. But it acknowledged a high sickness rate in some of the Japanese camps, which had reduced the amount of work they could perform. The report was understated. At this time, 10,344 Japanese on the island were either patients in hospital or were off duty and unable to work. The war diary listed 159 Japanese deaths in that week, most weak men taken by the effects of malaria and other diseases, but the toll would become much worse. The Australian adjutant, Captain William Foster, issued an order demanding an immediate improvement in malaria control, saying 'excuses will not be accepted'. While the Australian sickness rate was never high and rapidly diminished, the Japanese rate soared. The victors naturally felt that their own wellbeing had absolute priority. The Japanese were despised, as officers from an Australian Atrocities

Commission made a number of visits to interview potential Japanese war criminals. The adjutant Captain Foster perhaps indicated the army's mood in an order he wrote after discovering some trading between Australian and Japanese soldiers:

> The attention of all personnel is drawn to the brutal treatment to Australians prisoners of war, including nurses ... The apparent docility of Japs cannot be accepted at its face value and merely cloaks a deceptive and cunning mind.

When the 7th Battalion troops arrived back in Sydney in February 1946 they complained bitterly to newspapers about their conditions on Fauro Island and at Torokina on Bougainville, saying they had been poorly fed themselves and treated to the most unnecessary and irritatingly strict discipline enforced by their own senior officers.

*

In June 2008 the then Australian governor-general, Major General Michael Jeffery, proclaimed an annual 'Battle for Australia Day' of observance. Earlier he had described the Battle for Australia as a series of stirring events. He said hundreds of thousands of servicemen and women, and the civilian population of Australia, had ensured the country's survival and future prosperity:

> For the first time our nation's shores were attacked. And for some time after, we were told by our leaders that the Battle for Australia was for real and that air and naval attacks on our coastal cities and towns could develop into a full-scale invasion by a powerful and brutal enemy. Thus the nation mobilised; no part of our community unaffected; the entire population involved in a genuinely perceived struggle for national survival.

John Curtin's biographer David Day has written that although Curtin has been hailed as the 'saviour of Australia', this is an overblown claim. There was no Battle for Australia along the same lines of the Battle of Britain, he wrote. The Battle of Britain, from July 1940 until the last German night raids on London and other cities in May 1941, claimed the lives of more than 40,000 civilians. Day wrote that Curtin's great contribution to the defence of Australia was to recognise the flaws in the Singapore strategy, to develop closer ties with the United States and to welcome General MacArthur as supreme commander:

> His insistence on the return of Australian troops to defend Australia, despite strong pressure from both Churchill and Roosevelt to have them sent to Burma, also stands to his enduring credit.

The last surviving Australian general with Second World War experience, Major General Gordon Maitland, NSW branch president of the Battle for Australia Commemoration National Council, disagrees:

> Curtin's 'battle' with the Army started way back but he never bothered to try and understand it. He never fully understood the tactical and strategic implications involved in his decisions. He was so ill equipped to discuss matters with Blamey that he sidelined him. He was duped by MacArthur.
>
> I am surprised at the reverence paid to Curtin, particularly in respect of his resistance to Churchill's plan to divert the 7th Division to Burma. After all, Curtin had no other choice. His cabinet was in a state of panic and was insisting on the Division being brought back to Australia, and his Chief of the general Staff was going to resign if he didn't do so. Moreover, having regard to the non-tactical loading of the 7th Division's weapons and equipment there was little prospect of the division being able to alter the fate of Burma as contended by Churchill.
>
> Of its four AIF divisions Australia had already lost a substantial part of the 6th Division in Greece and Crete plus the whole of the 8th, so to lose the 7th in Burma would have been a complete disaster and political suicide. In addition Curtin already knew

that Churchill was anti Australia and not overly concerned about its fate.

Gordon Maitland says Curtin lied to the Australian people about the first bombing disaster at Darwin in February 1942 and lied about other critical issues, including the continuing danger from Japan:

Lies which were later described as being for morale purposes. However they conveniently enhanced Labor's 1943 election prospects. As for his failure to control the maritime, mining, and waterside unions, soldiers felt they were betrayed, even more so when critically needed stores were opened to find the contents missing – contents of no domestic value so it was clearly sabotage. I will never forget coming home to Sydney in a troop ship; it was joy unbounded; then some waterside workers were seen and the mood on the ship not only changed but became ugly . . .

[Curtin's] despondency was not due to his concern for Australia but because he was plagued by being ineffective. Curtin's work at times was so militarily astray that he either failed to consult with the service chiefs or ignored them.

War historian Gavin Long recalled Curtin as a great leader of his nation during perhaps the most critical period of its existence:

Austere, sensitive and devoted, it seems likely that worry and inner conflicts shortened his life.

Deputy Prime Minister and Army Minister Frank Forde, addressing the House of Representatives on the day Curtin died, said he was personally thankful that Curtin was spared long enough to guide the nation's destiny: .

John Curtin is as one today with those fighting men of our race who have given their lives that we might live. For them, interposing, as he himself put it, their bodies between us and the enemy, he worked day and night for many weary months and years that they might have the strength to hold out.

Curtin never resiled from his expressed belief that the Japanese had been out to invade Australia through their New Guinea operations:

The objectives of the Japanese were to establish themselves on the mainland of Australia and to sever or interrupt the sea communications to Australia through the Pacific Ocean. They had hoped to accomplish these by a continuation of their advances in a south-easterly direction through New Guinea and by a parallel advance down the Solomon Islands.

The British leader Winston Churchill who at times demonstrated greatness, was nevertheless prepared to sacrifice Australia to the Japanese, if it came to it, in what he termed the 'lesser war' in the Pacific, to maintain the pressure on his primary enemy, Germany. Churchill in 1942 foresaw the strong possibility of Japan landing in northern Australia and establishing footholds. Fortunately, his influence on President Roosevelt not to devote too many resources to the Pacific ahead of Europe was gradually undermined.

Curtin's anxiety and ill-health through the war years revealed with clarity the stresses that can consume those in public office in times of great crisis. The prime minister in January 1942 at least had the foresight to listen to his close colleagues and his doctor compelling him to leave Melbourne and go home at a most critical hour. His timing during the Japanese invasion of Rabaul prevented him from taking the rest he so needed. As time went on his unrelieved stress mounted and illness increased, eventually consuming him. As Curtin wrote in September 1944:

High office in normal times is always stressful. In war there are added the most grievous anxieties, increasing pressures and the sheer incapacity to relax either concentration or application to the many problems which governments confront.

From 2002, the concept that there was a Battle for Australia was ridiculed by a few historians in Canberra. They applied the same reinterpretation to Curtin's leadership, one saying that one of Curtin's lasting legacies was 'whipping up of the fear of invasion . . .' That erroneous claim was withdrawn some years later.

Curtin's enduring legacy will stand the test of time. Here was a poverty-stricken boy who ran barefoot along the streets of Creswick, Ballarat and Brunswick, who rose, with all his fears and shortcomings, to become national leader, asserting, above all else, the paramount interests and needs of Australia and of the Australian people. Governor-General Gowrie had no doubts about the threat when he said on leaving Australia after sixteen years in 1944:

There were moments when the fate of Australia trembled in the balance, and had it not been for superb courage and endurance of our lads, supported by our Allies from the United States, fighting under the most appalling conditions men have been called on to face, Australia would have suffered the horrors of invasion by a savage and ruthless foe.

NOTES

Abbreviations

AAP	Australian Associated Press
ABC	American–British Conversations or Australian Broadcasting Corporation
AG	Adjutant General
ANGAU	Australia New Guinea Administrative Unit
ANU	Australian National University
AWM	Australian War Memorial
DDA	*Digest of Decisions and Announcements and Important Speeches by the Prime Minister*, Commonwealth of Australia
GHQ	General Headquarters (US)
JCPML	John Curtin Prime Ministerial Library
LHCMA	Liddell Hart Centre for Military Archives, King's College London
NA	National Archives, United Kingdom
NAA	National Archives of Australia
NLA	National Library of Australia,
PRO	Public Record Office, United Kingdom
SLNSW	State Library of New South Wales

Note: For the sake of convenience, the four volumes of Winston Churchill's six-volume history/memoir *The Second World War* (Cassell, London, 1948–54) quoted in this book are referred to in the notes by their volume titles only: *The Gathering Storm*, *Their Finest Hour*, *The Grand Alliance*, *The Hinge of Fate*.

Chapter 1   Man on the brink

1   Summary of war situation in January 1942: records of war cabinet meetings in Melbourne, 20 and 21 January 1942, NAA, A5954, 807/2, and author's abridged record of events detailed in later chapters.

2   Rabaul and decision not to fight: John Moremon, *Remembering the War in New Guinea: Rabaul, 1942*, AWM, http://ajrp.awm.gov.au/ajrp/remember. nsf/Web-Printer/C6FD73CC5C579789CA256AC000135979; George Odgers, *100 Years of Australians at War*, New Holland, Sydney, 2003, p. 44; description of war cabinet room, Victoria Barracks, Melbourne: author's visit 2007; Agnes Hannan, *Victoria Barracks Melbourne: A Social History*, Australian Defence Force Journal Publication, Canberra, 1995, pp. 111–52.

3   Curtin's missed meeting: records of war cabinet meetings, January–February 1942, NAA, A5954, 807/2, and Advisory War Council meetings, NAA, A5954, 813/2; Curtin's clash with Churchill on war direction: minutes of war cabinet meeting, 21 January 1942, NAA, A5954, 807/2.

4   Curtin's warning to be on guard: *The Herald*, Melbourne, 27 December 1941; early days of Jack Curtin: David Day, *John Curtin: A Life*, HarperCollins, Sydney, 2006, pp. 29–35, 47–49, 52, 79; 1890s depression in Australia: Graeme Davidson (ed.), *The Oxford Companion to Australian History*, Oxford University Press, Melbourne, 2001, pp. 183–84; Bruce W. Pratt (ed.), *The Australian Encyclopaedia*, vol. 2, Grolier Society, Sydney, 1977, p. 311; starvation and social concerns in Melbourne: *The Argus*, 10, 22, 23 June 1892, 2 July, 1892.

5   Curtin and revolutionary socialism: *The Socialist*, 5 May 1906, JCPML00819/1, JCPML00819/34; Curtin becomes secretary of the Timber Workers' Union: Lloyd Ross, *John Curtin: A Biography*, Melbourne University Press, Melbourne, 1996, pp. 8–14, 15–29; Winston Churchill and Blenheim Palace: author's tour of the palace, 1999; John George Vanderbilt Henry Spencer-Churchill, 11th Duke of Marlborough, *Blenheim Palace*, Jarrold Publishing, Norwich, 1999, pp. 2–3, 10–19, 36–4.

6   Churchill's childhood and youth: William Manchester, *Winston Spencer Churchill: The Last Lion*, Visions of Glory: 1874–1932, Michael Joseph, London, 1983, pp. 91–94, 99–101, 112, 116–18.

7   Churchill on war during the Kaiser's visit: Martin Gilbert, *Churchill: A Life*, Henry Holt & Co., New York, 1992, p. 208; support for war: Ernest Scott, *Official History of Australia in the War of 1914–1918*, vol. 11, p. 286; Curtin on war and anti-militarism and defence of Australia: David Black (ed. and narrator), *In His Own Words: John Curtin's Speeches and Writings*, Paradigm Books, Perth, 1995, pp. 10–13, 26, 104; Fred Alexander: Lyall Hunt (ed.), *Westralian Portraits*, University of Western Australia Press, Perth, 1979, p. 228; Curtin, stress, drinking and Balaclava election: Day, *John Curtin*, pp. 202–203; Ross, *John Curtin*, pp. 42–44.

8   Curtin not a pacifist: Day, *John Curtin*, p. 257; Australian Gallipoli background: C. E. W. Bean, *Official History of Australia in the War of 1914–1918*, vol. 1, Angus & Robertson, Sydney, 1941, pp. 248–253; Odgers, *100 Years of Australians at War*, pp. 38–41, 46–57.

9   Dardanelles background and Gallipoli campaign: C. E. W. Bean's account of the landing at Gallipoli, Bean, *Official History of Australia in the War of 1914–1918*, vol. 1, pp. 250–56; Keith Murdoch's letter of 23 September 1915 to Prime Minister Andrew Fisher: Papers of Keith Arthur Murdoch, NLA, MS 2823/2/1.

10   Curtin 'cold and disturbed': David Black, *Friendship Is a Sheltering Tree: John Curtin's Letters, 1907 to 1945*, John Curtin Prime Ministerial Library, Perth, 2001, p. 79; Curtin's anguished letter to 'Dear Friends': 6 July 1915, Black, *Friendship Is a Sheltering Tree*, pp. 76–78; Hughes and conscription referendum: Day, *John Curtin*, pp. 238; L. F. Fitzhardinge, *Hughes, William Morris (Billy) (1862–1952)*, Australian Dictionary of Biography, National Centre of Biography, ANU, http://adb.anu.edu.au/biography/hughes-william-morris-billy-6761/text11689; Curtin's jailing and release: *Sydney Morning Herald*, 23 November 1916; letters of 15 and 27 December 1916, Black, *Friendship Is a Sheltering Tree*, pp. 99–105; Curtin's letter to Elsie Needham: 30 October 1916, Black, *Friendship Is a Sheltering Tree*, p. 97.

11   Asquith and Churchill at Dardanelles Committee: 10 Downing Street, 6 and 7 October 1915, NA, CAB 42/4/3 and CAB 42/4/4; Churchill's resignation: Violet Bonham Carter, *Winston Churchill as I Knew Him*, Eyre & Spottiswoode and Collins, London, 1965, p. 425; Gallipoli background and criticism: Bean, *Official History of Australia in the War of 1914–1918*, vol. 1, pp. 201, 248–53.

12   Clementine Churchill on her husband: Martin Gilbert, *Winston S. Churchill*, vol. III, 'The Challenge of War, 1914–1916', Heinemann, London, 1971, p. 473; Odgers, *100 Years of Australians at War*, pp. 38–41, 46–57; Churchill on his role in Dardanelles: Hansard, House of Commons, 15 November 1915, and Churchill Papers, Churchill Archives Centre, CHAR 9/51; Gallipoli inquiry: Churchill in Parliamentary Dardanelles Commission debate, Hansard, House of Commons, 20 March 1917; Churchill's ministerial appointment: *Morning Post*, London, 17 July 1917; Australians in Belgium: Bean, *Official History of Australia in the War of 1914–1918*, vol. 3, pp. 658–60, 803–805, 860. Passchendaele casualty figures: AWM, *Passchendaele: An Almost Universal Experience*, www.awm.gov.au/blog/ 2007/10/06/passchendaele-an-almost-universal-experience; AIF casualty figures over four months in 1918: AWM 3DPL/2316.

13   Anstey's letter to Curtin: 2 July 1916, Black, *Friendship Is a Sheltering Tree*, p. 93; Hughes on war as threat to Australia: W. Farmer Whyte, *William Morris Hughes: His Life and Times*, Angus & Robertson, Sydney, 1957, pp. 274–76.

14   Curtin appointed editor of *Westralian Worker* in Perth, 1917, and marriage: Day, *John Curtin*, pp. 259–61.

15   Curtin's horror: editorial, *Westralian Worker*, 15 November 1918, JCPML00302/89; Curtin's depression in 1919 and 1920: Day, *John Curtin*, pp. 293–94, 296–97; Perth election 1919: Day, *John Curtin*, p. 296; description of neurasthenia: Marie T. O'Toole (ed.), *Encyclopedia and Dictionary of Medicine, Nursing and Allied Health*, W. B. Saunders, Philadelphia, 1972, p. 1102.

16   Curtin's aborted attempts to travel east: Day, *John Curtin*, p. 296; Curtin ill again: *The Bulletin*, 23 September 1921, in Day, *John Curtin*, p. 272; Curtin's political career in 1929 and the early 1930s: Day, *John Curtin*, pp. 306–308, 322–24, 338–41.

17   German oath for Hitler: 18 October 1934, *Sydney Morning Herald*; Yamamoto on 'cut-and-dried' naval plan: *Sydney Morning Herald*, 19 October 1934; Hiroyuki Agawa, *The Reluctant Admiral: Yamamoto and the Imperial Navy*, Kodansha International, Tokyo, 1969, pp. 37–38; Curtin opposition leader: *Diary of a Labor Man, 1917–1945*, JCPML, http://john.curtin.edu.au/diary/opposition/index.html; Roosevelt on 'reign of terror': 'Quarantine speech', 5 October 1937, Documents for the Study of American History, www.vlib. us/amdocs/texts/fdrquarn.html;

American newsman Snow on Nanking: Edgar Snow, *Scorched Earth*, Victor Gollancz, London, 1941, pp. 60–63.

18   Curtin with daughter Elsie at Cottesloe beach and fear of Japan: Alan Chester, *John Curtin*, Angus & Robertson, Sydney, 1943, pp. 58–59; Menzies' war broadcast, 3 September 1939: A. W. Martin, *Robert Menzies: A Life*, vol. 1, Melbourne University Press, Melbourne, 1993, p. 284.

19   Menzies on justice for Germany: *The Times*, London, 11 September 1938; A. W. Martin, *Robert Menzies: A Life,* vol. 2, Melbourne University Press, Melbourne, 1999, p. 154; Curtin's appeasement in 1935 and 1937: E. M. Andrews, *Isolationism and Appeasement in Australia*, ANU, Canberra, 1970, pp. 27, 50–51, 92; Churchill's early opposition to Hitler and appointment as prime minister: Winston Churchill, *The Gathering Storm*, Cassell, London, 1948, pp. 525–27, 599.

20   Churchill on Dowding and the Fighter Command: Winston Churchill, *Their Finest Hour*, Cassell, London, 1949, pp. 285–86; Battle of Britain background: Edward Bishop, *The Battle of Britain*, Allen & Unwin, London, 1960, pp. 10, 28–36; Royal Air Force, *The Battle of Britain*, www.raf.mod.uk/history/thebattleofbritain.cfm; Chester Wilmot, *The Struggle for Europe*, Collins, Sydney, 1952, pp. 34–55; AWM, *Battle of Britain*, www.awm.gov.au/encyclopedia/battle_of_britain; Paterson Hughes: AWM summary, www.awm.gov.au/collection/REL/17986.003; Australian fighter pilots: AWM, *Empire Air Training Scheme*, www.awm. gov.au/units/ unit_14939.asp

21   Greek and Crete campaigns: Gavin Long, *The Six Years War: A Concise History of Australia in the 1939–1945 War*, AWM, Canberra, 1973, pp. 69–74, 81–85, 87; AWM, *The Greek Campaign, 1941*, www.awm. gov.au/encyclopedia/greek_campaign; Tobruk, Wavell and Churchill, and Churchill on evacuation of Greece and no regrets: Hansard, House of Commons, 30 April, 7 May 1940; Tobruk: Odgers, *100 Years of Australians at War*, pp. 123–24, 119–20; Churchill to Wavell on Syria, 21 May 1941: Winston Churchill, *The Grand Alliance*, Cassell, London, 1950, pp. 290–91; AWM, *Tobruk*, www.awm.gov.au/units/event_220. asp

22   Japanese advance through Indo-China, Long, *The Six Years War*, pp. 103, 113, 116; troops for Singapore, AWM, 2/20th Battalion, http://www.awm.gov.au/units/unit_11271.asp

23   Elsie Curtin preferring Cottesloe to Canberra: *Sun Pictorial*, 13 September 1943, Curtin Family Scrapbook, JCPML002972/3, part 2, item 323; Evatt

seeks national government with Menzies: Evatt letter, 24 May 1941, Menzies papers, NLA, MS 4936.

24 Curtin's birthday greeting letter to wife Elsie, 30 September 1941: Records of the Curtin Family, JCPML00402/37.

Chapter 2 Japan strikes

25 Menzies' designs on British leadership: David Day, *Menzies and Churchill at War*, Oxford University Press, Melbourne, 1993; Menzies seeks to revisit London, then resigns: Day, *John Curtin*, pp. 410–12; Fadden takes over from Menzies: Arthur Fadden, *They Called Me Artie: The Memoirs of Sir Arthur Fadden*, Jacaranda, Brisbane, 1969, pp. 64–72; Harold Cox on Curtin's stress: Cox interview, 6 April 1973: NLA ORAL TRC 121/43; JCPML01060/1.

26 Harold Cox on hearing from Curtin that he would be prime minister: Cox oral history interview, 6 April 1973: NLA ORAL TRC 121/43; JCPML01060/1; Fadden's conversation with Curtin before budget vote: Fadden, *They Called Me Artie*, pp. 68–72.

27 Curtin's 'birthday gift' to Elsie: telegram, 3 October 1941, JCPML00402/38; Fadden Government defeated: *Sydney Morning Herald*, 4 October 1941; *Sunday Times*, Perth, 5 October 1941; Curtin's health 'unequal to his new responsibilities': Don Whitington, *The House Will Divide: A Review of Australian Federal Politics*, Lansdowne Press, Melbourne, 1969, p. 90; Elsie Curtin and daughter at Cottesloe: *The Herald*, Melbourne, 4 October 1941 and *Sunday Sun*, Sydney, 5 October 1941, Curtin family scrapbook of press clippings, JCPML00297/1; 'Curtin gets his chance', *Sunday Times*, 5 October 1941.

28 Curtin's first ministry: Hansard, Senate, 8 October 1941.

29 Lord Gowrie to George VI, 10 October 1941: Gowrie Papers, NLA MS2852, 5/13; Pownall on Australian attitudes: Pownall diary references for 13 October, 15 November 1941, LHCMA, Pownall 2.

30 Brooke-Popham and Curtin statements at the Advisory War Council meeting of 16 October 1941: NAA, A2682, vol. 3; Brooke-Popham report on the Far East, 12 March 1942: LHCMA, 6/9/5.

31 Chiefs of staff to Brooke-Popham, 17 September 1941: LHCMA, 6/1/33; Brooke-Popham on Empire and reinforcements: letter to Sir Arthur Street, Air Ministry, London, 28 October 1941, LHCMA 6/3/16; Curtin on 'ominous portents' on Pacific horizon: *Sydney Morning Herald*, 20 October 1941.

32   Australia 'virtually naked': Mackay's personal notes, Ivan D. Chapman, *Iven G. Mackay: Citizen and Soldier,* Melway, Melbourne, 1975, p. 234; concern over industrial disputes during 1941, including Curtin and issues raised at the Advisory War Council meetings of 5 and 13 February 1941: NAA, A5954, 812/1; Darwin strike against army, 7 October 1941: *Sydney Morning Herald*; aircraft strike and Ipswich railway strike: *The Argus*, 7 October 1941; Lithgow arms factory strike: *The Argus* and *Canberra Times*, 8–9 October 1941; mine strike South Maitland: *The Argus*, 8 October 1941; Ward prevents army from unloading: *Canberra Times*, 9 October 1941.

33   Ward on 'irritation tactics' of employers: DDA, 9 November 1941, NAA, B5459/5; letters intercepted by Commonwealth censors from 17 to 30 November 1941: dated 18 December 1941, NAA, A11743, 3 Attachment; Earle Page special envoy to London: Ann Mozley (ed.), *Truant Surgeon: The Inside Story of Forty Years of Australian Political Life*, Angus & Robertson, Sydney, 1963, pp. 298–309.

34   Page to Churchill on 9th Division, 15 September 1941: NA, PRO, DO 114/114; Earle Page's Singapore comments: Mozley (ed.), *Truant Surgeon*, pp. 300–309; Page in London: Mozley (ed.), *Truant Surgeon*, pp. 311–15.

35   Proceedings of Imperial Conference of 5 and 12 November 1941: Nobutaka Ike (ed.), *Japan's Decision for War, Records of the 1941 Policy Conferences*, Stanford University Press, Palo Alto, California, 1967, pp. 208–38.

36   Japan's Combined Fleet Operational Order 1, 5 November 1941: Louis Morton, *Strategy and Command: The First Two Years*, Office of the Chief of Military History, Department of the Army, Washington DC, 1962, p. 109; Page in London: Mozley (ed.), *Truant Surgeon*, pp. 309–16.

37   Page report to Curtin on 12 November meeting with Churchill, 14 November 1941: NAA, A981, PACIFIC, 8, i.

38   Page diary references for 15 November 1941: Page diary in NLA MS1633, folder 2345; Portal comment to Page in Freudenberg, Graham, *Churchill and Australia*, Pan Macmillan, Sydney, 2008, p. 317 (the emphasis is the author's); Churchill and air cover for Malaya: Stanley Woodburn Kirby, *Singapore: The Chain of Disaster*, Macmillan, New York, 1971, pp. 87–88.

39   Japanese better fighters than thought: Pownall diary entry, 20 December 1941, LHCMA, Pownall 2; Foreign Minister Togo on fuel position: Shigenori Togo, *The Cause of Japan*, Simon & Schuster, New York, 1956, pp. 139–41.

40 Prime Minister Tojo's address to the diet in Tokyo: *Sydney Morning Herald*, 19 November 1941; Rory Burnett on his father, Captain Joseph Burnett: interview with the author, *The Bulletin*, 17 January 2006; loss of HMAS *Sydney*: G. Hermon Gill, *Royal Australian Navy, 1939–1942*, AWM, Canberra, 1957, pp. 449–61.

41 Curtin sees governor-general: Lloyd Ross, 'The story of John Curtin', *Sun-Herald*, 3 August 1958, Sydney, JCPML00788/1/7; Curtin on the sinking of the *Sydney*: DDA, no. 9, 30 November 1941 (the wreck of the *Sydney* was found in 2008 about 150 kilometres west of Steep Point, Shark Bay, and 23 kilometres from the *Kormoran*, which was discovered a few days earlier); HMAS *Sydney*: diary of Joe Alexander, 19 November and 3 December 1941, NLA, MS 2389.

42 Churchill's terse complaint to Curtin, 28 November 1941, and Curtin reply to Churchill, 29 November 1941: NA, PRO, PREM 4 50/1; Japan 'ready for action': Joe Alexander's diary, 30 November 1941, NLA, MS 2389.

43 Hirohito agrees on war: Ike (ed.), *Japan's Decision for War*, p. 262ff, 283; Takushiro Hattori, *The Complete History of the Greater East Asia War*, Hara Shobo, Tokyo, 1953, pp. 231–34; coded cable to Washington, 1 December 1941, Purple CA, #865 and #2444 on code machines, intercepted diplomatic message sent by Japanese Government: exhibit no. 1 of Joint Committee, Archives of US Congress.

44 Churchill's priorities and 'striking first': Churchill, *The Grand Alliance*, pp. 534–35; Curtin learns of Japanese burning papers: Gavin Long, Diary, AWM67,1/3, 2 October 1943, p. 27; Bob Wurth, *Saving Australia: Curtin's Secret Peace with Japan*, Lothian, Melbourne, 2006, pp. 145–46; Saturday reports on Japanese expeditionary force: *Sydney Morning Herald*, 6 December 1941; Curtin visits old friends of the family: Day, *John Curtin*, p. 429; Don Dowie: *Makan* (official journal of the 2/30th Battalion AIF Association), no. 235, June–August 1977.

45 Air reconnaissance reports from Singapore on Japanese fleets, including praise for RAAF crew: Brooke-Popham Papers, LHCMA, 6/5/29; RAAF Hudsons sighting Japanese fleet: Douglas Gillison, *Australia in the War of 1939–1945*, series 3: 'Air', vol. 1, 'Royal Australian Air Force, 1939–1942', AWM, Canberra, 1962, p. 201; Yamashita on signals to Saigon: John Deane Potter, *A Soldier Must Hang: The Biography of an Oriental General*, Four Square, London, 1963, p. 51.

46 Joe Alexander takes Don Rodgers to dinner in Melbourne and writes of the atmosphere of the time: diary, 6 December 1941, NLA, MS 2389; Ian

Fitchett reports from Malaya on Australians at work: *Sunday Telegraph*, 7 December 1941.

47   Brooke-Popham comment 'no real certainty' ships were an expedition: LHCMA, 6/5/30; controversy involving Brooke-Popham and convoy direction: Gillison, 'Royal Australian Air Force, 1939–1942', p. 201; Don Dowie: *Makan*, no. 235, June–August 1977.

48   Pownall on Vildebeest aircraft: Brian Bond (ed.), *Chief of Staff: The Diaries of Lieutenant-General Sir Henry Pownall*, vol. 2: '1940–1944', Leo Cooper, London, 1974, pp. 71–72.

49   Cranborne cable to Curtin on Japanese fleet: sent 0325 GMT, 7 December 1941, NAA, A816/1, 19/304/431; carrier strike force nears Hawaii and messages from Emperor and Yamamoto: Agawa, *The Reluctant Admiral*, p. 246; Gordon W. Prange, *At Dawn We Slept: The Untold Story of Pearl Harbor*, Penguin, New York, 1991, p. 468.

50   Japanese naval operation and Washington envoys meeting with Secretary of State Hull: Cordell Hull, *The Memoirs of Cordell Hull*, Macmillan, New York, 1948, pp. 1095–96; Joint Committee on the Investigation of the Pearl Harbor Attacks, 79th Congress of the US, Washington DC, 1946, part 14, p. 1238; *Department of State Bulletin*, vol. V, no. 129, 13 December 1941, Yale Law School Avalon Project, http://avalon.law. yale.edu/wwii/p3.asp; army and navy wouldn't compromise: Mamoru Shigemitsu, *Japan and Her Destiny: My Struggle for Peace*, Dutton, New York, 1958, p. 263; Japanese diplomat tried to interest British in negotiations: Toshikazu Kase, *Journey to the Missouri*, Yale University Press, New Haven, Connecticut, 1950, pp. 58–59.

51   Portal inspirational cable to Brooke-Popham, 8 December 1941: LHCMA 6/5/32; landings at Kota Bharu: report from China, 8 December 1941, NAA, A5954, 807/1; 'Let Thailand rip': Joe Alexander diary entries on Curtin and Churchill, 1–2 December 1941, NLA, MS 2389.

52   Pearl Harbor attack order given: Mitsuo Fuchida and Masatake Okumiya, *Midway: The Battle that Doomed Japan*, Naval Institute Press, Annapolis, Maryland, 1957, p. 27; fiasco involving MacArthur and Brereton in the Philippines over Japanese attack on US aircraft: Samuel Eliot Morison, *The Two-Ocean War: A Short History of the United States Navy in the Second World War*, Naval Institute Press, Annapolis, Maryland, 1963, p. 78.

53   Hull and Pearl Harbor: US Naval History and Heritage Command, *Overview of Pearl Harbor Attack, 7 December 1941*: www.history.navy.

mil/ faqs/faq66–1.htm; 8 December 1941: NAA, A5954, 807/1; Japanese attack on Clark Field and MacArthur's lack of preparation: Morison, 'The Rising Sun in the Pacific', pp. 169–74; John Costello, *The Pacific War 1941–1945*, Collins, London, 1981, pp. 141–42, Morison quote on incomprehensible surprise at Manila: Morison, *The Two-Ocean War*, p. 78.

54 Curtin hears news of Japanese attacks: Gavin Souter, *Acts of Parliament: A Narrative History of the Senate and House of Representatives Commonwealth of Australia*, Melbourne University Press, Melbourne, 1988, p. 344; Broadcasts monitored in Melbourne about Japanese attacks and incorrect Manila report: *The Argus*, 9 December 1941; *Sunday Telegraph*, Sydney (feature for first anniversary of outbreak of war), 6 December 1942; Curtin's strain and endurance described by Canberra correspondent Ross Gollan: *Sydney Morning Herald*, 8 December 1941.

55 Fred McLaughlin on Curtin's strength: letter to Hector Harrison, NLA, MS 6277; JCPML00472:4.

Chapter 3   Our darkest hour

57 Japan goes to war, scenes on Melbourne and Sydney streets: 8 December 1941, *The Argus, The Age, Sydney Morning Herald*, 9 December 1941; First bombing raid on Singapore: Geok Boi Lee, *Syonan: Singapore Under the Japanese 1942–1945*, Singapore Heritage Society, Singapore, 1992, pp. 18–24; Butcher and Wok, first bombings in Singapore: BBC Scotland, *Singapore 1942: End of Empire*, ep. 2; BBC Home, *WW2 Peoples' War*, www.bbc.co.uk/ww2peopleswar/stories/53/a5288853.shtml

58 Churchill war announcement: Hansard, House of Commons, 8 December 1941; war cabinet meeting, troops in ship for Rabaul Melbourne, 8 December 1941: NAA, A5954, 807/1.

59 Darwin labour problems and defence 'shortages', including rifles, 8 December 1941: NAA, A5954, 807/1.

60 Durnford on available aircraft: NAA, A5954, 807/1; various reports, including from the official Domei news agency, of Japanese attacks and Emperor Hirohito's Imperial Rescript: *Japan Times*, evening edition, 8 December 1941.

61 Curtin broadcast, 8 December 1941: DDA, no. 10, JCPML00110/15; Page's plan for full membership of higher direction of war groups: NAA, A1608, H33/1/2.

62 Churchill on 'Australia and New Zealand open to attack' and later hearing of sinking of *Prince of Wales* and *Repulse*: Churchill, *The Grand Alliance*, pp. 547, 551.

63 Lieutenant Albert Jacobs on the sinking of the battle cruiser *Repulse*: A. E. Jacobs, *The Loss of Repulse and Prince of Wales: A Participant's Account*, International Naval Research Organization, www.warship. org/no11986. htm; Curtin's reaction to battleship sinkings: letter from Fred McLaughlin to Very Rev. Hector Harrison, 1945, JCPML00472:4, Papers of Hector Harrison, NLA MS 6277; Curtin to Cranborne seeking urgent British appreciation on Far East situation, 11 December 1941: NAA, A981, WAR 49, I; Cranborne's reply to Curtin, 11 December 1941, NAA, A1608, V41/1/1.

64 Churchill to Roosevelt, 12 December 1941: PM Personal telegram T969, Churchill Papers, Churchill Archives Centre, CHAR 20/46, Martin Gilbert, *Winston S. Churchill*, volume VI, 'Finest Hour, 1939–1941', Houghton Mifflin, Boston, 1983, p. 1274; Joe Alexander's worries: Alexander diary, 10 December 1941, NLA, MS 2389.

65 Chockos and AIF: oral history interviews with Lawrie Howson and Private Norm Scowen, Keith Murdoch Sound Archive, AWM, S00501 and S00594; CMF troop dispositions in Australia, Papua and New Guinea and islands, and expansion of Australian army: Dudley McCarthy, *South-West Pacific Area: First Year: Kokoda to Wau*, AWM, Canberra, 1959, pp. 11–12.

66 Officers recalled to Australia: McCarthy, *South-West Pacific Area*, p. 13; Curtin's warning speech in Melbourne on enemy approaching, 11 December 1941: DDA, no. 11.

67 Admiral Moore's 'Future British Naval Strategy' memorandum, including imperial unity, 14 December 1941: NA, CAB 69/3, pp. 146–53; 'No depression' notice on Churchill's desk: author's visit to Cabinet War Rooms, London.

68 Curtin plea to Roosevelt for Pacific assistance, 12 December 1941: Lloyd Ross Papers, NLA, MS 3939/11; UK War Cabinet Chiefs of Staff Committee, 20 December 1941: NA, CAB 69/3, pp. 138–45.

69 Army personnel NSW industrial centres: McCarthy, *South-West Pacific Area*, p. 12; Japanese landings: Long, *The Six Years War*, pp. 131–32; Reasons for capturing Rabaul: Sadatoshi Tomioka's interview with US intelligence officers, Tokyo: US Army, *Statements of Japanese Officials on WWII*, vols 3–4, no. 61232, 10 September 1947; Pownall in Cairo,

worries about Malaya and on Churchill and capital ships: Pownall diary, 13 December 1941, LHCMA, Pownall 2, original emphasis.

70 Pownall on Malaya, air force and Churchill's priorities: Pownall diary, Calcutta, 20 December 1941, LHCMA, Pownall 2.

71 Curtin's telegram to Churchill on strengthening Malayan air defence, 17 December 1941: W. J. Hudson and H. J. W. Stokes (eds), *Documents on Australian Foreign Policy*, vol. V, Australian Government Publishing Service, Canberra, 1982, pp. 317–18; Churchill's cable to Curtin on Wavell appointment: 29 December 1941, NAA, A981, WAR 54.

72 Bennett private letter to Army Minister Forde, 16 December 1941: NAA, A1974/398,1.

73 Bennett cable to Sturdee, Sturdee to Brooke-Popham and Curtin cable to Brooke-Popham, 19 December 1941: NAA, A5954, 571/4; Eisenhower and Marshall on US supply operation for the Philippines via Australia, Eisenhower to Marshall, 17 December 1941, Marshall to Brett, 17 December 1941, Eisenhower on 'lightning speed' to General Walter Krueger, 20 December 1941: Dwight D. Eisenhower, *Papers of Dwight David Eisenhower: The War Years*, vol. 1, Johns Hopkins Press, Baltimore, Maryland, 1970, pp. 7–16; Curtin to Churchill on 'penny packet' dispositions, 20 December 1941: NAA, A12728/2.

74 General Brooke's Far East Policy Report: War Cabinet Chiefs of Staff Committee, 20 December 1941, NA, CAB 69/3; reinforcements for Sumatra and Java, 23 December 1941: NA, CAB 79/17; Bowden on British officials and Malaya air strength, 19 December 1941: NAA, A981, WAR 42; and 'secondary theatre of war': NAA, A3830, 1941, 3539.

75 War cabinet and air raid budget: Curtin announcement, 19 December 1941, DDA, no. 12; British leaders criticised in Singapore: AAP report in *The Argus*, 23 December 1941; Sir Ronald Cross in Australia: Kent Fedorowich, *At War With Canberra: Sir Ronald Cross and the British High Commission, 1941–42*, Menzies Centre for Australian Studies, King's College, London, 2008, pp. 8–10, 21–22, 26–29; Cross 'lecturing' Australian Ministers: Cranborne to Emrys-Evans, 31 August 1941, Emrys-Evans papers, British Library, Add. MSS 58240, folios 43–46; editorials in *Daily Express* and *The Times* in London: reported in *Canberra Times*, 23 December 1941.

76 Pownall on Singapore, 20 and 24 December 1941: LHCMA, Pownall 2; Churchill on Britain's pleasing home defence situation by the end of 1941: Churchill, *Their Finest Hour*, p. 553.

77   Churchill on defeating Germany first and recovering nations defeated by Japan: notes to his defence chiefs written aboard the *Duke of York* en route to the US, 'The Pacific Front', Defence Committee Memorandum, 17 December 1941, and memorandum '1943', 18 December 1941, Churchill Papers, Churchill Archives Centre, CHAR 4/235; Martin Gilbert, *Winston S. Churchill,* vol. VII, 'Road to Victory, 1941–1945', Heinemann, London, 1986, pp. 11–15; Churchill, *The Grand Alliance,* pp. 571, 578–81; Dr Charles Wilson (Lord Moran) on Churchill and his fear that the US strategy might now focus strongly on Japan: diary entry, 20 December 1941, Lord Moran, *Winston Churchill: The Struggle for Survival 1940–1965,* Sphere Books, London, 1968, pp. 24–25.

78   Sir Earle Page takes a holiday: David Day, *The Great Betrayal: Britain, Australia and the Onset of the Pacific War, 1939–42,* Angus & Robertson, Sydney, 1988, pp. 218–19; Page diary, 23–28 December 1941, NLA, MS 1633, folder 2345; US troops in Australia: Chapman, *Iven G. Mackay,* p. 250; Philippines blockade running and carriers plan: Forrest C. Pogue, *George C. Marshall: Ordeal and Hope, 1939–1942,* MacGibbon & Kee, London, 1968, p. 242; New Caledonia, Pogue, *George C. Marshall,* p. 254; Marshall and 'Beat Hitler First': Pogue, *George C. Marshall,* p. 260.

79   British troops withdraw over Perak River: Kirby, *Singapore,* p. 160; letter from Private Henry Ritchie, 2/20th Australian Infantry Battalion, in Mersing to Mrs E. Campbell, East Gordon, Sydney, 22 December 1941: papers of the late Mrs Christina Leal of Turramurra; shortages of weapons, ammunition and training: Lieutenant Frank Gaven, oral history interview with Don Wall, Keith Murdoch Sound Archive, AWM, S04104.

80   Vildebeest biplane drops bomb on Australians: Russell Braddon, *The Naked Island,* Pan Books, London, 1955, pp. 87–88.

81   General Ismay on American friends: Lord Ismay, *The Memoirs of General the Lord Ismay,* Heinemann, London, 1960, p. 243; Churchill, Roosevelt and officials at first meeting in Washington: Pogue, *George C. Marshall,* pp. 267–68; and on US Pacific strategy: Pogue, *George C. Marshall,* p. 273; minutes of first meeting, Chiefs of Staff Conference, 24 December 1941, Arcadia, ABC-337; Stilwell on British and Atlantic priority: diary entry, 29 December 1941, Joseph W. Stilwell, *The Stilwell Papers,* Macdonald, London, 1949, pp. 41–42; Bennett to chiefs of General Staff, Melbourne, on need for three divisions, and Curtin to Page on Malaya situation and reinforcements, 24 December 1941: NAA, A5954, 571/4; minutes of war cabinet meeting, NAA, A5954, 807/1.

82   Japanese landings with US–Filipino retreat to Bataan peninsula: John
      Toland, *The Rising Sun: The Decline and Fall of the Japanese Empire,
      1936–1945*, Penguin, London, 2001, pp. 250–53; Curtin and RAAF lunch
      Christmas Day: Ross, *John Curtin*, pp. 249–50.

83   John Curtin's Christmas telegram: 23 December 1941, JCPML00402/39;
      Churchill answers Curtin's 'penny packet' cable, 25 December 1941:
      Churchill, *The Grand Alliance*, pp. 592–93; Churchill reflecting on
      Australian Government's state of mind about Japan: Churchill, *The
      Grand Alliance*, p. 592.

84   Padre Barnett statement on Japanese atrocities at Stanley, 10 August
      1945: Oliver Lindsay, *The Lasting Honour: The Fall of Hong Kong,
      1941*, Sphere Books, London, 1978, pp. 152–56; Arnold on cramming
      men and arms in to Australia, 22 December 1941: Douglas MacArthur,
      Reminiscences, Naval Institute Press, Annapolis, Maryland, 1964, p. 65,
      MacArthur on the Philippines: MacArthur, *Reminiscences*, pp. 126–29.

85   Curtin 'encouraged' by Washington talks: national broadcast,
      26 December 1941, DDA, no. 13, pp. 7–10, JCPML00110/18; Curtin to
      wife Elsie Curtin in Perth: Day, *John Curtin*, p. 437; Roosevelt broadcast,
      Canberra Times, 27 December 1941.

86   Curtin article on 'task ahead': *The Herald*, Melbourne, 27 December
      1941; Black, *In His Own Words*, pp. 193–97; Don Rodgers on his author-
      ship of the article: JCPML00463/1/8; Churchill response to Curtin saying
      US Navy should protect Australia and New Zealand, 3 January 1942,
      NAA, A981, WAR 54.

87   Rodgers on reasons for the 'look to America' statement: letter from Don
      Rodgers to R. G. Neale, 7 May 1973, Hudson and Stokes, *Documents
      on Australian Foreign Policy*, vol. V, p. 405, n. 7 (Professor Neale at that
      time was a member of the editorial advisory board of *Documents on
      Foreign Policy* and later became head of the NAA); Churchill to Curtin
      on Singapore reinforcements: received Canberra, 28 December 1941,
      NAA, A3195, 1941, 1.29719 and A12728/1; Churchill cable to Curtin,
      29 December 1941, NA, PREM 4/50/15.

88   Churchill on relations with Australian Government and Churchill cable
      to Curtin 19 January 1942: Winston Churchill, *Hinge of Fate*, Cassell,
      London, 1950, p. 13, (entire Curtin–Churchill debate, pp. 7–17); Curtin
      in reply to Churchill's proposal: 19 January 1942, NAA, A981, WAR
      41B.

Chapter 4   Abandoning Australia

89   Philippines advances: Matome Ugaki, *Fading Victory: The Diary of Admiral Matome Ugaki 1941–1945*, University of Pittsburgh Press, Pittsburgh, 1991, p. 64; Yamashita's advance and his confidence in diary: Potter, *A Soldier Must Hang*, pp. 65–67.

90   Joint Chiefs of Staff Conference, Washington, 31 December 1941: ABC-4/CSI, in Louis Morton, *Strategy and Command: The First Two Years*, US Government Printing Office, Washington DC, 1962, pp. 158–59.

91   Curtin cable to Churchill on proposals isolating Australia, 1 January 1941: NAA, A3300, 219; Churchill to Curtin on labouring 'night and day' in Australia's interests, 3 January 1942: NAA, A981, WAR 54; ABDA command difficulties under Wavell: James MacGregor Burns, *Roosevelt: The Soldier of Freedom 1940–1945*, Harcourt Brace Jovanovich, New York, 1970, p. 203; D. M. Horner, *Crisis of Command: Australian Generalship and the Japanese Threat, 1941–1943*, ANU Press, 1978, pp. 37, 39, 43.

92   Serious talk of abandoning Australia and New Zealand and Admiral King's initiative: Samuel Eliot Morison, *History of United States Naval Operations in World War II*, vol. 4, 'Coral Sea, Midway and Submarine Actions', Castle Books, New York, 2001 (first published 1949), pp. 246–47; Morison background: www.history.navy.mil/bios/morison_s.htm

93   Admiral King on need for Pacific bases: George C. Marshall. H. H. Arnold and Ernest J. King, *The War Reports*, Lippincott, Philadelphia, 1947, p. 514; Pownall on British Far East policy and the United States: Pownall diary, 24 December 1941, LHCMA, Pownall 2 (author's emphasis); Admiral King and reason for initial defensive, not offensive action: Louis Caporale, 'The Pacific war – 1941–1945', *Marine Corps Gazette*, November 1985, www.mcamarines.org/gazette/pacific-war1941-1945.

94   Situation in Malaya in late December 1941, including Bennett: Lionel Wigmore, *The Japanese Thrust*, AWM, Canberra, 1957, pp. 181–82; Bowden to Evatt on defence 'landslide' in Malaya: Bowden to Evatt, received 24 December 1941, Naa, A981, WAR 33, Attachment B.

95   Industrial action: *Sydney Morning Herald*, 20 December 1941, 14 January 1942; anxious days for Australia in January 1942: David Day, *The Politics of War: Australia at War 1939–45 from Churchill to MacArthur*, HarperCollins, Sydney, 2003, pp. 231–32; Paul Hasluck, *Australia in the War of 1939–1945*, vol. 2, 'The Government and the People, 1942–1945',

AWM, Canberra, 1970, pp. 1–2; Hudson and Stokes (eds), *Documents on Australian Foreign Policy,* vol. V, pp. xii–xiv; Curtin and Industrial Relations Council: *The Argus*, 29 December 1941; Churchill on Australian anxieties: Churchill, *The Hinge of Fate*, pp. 4–5.

96   Governor-General Gowrie in national broadcast, 1 January 1942: Papers of Alexander Gore Gowrie, NLA, MS 2852; reverses in Malaya, Tokyo Radio, Japanese leaflets and civilians working with troops at home: *Army News*, 4 January 1942; *Sydney Morning Herald*, 6 January 1942; civilians helping soldiers with war preparations: *Sydney Morning Herald*, 6 January 1942.

97   Air raid shelter expenditure: war cabinet minutes, 26 January 1942, NAA, A5954, 807/2; Sydney GPO tower removed and buildings protected: NAA C4189/1 and A1200, L43868; Churchill's doctor, Sir Charles Wilson, in Washington: diary entry, 1 January 1942, Moran, *Winston Churchill*, p. 35; first Japanese raids on Rabaul: Bruce Gamble, *Darkest Hour: The True Story of Lark Force at Rabaul*, Zenith Press, St Paul, Minnesota, 2006, pp. 68–69; two raids at Rabaul: *The Argus* and *The Courier-Mail*, Brisbane, 5 January 1942; 2/22nd Battalion background: AWM, *2/22nd Battalion*, www.awm.gov.au/units/unit_11273.asp

98   Curtin letter to Elsie Curtin, 5 January 1942: Ross, *John Curtin*, p. 254; Day, *John Curtin*, p. 440.

99   Gollan on Rabaul raids and junior minister obstructionists in the Curtin ministry: *Sydney Morning Herald*, 5 January 1942; Curtin to Churchill on Australia ripe for Japanese attacks: 6 January 1942, NAA, A2937, A.B.D.A. STRATEGIC AREA 1941–1942; Churchill to Curtin, 8 January 1942, posing invasion in force question: NAA, A3195, 1942, 1.1112.

100 Sir Charles Wilson on Churchill's 'black dog': Moran, *Winston Churchill*, pp. 181–82; Wilson on Churchill in water: diary entries, Florida, 5 and 9 January 1942, Moran, *Winston Churchill*, pp. 36–37.

101 Admiral Ugaki, diary for 5 January 1942: Ugaki, *Fading Victory*, pp. 68–69; Fukudome invasion plan: Shigeru Fukudome, *Shosho No Kaiso (Recollections of Rear Admiral Shigeru Fukudome)* in Boeicho Boei Kenshujo Senshishitsu (ed.), *Senshi sosho: Japanese Army Operations in the South Pacific Area: New Britain and Papua Campaign, 1942–1943*, trans. Steven Bullard, AWM, Canberra, 2007; Imperial Headquarters' conception of stage 2 operations: Yamaguchi plan in Boeicho, *Daihon'ei, Kaigunbu*, vol. 2, pp. 304–307; John J. Stephan, *Hawaii Under the*

Rising Sun: Japan's Plans for Conquest After Pearl Harbor, University of Hawaii Press, Honolulu, 1984, pp. 101–105; Admiral Matome Ugaki on Yamamoto's plans: Ugaki, *Fading Victory*, pp. 121–25.

102 Imperial General Headquarters and navy/army differences on Australia: Takushiro Hattori, *Dai Toa Senso Zenshi* (*The Complete History of the Great East Asia War*), Hara Shobo, Tokyo, 1965, p. 52 (US military translation from Gordon W. Prange Papers, Special Collections, University of Maryland Libraries, courtesy Gordon W. Prange).

104 Prince Higashikuni background, proposed as prime minister, opposed by Lord Kido: Nobutaka Ike, *Japan's Decision for War: Records of the 1941 Policy Conferences*, p.185; Higashikuni's conversation with Tojo: James E. Auer (ed.), *From Marco Polo Bridge to Pearl Harbor: Who was Responsible?*, Yomiuri Shimbun, Tokyo, pp. 170–71; Reinforcements and Port Moresby situation in early 1942: Peter Ryan, essay on Second World War, Peter Ryan (gen. ed.), *Encyclopaedia of Papua and New Guinea*, vol. 2, Melbourne University Press, Melbourne, 1972, p. 1215.

105 Alexander speech on knocking out Germany first: *Canberra Times*, *West Australian*, *The Courier-Mail*, Brisbane, 12 January 1942.

106 Knox speech to mayors in Washington: *The Times*, London, 13 January 1942, *Sydney Morning Herald*, *The Argus*, *Cairns Post*, 14 January 1942; Knox and Gallup poll on Germany, Richard F. Hill, *Why the US Declared War on Germany*, Rienner, Boulder, 2003, pp. 120–21; Knox misunderstood: *Time* magazine, 9 February 1942; Knox on navy and doomed Pacific region: Henry L. Stimson and McGeorge Bundy, *On Active Service in Peace and War*, Harper & Brothers, New York, 1947, pp. 396–97; Knox's Massachusetts speech 30 June 1941, *Clear the Atlantic of the German Menace: We Can Wait No Longer*, www.ibiblio.org/pha/policy/1941/1941–06–30a.html; Casey called in by Knox, 20 January 1942: NAA, A981, WAR 49, I; *Time* magazine on Knox: 26 January 1942.

107 Eisenhower's diary and difficulty getting anything done in Australia: 4 January and 12 January 1942, Robert H. Ferrell (ed.), *The Eisenhower Diaries*, W. W. Norton, New York, 1981, pp. 40, 42; Brigadier General Barnes and Curtin at War Council, 12 January 1942: NAA, A5954, 813/2.

108 Submarines lay mines off Darwin: Professor Hiromi Tanaka, 'The Japanese Navy's operations against Australia', *Journal of the Australian War Memorial*, issue 30, April 1997; Bardolph broadcast on trade union councils and strikes, 20 January 1942: *Canberra Times*, 21 January 1942; National Security Coal Regulations introduced: *Canberra Times*,

12 January 1942; editorial on strikes: *Barrier Miner*, 14 January 1942; more strikes on news pages: *Barrier Miner*, 15 January 1942; Ward on forthcoming transport stoppage: *Canberra Times*, 16 January 1942; editorial, *The Courier-Mail*, Brisbane, 19 January 1942.

109 Curtin orders navy to unload steamer: *Sydney Morning Herald*, 19 January 1942; endorsed by war cabinet meeting: 21 January 1942, NAA, A5954, 807/2; further strikes by coalminers: *Canberra Times*, 20 January 1942, *The Argus*, 21 January 1942; Pownall on Singapore and Japanese advances, pins hopes on Hurricanes: Pownall diary, 19 January 1942, LHCMA, Pownall 2.

111 Rabaul troops and 'hostages to fortune': Royle to Casey, 12 December 1941, NAA, A1608, L41/1/5; Gamble, *Darkest Hour*, pp. 56–57; Signal from Lerew in Rabaul on 100 planes attacking: Gillison, 'Royal Australian Air Force, 1939–1942', p. 356; Situation Report No. 84, 20–21 January 1942, from Director, Combined Operational Intelligence Centre, Melbourne, AWM54 423/12/1 and 2; War in the Pacific: Chiefs of Staff Appreciation – Defence of Australia and adjoining areas, 15 December 1941.

112 Rabaul and decision to 'make the enemy fight': John Moremon, *Remembering the War in New Guinea, Rabaul, 1942*, AWM, http://ajrp.awm.gov.au/ajrp/remember.nsf/Web-Printer/C6FD73CC5C579789CA256AC000135979; decision to abandon the Australian troops at Rabaul: minutes of war cabinet meeting, 12 December 1941, NAA, A5954, 807/1 and A5954, 555/10; Page plea to evacuate civilians and *Herstein*: Douglas Aplin, *Rabaul 1942: 2/22nd Battalion AIF*, Lark Force Association, Melbourne, 1980, p. 352; Gillison, 'Royal Australian Air Force, 1939–1942', p. 356; Curtin, ministers and defence chiefs consider last minute requests for two guns and reinforcements for Rabaul, Page's plea for civilian evacuation: war cabinet meeting, 19 January 1942, and reply, 20 January 1942, NAA, A5954, 807/2.

114 Curtin 'overwhelmed': Professor Geoffrey Sawyer in oral history interviewed with Dr Errol Hodge, 1988, Keith Murdoch Sound Archive, AWM, S01524; Don Rodgers on Curtin's problems with alcohol: interviewed by Mel Pratt, 1971, NLA, TRC 121.14, JCPML00497.

115 Don Rodgers on Curtin's depression: JCPML00497/1, Day, *John Curtin*, pp. 135–36; Rabaul defenders saddened and frustrated by Australian authorities, Flight Officer Geoffrey Lempriere: Gamble, *Fortress Rabaul*, p. 34; Japanese fleet en route to Rabaul and 'all available aircraft' order: Gillison, 'Royal Australian Air Force, 1939–1942', pp. 356–357, p. 358;

Lerew cables: Gamble, *Darkest Hour*, p. 77; Bruce Gamble, *Fortress Rabaul*, Zenith Press, Minneapolis, 2010, pp. 33–35.

116 Coastwatchers see invasion vessels steaming for Rabaul: Eric Feldt, *The Coast Watchers*, Currey O'Neil, Melbourne, 1975, pp. 80–85; press release, Don Rodgers, 22 January 1942, NAA, A5954/69, 1882/3; Don Rodgers's press statement on Curtin going home to Perth, *The Argus*, 22 January 1942, *Sydney Morning Herald*, 23 January 1942; Curtin's fears of Rabaul as a Japanese base for attacking the islands, New Zealand and the east coast of Australia: Curtin to Dominions Secretary Attlee, 19 March 1942, NAA, A2684, 904.

Chapter 5   Flight of a prime minister

117 Victoria Barracks description: author's tour 2005; Agnes Hannan, *Victoria Barracks Melbourne: A Social History*, Australian Defence Force Journal Publication, Canberra, 1995, pp. 147–53; plethora of appalling news received in Australia: Situation Report No. 85, 0830 to 1500 hours, 21 January 1942, Combined Operational Intelligence Centre, AWM54 423/12/1 and 2.

118 The ABC's Jack Commins on the Canberra atmosphere in January 1942: Jack Commins in oral history interview with Mel Pratt, 22–26 May 1971, NLA, TRC 121/13, and JCPML01092/1; war cabinet discussion on evacuation of civilians from coast, 20 January 1942: NAA, A5954, 807/2.

119 Fuchida leads attack from carriers and critical of the unnecessary force used: Fuchida and Okumiya, *Midway*, pp. 36–37; Sadatoshi Tomioka on Rabaul in statement on the circumstances of the Japanese offensives on Midway Islands and the South Eastern Area: US Army, *Statements of Japanese Officials on World War II*, vols 1–2, no. 61232, 10 September 1947; Vice Admiral Shigeru Fukudome on navy discussions: interrogation, 9–12 December 1945, US Strategic Bombing Survey, Interrogation of Japanese officials, OPNAV-P-03–100 (USSBS No. 503).

120 Churchill on 21 January 1942 and re-evaluates Singapore over Burma: Wigmore, *The Japanese Thrust*, pp. 284–86.

121 Intelligence reports of Japanese attacks received at Victoria Barracks: Combined Operational Intelligence Centre, Situation Report No. 86, 1500 hours, 21 January 1942, to 0830 hours, 22 January 1942, AWM54 423/12/1 and 2.

122 Churchill to Curtin on invasion: 9 Jan, 1942, NAA, A5954, 555/4; Curtin to Churchill on protection of Australia and Rabaul situation: 21 January

1942, NAA, A3196, 1942, 0.2009; Curtin to Churchill on 21 January 1942 on danger of invasion of Australia, NAA, A3196, 1942, 0.2039 and A5459, 554/4; Curtin to Churchill on inadequate naval strength in Australian region, 21 January 1942, NAA A3196, 1942, 0.2009; Curtin protest re: Wavell command: cable to Cranborne, 21 January 1942, NAA, A3196, 1942, 0.2014.

123 Situation in Malaya, diary of General Bennett of 21 January 1942 in Bennett, *Why Singapore Fell*, p. 138; Japanese massacre at Parit Sulong bridge, AWM unit history, http://www.awm.gov.au/units/unit_11280. asp; Churchill to Curtin 19 January 1942, deeming Middle East more important and 'we must not be dismayed': NAA A3195, 1942, 1.2352.

124 Curtin to Churchill, 21 January 1942, on Pacific War Council: NAA, A2680, 14/1942; bombing of Lae, Salamaua and Bulolo: communique from Air Minister Drakeford in Australian newspapers, including *The Courier-Mail*, Brisbane, 22 January 1942; Lieutenant Bob Emery of ANGAU at Madang: transcript of oral history interview, Keith Murdoch Sound Archive, AWM, S00727; Curtin clash with Churchill on war direction: minutes of war cabinet meeting, 21 January 1942, NAA, A5954, 807/2.

125 Curtin's 'satisfactory' talks with Ward: *Sydney Morning Herald* and *The Advertiser*, Adelaide, 22 January 1942.

126 Tojo war aims and threats on 21 January 1942: *Sydney Morning Herald*, 22 January 1942; Curtin's missed twelve meetings: records of the January– February 1942 war cabinet meetings, NAA, A5954, 807/2, and Advisory War Council meetings, NAA, A5954, 813/2; Forde background: Neil Lloyd, 'Forde, Francis Michael (Frank) (1890–1983)', Australian Dictionary of Biography, National Centre of Biography, ANU, http://adb.anu.edu.au/biography/forde-francis-michael-frank-12504/ text22477.

127 War cabinet preliminary discussion on scorched-earth policy: 24 January 1942, NAA, A5954, 807/2; MacArthur on dangerous defeatism in Australia: MacArthur, *Reminiscences*, p. 151; Curtin meets Gowrie, 21 January 1942: vice regal notices, *The Argus* and *Canberra Times*, 22 January 1942.

128 Elsie Curtin on husband's lasting friendship with Gowrie: Elsie Curtin, 'The Curtin story: his greatest triumph', *Woman* magazine, 2 April 1951; Curtin's close relationship with Gowrie: Bob Wurth, 'Curtin's hand of friendship', *Griffith Review*, no. 9: Up North, August 2006,

http://griffithreview.com/edition-9-up-north/curtins-hand-of-friend-ship; McKernan on Curtin's health: public lecture by Dr Michael McKernan, JCPML Visiting Scholar, Curtin University of Technology, Perth, 20 October 2005, JCPML00955/1; letters from Gowrie to George VI mentioning Curtin's health: 10 October 1941 and 14 April 1942, Gowrie Papers, NLA, MS 2852/5/13 and 14.

129 Description of State Car No. 4, Victorian Railways: Chris Banger and Peter Medlin, 'Ninety years of the E cars', *Newsrail*, Australian Railway Historical Society, Victorian Division, August 1996, p. 236.

130 Gladys Joyce: interviewed by Isla Macphail for the John Curtin Prime Ministerial Library, 3 July 1997, JCPML00210; Intelligence about Rabaul: Situation Report No. 88, Combined Operational Intelligence Centre, AWM54 423/12/1 and 2; Japanese attack Rabaul, Boeicho Boei Kenshujo Senshishitsu (ed.), *Senshi sosho: Minami Taiheiyo Rikugun sakusen (1) Poto Moresubi–Gashima shoko sakusen* (*War History Series: South Pacific Area Army Operations (1), Port Moresby–Guadalcanal First Campaigns*), Asagumo Shinbunsha, Tokyo, 1968, pp. 50–51, trans. Steven Bullard, Australia–Japan Research Project translation, http://ajrp.awm.gov.au/ajrp/ajrp2.nsf/WebI/JpnOperations/$file/ JpnOpsText.pdf?OpenElement; defence of Rabaul: NAA, MP729/6, 16/401/493.

131 Muar River, Malaya background and Captain Beverley: Wigmore, *The Japanese Thrust*, pp. 237–49.

132 Colonel Anderson VC citation, www.awm.gov.au/units/people_8219. asp; Japanese atrocities at Parit Sulong: Wigmore, *The Japanese Thrust*, pp. 246–47; Potter, *A Soldier Must Hang*, pp. 87, 91; text of commemoration on interpretive panels at the Parit Sulong Memorial, Department of Veterans' Affairs.

133 General Arthur Percival on Australians at Muar: Arthur Percival, *The War in Malaya*, Eyre & Spottiswood, London, 1949, p. 233; Braddon on shambles of Muar battle: Russell Braddon, *The Other Hundred Years War: Japan's Bid for Supremacy 1941–2041*, Collins, London, 1983, p. 20; Scanlan and Lark Force rout: Wigmore, *The Japanese Thrust*, pp. 400–402.

134 Curtin and Prince of Wales carriage description: http://john.curtin.edu. au/education/tlf/R4143/2162_image/index.html; Australian Railway Historical Society, Victorian Division; Philippa Rogers, Heritage amd Museum Services, City of Wanneroo; John Burley memories of Curtin

and train, 1942, JCPML00154/1; *On Track: Curtin's Railway Journeys*, http://john.curtin.edu.au/railway/primeminister/index.html; Ian Jenkin, Australian Railway Historical Society (Victorian Division), letter to author, 13 April 2011; Commonwealth Railways, NAA, A5954, 718/2; A816, 56/301/57; Sydney Gray meets Curtin en route to Perth, 22 January 1942: written by Sydney G. Gray, JCPML00346/2; *Sydney Morning Herald*, 23 January 1942 (Gray's account and press reports differ in some detail on this meeting); additional quotes, Francis Shea, interview for the Battye Library, JCPML00013/1; Detail of Curtin's rail trip across the Nullarbor, in part assembled from various newspaper reports filed by reporters en route. Curtin speaks with press at Port Augusta and reports of fighting in Malaya: *The Advertiser*, Adelaide, 22 and 23 January 1942, *The Courier-Mail*, Brisbane, 23 February 1942; further information from Phillipa Rogers and the Railway Museum at Bassendean, Perth; Hazel Craig memories crossing the Nullarbor, interviewed July 1997, JCPML00209/1.

137   Singapore air raid: *The Argus*, 23 January 1942; life goes on in Singapore: *The Advertiser*, Adelaide, 23 January 1942; intelligence on Japanese advance: Situation Report No. 88, Combined Operational Intelligence Centre, AWM54 423/12/1 and 2.

138   General Bennett on reinforcements: diary, 23 January 1942, H. Gordon Bennett, *Why Singapore Fell*, Angus & Robertson, Sydney, 1944, pp. 146–47; Gordon Bennett diary, SLNSW, MLMSS 773; Lieutenant Arthur Tranter on the 2/29th being surrounded and Australians shooting their own men: recollections of Tranter in conversations with his son, Neville Tranter, of Bendigo, and Tranter papers held by his daughter, Brenda Tranter, of Caloundra, 2012; Gunner Russell Braddon on Australians killing their own and on Indian troops: Braddon, *The Naked Island*, pp. 68–69.

139   Karonie and landscape en route, Trans-Australian Railway timetable and description of route, washaway between Kalgoorlie and Karonie: Jim Averies, railways manager, 'Life at the outposts', Port Augusta, in Patsy Adam Smith, *Romance of Australian Railways*, Rigby, Adelaide, 1973, p. 221.

Chapter 6   Despair on the Nullarbor

141   Ross Gollan on Curtin's absence crossing the Nullarbor Plain and on fears of Curtin ministers, political backgrounder: 'The face of danger, mood of

the war cabinet', *Sydney Morning Herald*, 26 January 1942; Morse use by railways: Richie Bright, Morsecodians Fraternity of Western Australia.

142 Gift from David Crone to Curtin and Curtin's response, 23 January 1942: NAA, AM1415, 40.

143 Forde explaining Curtin's awareness on communications while en route to Perth: *Sydney Morning Herald*, 23 January 1942, *West Australian*, 26 January 1942; Evatt and Forde statements on A. V. Alexander's comments, 23 January 1942: DDA, no. 16, JCPML00110/21.

144 Curtin speaks with press on the train en route to Kalgoorlie: *Sun Pictorial*, Melbourne, 24 January 1942; Ward backs unionists in Industrial Relations Council issue and nationalisation and federal opposition: *The Advertiser*, Adelaide, 23 January 1942, *The Courier-Mail*, Brisbane, 24 January 1942; Curtin and his government scattered: *The Courier-Mail*, Brisbane, editorial, 23 January 1942.

145 Australia 'subordinate theatre of war': *Canberra Times*, 23 January 1942; 'This must not happen here', editorial, *The Argus*, 23 January 1942; Dismissive British attitude towards Australia, report filed from Kalgoorlie, 23 January 1942, *Daily Telegraph* 24 January 1942.

146 War cabinet deliberations, including Bostock: minutes of 23 January 1942, NAA, A5954, 807/2; Royle on invasion, Churchill's British reinforcements for Singapore: war cabinet meeting, 24 January 1942, NAA A5954, 807/2.

147 Frank Forde statements on 'enemy hammering at our gates' and report that some ministers were seeking total mobilisation of population and a scorched earth policy: *The Examiner*, Launceston, and *Sydney Morning Herald* reporting from Melbourne, 24 January 1942; DDA, no. 16, 23 January 1942.

148 Press statements by Beasley: 23 January 1942: DDA, no. 16; 'inexcusable betrayal' cable to Churchill in Curtin's name: NAA, A981, WAR 33, Attachment B; Page role: NAA, A5954, 571/4.

149 Three-point note handwritten and signed by Evatt referring to 'inexcusable betrayal': NAA, A5954, 571/4; Churchill response to 'inexcusable betrayal': Churchill, *The Hinge of Fate*, pp. 51–52; Australian soldier's description of landing near Vulcan: Wigmore, *The Japanese Thrust*, p. 403; AWM, *2/22nd Battalion*, http://www.awm.gov.au/units/unit_11273.asp

150 Fall of Rabaul and Japanese surrender pamphlet: Wigmore, *The Japanese Thrust*, pp. 403–411, 664; Rabaul 'surrender or go bush', Gamble, Bruce,

Fortress Rabaul, Zenith Press, Minneapolis, 2010, pp. 47–48; Lieutenant Anderson quoting Colonel Carr in 'report on events following the fall of Rabaul', NAA, MP1049/5, 2021/8/332; John Coates in Dennis (ed.), *The Oxford Companion to Australian Military History*, pp. 488–89.; Japanese bombs falling on Singapore: Rohan D. Rivett, *Behind Bamboo: An Inside Story of the Japanese Prison Camps*, Angus & Robertson, Sydney, 1946, p. 6.

151 Pownall on Singapore, Blamey and attitude of Australians: Pownall diary, 25 January 1942, LHCMA Pownall 2; Bond (ed.), Chief of Staff, vol. 2, '1940–1944', pp. 79–81; Curtin arrival at Kalgoorlie and 'challenging speech: *Melbourne Herald*, *The Advertiser*, Adelaide, *Daily News*, Perth, *Sydney Morning Herald*, *Sunday Times*, Perth, 24 January 1942.

152 Miners' deputation: *The Mirror*, Perth, 24 January 1942, *Sydney Morning Herald* and *The Argus*, 26 January 1942; Willcock sends his private carriage to Kalgoorlie: Premiers Office to Prime Minister's Department, 20 January 1942, NAA, A461, A418/3/5, PART 2.

153 Report from Kuala Lumpur: Intelligence Situation Report No. 89, covering 23 January 1942, Combined Operational Intelligence Centre, Melbourne, AWM54 423/12/1 and 2; Rodgers on Curtin's statement on the BBC: DDA, no. 16, 'Prime Minister's criticism', 24 January 1942.

154 Evatt and scorched-earth policy: minutes of the war cabinet, 24 January 1942, NAA, A5954, 807/2; 'The Enemy Thunders at Our Gates' and other propaganda posters: NAA, C934/91/Government advertising posters c 1942; Curtin comes home to Perth: *The Mail*, Adelaide, 24 January 1942; *West Australian*, 24 and 25 January 1942; Evatt on Japanese threat exaggerated: Commonwealth Parliamentary Debates, House of Representatives, 21 August 1941, pp. 91–93.

155 The Curtins at Sydney Gray's wedding and reception: records of Sydney Gray, JCPML00346/1 and 2; *Sunday Times*, Perth, 25 January 1942; *West Australian*, 26 January 1942; Imperial General Headquarters announcement on Rabaul: Board of Information spokesman Tomokazu Hori, 26 January 1942, Diplomatic Record Office, Ministry of Foreign Affairs, Tokyo.

156 'extreme alarm' in Australia: *Senshi sosho: Japanese Army Operations in the South Pacific Area: New Britain and Papua Campaign, 1942–1943*, trans. Steven Bullard, p. 33; British intelligence on Australia: British war cabinet Joint Intelligence Sub-Committee on Australia and New Zealand, meeting 25 January 1942, CAB 68/9/17, J.I.C. (42) Final.

157 Gollan on fears of Australian war cabinet ministers: *Sydney Morning Herald*, 26 January 1942; Hasluck observing Curtin: Paul Hasluck, *Diplomatic Witness: Australian Foreign Affairs 1941–1947*, Melbourne University Press, Melbourne, 1980, pp. 43–45.

158 Hasluck on Curtin Government's fear: Hasluck, 'The Government and the People, 1942–1945', pp. 127–29; Charles Bean on 'shakiest at the top': 'What is wrong with Australia?', *Sunday Herald*, Sydney, 13 February 1949; Sir James Plimsoll on government nerves: interviewed by Clyde Cameron, 28 March 1984, transcript of sound recording, pp. 134–35, NLA.

159 Japan's fear of Australia as a US base and Imperial Navy's invasion proposals: Sadatoshi Tomioka, *Kaisen to shusen: Hito to kiko to keikaku* (*The Opening and Closing of the War: The People, the Mechanism, and the Planning*), Mainichi Shinbunsha, Tokyo, 1968, pp. 116–18, trans. for the author by Kyal Hill, Tokyo; Vice Admiral Inoue's aggressive plans: John B. Lundstrom, *The First South Pacific Campaign: Pacific Fleet Strategy*, Naval Institute Press, Annapolis, Maryland, 1976, pp. 9, 40, 68; Inoue's character and his aggressiveness in the South Pacific: Richard B. Frank, *Guadalcanal: The Definitive Account of the Landmark Battle*, Random House, New York, 1992, pp. 21–23.

160 Interest in Australia from Vice Admiral Shigeyoshi Inoue and Rear Admiral Shikazo Yano: H. P. Willmott, *The Barrier and the Javelin: Japanese and Allied Pacific Strategies, February to June 1942*, Naval Institute Press, Annapolis, Maryland, 2008, p. 40; Historian Professor Hiromi Tanaka: interviewed by the author, Tokyo, 16 August 2007; Gulf between Australia and Britain: Board of Information spokesman, Tomokazu Hori, 26 January 1942, Diplomatic Record Office, Ministry of Foreign Affairs, Tokyo.

161 Curtin claim for representation: DDA, no. 16, 24 January 1942, JCPML00110/21; Irene Dowsing, *Curtin of Australia*, Acacia Press, Melbourne, 1969, pp. 112–15.

Chapter 7   Thundering at the gates

162 Australians carried on as usual: 'The stirring of a people', in Hasluck, *Australia in the War of 1939–1945*, vol. 2, 'The Government of the People, 1942–1945', pp. 55–69; Curtin's Australia Day speech: broadcast 26 January 1942, JCPML00652/2/15.

163 Curtin note to Roosevelt: 26 January 1942, with copy of cable to Churchill of 21 January 1942, in Alfred D. Chandler (ed.), *The Papers of Dwight*

David Eisenhower: The War Years, vol. 1, John Hopkins Press, Baltimore, Maryland, 1970, pp. 76–77.

164 Brereton on no adequate defence in Australia and Eisenhower on fighters for Australia: Eisenhower, *The Papers of Dwight D. Eisenhower*, vol. 1, pp. 76–78; Eisenhower on 'Germany first': Eisenhower, *The Papers of Dwight D. Eisenhower*, vol. 1, pp. 149–55; notes, US War Plans Division 4628-24; G. S. J. Barclay, 'Australia Looks to America, 1939–1942', *Pacific Historical Review*, vol. 46, no. 2, May 1977, p. 264.

165 Curtin on Australia's lack of fighters and being 'left almost defence-less': Curtin to Churchill, 27 January 1942, Churchill Archives Centre, CHAR 20/69A (49–50). Curtin's aircraft figures excluded Darwin, which he had previously suggested should come within the ABDA area: Peter Grose, *An Awkward Truth: The Bombing of Darwin, February 1942*, Allen & Unwin, Sydney, 2009, pp. 47–54; Curtin's 'badly-needed rest': *Sun Pictorial*, 27 January 1942.

166 Curtin speech at the Capitol Theatre, Perth, 27 January 1942: Alan Chester, *John Curtin*, Angus & Robertson, Sydney, 1943, pp. 130–31; *Daily News*, Perth, 27 January 1942; *West Australian*, 28 January 1942; Churchill on growing discord over his government: Churchill, *The Hinge of Fate*, pp. 53–54, 57–62.

167 Churchill background on the likelihood of the Japanese going to war: Churchill, *The Grand Alliance*, pp. 484–86, 526–29; British priorities on Russia and Far East: Ismay, *The Memoirs of General the Lord Ismay*, pp. 228, 239; British intelligence chiefs' report to chiefs of staff and General Ismay: Intelligence Assessment, Joint Intelligence Committee (41) 492, 29 December 1941, NA, CAB 79/16; Brooke-Popham's warning about Japan and Singapore: letter, 26 October 1940, 6/1/5; 'Notes on the Far East, 6/9/5, Papers of Air Chief Marshall Sir Henry Robert Brooke-Popham, LHCMA.

168 Churchill's intelligence regarding possibility of war with Japan, February 1941: Churchill, *The Grand Alliance*, pp. 157–58.

169 Churchill in parliamentary debates: House of Commons Official Report, 27 January 1942; House of Commons confidence debate, Hansard, 27–28 January 1942, http://hansard.millbanksystems.com/people/mr-winston-churchill/1942 (my emphasis); Anzac force ships in Fiji: Willmott, H.P., *Empires in the Balance, Japanese and Allied Pacific Strategies to April 1942*, Naval Institute Press, Annapolis, Maryland, 1982, p. 264.

170 Jack Holmfield on Rabaul and Curtin 'a real bastard': Herbert John (Jack) Holmfield interviewed by Hank Nelson for Keith Murdoch Sound Archive, AWM, S01043.

171 Kokopo plantation manager Kenneth Ryall: Mark Felton, *Slaughter at Sea: The Story of Japan's War Crimes*, Pen and Sword Maritime, Barnsley, UK, 2008, p. 19; minute to Department of the Army, 16 May 1942, NAA, A5954, 532/1.

172 Tol plantation massacre, including Private Bill Cook: report of Japanese atrocities presented to the Commonwealth Government by Sir William Webb, 15 March 1944, NAA, A1066, H45, 580/2/8/1 and A10943/1; Wigmore, *The Japanese Thrust*, pp. 667–68; Professor Hank Nelson, *The Tol Massacre*, Montevideo Maru Foundation, www.montevideomaru. org/ history/history-war-new-guinea/the-tol-massacre; first news of Tol plantation massacre: *Daily Bulletin*, Townsville, *The Courier-Mail*, Brisbane, 7 April 1942.

173 Japan's Board of Information: statement on atrocities, 16 April 1942, Diplomatic Record Office, Ministry of Foreign Affairs, Tokyo; Colonel Scanlan background: A. J. Sweeting, 'Scanlan, John Joseph (1890–1962)', Australian Dictionary of Biography, National Centre of Biography, ANU, http://adb.anu.edu.au/biography/scanlan-john-joseph-8349/text14653; nurses captured in Rabaul: AWM, *Second World War Nurses*, www.awm. gov.au/exhibitions/nurses/ww2; Curtin broadcast on 6KY, 28 January 1942: *West Australian*, 29 January 1942.

174 Rifle shortage: Curtin note to Forde, 3 February 1942, NAA, A367, M1416, 46; Tonkin on Curtin and defence situation: JCPML00019/1.

175 Curtin departs east on the Westland express: *West Australian*, 30 January 1942; Curtin to celebrate son's 21st birthday in Cottesloe, *The Age*, Melbourne, 22 January 1942; John Francis Curtin speaking of his father in earlier days: oral history interview by Heather Campbell, March–April 2004, JCPML00855/1. (John Curtin, the son, died in 2007 at the age of eighty-six.) Richard Hughes on Curtin's work in Perth and Western Australians: *Daily Telegraph*, Sydney, 1 February 1942, JCPML00297/2.

176 Editorial suggesting how the Australian Government should behave in dealings with Britain: *West Australian*, 29 January 1942; unrest among RAAF flyers in Britain and need to defend Australia, Cranborne and Eden: minutes of the British Defence Committee (Operations) of the war cabinet, 30 January 1942, NA, CAB 69/4; use of US Kittyhawk fighters

by RAAF: AWM, *P-40E-1-CU Kittyhawk fighter aircraft A29-133 : RAAF*, http://cas. awm.gov.au/item/REL/20242

177 Possibility of invasion of Australia: AAP report, *The Advertiser*, Adelaide, and other newspapers, 30 January 1942; Forde and Makin response: DDA, no. 17, 29 January 1942; Ambon defeat and massacre: Dennis (ed.) *The Oxford Companion to Australian Military History*, p. 31; AWM, *2/21st Battalion*, www.awm.gov.au/units/unit_11272.asp; Ambon background: Wigmore, *The Japanese Thrust*, pp. 437–40.

178 Laha massacre inquiry summary, NAA, A705/15, 166/43/989.

179 Gordon Bennett tells Sultan of Johore of escape plans, leaves Johore Bahru, writes of Wavell's statement in diary: Frank Legg, *The Gordon Bennett Story*, Angus & Robertson, Sydney, 1965, pp. 222–23; student Lee on 'end of the British Empire': Lee Kuan Yew, *The Singapore Story: Memoirs of Lee Kuan Yew*, Singapore Press Holdings/Marshall Cavendish, Singapore, 1998, pp. 44–45.

180 Combined Fleet invasion planning: *Senshi Sosho: Minami Taiheiyo Rikugun sakusen (1) Poto Moresubi–Gashima shoko sakusen (War History Series: South Pacific Area Army Operations (1), Port Moresby–Guadalcanal first campaigns)*, vol. 1, p. 355; Ugaki on Darwin and Timor: diary entry, 5 February 1942, Ugaki, *Fading Victory*, p. 85; British intelligence reports: cabinet minutes, 27 January and 5 February 1942, 'Possible Japanese action against Australia and New Zealand', presented in Washington on 31 January 1942, NA, CAB 79/17/30 and CAB 79/18/7.

181 Curtin back in Melbourne and newspaper criticism: *Canberra Times* and *The Courier-Mail*, Brisbane, 2 February 1942.

182 Mackay on abandoning Australian towns to their fate: Defence Appreciation, 4 February 1942, Chapman, *Iven G. Mackay*, pp. 235–36, 252–54.

183 National Bank measures, ordered 2 February 1942 by McConnan: Geoffrey Blainey and Geoffrey Hutton, *Gold and Paper 1858–1982: A History of the National Bank of Australasia Ltd*, Macmillan, Melbourne, 1983, p. 221; Gerow to board of economic warfare: 17 January 1942, National Record Administration, Washington, RG 165, WPD 4630.

184 Mark Jacobsen, 'US grand strategy and the defence of Australia', in Gavin Fry et al. (eds), *The Battle of the Coral Sea 1942: Conference Proceedings, 7–10 May 1992*, Australian National Maritime Museum, Sydney, 1993, pp. 21–22; General Shinichi Tanaka on Darwin: interview, Willoughby (ed.), *Reports of General MacArthur*, vol. 2, part I, p. 132n; Takushiro

Hattori on invasion plans: US Army interview, Tokyo, 5 October 1947, *Statements of Japanese Officials on World War II*, vols 1 and 2.

185 Australian troops to Port Moresby and details of raw recruits on the *Aquitania*: AWM, *53rd Battalion (West Sydney Regiment)*, www.awm.gov. au/units/unit_11966.asp

186 Japanese expansion of bases, Historian Shindo Hiroyuki: 'Japanese air operations in New Guinea', in Steven Bullard, Steven and Keiko Tamura (eds), *From a Hostile Shore: Australia and Japan at War in New Guinea*, AWM, Canberra, 2004, pp. 60–62; Jack Boland oral history interview: Keith Murdoch Sound Archive, AWM, S00506; Eleven squadron flying boats in Port Moresby: AWM, *11 Squadron RAAF*, http://www.awm.gov. au/units/unit_11039.asp

187 Army in Port Moresby not reinforced but hopes of US carrier-borne planes to protect the gateway: Gillison, 'Royal Australian Air Force, 1939–1942', pp. 446–47; Japanese navy and army reasons for the capture of Port Moresby: Hiromi Tanaka, 'Japanese and the Pacfic War in New Guinea', in Bullard and Tamura (eds), *From a Hostile Shore*, p. 36.

Chapter 8   Mounting disasters

188 Australians poorly armed and impossible terrain in waterlogged west coast of Singapore for 2/20th, including Private Henry Ritchie and Lieutenant Frank Gaven: oral history interview with Don Wall, Keith Murdoch Sound Archive, AWM, S04104; A Company 2/20th Battalion's vulnerable position on west coast of Singapore: Maynard, Roger, *Hell's Heroes: The Forgotten Story of the Worst P.O.W. Camp in Japan*, HarperCollins, Sydney, 2010, pp. 70, 88–89, 90–91.

189 Japanese attack on Australian positions on west coast of Singapore: Legg, *The Gordon Bennett Story*, pp. 235.

190 Description of Australian fighting in Singapore, Percival and Wavell: Wigmore, *The Japanese Thrust*, pp. 335–38; General Percival meeting with General Bennett: Percival, *The War in Malaya*, p. 275; Churchill cable to Wavell, 10 February 1942, on East Indies and fighting to bitter end: Churchill, *The Hinge of Fate*, pp. 87–88.

191 Wavell's orders and order of the day, 10 February 1942: Percival, *The War in Malaya*, pp. 238, 341–42, 343; Lieutenant Frank Gaven on Kranji 'schmozzle', confronts Bennett, 'fantasy' orders: oral history interview with Don Wall, Keith Murdoch Sound Archive, AWM, S04104.

192 2/20th Battalion casualties: Major Ron Merrett, oral history interview with Don Wall, Keith Murdoch Sound Archive, AWM, 21 May 1982, S04100; death of Private Henry Ritchie, AWM, Roll of Honour cards, 1939–1945 War, 2nd AIF (Australian Imperial Force) and CMF (Citizen Military Force), AWM147; description of Fort Canning 'labyrinth' underground headquarters: author's visit 2011; Romen Bose, *Secrets of the Battlebox: The History and Role of Britain's Command HQ During the Malayan Campaign*, Marshall Cavendish, Singapore, 2005, p. 17.

193 Last of Singapore's aircraft flown off: Wigmore, *The Japanese Thrust*, p. 341; teenaged Phua Tin Tua, Willie, on wartime Singapore: interviewed by the author, Singapore, 5 March 2009; Japanese bombs and shells hit Singapore city: Rivett, *Behind Bamboo*, p. 6; The Istana (Government House): Noel Barber, *The Singapore Story: From Raffles to Lee Kuan Yew*, Fontana, London, 1978, pp. 120–22; Alan Warren, *Singapore 1942: Britain's Greatest Defeat*, Grant Books, Singapore, 2002, p. 261; Phua Tin Tua, Willie, on air raids: interviewed by the author in Singapore, 1 and 7 December 2000. (Phua went on to become an ABCTV cameraman in Asia).

194 Bennett meeting with Percival and others at Fort Canning Battle Box, Thomas advises surrender, and scenes of utter devastation in Singapore: Bennett diary, Legg, *The Gordon Bennett Story*, pp. 243–45; last days of Singapore, including hospital massacre: Major General Kiyotake Kawaguchi statement in Foreign Service despatch no. 1498, Harlan B. Clark, US Embassy, Tokyo to State Department Washington, 30 June 1959; Colonel Masanobu Tsuji quoted in Ian Ward, *The Killer They Called a God*, Media Masters, Singapore, 1992, pp. 319–20.

195 Evatt cable to Vivian Bowden in Singapore: 10 February 1942, NAA, A981, AUSTRALIA 237B; escape and murder of Vivian Bowden: manuscript by Alan Robert Taysom, 'History of the Australian Trade Commissioner Service', Department of Trade, Canberra, 1983, NLA, NQ 354.9400827 T 247; Bob Wurth, *Saving Australia*, pp. 175–76; Mackay report to Forde: 'Preparedness of Home Forces for Active Operations', 13 February 1942, quoted in Chapman, *Iven G. Mackay*, pp. 257–58.

196 Forde to Curtin on Australia's defence state on eve of fall of Singapore: memo of 14 February 1942, NAA, A5954, 554/4; Curtin intervening in industrial disputes: *Sydney Morning Herald*, 9 February 1942; northern coal production lost: *Sydney Morning Herald*, 12 February 1942; Miners'

Federation on abandoning strikes: *The Argus* and *Sydney Morning Herald*, 14 February 1942.

197 Admiral Raeder to Hitler: Fuehrer Conferences on Naval Affairs, 13 February 1942, p. 371, Defence Academy, UK, www.da.mod.uk/colleges/jscsc/jscsc-library/archives/fuehrer-conferences; Bennett on commanders agreeing to surrender: Bennett diary, February 1942, quoted in Bennett, *Why Singapore Fell*, pp. 191–98; fear of Japanese rampage in Singapore: Kirby, *Singapore*, p. 245.

198 General Bennett's escape: Bennett, *Why Singapore Fell*, pp. 201–15; Percival and officers meet at Fort Canning and subsequent surrender at Bukit Timah, 15 February 1942: Kirby, *Singapore*, pp. 247–49.

199 Tojo warning to Australia and New Zealand: *Japan Times*, 16 February 1942; Japan's 'happier and more prosperous Asia': *Japan Times*, 17 February 1942; Japan's Foreign Office statement on Curtin: 18 February 1942, Board of Information. Diplomatic Record Office, Ministry of Foreign Affairs, Tokyo; Churchill shock on fall of Singapore: quoted in Churchill, *The Hinge of Fate*, p. 94; Churchill broadcast on loss of Singapore: AAP report, *Sydney Morning Herald*, 17 February 1942.

200 British and Australian press criticism of Churchill and his government: *The Argus*, 13, 14 and 16 February 1942, *Sydney Morning Herald*, 16 and 17 February 1942; editorial on 'disastrous' policy: *The Argus*, 16 February 1942; Wilson on Churchill's reaction to Singapore: Moran, *Winston Churchill*, p. 43.

201 Anthony Eden on Churchill's depression and 'nagging': Eden diary, quoted in Gilbert, 'Road to Victory, 1941–1945', p. 49; Forde statement on troops in Malaya, 17 February 1942, and Curtin on fall of Singapore: DDA no. 19, 16 February 1942.

202 Australians 'consumed by sloth and faction': 'Australia, arise', editorial, *Sydney Morning Herald*, 18 February 1942; Miners' Federation on aggressor at the door: *Sydney Morning Herald*, 16 February 1942.

203 Bishop Riley denounces strikes: *The Argus*, 17 February 1942; Curtin Government introduces coal production legislation, Curtin warns striking New South Wales miners, Victorian Railways 'dwindling' coal supplies: *The Argus*, 25 February 1942; Churchill message to Wavell, 15 February 1942, regarding opportunities for escape: NA, CHAR 20/70; union stoppages including Curtin's intervention in Melbourne: *West Australian*, 16 March 1942.

204 Lieutenant Arthur Tranter and Australians escaping Singapore and crossing Sumatra to Padang: recollections of son, Neville Tranter, and records of Arthur Tranter held by his daughter, Brenda Tranter, Caloundra, Queensland.

205 Sister Bullwinkel and Australian army nursing sisters: Betty Jeffrey, *White Coolies*, Angus & Robertson, Sydney, 1954, pp. 4–25; account by Sister Bullwinkel in a narrative by Sister Veronica Clancy, who was also on the *Vyner Brooke* and was interned with Bullwinkel: Wigmore, *The Japanese Thrust*, pp. 286–87; New Zealand prime minister, Peter Fraser, correspondence with Churchill and Roosevelt: 17 February 1942, NA, CHAR 20/70.

206 Curtin's gastritis: *Sydney Morning Herald* and *The Argus*, 19 February 1942; Day, *John Curtin*, pp. 495–96.

207 Curtin speech at Liberty loan drive, Sydney: DDA, no. 18, 17 February 1942; Liberty loan coverage: *Sydney Morning Herald*, *Canberra Times*, 18 February 1942.

208 Curtin unwell: 'Curtin ill', *Daily News*, Perth, 18 February 1942; message from Father McGrath warning Darwin of aircraft sighted over Bathurst Island: Douglas Lockwood, *Australia's Pearl Harbour: Darwin 1942*, Cassell, Melbourne, 1966, pp. 22–24.

209 DCA operator Acland: Lockwood, *Australia's Pearl Harbour*, pp. 40–42; Detail on bombing of Darwin, Lockwood, *Australia's Pearl Harbour*, pp. 57–59; Darwin bombing general background: Dennis (ed.) *The Oxford Companion to Australian Military History*, pp. 201–202; Odgers, *100 Years of Australians at War*, pp. 140–41; Japanese version of attack on Darwin and reason for the raid from Air Commander Mitsuo Fuchida: Fuchida and Okumiya, *Midway*, pp. 38–40.

210 USS *Peary* detail: E. Andrew Wilde Jr (ed.), *The USS Peary (DD-226) in World War II, Manila to Darwin, 12/10/41–2/19/42: Documents and Photographs*, E. Andrew Wilde, Needham, Massachusetts, 2007; Destoyer History Foundation, *USS Peary, Destroyer No. 226; DD 226*, http://destroyerhistory.org/flushdeck/usspeary; hospital ship *Manunda*: Allan S. Walker, *Australia in the War of 1939–45*, series 5, 'Medical', vol. 4, 'Medical services of the R.A.N. and R.A.A.F., with a section on women in the army medical services', AWM, Canberra, 1961, pp. 63–64.

211 Administrator Charles Abbott on attack: C. L. A. Abbott, *Australia's Frontier Province*, Angus & Robertson, Sydney, 1950, pp. 80–81; 21st Battalion letters intercepted by Commonwealth censors: 17–30

November 1941, dated 18 December 1941, NAA, A11743, 3 Attachment; Japanese spies as guests at Government House: Abbott, *Australia's Frontier Province*, pp. 133–34; NAA, A8911/1:11; Japanese espionage, NAA, A8911/1:8; further detail on Japanese activities obtained from historian– researcher Barbara Winter, Brisbane.

212 Commissioner Charles J. Lowe report, 27 March 1942: NAA, A431, 1949/687; air raids on Australian mainland, AWM, *Bombing of Darwin*, www.awm.gov.au/units/event_59.asp; Rex Ruwoldt and Jack Mulholland: *Sunday Territorian*, Darwin, souvenir edition, 19 February 2012, p. 8.

213 Author's description second bombing raid on Darwin, 19 February 1942: as seen on Japanese propaganda film archives, CriticalPast LLC, www.criticalpast.com/products/location_history/Darwin_Australia/1940/1942; air strength that day: Gillison, 'Royal Australian Air Force, 1939–1942', pp. 245–46.

214 Administrator Abbott's report to Department of the Interior, 27 February 1942, and Abbott on police sergeants: Grose, *An Awkward Truth*, pp. 158, 196, 211; Damage to Darwin: General Sturdee, Report on war damage to defence facilities and Darwin port, 23 February 1942, NAA, A2684, 872.

215 Front page report: 'Darwin bombed', *Daily News*, Perth, 19 February 1942; Curtin statements from hospital: *Sydney Morning Herald*, 20 February 1942; Curtin statement on change in war aim: DDA, no. 19, 16 February 1942.

216 Curtin statement on seventeen deaths: *The Argus*, 21 February 1942; Curtin to pressmen on 'interests of security' and death toll at Darwin: Grose, *An Awkward Truth*, pp. 183–84; Curtin on Japanese able to establish bridgehead on Australia: notes of Fred Smith, AAP bureau chief, Canberra, quoted in Clem Lloyd and Richard Hall (eds), *Backroom Briefings: John Curtin's War*, NLA, Canberra, 1997, p. 94; Hasluck quoting Frederick Shedden: Hasluck, *Diplomatic Witness*, pp. 43–45; 'Every city can face assault', Curtin: *Sydney Morning Herald*, 23 February 1942.

217 Tokyo Radio and Japanese daily newspaper editorial summaries: translations reprinted in English-language newspaper *Japan Times*, 21–23 February 1942.

218 How the Darwin attack came about: Fuchida and Okumiya, *Midway*, pp. 38–39; Colonel Kotani and Captain Tomioka clash over an invasion of Australia: Army General Staff, *Daihon'ei kimitsu senso nisshi*, entry for 20 February 1942, quoted in Henry P. Frei, *Japan's Southward*

Advance and Australia: From the Sixteenth Century to World War II, p. 166;
Australians 'shocked and scared stiff', *Japan Times*, 25 February 1942;
'Last vestiges of doubt' dissipated: 'War Comes to Australia', editorial,
The Age, 20 February 1942.

Chapter 9   'They're coming home!'

219 Surrender details and Singapore prisoner and casualty figures: Kirby,
Singapore, pp. 244–50; Odgers, *100 Years of Australians at War*, p. 137;
summaries in this chapter of Malaya and Singapore campaigns: Odgers,
100 Years of Australians at War, pp. 132–37; Dutch East Indies, pp. 141–46;
Malaya–Singapore, Dennis (ed.), *The Oxford Companion to Australian
Military History*, pp. 375–81, Dutch East Indies, pp. 418–20; Curtin on
Australia's scant air support: cable to Wavell, 19 February 1942, NAA,
A816, 52/302/142.

220 War cabinet approves new fighter interceptor (Boomerang), 18 February
1942: NAA, A5954, 807/2; RAAF Museum, *CAC Boomerang A46-30*,
www.airforce.gov.au/raafmuseum/exhibitions/hangar180/boomerang.
htm; AIF 6th and 7th divisions return to Australia: Wigmore, *The
Japanese Threat*, pp. 444–49; Mark Johnston, *The Silent Seventh: An
Illustrated History of the 7th Australian Division 1940–46*, Allen & Unwin,
Sydney, 2005, p. 77; General Kenney quoting generals Marshall and
Arnold on US casual attitude towards the Pacific: George C. Kenney,
General Kenney Reports: A Personal History of the Pacific War, Office of Air
Force History, United States Air Force, Washington DC, 1987, pp. 10–11.

221 Roosevelt to Morgenthau on Australia: Robert Dallek, *Franklin D.
Roosevelt and American Foreign Policy, 1932–1945*, Oxford University
Press, New York, 1995, p. 338; Message to Curtin from Dominions
Office and speculation about Darwin: cable from UK Dominions Office
to Sir Ronald Cross, UK High Commissioner in Australia, 2 March
1942, NAA, A2937, FAR EAST POSITION 1942; Curtin to Churchill,
4 March 1942, NAA, A816, 14/301/223A.

222 Japanese invasion of Timor: Wigmore, *The Japanese Thrust*, pp. 476–80;
AWM, *Fighting in Timor, 1942*, www.awm.gov.au/atwar/timor.asp;
Christopher C. H. Wray, *Timor 1942: Australian Commandoes at War with
the Japanese,* Hutchinson, Melbourne, 1987, pp. 14–15; Consul Ross on
Japanese troop strengths and state of commandoes: report to the govern-
ment, 28 July 1942, NAA, A6779, 21; Timor background: Wigmore, *The
Japanese Thrust*, pp. 466–74.

223 Life in Singapore under the Japanese, Sook Ching massacres; Chan Cheng Yean on the massacres: Beng Luan Tan and Irene Quah, *The Japanese Occupation 1942–1945*, National Heritage Board of Singapore, Times Editions, Singapore, 1996, pp. 67–74.

224 Colonel Masanobu Tsuji's involvement in massacres: statement by Major General Kiyotake Kawaguchi, despatch no. 1498, Harlan B. Clark, US Embassy Tokyo to State Department Washington, 30 June 1959; Wurth, *Saving Australia*, pp. 173, 243, 247, 275–76, 284.

225 Battles for Java, sinking of HMAS *Perth*: Hermon G. Gill, *Royal Australian Navy, 1939–1942*, pp. 621–22; Ronald McKie, *Proud Echo*, Angus & Robertson, Sydney, 1953, pp. 46–47, which narrates the experiences of ten survivors from the *Perth*; AWM, *The loss of HMAS Perth, 1 March 1942*, www.awm.gov.au/encyclopedia/perth/loss.asp

226 Seaman Frank McGovern: Veterans' Affairs, www.australiansatwar filmarchive.gov.au/aawfa/interviews/28.aspx; Michael Caulfield (ed.), *Voices of War: Stories from the Australians at War Film Archive*, Hodder, Sydney, 2006, pp. 161–90; Long, *The Six Years War*, pp. 165–167; http://www.navy.gov.au/hmas-perth-i

227 Background on *Perth* casualties: Dennis (ed.), *The Oxford Companion to Australian Military History*, p. 343; sinking of HMAS *Yarra*: Gill, *Royal Australian Navy, 1939–1942*, pp. 629–31; firing to the last: from a report identified as by John P. Murphy, of *Stronghold* in Gill, *Royal Australian Navy, 1939–1942*, p. 631.

228 Ronald Taylor ignoring orders: Greg Swindon,'*Their Finest Hour': The Story of Leading Seaman Ron Taylor and the Loss of HMAS* Yarra, *4 March 1942*, Naval Historical Society of Australia, Sydney, 1996; Curtin statement on loss of the *Perth* and the *Yarra*, Canberra, 13 March 1942: *West Australian*, 14 March 1942; Japanese operations in Dutch East Indies after the fall of Singapore: *Sydney Morning Herald*, 16–20 February 1941; Australians and the campaign in Java: Long, *The Six Years War*, pp. 165–169; John Coates, essay in Dennis (ed.), *The Oxford Companion to Australian Military History*, pp. 418–420; Wigmore, *The Japanese Thrust*, pp. 495–503.

229 Frank Forde on early casualty figures: statement, 12 March, DDA, no. 22, 11–25 March 1942; prisoners of the Japanese: Wigmore, *The Japanese Thrust*, pp. 511–12, 515.

230 Russell Braddon on Changi: Hank Nelson, *POW Prisoners of War: Australians Under Nippon*, ABC, Sydney, 1985, p. 34; Burma neglected

by British: S. Woodburn Kirby, *The War Against Japan*, vol. 2, 'India's Most Dangerous Hour', Navy and Military Press, Uckfield, UK, 2004, pp. 100–101; six changes in command structure, Kirby, 'India's Most Dangerous Hour', p. 103; Pownall on need for British withdrawal from Burma: Pownall diary, 25 January 1942, LHCMA, Pownall 2; Churchill's Pacific War Council established in London: *Canberra Times*, 17 February 1942 (Roosevelt had already established a Pacific War Council in Washington); Churchill on keeping Burma Road open to supply Chinese: Churchill to General Ismay, 20 January 1942, quoted in Churchill, *The Hinge of Fate*, p. 47.

231 Churchill's 'painful episode' in relations with Australia, 20 February 1942: quoted in Churchill, *The Hinge of Fate*, pp. 136–39; Japanese thrust into Burma and Wavell, quoting confident commanders, mid-February 1942: Wigmore, *The Japanese Thrust*, pp. 459–63; original plan for AIF redeployment and Curtin's reasoning on 7th Division diversion: telegram, Curtin to Churchill, 23 February 1942, quoted in Hasluck, 'The Government and the People, 1942–1945', pp. 74–75, 84.

232 Churchill agreeing that Australian troops and air squadrons overseas must move homewards for defence of Australia: minute 3 of the British war cabinet, 27 January 1942, NA CAB 65/29/8, p. 25; Page to Curtin on recommendation that seaborne Australian 7th Division be diverted to Burma, 18 February 1942: NAA, A816, 52/302/142; Churchill's threat of grave US repercussions to Curtin, 20 February 1942: Churchill, *The Hinge of Fate*, pp. 136–39.

233 Roosevelt backs Churchill's bid for Australian reinforcements in Burma, Casey to Curtin, 21 February 1942, NAA A981, WAR 33 I; Curtin's reply to Roosevelt: Curtin to Casey, 22 February 1942, NAA, A3196, 1942, 0.5404; Churchill on Burma and cables to Curtin and Roosevelt about diverting Australian reinforcements to Burma: Churchill, *The Hinge of Fate*, pp. 136–51; Churchill 'could not contemplate' an Australian refusal: Churchill, *The Hinge of Fate*, p. 143; NAA, A816, 52/302/142; 7th Division diversion by Churchill and Curtin's stress and responses: Day, *John Curtin*, pp. 452–58; Churchill's relationship with Curtin: Churchill, *The Hinge of Fate*, pp. 137–38; Curtin 'primary obligation to save Australia': Churchill, *The Hinge of Fate*, p. 144; NAA, A3196, 1942, 0.5424.

234 Curtin cable to Blamey, 20 February 1942: NAA, A3196, 1942, 0.5295.; *Sun Pictorial* newsman Harold Cox on two conversations with Curtin

in parliament about Australian troops at sea, Cox interview on Curtin's stress during Burma decision-making process: Harold Cox, oral history interview, 6 April 1973, NLA, ORAL TRC 121/43 and JCPML01060/1.

235 Frank Green recollecting Curtin's appearance and anxiety about 7th Division returning: Frank C. Green, *Servant of the House*, Heinemann, Melbourne, 1969, pp. 127–28.

236 Stanley Bruce on Cripps and Churchill's stress: Bruce to Curtin 23 February 1942, NAA M100, February 1942; Page supports Churchill: Hasluck, 'The Government and the People, 1942–1945', pp. 78–79; special envoy Page supporting Churchill's Burma relief plans: Mozley (ed.), *Truant Surgeon*, pp. 333–43.

237 Historian Lionel Wigmore on repercussions if Australians had landed at Rangoon: Wigmore, *The Japanese Thrust*, pp. 464–65; General Lavarack advice to Advisory War Council on Burma, Canberra, 24 February 1942: NAA, A5954, 813/2; General Hutton certain that Rangoon would fall despite reinforcements: Kirby, 'India's Most Dangerous Hour', pp. 103–104; Churchill did not inform Curtin of General Hutton's views: Kim E. Beazley, *John Curtin: An Atypical Labor Leader*, ANU Press, Canberra, 1972, p. 15; Curtin's decision correct, see strategic report from Australia's defence chiefs: Advisory War Council minutes, 28 February 1942, NAA, A5954, 813/2.

239 General Pownall on Australian troops and the Curtin Government's terror: Pownall diary, 25 February 1942, LHCMA, Pownall 2; Joe Alexander on secret intelligence from Curtin: J. A. Alexander, oral history interview with Mel Pratt, 2 March 1971, NLA, AGY009, SER0016 and JCPML00551; Elsie Curtin on her father's worries: Elsie Curtin, interview with Ronda Jamieson, 10 May 1994 and 20 February 1995, JCPML00012.

240 7th Division arrival and background: AWM, *Shaggy Ridge Operations*, www. awm.gov.au/units/event_347.asp; Eisenhower on Australia, Europe and new priorities: Eisenhower diary, quoted in Ferrell (ed.), *The Eisenhower Diaries*, 30 January 1942, pp. 46, 49, 50.

241 Churchill in conversation with George VI, 24 February 1942: John Wheeler-Bennett, *King George VI: His Life and Reign*, Macmillan, London, 1958, p. 538; Gilbert, *The Second World War*, pp. 303–304.

242 Gowrie on invasion and Curtin's plans for Defence Act changes: letter to George VI, 26 February 1942, Gowrie Papers, NLA, MS 2852.

243 Defence chiefs' views on Japanese threat to Australia: Strategic report from Australia's defence chiefs, Advisory War Council minutes, 28 February 1942, NAA, A5954, 813/2; General Blamey's apprehension: John Hetherington, *Blamey: The Biography of Field-Marshal Sir Thomas Blamey*, Cheshire, Melbourne, 1954, pp. 134–36.

Chapter 10   The last bastion

244 Imperial Army and Navy debates on Australia: *Senshi sosho: Japanese Army Operations in the South Pacific Area: New Britain and Papua Campaign, 1942–1943*, trans. Steven Bullard, AWM. The meeting of 27 February is discussed on pages 474–75, of vol. 35. Diary notes were taken by Commander Kowashi Sanagi; Sturdee and defence appreciation on Australia's vulnerability: 29 January 1942, NAA, A5954, 555/4 and A5954, 563/1; US troops in Australia, end of 1942: Hasluck, 'The Government and the People, 1942–1945', pp. 224–25.

245 Tokyo liaison conference detail: Hajime Sugiyama, diary entry for 28 February 1942, agenda item 4, in Hajime Sugiyama, *Sugiyama Memo*, Honbu Sanbo, Tokyo, 1967, trans. for the author by Kyal Hill, Tokyo.

246 Studies of isolating Australia and feasibility of invading Australia: Stephan, *Hawaii Under the Rising Sun*, pp. 106–107.

247 Shigetaro Shimada on Australia: Koichi Kido, *Kido Koichi nikki* (Kido Koichi Diaries), Tokyo University Press, Tokyo, 1966, pp. 927–28.

248 Shigetaro Shimada: interviewed by historian Gordon Prange, no. 1, 9 July 1947, Gordon W. Prange Papers, Special Collections, University of Maryland Libraries, College Park; Toshikazu Ohmae on Australia: US Interrogation Files, G-2, Historical Section, GHQ, Far East Command, quoted in Willoughby (ed.), *Reports of General MacArthur*, vol. 1, p. 38n; Governor-General Gowrie on invasion prospects: letter to George VI, 26 February 1942, Gowrie Papers, NLA, MS 2852.

249 Eisenhower on minimalising US role in south-west Pacific: Eisenhower memo for Marshall, 'Strategic conceptions and their applications to Southwest Pacific', 28 February 1942, George C. Marshall Library, Lexington, Virginia, RG165, Reel 105, item 2528.

250 Rabaul escapees reach Moresby early March: Osmar White, *Green Armour: The Story of the Fighting Men in New Guinea*, Wren Publishing, Melbourne, 1972, pp. 39–40; messages from 2/22nd Battalion survivors: Joanne and Jenny Evans, *Lost Lives: The Second World War and the Islands of New Guinea*, entries from an album kept by the family

of William Ladner's sister, www. jje.info/lostlives/transcripts/D00063. html

251 Lieutenant Bob Emery of the NGVR recollections of Madang bombing and rescue operation to New Britain: Bob Emery, *When the Japanese Bombed Madang*, transcript of interview, *Una Voce*, September 1996, Papua New Guinea Association of Australia, www.pngaa.net/Library/ BombMadang.html; J. K. McCarthy's exploits as coastwatcher: Eric Feldt, *The Coast Watchers*, Currey O'Neil, Melbourne, 1975, pp. 59–65.

252 Curtin welcomes Bennett into war cabinet for Malaya: report, 2 March 1942, NAA, A5954, 808/1; Bennett scorned by defence chiefs, Legg, *The Gordon Bennett Story*, p. 265.

253 Background on Broome and Wyndham air raids, 3 March 1942: AWM54 812/3/12 and AWM52, 5/27/1; Australia Remembers Taskforce, *Australia Remembers 1945–1995: Commemorating the 50th Anniversary of the End of World War II: Background Information*, Department of Veterans' Affairs, Canberra, 1994; Dutch aviators: W. F. A. (Gus) Winckel interviewed about Broome attack, *Dimensions in Time*, ABC TV, filmmaker David Batty, broadcast 23 April 2002; Winckel, Netherlands Ex-Servicemen and Women's Association, New South Wales Branch, www.neswa.org. au; Rod Torrington and Wyndham air raid, 3 March 1942: Roger Meyer, *The DCA's Role in the Second World War: Part 3*, www.airwaysmuseum. com

254 Catalina resilience: Flying Officer Cliff Hull oral history interview with Harry Martin, 1989, Keith Murdoch Sound Archive, AWM, S00734; air raids on Port Moresby, McCarthy, *South-West Pacific Area*, pp. 65–66; war correspondent on young troops, *Sydney Morning Herald* 8 August 1942.

255 War correspondent on young troops, *Sydney Morning Herald*, 8 August 1942; youngsters of the 39th, observations of Osmar White: White, *Green Armour*, p. 51; Japanese invasion of Lae and Salamaua, 7 March 1942: McCarthy, *South-West Pacific Area*, pp. 57–58.

256 US carrier raid on Lae and Salamaua: Morison, *History of the US Naval Operations in World War II*, vol. 3, 'The Rising Sun in the Pacific', pp. 388–89; liaison conference details, Tokyo, 4 March: *Sugiyama Memo*, diary entries for that date.

257 Japan's Foreign Office on British failure to assist Australia: Board of Information statement, 6 March 1942, Diplomatic Record office, Ministry of Foreign Affairs, Tokyo.

258 Board of Information statement on 'Salvation of Australia': 11 and 13 March 1942, Diplomatic Record Office, Ministry of Foreign Affairs, Tokyo; US assessment on invasion prospect: Japanese approaching Australia's doorstep, Willoughby (ed.), *Reports of General MacArthur*, vol. 1, pp. 26–27; General Brett on likely Japanese trust into Australia: Brett to Adjutant General, 4 March 1942, War Department file RG165, OPD 381, quoted in Dr Mark Jacobsen, 'Defence of Australia', *The Battle of the Coral Sea: Conference Proceedings, 7–10 May 1992*, Australian National Maritime Museum Sydney; Bennett on invasion in the north: broadcast, 8 March, reported in *Canberra Times*, 9 March 1942; *Times* of London on invasion of northern Australia: quoted in *The Mercury*, Hobart, 24 February 1942.

259 Curtin broadcast to the US, 14 March 1942: DDA, no. 22, 11–25 March 1942; Blamey on Japanese threat to Western Australia: Hetherington, *Blamey*, pp. 134–36.

260 Signal Roosevelt to MacArthur on Corregidor: 'Mac. Personal, Feb. 1942', MacArthur Memorial Archives, Norfolk, Virginia, R6–2: USAFFE, B.2, F.4; MacArthur on preparedness in the Philippines, 7 December 1942: MacArthur, *Reminiscences*, p. 114.

261 MacArthur and group leave Corregidor for Mindanao by boat and arrival in Australia: MacArthur, *Reminiscences*, pp. 140–45; MacArthur's 'primary object . . . relief of the Philippines', *The Advertiser*, Adelaide, 21 March 1942; MacArthur's arrival in Australia, including 'I shall return' statement: MacArthur, *Reminiscences*, pp. 145–46. (MacArthur in his *Reminiscences* says he addressed the press in Alice Springs when in fact it was at Terowie, South Australia.)

262 Curtin statement on McArthur's arrival: DDA, no. 22, 18 March 1942; Curtin 'take back that which has been lost': *The Argus*, 21 March 1942; General Brett on Australia at the time of MacArthur's arrival: quoted in Willoughby (ed.), *Reports of General MacArthur*, vol. 1, p. 37; MacArthur 'to begin offensive': *The Courier-Mail*, Brisbane, and *Canberra Times*, 21 March 1942.

263 Professor Stephen Roberts on the meaning of Curtin's arrival in Melbourne: *The Argus*, 21 March 1942; MacArthur told of shortages en route to Melbourne: Wesley Craven and John Cate, *The Army Air Force in World War II: The Pacific, Guadalcanal and Saipan*, University of Chicago Press, Chicago, 1950, pp. 410–11; Gamble, *Fortress Rabaul*, pp. 111–12; highly discouraging Australian situation: Willoughby (ed.),

Reports of General MacArthur, vol. 1, pp. 4, 22; Report of Organization and Activities, US Army Forces in Australia, AG GHQ 314.7; 'Great welcome to General MacArthur', *The Argus*, 23 March 1942.

264 MacArthur finds Australia 'desperate' and 'weak', with only five bombers in a condition to fly: MacArthur, *Reminiscences*, p. 152, 157; analysis of Japan's intentions: article by Professor Stephen Roberts in *The Argus* and *Canberra Times*, 21 March 1942.

265 Curtin and Churchill row over Australian Minister to the US Richard Casey's British appointment: Hudson and Stokes, *Documents on Australian Policy*, vol. V, notes pp. 658–59, 666–67; NAA, A3195, 1942, 1.11420, A3195, 1942, 1.11693; hero worship of MacArthur: *The Advertiser*, Adelaide, 24 March 1942; Bataan death march and 'Beat Hitler first' policy, MacArthur, *Reminiscences*, pp. 146–47.

266 Corregidor surrender: Louis Morton, *The Fall of the Philippines*, Center of Military History, US Army, Washington DC, 1953, pp. 460, 564.

267 MacArthur speech at parliamentary dinner, 26 March 1942: *Sun News Pictorial* and *The Argus*, 27 March 1942; General Herring at Darwin and build-up of forces and facilities in in the north: McCarthy, *South West Pacific Area*, pp. 72–74; Paul Hasluck, 'The Government and the People, 1942–1945', p. 224; AWM, *United States Forces in Australia*, www.awm. gov.au/encyclopedia/homefront/us_forces; Curtin speech in parliament, 25 March 1942, DDA, no. 23, JCPML00110/28.

268 US servicemen in Australia and return of AIF in 1942: minutes of Advisory War Council, 1 April 1942, NAA, A5954, 554/4; diversion of part of 6th Division to Ceylon: McCarthy, *South West Pacific Area*, pp. 78–79; AWM, *2/6th Battalion*, www.awm.gov.au/units/unit_11257. asp; Professor Hiromi Tanaka on Curtin and MacArthur: interview with the author, Tokyo, 24 May 2011, interpreters Haijime Muratani and Kyal Hill.

269 MacArthur finds a concept of 'passive defense' in Australia and first meeting with Curtin in Canberra: MacArthur, *Reminiscences*, pp. 151–52.

270 War cabinet and scorched-earth policy, 4 February 1942: NAA, A5954, 807/2; secret plans made by army authorities: *Cairns Post*, 2 February 1942; Curtin statement on purpose of scorched-earth policy: *Army News*, Darwin, 5 February 1942; demolition orders: NAA, BP262/2, 9352; Curtin letter to Queensland premier, 30 July 1942, and war cabinet: NAA, A2671, 182/1942; Curtin's circulars to state premiers, 30 July 1942 and 26 May 1943: State Records of Western Australia, AN68/1,

Acc 1005, Acc 756/42, JCPML00169/1 (the emphasis in first circular is Curtin's); MacArthur on 'dangerous defeatism' in Australia: MacArthur, *Reminiscences*, p. 151; Mining transport facilities in Cairns: Timothy Bottoms, *Defending the North: Frontline Cairns (1940–1946) – An Historical Overview*, etropic, vol. 8, 2009, www.jcu.edu.au/etropic/ET8/Bottoms.htm

Chapter 11   Churchill's 'lesser war'

272 Joint US and Australian assessments on Japanese moves: message from MacArthur to General Marshall in Washington, No. 70, CM-IN 1069, 4 April 1942; Samuel Milner, *United States Army in World War II: The War in the Pacific*, US Department of the Army, Washington DC, 1957, p. 25; Assessment in US signals in April 1942: G-3 GHQ, SWPA Journal and AHQ operational instruction no. 50, 9 April 42, G-3, SWPA Admin 370 (S), in Willoughby (ed.), *Reports of General MacArthur*, vol. 1, p. 34.

273 Defence appreciation sent to Evatt: Advisory War Council minute 893, 'Defence of Australia: Appreciation for Dr Evatt', 8 April 1942, NAA, A5954, 563/1.

274 Cables Churchill to Curtin: 30 March and 1 April 1942, in Advisory War Council minutes, NAA, A5954, 814/1; Curtin/MacArthur proposal for Australia as a base for offensive action: 17 April 1942, NAA, A981, WAR 33, Attachment C; Evatt to Curtin, 19 April 1942, NAA, A4764, 2; Lord Gowrie letter to George VI on situation in Australia and Curtin's health: 14 April 1942, Gowrie Papers, NLA, MS 2852/5/14.

275 Brooke on Indian Ocean and Australia and New Zealand: Brooke diary, 7 April 1942, and notes for his memoirs, quoted in Arthur Bryant, *The Turn of the Tide 1939–1943: A Study Based on the Diaries and Autobiographical Notes of Field Marshal the Viscount Alan Brooke*, pp. 282–83.

276 Churchill to Bruce on invasion: 3 April 1942, NA, CHAR 20/53B/178–179; British defence chiefs and Churchill on US and Japan: Minutes of Defence Committee at War Cabinet, 16 April 1942, NA, CAB 69/4; Curtin's private discussion with Gavin Long regarding offensive from Australia: Gavin Long, diary, 2 October 1943, referring to his notes of April 1942, AWM67, 1/3.

277 Japanese plans to invade Port Moresby and Tulagi: US GHQ, 10 September 1947, Far East Command, *Statements of Japanese Officials*, vols. 3–4; Sadatoshi Tomioka, *Kaisen to Shusen*, pp. 116–18; Australia and Japanese Navy High Command priorities: Hiroyuki Shindo, 'Japanese

air operations over New Guinea during the Second World War', *Journal of the Australian War Memorial*, vol. 34, June 2001.

278 Hiromi Tanaka on reasons for invasion of Port Moresby and Tulagi: Tanaka, 'Japan in the Pacific War and New Guinea', pp. 32–34.

279 Higashikuni's conversation with Tojo: Auer (ed.), *From Marco Polo Bridge to Pearl Harbor*, pp. 170–71, quoting Higashikuni, *Ichi-kozoku no Senso Nikki (War Diary by an Imperial Family Member)*, Nihoa Shuhosha, Tokyo, 1957, p. 106; Tojo denial of invasion plans for Australia while awaiting execution: Oliver A. Gillespie, *The Official History of New Zealand in the Second World War, 1939–1945: The Pacific*, Historical Publications Branch, Wellington, 1952, p. 211; Shigemitsu on invasion of Port Moresby and crossing to Darwin: Shigemitsu, *Japan and Her Destiny*, pp. 275–76; Tojo statement on Australia and invasion: Gill, *Royal Australian Navy, 1939–1942*, p. 643.

280 Australia 'has weakened her defences': *Washington Post*, 20 March 1942; Mrs Cronin and rings sent to Curtin and returned: prime minister's correspondence, 20 March 1942, NAA, M1415, 40 (a ring keeper is a cheaper ring to prevent the loss of a valuable ring).

281 Airstrip construction, Mareeba: Bottoms, 'Defending the North'; Churchill on war in the Pacific: Parliamentary Debates, House of Commons Official Report, 27 January 1942; House of Commons confidence debate, Hansard, 27–28 January 1942.

282 Churchill's House of Commons secret speech, 23 April 1942: NA, CHAR 9/155A/34; Charles Eade (ed.), *Winston Churchill's Secret Session Speeches*, Simon & Schuster, New York, 1946, pp. 51–88; *Life* magazine, New York, 28 January 1946; Churchill's handwritten changes to speech deleting Japan as the 'minor enemy': NA, CHAR/9/155A/95; Churchill's scored-out paragraph: pp. 2 and 3 of his notes, NA, CHAR9/155A/36 and 37.

283 Parliamentary proceedings in secret sessions: Thomas Erskine May, *Erskine May's Treatise on the Law, Privileges, Proceedings and Usage in Parliament*, Butterworth, London, 1976, pp. 308–309.

286 Curtin in UK/Australian broadcast: 28 April 1942 in London, 29 April 1942 in Australia, text in Gowrie Papers, NLA, MS 2852 and JCPML00652/1/14. (After the war, both the Australian Government and opposition did not encourage 'unproductive post-mortems' and reaction to the release of Churchill's secret speech was generally somewhat muted); Admiral King on threat to Melanesia and Australia before Coral Sea Battle: King, *US Navy at War 1941–1945*, pp. 45–46.

287   MO operation and Coral Sea Battle: Morison, *History of the US Naval Operations in WWII*; Port Moresby the key to dominance: Morison, *History of the United States Naval Operations*, vol. 4, p. 10.

288   Proposed carrier attack on Townsville and seizure of islands: Morison, *History of the US Naval Operations in WWII*, pp. 10–13; operation during 1–6 May 1942, Morison, *History of the US Naval Operations in WWII*, pp. 21–28; Long, *The Six Years War*, pp. 190–92; war situation beginning of May 1942: McCarthy, *South West Pacific Area*, pp. 79–82.

289   Admiral Crace and attacks on his Anzac force ships by Japanese and American aircraft: Gill, *Royal Australian Navy, 1942–1945*, pp. 49–50.

290   Captain Harry Howden's techniques: R Scrivener, 'This Man Howden – Captain Harry L. Howden, CBE, RAN', Naval Historical Society of Australia Review, December 1974, www.navyhistory.org.au/this-man-howden-captain-harry-l-howden-cbe-ran

292   Curtin statement on Coral Sea Battle in the House of Representatives, 8 May 1942, DDA No. 28; Don Rodgers on Curtin's address: JCPML00497/1/10; Shigemitsu on effects of Coral Sea Battle: Shigemitsu, *Japan and Her Destiny,* pp. 275–76.

293   Admiral Ugaki diary on Coral Sea Battle: Ugaki, *Fading Victory*, p. 124.

294   Admiral King on threat to Australia after Coral Sea Battle: King, *US Navy at War 1941–1945*, p. 47.

295   Gowrie on lull after Coral Sea Battle: letter to George VI, 19 May 1942, Gowrie Papers, NLA, MS 2852/5/14; cable from Curtin in Canberra to Evatt in London, 13 May 1942: NAA, A981, WAR 33, Attachment C.

296   MacArthur tells Curtin of possible 'disaster' and Churchill complains about requests to Roosevelt: Gavin Long, *MacArthur as Military Commander*, Combined Publishing, Pennsylvania, 1969, p. 98, plus note; Curtin on coal disputes: DDA, no. 29, 13–21 May 1942 and no. 30, JCPML00110/34 and 35; editorials and news items: *Sydney Morning Herald*, 12 May and 14 May 1942, *Canberra Times*, 14 May 1942.

297   Curtin 'worried himself sick' over strikes and industrial background: Hasluck, 'The Government and the People, 1939–1941', Appendix 6, pp. 603–608; Japan's successful war situation in May 1942: Wigmore, *The Japanese Thrust*, pp. 507–508.

298   Evatt cable from London to Curtin revealing details of the 'Beat Hitler first' strategy, 28 May 1942: NAA, A4764, 2; MacArthur on 'other factors': notes on address to the Advisory War Council, 26 March 1942, NAA, A5954, 3/5.

299   Evatt cable from London to Curtin and Churchill's promises: 28 May 1942, NAA, A4764, 2; Lord Gowrie concerns for Curtin: letter to Viceroy of India, Lord Linlithgow (Victor Hope), 14 January 1943, Gowrie Papers, NLA, MS 2852/5.

Chapter 12   Pacific turning point

300   Preparations for midget submarine raid on Sydney: pilot Susumu Ito interview with author, 11 August 2007, Iwakuni, Japan, interpreter Kyal Hill.

301   Navy Office summary report on midget attack with reference to 'no reported submarine activity' on east coast since 16 May: report dated 1 August 1942, AWM124, 4/474; sinking of *Wellen*: Gill, *Royal Australian Navy, 1942–1945*, pp. 62–63, www.awm.gov.au/collection/records/awmohww2/navy/vol2/ awmohww2-navy-vol2-ch3.pdf. (Note: Gill uses the Japanese identification *M-14* for Ban's midget. The Australian identification was *M-24*, corresponding with the number for the mother sub).

302   Navy Office report, 1 August 1942, referring to a 'good deal of traffic', reason for errors: AWM124, 4/474.

303   James Cargill on finding something in the net: letter to Rear Admiral Muirhead-Gould, 3 June 1942, archives, Maritime Services Board of NSW, Sydney; progress of second midget: Katsuhisa Ban in letter quoted in Lewis Lind, *The Midget Submarine Attack on Sydney*, Bellrope Press, Sydney, p. 21; midget in boom net and reactions: Horace Doyle reminiscences, AWM, PRO3229; James Nelson in Carruthers, Steven L., *Japanese Submarine Raiders, 1942*, Casper Publications, Sydney, 2006, p. 136. (For extensive coverage of the midget submarine raid on Sydney Harbour, see Bob Wurth, *1942: Australia's Greatest Peril*, Pan Macmillan, Sydney, 2010, pp. 221–43.)

304   USS *Chicago* opens fire on *M-24* and Garden Island wharf witness: Gill, *Royal Australian Navy, 1942–1945*, p. 68; *Kuttabul* sinking: Ernest Jamieson recollection in AWM, PR03013; aboard *Kuttabul*: Neil Roberts's statement, AWM PO2534.001; Lord and Lady Gowrie at Admiralty House: letter from Gowrie to George VI, 9 June 1942 and attached draft of same letter, Gowrie Papers, NLA, MS 2852/5/14; details of harbour firing in attack: Navy Office summary report, 1 August 1942, AWM124, 4/474; chaos on Sydney Harbour: *Sydney Morning Herald*, 2 June 1942.

305   Trawler *San Michele* spots submarine: sub signals 1 Jun, 1942, NAA B6121/3, 162K; HMAS *Yandra* strikes the midget M-22, see http://www.

navy.gov.au/hmas-yandra; ferries ordered to keep operating: Muirhead-Gould in appendix B, preliminary report, 22 June 1942, BS 1518/201/37; Official report of Rear Admiral in Charge of Sydney Harbour Defences, 16 July 1942, BS1749/201/37, and background in NAA, A6769, MUIRHEAD-GOULD GC.

306 Communique issued by Defence Headquarters: quoted in *Sydney Morning Herald*, 2 June 1942; Makin on Sydney raid: 2 June 1942, DDA, no. 30, JCPML00110/35; 'exciting experience': *Sydney Morning Herald*, 2 June 1942.

307 Raid on Moresby: George Johnston, *War Diary 1942*, Collins, Sydney, 1984, p. 58; Japanese reconnaissance of Gona and Buna: Gill, *Royal Australian Navy, 1942–1945*, pp. 75–76; attack on the *Barwon* and suspicious sighting by the *Canberra* near Cape Moreton: *Sydney Morning Herald*, 2 June 1942.

308 Suspicious sighting by the *Canberra* near Cape Moreton: Gill, *Royal Australian Navy, 1942–1945*, pp. 75–76; reports of submarine shelling of Sydney, including M. Lanham at 'Woollahra': *Sydney Morning Herald*, 8 June 1942, and other newspapers.

309 Curtin defence statement regarding destruction of seven and probably eight Japanese submarines: 7 June 1942, DDA, no. 30, JCPML00110/35; Susumu Ito on Newcastle shelling: interviewed by the author, 11 August 2007, Iwakuni, Japan; details of RAN funeral service for the four submariners: Major G. B. Walker to Muirhead-Gould, 8 June 1942, Hedinger to Kawai, c. 15 June 1942, NAA, 3741/5, V/11189; see also return of submariners' ashes in Wurth, *1942: Australia's Greatest Peril*, pp. 276–77, 289–91.

310 Discovery of the *M-24*: Bob Wurth, 'Midget sub discovery stirs ghosts of the past', *Sydney Morning Herald*, 13 December 2006; Coalmine strikes: editorial, *The Argus*, 4 June 1942.

311 Combined intelligence establishment in Australia and Ultra background: Jack Bleakley, *The Eavesdroppers: The Best Kept Secret of World War 2*, self published, Melbourne, 1992, pp. xiv–11; Special Intelligence Organisation: NAA, A5799, 104, 1941; Ultra: Dennis (ed.), *The Oxford Companion to Australian Military History*, p. 598; Melbourne special group established: memo, Colonel C. G. Roberts, Director of Military Intelligence, NAA. A6923, 51/2.

312 Details of 'Ultra Top Secret' intercepts received in Australia concerning Midway attack: NAA, B5555, 4.

314 Doolittle raid on Tokyo: Morrison, *History of the United States Naval Operations, Vol. 3*, pp. 389–398; Fuchida on Yamamoto's thinking about Midway operation: Fuchida and Okumiya, *Midway*, pp. 76–79.

315 Japanese Carrier Strike Force advancing on Midway and lack of Japanese intelligence: Fuchida and Okumiya, *Midway*, pp. 123–30; Curtin's confident Liberty loan speech: 2 June 1942, DDA, no. 16.

316 Fuchida's eyewitness account from the *Akagi*: Fuchida and Okumiya, *Midway*, pp. 177–79.

317 Sinking of the *Yorktown*: recollections of Lieutenant Joseph P. Pollard, History section, Bureau of Medicine and Surgery, US Navy, archives of Naval Historical Center, Washington.

318 Dive bombers sink carriers: Morison, *History of United States Naval Operations in World War II*, vol. IV, pp. 121–31.

319 Midway background: Morison, *History of United States Naval Operations in World War II*, vol. IV, pp. 87–93; sinking of *Hiryu*, Morison, *History of United States Naval Operations in World War II*, vol. IV, pp. 132–40; Admiral Nimitz quote on use of intelligence: Morison, *History of United States Naval Operations in World War II*, vol. IV, pp. 156–59.

320 Japanese Government propaganda campaign six months after Hirohito's war declaration: *Japan Times*, 8 June 1942; Curtin discloses to reporters secret intelligence on Midway: Joe Alexander diary, 8 June 1942, NLA, MS 2389.

321 MacArthur 'security of Australia has now been assured': MacArthur meeting with Curtin, Melbourne, 11 June 1942, NAA, A461/7, R4/1/12; Professor David Black on Curtin and public's war effort: Day, *John Curtin*, pp. 475–76; David Black, *The General and the Prime Minister: Douglas MacArthur and John Curtin*, http://john.curtin. edu.au/macarthur/print.html#; Curtin broadcast on invasion threat remaining: 17 June 1942, JCPML00652/2/9; Curtin 'whipping up of the fear of invasion': historian Dr Peter Stanley, 'Remembering 1942' conference, AWM, 2002 (Dr Stanley retracted this statement in 2008); Curtin's fears and Rowell on decision to send wrong troops to Moresby: Rowell, Foreword, in Raymond Paull, *Retreat from Kokoda*, Heinemann, Melbourne, 1958, p. xv; Japanese troops strength and gains in Rabaul, East Indies, Borneo and northeast coast of New Guinea: *US Strategic Bombing Survey: Air Campaigns of the Pacific War*, Military Analysis Division, July 1947, US Government Printing Office, pp. 13–14.

323 John Dedman on danger persisting into 1943: unpublished manuscript, 1 August 1969, Papers of John Dedman, NLA, MS 987, pp. 40–42; David Horner on invasion not eventuating: David Horner lecture, Curtin University of Technology, 5 October 2006, JCPML01044; Northern Australia invasion option kept open: Paul S. Dull, *A Battle History of the Imperial Japanese Navy 1941–1945*, Naval Institute Press, Annapolis, Maryland, 1978, p. 118; Curtin and Ultra, *The Canberra Times*, 11 May 1942; Curtin's actions in Layton, Edwin T., *And I was there*, Bluejacket Books, Annapolis, 2006, pp 416–419.

Chapter 13   Tragedy and retreat

324 Sailing of the *Montevideo Maru* from Rabaul and sinking on 1 July 1942 by the USS *Sturgeon*: Wigmore, *The Japanese Thrust*, pp. 593, 674; Ian Hodges, 'The sinking of the *Montevideo Maru*', AWM talk, 1 July 2002, AWM PASU0174, www.awm.gov.au/atwar/remembering1942/monte-video/transcript.asp.

325 USS *Sturgeon*: Gamble, *Darkest Hour*, pp. 226–28; report of Major Williams in Tokyo on *Montevideo Maru*, 6 October 1945: AWM54, 779/1/1; Mrs Frances Ryan on pension and suffering of family: letter to Prime Minister Chifley, 9 December 1946, NAA, A1066, IC45/55/3/19; additional information, Member of Ballarat, Catherine King, House of Representatives, 21 June, 2010, Hansard.

326 *Montevideo Maru* POWs: Yoshiaki Yamaji and Professor Hank Nelson, ABCTV, *7.30 Report*, 6 October 2003, reporter Mark Simkin, www.abc.net. au/7.30/content/2003/s961016.htm

327 British Government declines to accept Curtin's refusal on Spitfires: Gillison, 'Royal Australian Air Force, 1939–1942', pp. 650–651; Curtin's Pacific concerns and Spitfires: diary notes, 30 June and 1 July 1942, Fred Smith, bureau chief of the newsagency Australian United Press (AUP), quoted in Lloyd and Hall, *Backroom Briefings*, pp. 49–51.

328 Bert Kienzle on Japanese raids, cavalier expeditions and essential air drops: report to ANGAU, quoted in McCarthy, *South West Pacific Area*, pp. 117–18.

329 MacArthur background and speaking at Curtin's off-the-record press conference in Canberra, 17 July 1942: typed 'secret' transcript of diary of Joe Alexander, NLA, MS 2389, 12/4/11; Kenney's meeting with MacArthur in Brisbane in August 1942 on poor state of US air force: Kenney, *General Kenney Reports*, pp. 31–32.

330 Major General Gordon Maitland on Australia's plight: notes to the author, 23 February 2013; Gordon Maitland, *The Battle History of the Royal New South Wales Regiment: 1939–1945*, Kangaroo Press, Sydney, 2001, pp. 326–29; planning of second Port Moresby invasion attempt (RI Operation Study), including Prince Takeda of 17th Army on road to Port Moresby, *Senshi sosho*, pp. 109–117.

331 Tsuji's planning work: *Senshi Sosho*, p. 122; invasion force leaves Rabaul: *Senshi sosho*, pp. 124–25 (the history makes no mention of Tsuji's involvement in atrocities); Professor Dull on *Senshi sosho*: Paul S. Dull, *A Battle History of the Imperial Japanese Navy 1941–1945*, p. 133.

332 Eric Damai and trek from Gona to Buna: from the author's Kokoda Track essays for *Sydney Morning Herald*, May–June 1977; MacArthur disregards second threat to Port Moresby: David Horner, 'High command and the Kokoda Campaign', AWM 2002 History Conference – Remembering 1942, www.awm.gov.au/events/conference/2002/horner.asp

333 Last letter from Mavis Parkinson: to her parents, 5 August 1942, *Australian Women's Weekly*, 1 May 1943, Ruth Henrich, *South Sea Epic: War and the Church in New Guinea*, Society for the Propagation of the Gospel, London, 1944, http://anglicanhistory.org/aus/png/epic1944/08.html

334 Report of Justice William Webb: NAA, A10943, 1; missionaries killed: McCarthy, *South West Pacific Area*, p. 139; Margaret Bride, *I Wait for the Lord*, online resource book of the Martyrs of Papua and New Guinea, Anglican Board of Mission, Australia, www.abmission.org; atrocities on Buna beach: *Canberra Times*, 17 May 1943, *The Times*, London, 18 May 1943, *Sydney Morning Herald*, 11 September 1945; Paull, *Retreat from Kokoda*, p. 51. (Details of exactly when and how each of the victims of the Japanese was killed sometimes differ.)

335 Bert Kienzle prepares staging posts: interviewed by the author at Mamba Estate near Kokoda, 26 May 1977, broadcast on 2BL, ABC Radio, Sydney and other stations; formation of 39th Battalion: AWM, *39th Battalion (Hawthorn Kew Regiment)*, www.awm.gov.au/units/unit_11908.asp

337 Seizure of Kokoda and death of Colonel Owen: described by Charlie Pyke in Patrick Lindsay, *The Spirit of Kokoda: Then and Now*, Hardie Grant, Melbourne, 2003, pp. 38–41; Owen and re-occupying Kokoda: McCarthy, *South West Pacific Area*, pp. 126–28.

338 Retreat to Deniki and Kienzle's discovery of Lake Myola: Paull, *Retreat from Kokoda*, pp. 66–69; Curtin's sickness in early August: *Daily Telegraph*,

16 August 1942; Curtin to Churchill on landing in Papua: cable, 30 July 1942, NAA, A4763.

339 Tojo broadcast warning Australians: *Sydney Morning Herald*, 28 July 1942; Kokoda Track topography and weather: Bert Kienzle interview with the author, 26 May 1977; author walking the Track, *Sydney Morning Herald* and ABC Radio series, May–June 1977; Kienzle on 'some of the roughest country': McCarthy, *South West Pacific Area*, p. 117; MacArthur on move away from passive defence: MacArthur, *Reminiscences*, p. 133.

340 General Morris and supply difficulties over Kokoda Track: McCarthy, *South West Pacific Area*, p. 140.

341 Morris replaced by General Rowell: McCarthy, *South West Pacific Area*, p. 140; Guadalcanal and Tulagi: John Miller Jnr, *United States Army in World War II, Guadalcanal: The First Offensive*, BDD Special Editions (first printed by Center of Military History), Washington DC, 1949, pp. 1–16; Odgers, *100 Years of Australians at War*, pp. 158–60; Admiral King and US politics: H. W. Brands, *Traitor to His Class*, Anchor Books, New York, 2009, pp. 680–81; King quotes on offensive: *US Navy at War 1941–1945*, www.ibiblio.org/ hyperwar/USN/USNatWar/USN-King-1.html - V

342 HMAS *Canberra*: Gill, *Royal Australian Navy, 1942–1945*, pp. 144–45, http://www.awm.gov.au/collection/records/awmohww2/navy/vol2/awmohww2-navy-vol2-ch5.pdf

343 Major Cameron and Maroubra force: Paull, *Retreat from Kokoda*, pp. 70–71.

344 Deniki fighting: McCarthy, *South West Pacific Area*, pp. 134–37; Colonel Honner at Isurava: Lindsay, *The Spirit of Kokoda*, pp. 46–52.

345 Japanese destroy US aircraft at Moresby: Paull, *Retreat from Kokoda*, p. 105; Lindsay, *The Spirit of Kokoda*, p. 53.

346 Withdrawing along the Track and Kienzle redoubling carrier effort: McCarthy, *South West Pacific Area*, pp. 196–98; Horii's forces for Kokoda campaign: McCarthy, *South West Pacific Area*, p. 145; Kingsbury VC: McCarthy, *South West Pacific Area*, p. 206; Lieutenant Avery on Kingsbury: Lindsay, *The Spirit of Kokoda*, pp. 79–80.

347 Withdrawal from Isurava to Alola: McCarthy, *South West Pacific Area*, pp. 199–210; 2/14th difficulties and casualties: McCarthy, *South West Pacific Area*, pp. 211–13.

348 Osmar White on Kokoda Track: oral history interview with Peter Jepperson, 1990, Keith Murdoch Sound Archive, AWM, S00981; White, *Green Armour*, pp. 196–97, 202–204.

349   Professor Hiromi Tanaka on the Japanese Kokoda campaign and potential threat to Australia: interviewed by the author, Tokyo, 24 May 2011;
Tanaka, 'Japan in the Pacific War and New Guinea'.

Chapter 14   Taking the offensive
351   State of Japanese and US navies mid-1942: US Naval Institute, *The
Imperial Japanese Navy after Midway*, 23 July 2009, http://blog.usni.
org/2009/07/23/ the-imperial-japanese-navy-after-midway
352   Evatt to Admiral King: cable, 14 August 1942, NAA, A981, WAR 33,
Attachment C; strategy of Milne Bay for Allies and Japanese: McCarthy,
South West Pacific Area, pp. 145, 155.
353   2/12th Battalion at Milne Bay: AWM, *2/12th Battalion*, www.awm.gov.
au/ units/unit_11263.asp; background: Dr Peter Londey, *Remembering
1942: Milne Bay, 5 September 1942*, www.awm.gov.au/atwar/remembering1942/milnebay/transcript.asp; AWM, *Battle of Milne Bay*, www.
awm.gov.au/units/event_345.asp
354   Sergeant Colin Hoy: Peter Brune, *A Bastard of a Place: The Australians
in Papua*, Allen & Unwin, Sydney, 2004, p. 272; Major General Clowes
occupying and building the Milne Bay defences: Brune, *A Bastard of a
Place*, pp. 263, 269–71; RAAF's Colin Lindeman talks about Milne Bay:
oral history interview, 19 May 1989, Keith Murdoch Sound Archive,
AWM, S00548.
355   Primitive conditions of Milne Bay airfield: Colin Lindeman oral history
interview, 19 May 1989, and Bruce Brown, oral history interview, 9 June
1989, Keith Murdoch Sound Archive, AWM, S00548 and S00583.
356   Fighting in the first days of the Japanese landing, McCarthy, *South West
Pacific Area*, pp. 166–72; Gili Gili defence, McCarthy, *South West Pacific
Area*, pp. 160–61; Arthur Gould on flying Kittyhawks over Japanese:
Michael Caulfield, *Voices of War: Stories from the Australians at War
Film Archive*, Hodder, Sydney, 2006, p. 128; General Rowell and Major
General Clowes: McCarthy, *South West Pacific Area*, pp. 155, 158–59;
MacArthur's concerns about Clowes and Milne Bay: McCarthy, *South
West Pacific Area*, pp. 173–75.
357   Attack on number three strip: 31 August 1942, Brune, *A Bastard of a
Place*, pp. 358–61; General Clowes: Karl James, 'General Clowes of Milne
Bay', *Wartime* magazine, AWM, no. 59, July 2012, www.awm.gov.au/
wartime/59/ general-clowes; ensuring Japanese were dead: McCarthy,
South West Pacific Area, pp. 177–78; actions of Corporal John French

and detail from the recommendation that French be awarded the VC: McCarthy, *South West Pacific Area*, pp. 182–83; Long, *The Six Years War*, p. 214.

358 Point King, Milne Bay, mutilations and murders: McCarthy, *South West Pacific Area*, pp. 177–78.

359 Report by Justice Sir William Webb into Japanese atrocities at Milne Bay: NAA, A10943, 2, pp. 122–25 and J1889, BL43895/14; Japanese officers ordered atrocities: evidence at the Tokyo War Crime Trials, *West Australian*, 3 January 1947; Australian war crimes trials summary: Sissons, 'Sources on Australian investigations into Japanese war crimes in the Pacific', *Journal of the Australian War Memorial*, no. 30, April 1997, www.awm.gov.au/journal/ j30/sissons.asp

360 Cook shooting a Japanese pilot: RAAF Kittyhawk pilot Arthur Gould of 75 Squadron, video interview, Department of Veterans' Affairs, http:// kokoda.commemoration.gov.au/australian-veterans-accounts/veterans-accounts_arthur-gould.php; Curtin ill, premiers' conference: *Sydney Morning Herald*, 10 August 1942; Curtin tells premiers of 'life and death struggle': *Canberra Times* and *The Argus*, 11 August 1942; Curtin neuritis and rheumatism and 'brooding in the dark': *Daily Telegraph*, 16 August 1942, JCPML00964/68.

361 Curtin's worries about Moresby and Darwin, announces austerity campaign: national broadcast by the prime minister, 3 September 1942, DDA, no. 39, JCPML00110/44; Curtin on holding Milne Bay at press briefing: notes from Fred Smith, 28 August 1942, Lloyd and Hall (eds), *Backroom Briefings*, p. 79.

362 Benefits of Milne Bay campaign and MacArthur to Marshall, 6 September 1942, seeking ships: McCarthy, *South West Pacific Area*, pp. 187–88; Vasey on GHQ, Rowell on Kokoda Track threat to Moresby: McCarthy, *South West Pacific Area*, p. 225.

363 MacArthur on Australians unable to match enemy: McCarthy, *South West Pacific Area*, p. 225; disenchanted Curtin, 9 September 1942, on Admiral King visit and US priorities: media briefing notes by Fred Smith, Lloyd and Hall (eds), *Backroom Briefings*, pp. 82–83; Japanese lack rations: McCarthy, *South West Pacific Area*, p. 86.

364 Curtin's fears of invasion: letter to Dixon for Roosevelt, 11 September 1942, and reply from Roosevelt, 16 September 1942, Defence: Special Collection II, Bundle 5, Strategical Policy-SWPA, File No. 3, 48/1942 and NAA, A981, WAR 33, Attachment C; Curtin review of defence

policy in parliament: 7 October 1942, NAA, A5954, 587/7; Osmar White on the Kokoda Track and diggers not prepared: White, *Green Armour*, p. 198.

365 Couldn't see enemy: White, *Green Armour*, p. 200; Osmar White passes Digger with leg blown off: Paull, *Retreat from Kokoda*, p. 174; 53rd Battalion 'folding up' and 'spectator to disaster', White, *Green Armour*, pp. 201–202.

366 Signalman Norman Ensor: *Battle for Australia*, DVD, Battle for Australia Commemoration Committee NSW Inc., The History Channel, Foxtel; Japanese mountain guns and death of Sergeant Sid Johnston: told by Sergeant Dudley Warhurst, quoted in Lindsay, *The Spirit of Kokoda*, p. 109.

367 Sergeant Eric Williams of 2/16th on Ioribaiwa shelling: video interview, Department of Veterans' Affairs, http://kokoda.commemoration.gov. au/ australian-veterans-accounts/veterans-accounts_eric-williams.php; withdrawal to Imita Ridge and ramifications: McCarthy, *South West Pacific Area*, pp. 230–33; Japanese starving, Paull, *Retreat From Kokoda*, pp. 227–28.

368 Conversation about withdrawal between Allen and Eather: Steve Eather, *Desert Sands, Jungle Lands: A Biography of Major General Ken Eather*, Allen & Unwin, Sydney, 2003, p. 75; Imita Ridge artillery: Brune, *A Bastard of a Place*, p. 240; Lindsay, *The Spirit of Kokoda*, pp. 184–85; description of Golden Staircase and route to Owers' Corner: author's recollection from 1977 trek; Brune, *A Bastard of a Place*, p. 85.

369 Curtin note of Secraphone conversation between MacArthur and Curtin: Canberra, 17 September 1942, Defence: Special Collection II, Bundle 5, Strategical Policy – SWPA, File No. 3, 48/1942; MacArthur and Australian 'lack of efficiency' on Kokoda Track: McCarthy, *South West Pacific Area*, pp. 246–49; MacArthur requests to Curtin on Blamey and Rowell: Curtin in war cabinet, 6 October 1942, NAA, A5954, 808/2.

370 Vasey on Curtin's confession of command ignorance: Paull, *Retreat from Kokoda*, p. 248; Curtin's confidential press briefings in Canberra: notes by Fred Smith, 18 and 21 September 1942, quoted in Lloyd and Hall (eds), Backroom Briefings, pp. 88–93.

372 Correspondent Seizo Okada with General Horii when retreat order is received: McCarthy, *South West Pacific Area*, pp. 304–305.

373 MacArthur visit to Owers' Corner: Long, *The Six Years War*, p. 226; Frank Forde reports to war cabinet: 6 October 1942, NAA, A5954, 808/2;

Forde quoting MacArthur on Moresby: war cabinet meeting, 6 October 1942, NAA, A5956, 808/2.

374 MacArthur order to push the Japanese over the Kokoda Track: 1 October 1942, McCarthy, *South West Pacific Area*, p. 260; MacArthur's signal 'no serious effort' to displace Japanese, sent by Blamey to Allen, and Allen's dismissal: Long, *The Six Years War*, pp. 227–29; Allen's draft response to MacArthur 'if you think you can do any better': David Horner, *Blamey: Commander in Chief*, Allen & Unwin, Sydney, 1998, p. 346; Paul Ham, *Kokoda*, HarperCollins, Sydney, 2005, pp. 355–56; Allen relieved of command: David Horner, 'MacArthur, Douglas (1880–1964)', Australian Dictionary of Biography, National Centre of Biography, ANU, http://adb.anu.edu.au/biography/macarthur-douglas-10890/text19337; Sutherland's proposal to block Kokoda Track with explosives: McCarthy, *South West Pacific Area*, p. 141.

375 Japanese cannibalism and Yasuoka Fumitoshi: Paull, *Retreat from Kokoda*, pp. 273–74.

376 Bert Kienzle on Fuzzy Wuzzy Angels: interview with the author, 26 May 1977; Papuans hanged: ABC TV, *Foreign Correspondent*, www.abc.net.au/foreign/content/2007/s2109947.htm; Dr Geoffrey Gray, symposium paper, *Remembering the War in New Guinea: The coming of war to the Territories,* http://ajrp.awm.gov.au/AJRP/remember.nsf/ Web-Printer/ 2BA56E46D717A652CA256A99001D9F10; Hank Nelson, 'Grahamslaw, Thomas (1901–1973)', Australian Dictionary of Biography, National Centre of Biography, ANU, http://adb.anu.edu.au/biography/grahamslaw-thomas-10340/text18305; Reverend George Ambo, interviewed by the author at Gona, 18 May 1977; John Fowke on punishments: John Fowke, 'The war in Papua – the executions at Higaturu', Australian School of Pacific Administration, http://asopa.typepad.com/asopa_people/files/the_higaturu_hangings.pdf; Curtin goes home and 'Leave Curtin alone': *The Mirror*, Perth, 25 October 1942; Curtin's illness on train from Adelaide to Melbourne: *West Australian* and *Sydney Morning Herald*, 12 November 1942.

377 Mine strikes in New South Wales: *The Argus*, 10 November 1942; Curtin dilemma and introduces conscription beyond Australia's territories: Dennis (ed.) *The Oxford Companion to Australian Military History*, pp. 176–77; Hasluck, 'The Government and the People 1942–1945', p. 349; David Black, 'The art of the possible', JCPML00907/2.

378 Attacks on Curtin by Calwell at ALP conference: *Sydney Morning Herald*, 6 January 1943; death of General Tomitaro Horii: *Senshi sosho*, vol. 2, pp. 212–15; Justice Webb report on cannibalism in Papua: 15 March 1944, NAA, A10943, 2; Eather diary: Eather, *Desert Sands, Jungle Lands*, p. 119.

379 US troops in Buna–Sanananda operations: 16 November 1942 – 23 January 1943, Center of Military History, United States Army, Washington DC, 1990, www.ibiblio.org/hyperwar/USA/USA-A-Papua

380 'wretched-looking' American soldiers: E. J. Kahn, *G. I. Jungle: An American soldier in Australia and New Zealand*, Simon & Schuster, New York, 1943, pp. 121–22; Gona reinforced: Eather, *Desert Sands, Jungle Lands*, p. 71; Americans at Buna and MacArthur's direction to Eichelberger: Robert L. Eichelberger, *Our Jungle Road to Tokyo*, Viking, New York, 1950, pp. 21, 61.

381 General Blamey to Curtin on his lack of faith in US troops and threat to Australia: 4 December 1942, US forces in Papua, NAA, A5954, 654/26; McCarthy, *South West Pacific Area*, pp. 449–50; Papua operation: John Moremon, 'Remembering the war in New Guinea: Kokoda campaign', http://ajrp.awm.gov.au/ajrp/remember.nsf; tactical superiority over Japanese: Long, *The Six Years War*, p. 259.

382 Wau operations, topography and airstrip: reminiscences of the author in Wau 1970–1972; Odgers, *100 Years of Australians at War*, pp. 163–64; McCarthy, *South West Pacific Area*, pp. 89–92, 538, 554–63, 588–90; Willoughby (ed.) *Reports of General MacArthur*, vol. 2, part 1, pp. 190–92.

383 Curtin, 30 December 1942, bemoans Australia's plight to newsmen: notes by Fred Smith, quoted in Lloyd and Hall (eds), *Backroom Briefings*, pp. 119–23.

384 Blamey quotes on 'rabbits': Paull, *Retreat from Kokoda*, pp. 257–58; McCarthy on General Blamey's leadership, McCarthy, *South West Pacific Area*, p. 591; Professor Hiromi Tanaka on Blamey: interviewed by the author, Tokyo, 24 May 2011; Curtin's disheartening statement and personal fears, return of the 9th Division to Sydney: Fred Smith, 24 February 1943, quoted in Lloyd and Hall (eds), *Background Briefings*, pp. 139–140.

385 McCarthy on Japanese threat passing: McCarthy, *South West Pacific Area*, p. 591; Australian 9th Division in North Africa background: AWM, *2/28th Battalion*, www.awm.gov.au/units/unit_11279second_world_war. asp

386 Battle of the Bismarck Sea: Brad Manera, 'Battle of the Bismarck Sea, 2–4 March 1943', www.awm.gov.au/atwar/remembering1942/bismark; Flight Lieutenant Newton, VC, and Flight Sergeant Lyon: AWM, http://cas.awm.gov.au/item/RELAWM32315.001; strafing Japanese life rafts: Gillison, *Royal Australia Air Force, 1939–1942*, pp. 694–95

387 Spitfires at Darwin: George Odgers, *Australia in the War 1939–1945*, series 3, 'Air', vol. 2, 'War against Japan', p. 39; notes on threat to Australia after enemy air raid, 15 March 1943, and secret telephone conversation between MacArthur and Curtin, 16 March 1943: NAA, A5954, 524/6; notes of conversations between Curtin and MacArthur: 15 March 1943, NAA, A5954, 524/6; minutes of the war cabinet, 16 March 1943, NAA, A5954, 809/1; 1943 invasion scare: Odgers, 'War Against Japan', p. 39; Curtin secret briefing to reporters: 21 September 1942, typewritten notes, Joe Alexander diary, NLA, MS 2389, 12/4/11.

388 Yamamoto's death, 18 April 1943: Agawa, *The Reluctant Admiral*, pp. 344–68; Toland, *The Rising Sun*, pp. 440–44; Bleakley, *The Eavesdroppers*, pp. 93–97.

Chapter 15 Descent of a leader

389 MacArthur and Curtin meet to discuss future, emerge smiling, 8 June 1943: *Sydney Morning Herald*, 10 June 1943; Curtin privately admits that Japanese invasion is off: the agenda, briefing to political reporters, 9 June 1943, Fred Smith's diary, quoted in Lloyd and Hall (eds), *Background Briefings*, p. 156.

390 Curtin announces publicly that he does not think that Japan can invade Australia, 10 June 1943: *Sydney Morning Herald*, *West Australian* and other daily newspapers, 11 June 1943; Curtin on 'defeatist attitude' of previous governments: Labor conference report, *Sydney Morning Herald*, 7 June 1943; opposition response: *Sydney Morning Herald*, 8 June 1943; Curtin obtains two-to-one support from Labor conference on conscription: *Sydney Morning Herald*, 7 June 1943.

391 Keith Pryor, merchant navy: *Battle for Australia*, DVD, Battle for Australia Commemoration Committee NSW Inc., History Channel, Foxtel; merchant shipping attacks and deaths: Don Fraser, 'Men of a service: Australian merchant seamen', *Wartime*, AWM, no. 5, Summer 1999, pp. 53–57; AHS *Centaur* sinking: Long, *The Six Years War*, p. 291; AWM, *Centaur (Hospital Ship)*, www.awm.gov.au/encyclopedia/centaur; Curtin Independence Day broadcast to America: JCPML00110/65.

392 Industrial disputes in mines and factories, editorial castigating strikers: *Sydney Morning Herald*, 8 and 9 June 1943; Curtin, anti-strike code and illness: *Sydney Morning Herald*, 18 June 1943.

393 MacArthur on Japanese 'forced to loosen . . . hold' on New Guinea: MacArthur, *Reminiscences*, p. 180.

394 Curtin opening fourth Liberty loan in Sydney, 4 October 1943: *Sydney Morning Herald* and *The Argus*, 5 October 1943; Curtin transcript, http://john.curtin.edu.au/diary/primeminister/1943.html

395 Journal and covering letter by Lieutenant Arthur Tranter, written at Gloegoer, Sumatra: in the papers of Brenda Tranter, Caloundra, Queensland, and author interviews with Brenda Tranter, 2012.

396 Sir Archdale Parkhill and his son: exchange of letters with Curtin, 25 and 27 February 1943, war cabinet and defence chiefs, 30 January 1942, NAA, A5954, 532/13.

397 Curtin hospitalised in Melbourne and eventually moves back to the Lodge: *The Argus*, 28 December 1944 and *Canberra Times*, 3 January 1945; Calwell as 'enfant terrible': *Sydney Morning Herald*, 30 November 1944; Curtin in no hurry for bank nationalisation: *Sydney Morning Herald*, 17 December 1943.

398 Calwell rebuked by Curtin, 19 January 1944, and Calwell on Curtin 'losing his grip': A. A. Calwell, *Be Just and Fear Not*, Lloyd O'Neil/Rigby, Melbourne, 1972, pp. 57–58, transcript of Chapter 6, JCPML00972/2; Curtin ill again: *The Argus*, 11 December 1943; Curtin coming home for 'complete rest': *West Australian*, 28 December 1943; Curtin home for 59th birthday: Associate Professor Bobbie Oliver, 2012 JCPML Visiting Scholar, 'The Secret Life of Elsie Curtin', lecture, JCPML, 17 October 2012, http://john.curtin.edu.au/events/speeches/oliverlecture.html

399 Curtin at conference in Canberra: *Sydney Morning Herald*, 14 December 1943; Curtin on 'hostages to fortune': statement of 18 January 1944, DDA, no. 72, JCPML00110/77; Beasley and senior ministers overworked: Ross Gollan, *Sydney Morning Herald*, 24 January 1944.

400 Background on 1944 trip, Curtin, Churchill and Roosevelt: JCPML, http:// john.curtin.edu.au/artofthepossible/leaders.html; Curtin depressed, sails for the US: Day, *John Curtin*, pp. 532–36; David Horner, *High Command: Australia and Allied Strategy*, AWM/Allen & Unwin, Canberra/Sydney, 1982, p. 507; Curtin giving war summary speech: Washington, 24 April 1944, transcript from newsreel footage, University of South Carolina, MVTN 51–728; Curtin's illness in the United States:

The Herald, Melbourne, 27 April 1944, *The Sun*, Sydney, 28 April 1944; Day, *John Curtin*, p. 538; Curtin referring to 'hostages of fortune': DDA, no. 72, 28 January 1944, JCPML00110/77; Curtin summary on the progress of the war through to 1944, on MacArthur, and on 'Beat Hitler first': broadcast from Washington, 26 April 1944, together with press statement 27 April 1944, JCPML00652/2/3.

401 Don Rodgers on Curtin's overseas trip and losing the will to live: undated speech, Don Rodgers Papers, NLA, MS 1536, Box 9, Folder '1926–78'; Curtin's humanity, letter from Mrs Lucy Nicholson and Gunner Joseph Nicholson: Mrs Lucy Nicholson, Rutherglen, to Curtin, 7 May 1944, F. A. McLaughlin to Mrs Nicholson, 16 May 1944, and F. A. McLaughlin to Gunner Nicholson, 5 July 1944, NAA, M1415,449.

402 Historian Michael McKernan on Curtin's correspondence and health: 20 October 2005, JCPML00955/1; Cox on Curtin's and Rodgers's remarks: 21 August 1944, Papers of E. H Cox, NLA, MS 4554, Folder 1, and JCPML00546/1.

403 Curtin writing to cousin Mollie White, 31 August 1944: Papers of Lloyd Ross, NLA, MS3939/11; Gowrie background: Chris Cunneen, 'Gowrie, first Earl of (1872–1955)', Australian Dictionary of Biography, National Centre of Biography, ANU, http://adb.anu.edu.au/biography/gowrie-first-earl-of-6441/text11023; Gowrie's farewell letter to Curtin: Elsie Curtin, 'The Curtin Story', *Woman* magazine, 2 April 1951, JCPML0057714; Curtin ordered to rest and strain on ministers: Canberra correspondent, *Sydney Morning Herald*, 7 November 1944; Creighton Burns, *The Argus*, 7 November 1944.

404 Curtin's heart condition between November 1944 and January 1945 and doubts about recovery: Long, *The Six Years War*, p. 468; Harold Cox on Curtin's health: Harold Cox, notes to Keith Murdoch, 30 September 1944, 9 February, 5 March, 19, 22, 29 March and 9 April 1945, Papers of E. H. Cox, NLA, MS 4554, Folder 1 and JCPML00546/1.

405 Hector Harrison visits Curtin in hospital in Canberra: Records of NLA, interview of Hector Harrison, 1973, NLA, MS 6277, JCPML00016/1; Hitler dead: *Sydney Morning Herald*, 1 May 1945; Mrs Elsie Curtin speaking about her husband and his death: Elsie Curtin, 'The Curtin Story', part 5, *Woman* magazine, 9 April 1951, JCPML00577/5.

406 Curtin a war casualty: Geoffrey Serle, 'Curtin, John (1885–1945)', Australian Dictionary of Biography, National Centre of Biography, ANU, http://adb.anu.edu.au/biography/curtin-john-9885/text17495;

Curtin funeral: Associate Professor Bobbie Oliver, 'The Secret Life of Elsie Curtin': fall of Okinawa and Japanese surrender at war's end: Antony Shaw, *World War II: Day by Day*, Lifetime Distributors, Sydney, 2000, pp. 183–85; Hirohito's Imperial Rescript: *Nippon Times*, 16 August 1945; MacArthur takes surrender of Japan on USS *Missouri*, 2 September 1945: MacArthur, *Reminiscences*, pp. 265–69.

407 Prisoner of war figures, Long, *The Six Years War*, p. 470; Colonel 'Weary' Dunlop: letter on conditions to Brigadier Blackburn, 23 September 1945, quoted in Sue Ebury, *Weary: The Life of Sir Edward Dunlop*, Penguin, Melbourne, 1995, pp. 521–22; background on prisoners: Peter Hartley, *Escape to Captivity*, Dent, London, 1952, p. 192.

408 Journal and covering letter of Lieutenant Arthur Tranter, written at Gloegoer, Sumatra: in the papers of Brenda Tranter, Caloundra, Queensland, and author interviews with Brenda Tranter, 2012; Sandakan death march: Dennis (ed.), *The Oxford Companion to Australian Military History*, p. 527; AWM, *Stolen Years: Australian Prisoners of War*, www.awm.gov.au/exhibitions/stolenyears/ww2/japan/sandakan

409 Nursing sister Joan Crouch on Indian survivors: oral history interview with Angie Michaelis, Keith Murdoch Sound Archive, AWM, S00538; Australians overseas and anxious to get home: Karl James, 'Soldiers to citizens', *Wartime* magazine, AWM, no. 45, www.awm. gov.au/wartime/45/ soldiers-to-citizens 410 Professor Hiromi Tanaka on deaths on Muschu and Fauro islands: interview with the author, Tokyo, 24 May 2011, interpreter Hijime Murutani; additional information about Australians on Muschu and Fauro islands: Iwao Otsuki, *Solomon Shuyojo (Solomon Prisoner Camps)*, Tosho Shuppan, Tokyo, 1985, pp. 131–32, 139, 143; starvation diet: Otsuki, *Solomon Shuyojo*, p. 204.

411 Bodies of men from Ponape outside morgue: Otsuki, *Solomon Shuyojo*, p. 216; Japanese killings on Nauru and deaths by shelling and on Truk Island by Japanese: Professor Yuki Tanaka, 'Japanese atrocities on Nauru during the Pacific war: The murder of Australians, the massacre of lepers and the ethnocide of Nauruans', *Asia-Pacific Journal: Japan Focus*, http://japanfocus. org/-Yuki-TANAKA/3441; deaths of five Australians on Nauru: McCarthy, *South West Pacific Area*, pp. 38–39.

412 Japanese sickness and deaths on Fauro Island after war and Australian comments: War Diary of the 7th Infantry Battalion (AIF), AWM52 8/3/44/23.

413   AIF 7th Division troops complain about their treatment on Fauro Island: *Sydney Morning Herald*, 18 February 1946; Governor-General Michael Jeffery: Battle for Australia Commemorative Ceremony address, AWM, Canberra, 6 September 2006.

414   Major General Gordon Maitland on Curtin: note to the author, 23 February 2013, taken from his writings about the battle history of the Royal New South Wales Regiment.

415   Curtin's worry and inner conflicts shortened his life: Long, *The Six Years War*, p. 468; Frank Forde tribute to Curtin: House of Representatives, Hansard, 5 July 1945.

416   Curtin on war objectives of Japanese towards Australia: JCPML00652/2/3; Curtin's remarks on pressures on prime minister in wartime: letter to Mr G. Fitzpatrick, Win the War Movement, Sydney, 21 September 1944, revealed in NLA interview with Frank Forde, JCPML00439/1.

417   'whipping up of the fear of invasion' comment: Dr Peter Stanley, *Griffith Review*, no. 9: Up North, August 2006; Stanley's change of view on Curtin: Richard Glover program, 702 ABC Sydney, 5 September 2008; fear of invasion legacy, Dr Stanley on exaggerated threat to Australia: transcript from Geraldine Doogue's *Saturday Extra* on Radio National, 30 August 2008; Lord Gowrie's farewell broadcast on leaving Australia: *The Argus*, 11 September 1944.

SELECT BIBLIOGRAPHY

Agawa, Hiroyuki, *The Reluctant Admiral: Yamamoto and the Imperial Navy*, Kodansha International, Tokyo, 1969.

Asada, Sadao, *From Mahan to Pearl Harbor: The Imperial Japanese Navy and the United States*, Naval Institute Press, Annapolis, Maryland, 2006.

Bennett, H. Gordon, *Why Singapore Fell*, Angus & Robertson, Sydney, 1944.

Black, David, *Friendship Is a Sheltering Tree: John Curtin's Letters, 1907 to 1945*, John Curtin Prime Ministerial Library, Perth, 2001.

_____, *In His Own Words: John Curtin's Speeches and Writings*, Paradigm Books, Curtin University, Perth, 1995.

Boeicho Boei Kenshujo Senshishitsu (ed.), *Senshi sosho* (Japanese War History Series, part of 102 volumes), Military History department of Asagumo Shinbunsha (National Institute for Defense Studies), Tokyo, 1968. (In Japanese.)

Bond, Brian (ed.), *Chief of Staff: The Diaries of Lieutenant-General Sir Henry Pownall*, vol. 2: '1940–1944', Leo Cooper, London, 1974.

Brune, Peter, *A Bastard of a Place: The Australians in Papua*, Allen & Unwin, Sydney, 2004.

Bullard, Steven, (trans.) *Senshi sosho: Japanese army operations in the South Pacific Area: New Britain and Papua campaigns, 1942–43*, Australian War Memorial, Canberra, 2007.

_____ & Tamura, Keiko (eds.), *From a hostile shore: Australia and Japan at war in New Guinea*, Australia-Japan Research Project, AWM, Canberra, 2004.

Calwell, A.A., *Be Just and Fear Not*, Lloyd O'Neil, Melbourne, 1972.

Carruthers, Steven L., *Japanese Submarine Raiders, 1942*, Casper Publications, Sydney, 2006. (Also titled *Australia Under Siege*, Solus Books, Sydney, 1982.)

Chapman, Ivan D., *Iven G. Mackay: Citizen and Soldier,* Melway, Melbourne, 1975.

Churchill, Winston, *The Second World War,* Cassell series, London, 1948–1954.

Davidson, Graeme (ed.), *The Oxford Companion to Australian History*, Oxford University Press, Melbourne, 2001.

Daihon'ei, *Communiques issued by the Imperial General Headquarters: from December 8, 1941 to June 30, 1943*, Mainichi, Tokyo, 1943.

Day, David, *John Curtin: A life*, HarperCollins, Sydney, 2006.

_____, *The Great Betrayal: Britain, Australia and the Onset of the Pacific War, 1939–1942,* Angus & Robertson, Sydney, 1988.

_____, *Reluctant nation: Australia and the Allied Defeat of Japan 1942–1945*, Oxford University Press, Melbourne, 1992.

_____, *Menzies and Churchill at War*, Oxford University Press, 1993.

_____, *The Politics of War: Australia at War 1939–45 from Churchill to MacArthur*, HarperCollins, Sydney, 2003.

Dower, John W., *Embracing Defeat: Japan in the Wake of World War II,* Norton/New Press, New York, 1999.

Dull, Paul S., *A Battle History of the Imperial Japanese Navy 1941–1945,* Naval Institute Press, Annapolis, Maryland, 1978.

_____, *Guadalcanal: The Definitive Account of the Landmark Battle*, Penguin, New York, 1992.

Eade, Charles (ed.), *Winston Churchill's Secret Session Speeches*, Simon & Schuster, New York, 1946.

Eisenhower, Dwight D., *Papers of Dwight David Eisenhower: The War Years*, Vol. I, Johns Hopkins Press, Baltimore, 1970.

Fuchida, Mitsuo and Okumiya, Masatake, *Midway: the Battle that Doomed Japan: the Japanese Navy's story*, Naval Institute Press, Annapolis, Maryland, 1955.

Gamble, Bruce, *Darkest Hour: The True Story of Lark Force at Rabaul*, Zenith Press, St. Paul, Minnesota, 2006.

_____, *Fortress Rabaul: The Battle for the Southwest Pacific,* Zenith Press, St. Paul, Minnesota, 2010.

Gilbert, Martin, *Winston S. Churchill,* volume VI, 'Finest Hour, 1939–1941', Houghton Mifflin, Boston, 1983.

_____, *Winston S. Churchill*, vol. VII, 'Road to Victory, 1941–1945', Heinemann, London, 1986.

Gill, G. Hermon, *Royal Australian Navy 1942–1945*, Collins, Sydney, in association with the Australian War Memorial, Canberra, 1985.

Gillison, Douglas, *Australia in the War of 1939–1945,* series 3: 'Air', vol. 1, 'Royal Australian Air Force, 1939–1942', AWM, Canberra, 1962

Goldstein, Donald M. and Dillon, Katherine V. (eds), *The Pacific War Papers: Japanese Documents of World War II*, Potomac, Washington, 2004.

Grose, Peter, *A Very Rude Awakening,* Allen & Unwin, Sydney, 2007.

Ham, Paul, *Kokoda*, HarperCollins, Sydney, 2004.

Hasluck, Paul, *Diplomatic Witness: Australian Foreign Affairs 1941–1947*, Melbourne University Press, Melbourne, 1980.

_____, *Australia in the War of 1939–1945,* Vol. 2, 'The Government and the People', Australian War Memorial, Canberra, 1970.

Horner, David, *Crisis of Command: Australian Generalship and the Japanese Threat 1941–1943*, Australian National University Press, Canberra, 1978.

_____, *High Command: Australia and Allied Strategy, 1939–1945*, George Allen & Unwin, Sydney, in association with the Australian War Memorial, Canberra, 1982.

_____, *Inside the War Cabinet: Directing Australia's War Effort, 1939–45*, Allen & Unwin, Sydney, 1996.

Hattori, Takushiro, *The Complete History of the Greater East Asia War*, Hara Shobo, Tokyo, 1953. (US military translation from Japanese, from Gordon W. Prange Papers, University of Maryland Libraries.)

Hudson, W.J. & Stokes, H.J.W. (eds.), *Documents on Australian Foreign Policy, 1937–49,* Vols. IV & V, Department of Foreign Affairs, Canberra, 1980 & 1982.

Ienaga, Saburo, *The Pacific War, 1931–1945*, Pantheon Books, New York, 1978.

Jacobsen, Marc, 'US grand strategy and the defence of Australia', in Gavin Fry et al. (eds), *The Battle of the Coral Sea 1942: Conference Proceedings, 7–10 May 1992*, Australian National Maritime Museum, Sydney, 1992.

Kenney, George C., *The MacArthur I Know*, Duell, Sloan and Pearce, New York, 1951.

_____, *General Kenney Reports, A Personal History of the Pacific War*, Office of Air Force History, Washington, 1987.

King, Ernest J., *US Navy at War 1941–1945: Official Reports to the Secretary of the Navy*, United States Navy Department, Washington, 1946.

Kirby, Stanley Woodburn, *Singapore: The Chain of Disaster*, Macmillan, New York, 1971.

Lind, Lewis, *The Midget Submarine Attack on Sydney*, Bellrope Press, Sydney, 1990.

Lindsay, Patrick, *The Spirit of Kokoda: Then and Now*, Hardie Grant Books, Melbourne, 2003.

Lloyd, Clem and Hall, Richard (eds), *Backroom Briefings: John Curtin's war*, National Library of Australia, Canberra, 1997.

Lockwood, Douglas, *Australia's Pearl Harbour: Darwin 1942*, Cassell Australia, Melbourne, 1966.

Long, Gavin, *The Six Years War: A Concise History of Australia in the 1939–1945 War*, the Australian War Memorial and the Australian Government Publishing Service, Canberra, 1973.

Lundstrom, John B., *The First South Pacific Campaign: Pacific Fleet Strategy*, Naval Institute Press, Annapolis, Maryland, 1976.

MacArthur, Douglas, *Reminiscences*, Bluejacket Books, Naval Institute Press, Annapolis, Maryland, 2001.

Manchester, William, *Winston Spencer Churchill: The Last Lion*, Visions of Glory: 1874–1932, Michael Joseph, London, 1983.

Matloff, Maurice & Snell, Edwin M, *United States Army in World War II: Strategic Planning for Coalition Warfare 1941–1942*, Military History Department of the Army, Washington, 1953.

Milner, Samuel, *United States Army in World War II: The War in the Pacific*, US Department of the Army, Washington, 1957.

McCarthy, Dudley, *South-West Pacific Area: First Year, Kokoda to Wau*, Australian War Memorial, Canberra, 1959.

Moran, Lord, *Winston Churchill: The struggle for survival 1940–1965*, Constable, London, 1966.

Morison, Samuel E., *The Two Ocean War*, Little, Brown and Co., Boston, 1963.

————————, *History of the United States Naval Operations WWII*, vol. 3, 'The Rising Sun in the Pacific', Castle Books, Edison, New York, 2001.

————————, *History of the US Naval Operations WWII*, vol. 6, 'Breaking the Bismarcks Barrier', Castle Books, Edison, New York, 2001.

————————, *History of United States Naval Operations in World War II*, vol. 4, 'Coral Sea, Midway and Submarine Actions', Castle Books, Edison, New York, 2001.

Morton, Louis, *Strategy and Command: The First Two Years*, Office of the Chief of Military History, Department of the Army, Washington, 1962.

Odgers, George, *100 Years of Australians at War*, New Holland, Sydney, 2003.

Page, Earle, in *Truant Surgeon: The Inside Story of Forty Years of Australian Political Life*, Mozley, Ann, ed., Angus & Robertson, Sydney, 1963.

Paull, Raymond, *Retreat from Kokoda*, Heinemann, Melbourne, 1958.

Percival, Arthur, *The War in Malaya*, Eyre & Spottiswood, London, 1949.

Pogue, Forrest C., *George C. Marshall: Ordeal and Hope, 1939–1942*, MacGibbon & Kee, London, 1968.

Potter, John Deane, *A Soldier Must Hang: The Biography of an Oriental General*, Four Square, London, 1963.

Prados, John, *Combined Fleet Decoded: The Secret History of American Intelligence and the Japanese Navy in World War II*, Naval Institute Press, Annapolis, Maryland, 1995.

Ross, Lloyd, *John Curtin: A biography*, Melbourne University Press, 1996.

Rowell, S.F., *Full Circle*, Melbourne University Press, 1974.

Sakaida, Henry, *The Siege of Rabaul*, Phalanx, St Paul, 1996.

Shigemitsu, Mamoru, *Japan and Her Destiny*, Dutton, New York, 1958.

Togo, Shigenori, *The Cause of Japan*, Simon & Schuster, New York, 1956.

Toland, John, *The Rising Sun: The Decline and Fall of the Japanese Empire 1936–1945*, Penguin, London, 2001.

——————, *But Not in Shame*, Random House, New York, 1961.

Tomioka, Sadatoshi, *Kaisen to shusen: Hito to kiko to keikaku* (*The Opening and Closing of the War: The People, the Mechanism, and the Planning*), Mainichi Shinbunsha, Tokyo, 1968. (In Japanese.)

Ugaki, Matome, *Fading Victory: The Diary of Admiral Matome Ugaki 1941–45*, translated by Masataka Chihaya, with Donald M. Goldstein and Katherine V. Dillon, University of Pittsburgh Press, 1991.

US War Department, *The World at War, 1939–1944*, War Dept., Washington, 1945.

Wigmore, Lionel, *The Japanese Thrust*, Australian War Memorial, Canberra, 1957.

Willoughby, Charles A. (ed.), *Reports of General MacArthur: The Campaigns of MacArthur in the Pacific*, (two volumes) US Department of the Army, US Government Printing Office, Washington, 1966.

White, Osmar, *Green Armour: The Story of the Fighting Men in New Guinea*, Wren, Melbourne, 1972.

Whitington, Don, *The House Will Divide: A Review of Australian Federal Politics*, Lansdowne Press, Melbourne 1969.

Wurth, Bob, *Saving Australia: Curtin's Secret Peace with Japan*, Lothian, Melbourne, 2006.

——————, *1942: Australia's greatest peril*, Pan Macmillan, Sydney, 2008.

Principal centres of research visited by the author:

Australia: John Curtin Prime Ministerial Library, Curtin University, Perth; Museum of Australian Democracy, Old Parliament House, Canberra; National Library of Australia, Canberra (including the manuscripts archive and the online resource of the Trove newspaper archive); National Archives of Australia, Canberra; Australian War Memorial, Canberra (including the Memorial's online research facilities); The University of Queensland Library, Brisbane.

Singapore: National Museum of Singapore; National Library of Singapore.

Japan: National Diet Library, Tokyo; National Institute for Defense Studies, Tokyo; Diplomatic Record Office, Ministry of Foreign Affairs, Tokyo.

Britain: Churchill Archive Centre, Churchill College, Cambridge; Imperial War Museum, Duxford; Liddell Hart Centre for Military Archives, King's College, London; Imperial War Museum, London; National Archives, Kew, London.

An extended bibliography for this book can be found at the author's website: www.bobwurth.com

ACKNOWLEDGEMENTS

As a young journalist working for the ABC in Sydney in the mid-1960s, there was a cadet counsellor by the name of Warren Denning and an industrial reporter called Les Thomas in our radio newsroom at William Street, King's Cross. Denning was kindly, knowledgeable and reserved. Thomas, known to his senior colleagues as Tiger, was fiery, witty and outspoken. Both had been senior political journalists in Canberra during the war and were part of 'Curtin's Circus': the group of journalists with whom the prime minister, remarkably, revealed almost his every secret.

Both Denning and Thomas would often engage younger journalists in the newsroom with talk about John Curtin and their experiences. Shamefully, I must say, I wasn't much interested. I never asked these men, who had been at such close quarters with Curtin during the war, any questions. The memory of what they said about Curtin is something of a blur. It was history, you see, something old, buried in the past. Other far more interesting issues were afoot in the sixties, like the escalating war in Vietnam. A tinge of regret at my foolish disinterest lives with me today. What inside stories they had! It is perhaps a lesson for today's younger journalists. Our history somehow becomes more interesting and the need to know more compelling as you grow older.

One of the recollections that remained in biographer David Day's mind after he had completed his classic biography *John Curtin: A life* was the spectre of Prime Minister John Curtin suddenly walking out of Victoria Barracks in Melbourne in January 1942 to take a train home to Perth at a most critical period. 'Look further into that', he advised, 'there's more to be told'. That wise counsel soon led to yellowing yet fascinating documents, stacks of books, talks with railway historians, even inspections of old Commonwealth carriages and steam trains at the Railway Museum at Bassendean in Perth's north east. The investigation became more than one about a train journey, but more a voyage into Curtin's thinking and his depression at a crucial time. To David Day, I am indebted for helpful observations over good pasta. My thanks also to Phillipa Rogers – Coordinator Heritage and Museum Services, City of Wanneroo; and Ian Jenkin – Australian Railway Historical Society, Victoria.

I gratefully acknowledge two fellowships granted to me by the Australian Prime Ministers Centre at the Museum of Australian Democracy, Canberra, which enabled me to undertake research trips for this book to Canberra at the Museum of Australian Democracy, the National Archives of Australia, the National Library of Australia and the Australian War Memorial. The Memorial provided me with permission to quote from the Australian official war histories. Of particular use to the writer is the Trove Australian newspaper archive established by the NLA online.

In Singapore, fellowship research was conducted at the National Library of Singapore, the National Museum of Singapore, the Fort Canning 'Battle Box' and Fort Siloso on Sentosa island, with much assistance provided by my friend Phua Tin Tua (Willie). In Tokyo, research took me to the National Diet Library and the National Institute for Defense Studies, with a visit to the Japanese Overseas Migration Museum, Yokohama. Historian Professor Hiromi Tanaka once again provided me with insightful observations about the Japanese high command in relation to Australia and the fighting in New Guinea. I was also able to visit Manazuru to speak with Toshiro Takeuchi. In London, I spent some time at the Liddell Hart Centre for Military Archives at King's College, the National Archives at Kew and the Imperial War Museum research centre. In Cambridge I stayed at the Churchill College and accessed documents of Sir Winston Churchill, including his secret speeches, at the Churchill Archive Centre. My thanks to the Royal Archives, Windsor Castle, Berkshire, and registrar Pamela Clark for provision of the diary notes of King George VI with the permission of Her Majesty, Queen Elizabeth II.

I very much appreciate the valuable research assistance, records and photographs provided by the John Curtin Prime Ministerial Library at Curtin University, Perth, Western Australia, especially manager Deanne Barrett and archivist Sally Laming; also Lesley Wallace, former manager, and David Wylie, former archives technician. Professor David Black, historical consultant to the John Curtin Prime Ministerial Library, has provided valuable guidance over many years. Thanks also to Professor Alan Rix, Pro Vice Chancellor, the University of Queensland; Rev. Peter Holloway, 39th Battalion Association; author Patrick Lindsay, Kokoda Track Foundation; Prange and Goldstein Collection, the University of Pittsburgh and writer Bob Johnston for his early editing assistance.

My thanks to Major General Gordon Maitland, author, war historian and president of the Battle for Australian Commemoration Committee (NSW), for his insights, comments and contributions.

Structural editing by Deonie Fiford significantly improved the manuscript while Macmillan Publishers' senior editor Vanessa Pellatt contributed her professionalism and knowledge and polished a manuscript into a book to make an author proud.

Bob Wurth

INDEX

ALSO BY BOB WURTH IN PAN MACMILLAN

1942

1942 was the year of Australia's greatest peril as the nation awaited invasion from Japan. Darwin was devastated by bombing, Australian ships were torpedoed within sight of our coast, midget Japanese submarines attacked shipping in Sydney Harbour, and Japanese forces on their inexorable march south invaded New Guinea and islands to Australia's near north. This is the true story of the genuine and imminent threat to Australia in that fateful year.

On the beautiful Inland Sea of Japan – the heartland of the Imperial Japanese Navy – and in frenetic wartime Tokyo, radical and passionate staff officers and their illogical admirals debated the invasion of an almost defenceless nation. The Imperial Japanese Army, meanwhile, opposed the attack, foreseeing a looming military quagmire. Behind the scenes, Australian, British and American defence chiefs all but dismissed the chances of holding Darwin and the north. Australia's fate hung in the balance.

1942 is a story of desperate bravery and criminal stupidity. Most of all, it is the story of Australians left high and dry in those first few months of 1942, under the looming shadow of invasion, and the steps that an inexperienced leader, John Curtin, took to help save his country in its darkest days.